Transnational Corruption and Corporations

Regulating Bribery through Corporate Liability

SIMEON OBIDAIRO

African Development Bank, Tunis, Tunisia

Routledge
Taylor & Francis Group
LONDON AND NEW YORK

First published 2013 by Ashgate Publishing

2 Park Square, Milton Park, Abingdon, Oxfordshire OX14 4RN
52 Vanderbilt Avenue, New York, NY 10017

Routledge is an imprint of the Taylor & Francis Group, an informa business

First issued in paperback 2020

British Library Cataloguing in Publication Data
Obidairo, Simeon.
Transnational corruption and corporations: regulating bribery through corporate liability.
1. International business enterprises – Corrupt practices. 2. Bribery. 3. Foreign trade regulation. 4. International business enterprises – Law and legislation.
I. Title
364.1'68-dc23

The Library of Congress has cataloged the printed edition as follows:
Obidairo, Simeon.
Transnational corruption and corporations: regulating bribery through corporate liability / By Simeon Obidairo.
pages cm.
Includes bibliographical references and index.
ISBN 978-1-4094-5520-2 (hardback: alk. paper)
1. Corporations—Corrupt practices. 2. Bribery. 3. Criminal liability of juristic persons. 4. Criminal liability (International law) I. Title.
K5216.O25 2013
345'.04—dc23

2012044667

ISBN 978-1-4094-5520-2 (hbk)
ISBN 978-0-367-60126-3 (pbk)

Contents

List of Cases

United Kingdom

Anglo-Iranian Oil Co. v Jaffrate [The Rose Mary] [1953], 1 W.L.R. 246.
Attorney-General's Reference (No. 2 of 1999) [2000], Crim. App. Eng.
Blad v Bamfield [1974], 3 Swans, 604.
Bradford Election Case (No 2) [1869], 19 LT 723.
Calland [1967], Crim LR 236.
Carr-Briant [1943], K.B. 607.
Compania Naviera Vascongado v Critina SS [1938], A.C. 485.
Cooper v Slade [1856], 10 E.R. 1488.
Czarnikow v Rolimpex [1978], 3 W.L.R. 274.
Dobree v Napier [1836], 2 Bing. N.C. 781.
Duke of Brunswick v King of Hanover [1848], 2 H.L. Cas. 1.
H.L. Bolton (Engineering) Co. v T.J. Graham & Sons, Ltd. [1957], 1 Q.B. 159.
Harrison [1800], 1 East PC 383.
In re Claim by Helbert Wagg & Co. [1956], 1 Ch. 323.
Lindley [1957], Crim LR 321.
Llewellyn-Jones [1968], 1 Q.B. 429.
Lonrho Ltd. v Shell Petroleum Co. Ltd. [1980], 1 W.L.R. 627 (H.L.).
Luther v Sagor [1921], 3 K.B. 532.
MacKinnon v Donaldson Lufkin & Jenrette Securities Corp. [1986], 1 All E.R. 653.
MacKinnon v Donaldson Lufkin & Jenrette Securities Corp. [1986], All E.R. 653.
Meridian Global Funds Management Asia Ltd v Security Commission [1995], 2 A.C. 500.
Nissan v Attorney General [1970], A.C. 179.
Oppenheimer v Cattermole [1975], 1 All E.R. 539 (H.L.).
Pomfriet v Brownsal [1600], 78 E.R. 968.
Queen v Great North of England Railway Co. [1846],L 115 Eng. Rep. 1294 (Q.B.)
R (Corner House Research and Campaign Against Arms Trade) v Director of the Serious Fraud Office [2008], EWHC 714 (Admin).
R (Corner House Research and Campaign Against Arms Trade) v Director of the Serious Fraud Office [2008], EWHC 714 (Admin), at pars 57-60.
R v Andrews-Weatherfoil Ltd., [1972], 1 All E.R. 65 (C.A.).
R v Associated Octel Co Ltd [1996], 1 W.L.R 1543.
R v Braithwaite [1983], 2 All E.R. 87.
R v Gateway Foodmarkets Ltd [1997], IRLR 189.
R v Grossman [1981], 73 Cr.App.R. 302.

R v Gurney [1867], 10 Cox CC 550.
R v H. M. Coroner for East Kent, [1987] 88 CA. 10 (Q.B).
R v Natchi [2002], 2 Cr.App.R 20.
R v P&O Eur. Ferries (Dover), Ltd., [1990], 93 CA 72.
R v Parker [1985], Crim LR 589.
R v Smith [1960], 2 Q.B. 423 (CA).
R v Wellburn [1979], 69 Cr.AppRep 254.
Rio Tinto Zinc Corp. v Westinghouse Elec. Corp. [1978], A.C. 547 (H.L.).
Salomon v Salomon & Co. [1897], A.C. 22.
Tesco Stores Ltd v London Borough of London Borough of Brent (1993), [2 All E.R. 718]
Tesco Supermarkets, Ltd. v Nattrass [1972], A.C.. 153 (H.L.).
Vaughan [1769], 98 E.R. 308.
X AG v A Bank [1983], 2 All E.R. 464.

United States

Alfred Dunhill of London, Inc. v Republic of Cuba, 425 U.S. 682 (1976).
American Banana Co. v United Fruit, 213 U.S. 347 (1909).
Angelo Tomasso, Inc. v Armor Constr. & Paving, Inc., 447 A.2d 406 (Conn. 1982).
Asahi Metal Indus. Co., Ltd. v Superior Court, 107 S. Ct. 1026 (1987).
Associated Radio Service Co. v Page Airways, Inc., 624 F.2d 1342 (5th Cir. 1980).
Automotriz del Golfo de California S. A. de C. V v Resnick, 306 P.2d 1 (Cal. 1957).
Banco Nacional de Cuba v Sabbatino, 376 U.S. 398 (1964).
Bank of Augusta v Earle, 38 U.S. (13 Pet.), 519 (1839).
Calnetics Corp. v Volkswagen of America, 532 F.2d 674 (9th Cir. 1976).
Carpenter v United States, 484 U.S. 19 (1987).
Collet v American Nat'l Stores, Inc., 708 S.W.2d 273 (Mo. Ct. App. 1986).
Commonwealth v Proprietors of New Bedford Bridge, 68 Mass. (2 Gray) 339 (1854).
Dooley v United Technologies Corp., 803 F. Supp. 428 (D.D.C. 1992).
Enron Corp. Sec., Derivative & ERISA Litig., No. H-01-3624, 2003 U.S. LEXIS 1668, at *32 (S.D. Tex. Jan. 28, 2003).
Environmental Tectonics v W.S. Kirkpatrick, Inc., 847 F.2d 1052 (3rd Cir. 1988).
Evans v United States, 504 U.S. 255, 266 (1992).
Granite Constr. Co. v Superior Court, 149 Cal. App. Cal. Rptr. 3 (1983).
Harrison v Equitable Life Assurance Society of the U.S., 435 F. Supp. 281(W.D. Mich. 1977).
Hartford Fire Ins. Co. v Cal., 509 U.S. 764 (1993).
In re Grand Jury Proceedings (United States v Field), 532 F.2d 404 (5th Cir. 1976).
In re Sarrio S. A., 1995 WL 598988 (S.D.N.Y. Oct. 11, 1995).
Ings v Ferguson, 282 F.2d 149 (2d Cir. 1960).
Interstate Circuit, Inc. v United States, 306 U.S. 208 (1939).

Int'l Shoe Co. v State of Wash., 326 U.S. 310.
Kahn v. Lynch Communication Sys., Inc., 638 A.2d 1110, 1114-1115 (Del. 1994).
Lamb v Phillip Morris, Inc., 915 F.2d 1024 (6th Cir. 1990).
Louis K. Liggett Co. v Lee, 288 U.S. 517 (1933).
Ludwig v Western Union Tel. Co., 216 U.S. 146 (1910).
McGee v Int'l Life Ins. Co., 355 U.S. 220 (1957).
McNally v United States, 483 U.S. 350 (1987).
Milliken v Meyer, 311 U.S. 457 (1940).
Municipality of Anchorage v Hitachi Cable, Ltd., 47 F. Supp. 633 (D. Alaska 1982).
New York Central & Hudson River Railroad v United States, 212 U.S. 481 (1909).
Parmelee Transportation Co. v Keeshin, 292 F.2d 794 (7th Cir. 1961).
Pullman Co. v Kansas, 216 U.S. 56 (1910).
Railroad Tax Cases, 13 F. 722 C.C.D. Cal. (1882).
Securities and Exchange Commission v Banca Della Svizzera Italiana, 92 F.R.D. 111 (S.D.N.Y. 1981).
Societe Internationale pour Participations Industrielles et Commerciales, S.A. v Rogers, 357 U.S. 197 (1958).
Societe Internationale v McGranery, 111 F. Supp. 435 (D.D.C. 1953).
Societe Nationale Industrielle Aerospatiale v U.S. District Court (S.D. Iowa), 107 S.Ct. 2542 (1987).
Southern Ry. v Greene, 216 U.S. 400 (1910).
Standard Oil Co. of New Jersey v United States, 221 U.S. 1 S.Ct. 502 (1911).
State v Morris & Essex Railroad Co., 23 N.J.L. 360 (1852).
Sterling Nelson & Sons, Inc. v Rangen, Inc., 235 F. Supp. 393 (N. Idaho 1964).
Sugar Inst., Inc. v United States, 297 U.S. 553 (1936).
Timberlane Lumber Co. v Bank of America, 549 F.2d 597 (9th Cir. 1976).
Trade Dev Bank v Continental Ins. Co., 469 F.2d 35 (2d Cir. 1972).
Trustees of Dartmouth College v. Woodward, 17 U.S. (4 Wheat.) 518, (1810).
Underhill v Hernandez, 168 U.S. 250, 252 (1887).
United States v Aluminum Co. of America, 148 F.2d 416 (2d Cir. 1945).
United States v American Totalisator Co., 3 FCPA Rep. 699.067 (D. Md. 1993).
United States v Bank of New England, 821 F.2d 844 (1st Cir. 1987).
United States v Barber, 668 F.2d 778 (4th Cir. 1982).
United States v Barta, 635 F.2d 999 (2d Cir. 1980).
United States v Basic Constr. Co., 711 F.2d 570 (4th Cir. 1983).
United States v Basu, (D.D.C. 2002).
United States v Bronston, 658 F.2d 920 (2d Cir. 1981).
United States v Bryza, 522 F.2d 414 (7th Cir. 1975).
United States v Cauble, 706 F.2d 1322 (5th Cir. 1983).
United States v First National Bank of Chicago, 699 F.2d 341 (7th Cir. 1983).
United States v First National City Bank, 396 F.2d 897 (2d Cir. 1968).
United States v Harris Corporation, John D. Iacobucci and Ronald L. Schultz, (Cr. No. 90-0456), N.D. Cal., 1990.
United States v Holzer, 816 F.2d 304, (7th Cir. 1987).

United States v Illinois Cent. R.R., 303 U.S. 239 (1938).
United States v Isaacs, 493 F.2d 1124 (7th Cir. 1974).
United States v Kenny, 462 F.2d 1205, 1210 (3d Cir. 1972).
United States v Margiotta, 688 F.2d 108 (2d Cir. 1982).
United States v Mead, 3 FCPA Rep. 699.533 (D.N.J. 1998).
UnitedStates v Metcalf & Eddy, 3 FCPA Rep. 699.749 (D. Ma. 1999).
United States v Morton Salt, 338 U.S. 632 (1950).
United States v Rauhoff, 525 F.2d 1170 (7th Cir. 1975).
United States v Sawyer, 85 F.3d 713 (1st Cir. 1996).
United States v Sengupta, No. 1:02CR00040 (D.D.C. 2002).
United States v Silvano, 812 F.2d 754 (1st Cir. 1987).
United States v Sun Diamond Growers, 526 U.S. 398 (1999).
United States v Turkette, 452 U.S. 576 (1981).
United States v Vitusa Corp., 3 FCPA Rep. 699.155 (D.N.J. 1994).
United States v Weiss, 752 F.2d 777 (2d Cir. 1985).
Vuitch v Furr, 482 A.2d 811 (D.C. 1984).
W. S. Kirkpatrick & Co. v Environmental Tectonics Corp., 493 U.S. 400 (1990).
Western Union Tel. Co. v Kansas, 216 U.S. 1 (1910).

Australia

Hamilton v Whitehead, 166 C.L.R. 121 (1988).
Kehoe v Dacol Motors (Pty.), Ltd., 1972 Q.R 59, 74-75 (Queensl. Crim. App. 1971).

Canada

Canada (Human Rights Commission) v Canadian Liberty Net [1998], 1 S.C.R. 626.
Canadian Dredge & Dock Co. v R [1985], 1 S.C.R. 691.
R v Hammerbeck [1993], R.F.L. (3d) 265, 26 B.C.A.C. 1.
R v Libman [1985], 2 S.C.R. 178.
United States of America v Lépine [1994], 1 S.C.R. 286.

New Zealand

Nordik Indus., [1976] 1 NZLR 199.
R v McDonald [1993], 3 NZLR 354.

List of Abbreviations/Acronyms

ATC	American Totalisator Company
BPI	Bribe Payers Index
BSI	Banca Della Svizzera Italiana
CIME	Committee on International and Multilateral Enterprises
CPI	Corruption Perception Index
DOJ	US Department of Justice
FCPA	Foreign Corrupt Practices Act
FDI	Foreign Direct Investment
GDP	Gross Domestic Product
GoI	Government of Iraq
IMF	International Monetary Fund
NGO	Non-Governmental Organisation
OAS	Organization of American States
OECD	Organisation for Economic Cooperation and Development
OFFP	Oil-for-Food Programme
PTIA	British Protection of Trading Interests Act of 1980
RICO	Racketeer Influenced and Corrupt Organization Act
Saybolt	Saybolt Incorporated
SC	Security Council

SEC	Securities and Exchange Commission
SOMO	Iraq's State Oil Marketing Organization
TI	Transparency International
UK	United Kingdom
UN	United Nations
UNCAC	United Nations Convention against Corruption
US	United States

Foreword

It is an absolute pleasure providing the foreword to this book, *Transnational Corruption and Corporations*. The author makes a significant contribution to the corpus of existing legal, economic and political literature on the issue of corruption particularly in the transnational context. I enthusiastically welcome the valuable insight this work offers. The book starts to provide robust insight on the broad question that I have grappled with: how do we ensure that corruption does not roll back the modest developmental gains? This broader question is narrowed down in the book to the question: what are the challenges to the prevention of transnational bribery by transnational corporations in international business transactions?

There is some, but not unanimous, consensus on the point that corruption poses a very real challenge to growth in emerging economies. The controversy surrounding the relationship between corruption and growth spans several decades and is a three-way split between studies that find a negative, positive and an agnostic relationship between corruption and development. Attempting to summarize the salient features of the corruption and growth conundrum, and at a significant risk of reductionism, it would appear that corruption control has been successful in some countries that have registered higher levels of growth, but not others, and with an overall trend that is still the subject of vociferous debate. Since disputes continue about the determinants of economic growth more broadly, the corruption–growth relationship will continue to be a matter of sharp debate for some time. There is no question that this three decade long debate and the antecedent research that it has spurned has done a great deal to advance the development agenda, particularly in emerging economies.

Attention to the theoretical basis of the ideological disagreement on the relationship between effective control of corruption and growth, one would expect, would assist in drawing attention to the political and economic choices inherent in the substitution of one ideological development choice for another. Unfortunately, the precise opposite has been the case. The lofty goal of reaching an ideological consensus on the corruption and growth relationship has further obfuscated our focus, replacing attention to the economic and political tradeoffs inherent in the choice of a development paradigm with alternative ideas about the impact of corruption on development. As the author makes clear in the book, there exists both a supply-side and a demand-side to combating transnational bribery. The demand-side refers to requests for bribes by public officials while the supply-side refers to offers of bribes to public officials. A corrupt transaction, notably, can be effected either way. There is, thus, a need to generate viable supply-side solutions and demand-side solutions that will curb transnational bribery by corporations. Necessarily, the supply-side solutions will need to impede prospective bribe-givers from offering or paying bribers while the demand-side solution will need to discourage prospective bribe-takers from accepting or requesting bribes. In addition to skillfully addressing the complex interplay between corruption control and economic choices, the author convincingly points out that the current multilateral efforts to curb transnational bribery by corporations are unlikely to result in a reduction of the prevalence of bribery in international business transactions without a focus on both demand- and supply-side interventions.

Linking the theoretical basis of the ideological disagreement on corruption and growth to the practical issue of developing effective demand-side and supply-side solutions, I am advocating for a refocus of the debate on the impact of the assumptions embedded in the economic and political policy choices and the distributional impact of these choices on development within the African continent. In this regard, the intention is not to be overly polemical, but I do argue that the debate in essence distorts action for change to the existing world system. By focusing on the relationship between corruption and growth, the discourse ignores and fails to contest background political, economic and social features of the system in ways that that ignore fundamental inequities that dominate in the interstices.An example utilized in this book to buttress this point is the United Nations' Oil-for-Food Programme in Iraq and the many corporate entities around the world that share in the illicit benefits from, and in responsibility for, schemes that leave the population of Iraq undernourished despite the many billions of dollars deployed, in theory, to feed them. In this context, we speak about corruption retarding development by promoting waste but ignore the way in which the background rules shape and even undermine developmental goals.

It is because this book both ambitiously and effectively starts the process of addressing these issues that I consider it particularly useful. In line with its title, the book is a compendium of essential and contemporary issues of law and practice on the subject. It is well researched, very comprehensive and contains interesting topics. I am aware of the cynicism that people have with regard to combatting corruption. Indeed, progress in the fight against corruption requires an equal measure of realism and optimism. We have to be realistic that tackling corruption is very difficult. We have to be realistic that many suspicions and obstacles have to be overcome. We have to be realistic as well that sometimes, it is two steps forward and three steps back before it can be two steps forward and one step back. I do have a great sense of optimism about tackling corruption. This optimism is important because without optimism, there is no progress. Without optimism and a focus on the possibilities, nothing changes, nothing gets better.

Gbenga Oyebode MFR
Managing Partner, Aluko & Oyebode
Lagos
August 2013

Acknowledgements

This book is the product of several years of effort, many more of procrastination, and a significant amount of assistance. Over the average 30 words per day that it took to complete, between the effort and procrastination, the book certainly would not have been completed without the tremendous assistance I received from my colleagues, friends and family who were either interested in the subject of the book or in my finishing the work. It is not out of adherence to convention that I first acknowledge Dr Matthew Craven. Quite simply, if not for him, I would have given up on the subject area not too long after I started. I would like to thank him for advising me no more than necessary, and no less than sufficient. I would like to thank the staff at Ashgate Publishing, particularly Alison Kirk and Patrick Smith, for the care they have bestowed in the publication of this book. I would also like to thank my mentors, Dr Ngozi Okonjo-Iweala, Anna Bossman and Vinay Sharma: your guidance has been very much appreciated.

I have met many nice people whose kindness has had a significant impact and contributed in no small measure to the completion of this book. I would like to thank Amaka Aboh, whose tragic passing early on was a tremendous loss. Thank you to my good friend, Ana-Paula Linares, for comments on early drafts. For reading early drafts and her friendship, I would like to thank Pia Brosinovich. During my time in Geneva, I was very fortunate to be supported by lots of solid friends. Fernando and Marisol, words fail to express my appreciation. I would also like to thank Efua Dorkenoo, who gave me an opportunity when she had no reason to. Samantha Bell-Shiers, thank you. Although we have not kept in touch, your friendship and assistance really made the difference. Nan Kasonde, thanks for your friendship, to me and my family.

There are some of my friends who have remained so for many years. I would like to thank Ada Obi, Jano Ikpasa and Anne Thompson. I would like to thank Manisha Bharti, a friend and a colleague who provided very useful comments on early drafts. My gratitude goes to (Special Agent!) Karen Naimer for her encouragement, Emily Bolton for her invaluable comments and Gabriele Dunker for her friendship. I owe a larger than usual debt of gratitude to my dear friend Rachel Levy – congratulations with Max! I would also like to thank my former colleague and friend Dr Lisa Nichols for leading the way. Many thanks to Adam Shayne, Rune, and Lisa, your help has always been much appreciated. Jamie Johnson (JJ), Kim Gunthorpe – thanks for the editing. I would also like to thank Kemesha Naidoo, Rhoda Mshana, Elisha Sulai, Tunde Fagbohunlu, Natasha Glynn, Aina Ogunade-Paul, Funmi Akinosi, Johann Benohr, Chisom Nnabuihe, and Lisa Nzama.

I would like to dedicate this book to my family. To my father and mother, who sacrificed everything so that I would not need to. Thank you for having always removed any barriers that lay in my path. Thank you for showing me the joy of intellectual pursuit. To Dapo and Bukky, one could not ask for a better brother and sister-in-law. To my sisters Ronke and Kemi, words fail me to express my appreciation. To Hani, one could not ask for a better brother. To my parents-in-law, Eric and Tove Danielsen. Your patience and understanding whilst I spent family holidays working on this book has been admirable. To my siblings-in-law Hanne and Soren, thank you for your encouraging support. To Skip and Andy, your presence in our lives has truly been a gift. Thank you Uncle John for stimulating my interest in the law.

To my daughters, Emma and Nina, I am exceedingly fortunate to be parent to you. Much of the motivation for completing this book comes from you both. To my wife Charlotte, who has turned a blind eye to the dereliction of duty that occurred in our family over the past few years. Your dedication and persistent confidence in me has taken the load off my shoulder. I owe you for unselfishly letting your passions, and ambitions collide with mine. Thank you for enduring the last 13 years. I can't guarantee this book will turn out to be worth it but I promise that I'll try to make it up to you in our future together.

S.O

Chapter 1
Introduction

Multilateral Regulation of Corruption and Corporations

Building an effective regulatory and liability framework to curb the incidents of transnational corruption by corporations is a complicated endeavour. On the one hand, you have all the problems associated with trying to regulate conduct that is notoriously fuzzy to define. Most of us cannot agree on the definition, but we all assume that we can recognize it when we see it. This is great for slapping judgement on conduct after the fact, but hardly the stuff that we can design appropriately worded legislation to control. Throw in the fact that the word corruption is a culturally laden term. By culturally laden, I do not mean that some cultures condone corruption; rather I am suggesting that there is a spatial and temporal element to what constitutes corruption. This does not suggest that there are no commonly accepted notions of what constitutes corruption. Rather, because of the cultural variations, what morally constitutes corruption is not uniform, and the moral aspect obviously informs the legal. You can only determine whether conduct is corrupt by reference to what is acceptable at the time and place where the conduct occurs. In other words, labelling conduct as corrupt does not travel well. Also complicating the problem is the fact that corruption is difficult to measure (most of the people engaging in conduct labelled as corrupt do not advertise) and its effect are tricky to quantify (one of the enduring debates in the literature centres around whether or not corruption is harmful).

In addition to the specific issues associated with labelling conduct as corrupt, there are many issues associated with regulating transnational corporations and imposing liability on legal persons. The typical context in which a transnational bribery transaction occurs serves to highlight some of the difficult issues that national legal systems have to grapple with to ensure an effective liability regime for legal persons. The typical scenario for a transnational bribe transaction often presents itself in the following manner. A corporation incorporated in a developed country (State A) decides to conduct business in a developing country (State X). The corporation incorporates a wholly owned subsidiary in State A, and the wholly owned subsidiary incorporates a subsidiary in State X. The State X subsidiary designates itself the owning company and incorporates an operating subsidiary in the same state. In the course of doing business in the developing country, the State A corporation concludes that the only way it could obtain certain lucrative contracts would be to bribe officials in State X. An agent of the operating corporation in State X pays a bribe to the State X official. The operating corporation is successfully prosecuted for violating the bribery statute in state X and is fined.

The capacity of the host state to impose a sanction on the operating corporation, however, may be limited. The operating corporation does not own any significant assets and therefore cannot pay the fine. The State X authorities can bankrupt the operating entity, but the effect on the parent corporation, the subsidiary of the State A corporation, is minimal.[1] The owning entity will still have all the relevant assets, which the operating entity's creditors cannot touch. The owning entity can simply find or create a new operating entity and carry on as before. In State A, the public prosecutor brings an action against the corporation for violating the prohibitions against the bribery of foreign public officials.

The preceding situation is the typical context in which transnational bribery by corporations occurs and it raises a number of issues pertinent to state legal systems. For instance, in the context of the transnational bribery transaction described previously, one of the primary questions that would determine the efficacy of prohibitions against transnational bribery is whether the legal system of both jurisdictions imposes criminal liability on corporations. There has already been considerable discussion within the academic literature on the justification for imposing criminal liability and sanctions on corporations.[2] Where the legal system does recognize the imposition of criminal liability on corporations, the debate often focuses on the potential benefits of prosecuting corporations as opposed to individuals.[3] Other questions debated in academic circles include the means and circumstances required to impute the actions of the agent to the corporation.[4]

The determination that the actions of the agent are those of the corporation hardly ends the array of issues raised by this typical transnational bribery transaction. Other key issues include whether or not the parent corporation should be held liable for the actions of the subsidiary. For instance, using agency principles as the basis for liability, some courts impute criminal liability on a parent for the actions of a subsidiary. The basis for the liability of the parent corporation rests on the principle that where the parent controls the subsidiary corporation, the subsidiary acts not for itself but for the parent. Thus, the parent is liable for the acts of the subsidiary within the scope of its authority even when the subsidiary is a foreign

1 See Williams, C [2002]: 'Corporate Social Responsibility In An Era Of Economic Globalisation', in Vol. 35, *UC Davis Law Review*, 705, at 769, discussing the issue of judgement-proof corporations in developing countries held by solvent developed country corporations.

2 See Khanna, V [1996]: 'Corporate Criminal Liability: What Purpose Does It Serve?', in Vol. 109, *Harvard Law Review*, at 1477 for a discussion on the merits and demerits of imposing criminal liability on corporations.

3 See Khanna, V [2000]: 'Corporate Liability Standards: When Should Corporations be Held Criminally Liable?', in Vol. 37, *American Criminal Law Review*, 1239.

4 For a discussion on the imputation of criminal liability see Lederman, E [2000]: 'Models for Imposing Corporate Criminal Liability: From Adaptation and Imitation Toward Aggregation and the Search for Self-Identity', in Vol. 4, *Buffalo Criminal Law Review*, 641.

corporation. There is even precedent to suggest that liability may be based on the parent's acquiescence in the subsidiary's criminal activity.

The yardstick of the liability of the parent for the actions of the subsidiary is the involvement of the parent in the affairs of the subsidiary. In holding the parent liable, the courts look beyond the formal separateness to disregard the rule of limited liability. This process is commonly referred to as 'piercing or lifting the veil' or 'disregarding the entity'. The decision to pierce the corporate veil raises a host of other considerations. These include the decision on when corporations are sufficiently affiliated with one another that the veil of limited liability would be lost. For instance, it is presumed that only controlling shareholders should lose the safeguard of limited liability. Determining whether one corporation controls another is easy when a parent owns all of the stock of a subsidiary, but what about cases in which the alleged parent owns, for example, 25 percent of the subsidiary's stock? Should it make a difference if the shareholders are individuals? Should these individual shareholders lose the protection of limited liability?

Multilateral Initiatives to Control Corruption

Clearly, developing and implementing an effective regulatory and liability regime to curb corruption by transnational corporations is a complex affair. So complicated in fact, that the international community has demonstrated a concerted effort towards the regulation of transnational corruption in general and corruption by transnational corporations in particular. A fundamental assumption underlying the collaborative efforts is the belief that a transnational business community operating on a level playing field would maximize the interaction and competition between industry players and in turn realize greater market efficiencies for society.[5] There are also several other reasons for the increased collaboration such as attitudinal changes to the acceptability of the high levels of corruption, technological advances that have created border-less capital markets, the closer integration of economies, international mergers, and the growing international awareness that transnational corruption has economic costs.

On the international level, several multilateral institutions and organisations have made considerable progress in the efforts to regulate transnational bribery, such as through the efforts of the Organisation for Economic Cooperation and Development (OECD) member countries. These efforts culminated in the signing of the OECD Convention on Combating Bribery of Foreign Public Officials (OECD Convention), which is undoubtedly an important milestone in the effort to combat transnational bribery and corruption in international business transactions. Following the OECD Convention has been the adoption of the Inter American

5 See Unzicker, A [2000]: 'From Corruption to Cooperation: Globalization Brings a Multilateral Agreement Against Foreign Bribery', in Vol. 7, *Indiana Journal of Global Legal Studies*, 655, at 666–8.

Convention on Corruption (the Organization of American States [OAS] Convention) and very recently, the United Nations Convention against Corruption (UNCAC). The speedy ratification of these conventions and subsequent implementation of domestic legislation are a tribute to the success of these initiatives.

Despite the adoption of these multilateral initiatives and the broad attack on transnational bribery by corporations, a significant limitation exists in the form of the sovereign right of every state to regulate criminal activities that occur within their territory. The limitation imposed by such a right poses fundamental challenges to the efforts to control transnational bribery in general and by corporations in particular. Transnational bribery transactions, by their very nature, consist of actions or actors in more than one state. Transnational bribery by corporations further complicates the regulation of corruption because the transnational activity of these corporations implicates the home and host state, each with its own interests. These interests, and the legal control of each state over a corporation, are not always perfectly aligned. For instance, the jurisdictions of each state could either overlap or (worse) contain a jurisdictional lacuna where the corporation is not subject to the law of either state because of the disparity of law in different states. A typical example of this jurisdictional lacuna applies in the states that have yet to criminalize transnational bribery. Corporations of those states operating through a subsidiary are not liable for transnational bribery in states that have a rigid veil piercing law.

The disparity between the regulatory regimes in various states is also a source of additional challenges to the regulation of corporate transnational bribery. The regulation of criminal conduct requires the development of domestic regulatory capacity as a precursor to the effective regulation of transnational bribery. However, there are serious disparities between states in their domestic regulatory capacity and their ability to enforce the regulatory regime prohibiting transnational bribery. In theory, the regulatory regimes prohibiting transnational bribery by corporations in some states may accord prohibitions similar to the regulatory regimes in other states. Nevertheless, the impediments to an effective legal regulatory apparatus are many. First, there are cultural obstacles, where laws may be enforced on a very flexible, negotiable, and non-confrontational basis. Here, informal relationships between parties may override any formal legal arrangements that exist between them. Second, the administrative and institutional capacity to enforce laws is crucial to the effective prohibition of transnational bribery. Very often, the sheer lack of capacity results in the inconsistent or ineffective application of the laws that prohibit transnational bribery. Criticisms of the shortcomings of many developing states in their efforts to regulate transnational bribery remain commonplace in much of the contemporary commentary on the regulation of transnational bribery.

The main condemnation of the current efforts to regulate transnational bribery relates to the prevalence of transnational bribery despite extensive legal devices to control the practice.[6] In these criticisms, domestic regimes seem too weak to pursue adequate regulation on their own while being ensconced in notions of sovereignty and jurisdiction, which hamper efforts to respond adequately with the cross-jurisdictional cooperation requisite to the effective regulation of transnational bribery. In addressing the strategies for tackling corruption, Salbu argues that fighting corruption by legal decree is naïve, as these decrees do not address the entrenched political, social, and economic causes of corruption.[7] McClenahen similarly suggests that anecdotal evidence and experience support his contention that legislation cannot effectively curb transnational bribery. In support of this assertion, he cites as an example the Foreign Corrupt Practices Act (FCPA) and other domestic forms of legislation that have been ineffectual in curbing transnational bribery.[8]

The assertion that the curbing of transnational bribery by legal decree is naïve is contested by Nichols, who argues that the majority of transnational bribery transactions do not involve the United States (US) or US businesses because of the impact of the FCPA.[9] Salbu counters this point with evidence, which suggests that more than 90 percent of US company directors believe their competitors outside the US occasionally or regularly use intermediaries to circumvent anti-corruption legislation in competing for contracts in developing countries.[10] He argues that much of the corruption faced by US corporations bidding for overseas contracts continues to be attributable to US competitors. In effect, even if these corporations are complying with the FCPA, they are still engaging in transnational bribery. Salbu qualifies his argument in response to Nichols by suggesting that his argument is not that the laws are entirely ineffectual in combating transnational bribery. Rather, he opines that the law serves a very limited role, and the limited role of the law must be taken into account and incorporated into public policy. In his view, the most likely benefit of legislation is convincing the world that bribery and corruption are serious problems. Beyond this, the role of the law in effecting social change is questionable.[11]

---

6 Johnston, M [2012]: 'Why Do So Many Anti-Corruption Efforts Fail?', in Vol. 67, *New York University Annual Survey of American Law*, 467, at 472. He notes that while the anti-corruption movement has gained strength nearly everywhere, it has had difficulty succeeding anywhere.

7 See Salbu, S [2000]: 'A Delicate Balance: Legislation, Institutional Change, and Transnational Bribery', in Vol. 33, *Cornell Journal of International Law*, 657, at 678.

8 See McClenahen, J [1998]: 'Bribery Remains Widespread', in *Industry Week*, Oct. 19, 1998, at 16.

9 See Nichols, P. [1999b]: 'Regulating Transnational Bribery in Times of Globalization and Fragmentation', in Vol. 24, *Yale Journal of International Law*, 257, at 286.

10 Salbu, S [2001]: 'Information Technology in the War Against International Bribery and Corruption: The Next Frontier of Institutional Reform', in Vol. 38, *Harvard Journal on Legislation*, 67, at 83.

11 See Salbu [2000: 681].

Without taking a position on the efficacy of the law in effecting social change, it is indisputable that legislative strategies to combat transnational bribery have both a supply and demand side. The demand side of bribery refers to demands or requests for bribes by public officials. The supply side of bribery refers to offers of bribes to public officials. A corrupt transaction can be initiated in either way. There are, therefore, supply-side solutions and demand-side solutions to curbing transnational bribery by corporations. The supply-side solutions seek to impede prospective bribe-givers from offering or paying bribers. The demand-side solution discourages prospective bribe-takers from accepting or requesting bribes. Initial efforts at curbing bribery focused on the demand side, with most countries enacting legislation prohibiting the receipt of bribes. In recent years, these have been supplemented by supply-side solutions to transnational bribery through the adoption of extra-territorial prohibitions on transnational bribery. In part, at least, this has been a response to the perceived ineffectiveness of mechanisms for the regulation or control of bribery in the place of its commission.

Framing the Arguments on the Multilateral Framework to Control Corruption

This book sets out the argument that the current multilateral and domestic efforts to curb transnational bribery by corporations are unlikely to result in a reduction of the prevalence of bribery in international business transactions. The shortcomings are linked, among other issues, to the challenge presented by transnational corporations. The challenge posed by transnational corporations is that although commercial relationships increasingly transcend political borders, the laws regulating these transactions and the responsibility for enforcement remains determined by national regulatory institutions. These national institutions are, more often than not, too weak to regulate transnational bribery by corporations adequately. Theoretically, these national institutions would benefit from the support provided by an effective international regime for the regulation of transnational bribery. Unfortunately, the international regime has, however, been rendered ineffective by an overwhelming number of substantive and procedural impediments requisite to an effective regime to regulate transnational bribery by corporations.

There are at least two identifiable propositions explaining why the current multilateral regulatory regime to curb transnational bribery by corporations has not been effective. The first position, put forward by the proponents of the current multilateral efforts to regulate transnational bribery by corporations, link the failure of the current multilateral efforts to deficiencies in pursuing the existing regulatory interventions aggressively enough.[12] The second position, put forward by the opponents of the current multilateral efforts, locates the ineffectiveness of

12 Nichols [1999b: 258–303]. For a similar argument, see Tarullo, D [2004]: 'The Limits of Institutional Design: Implementing the OECD Anti-Bribery Convention', in

the current multilateral efforts, not in the failure to pursue the interventions but in the multilateral initiatives themselves. They argue essentially that multilateral initiatives against corruption are unacceptable forms of moral imperialism because the global community has yet to develop into a single viable community that can be effectively subjected to a single set of extrinsically imposed rules.[13] Both the proponents and opponents of the current multilateral efforts to regulate transnational bribery by corporations through multilateral cooperation typically begin at the same point and then diverge. The two positions both agree on the basic notion that the legal efforts to curb the prevalence of transnational bribery have thus far been ineffective. From this point, the two positions diverge regarding their diagnosis of the problem and in their appreciation as to what solutions might be used to reduce the levels of transnational bribery.

This argument set forth in this book offers a supplementary explanation for the failure of the current multilateral regime to curb the incidents of transnational bribery by corporations. In seeking to answer the question of why the regulation of transnational bribery by corporations has remained ineffective despite multilateral efforts, several factors weaken the explanatory power of the arguments of both the proponents and opponents of the current multilateral initiatives. First, whilst opponents of the current multilateral efforts suggest that the multilateral initiatives are to blame for the failure to curb transnational bribery by corporations, it is argued here that multilateral efforts have in fact managed to produce a remarkable degree of uniformity in the substantive laws regulating transnational bribery by corporations. If, then, there remain few substantive differences between states in their prohibition of transnational bribery by corporations, it is difficult to argue that the multilateral approach itself is responsible for the inefficacy of the regulatory regime.

Second, the book also supplements the arguments of the proponents of the current multilateral efforts to regulate transnational bribery by corporations that ascribe the variations in the efficacy of transnational prohibitions of bribery to differences in enforcement mechanisms. Whilst the incentives for regulation may differ from one state to another, there is still insufficient evidence to suggest that a more aggressive stance on the enforcement of transnational bribery through the passage of provisions prohibiting transnational bribery will improve the efficacy of the regime regulating transnational bribery by corporations. One needs only to look at the record of the FCPA and the continued engagement of US businesses in transnational bribery transactions for support for the assertion that an aggressive stance through the passage of legislation and its enforcement does not necessarily translate into a decrease in the prevalence of transnational bribery by corporations.

In sum, the impossibility of the position of the opponents of the current multilateral efforts and the indeterminacy of the position of the proponents of

---

Vol. 44, *Virginia Journal of International Law*, 665, at 666–9. He argues that the signatories to the OECD Convention either lack the will or capacity to meet their obligations.

13 Salbu [1999b]: 'Extraterritorial Restriction of Bribery: A Premature Evocation of the Normative Global Village', in Vol. 24, *Yale Journal of International Law*, 223, at 226.

the current multilateral efforts to curb transnational bribery by corporations leave many issues unexplained in the regulation of transnational bribery and therefore weaken the explanatory power of both positions. Still, if these explanations fail or at least seem implausible, and fail to describe adequately the causes of the inefficacy of the regulatory regime, what alternative explanation could account for the inability of the current multilateral efforts to curb transnational bribery by corporations? The arguments developed in the subsequent chapters seek to supplement the explanations in two main areas. First, the book attempts to explore the connection between the multilateral agreements and the changes in the national regulatory regimes. Second, the book attempts to relate the causes of the failure of the multilateral efforts to the interaction between the transnational prohibitions and the underlying regulatory regime. Consequently, the argument developed suggests that the reasons for the lack of effectiveness of the multilateral efforts can be better understood in terms of the basic tension exhibited between these prohibitions and the underlying regulatory regime. These tensions pre-exist the prohibitions against transnational, but are certainly substantially intensified by them.

The framework for analysis examines two particular constraints that operate upon the multilateral efforts to regulate transnational bribery. The first constraint concerns the limits of international cooperation in the regulation of transnational bribery. The domestic legal regime is better disposed to provide a legal framework to regulate transnational bribery by accommodating the economic, social, and cultural concerns implicated in the regulation of transnational bribery. The notion of territoriality inherent in the regulation of criminal conduct requires that the development of the domestic regulatory capacity is a necessary precondition to effective efforts to regulate transnational bribery by corporations. There are nevertheless serious disparities between states in their individual capacity to effectively regulate and enforce the transnational bribery prohibitions against transnational corporations. Some of the challenges that these domestic jurisdictions face include the lack of enforcement resources and skills, weak judicial capacity, and the lack of political will to confront large transnational corporations that engage in bribery.[14] These challenges counter the perception that the regulation of transnational bribery can only be effective through higher levels of compliance by states, which, tragically, the current multilateral efforts are unable to secure. It argues that the ideological and substantive legal convergence that those efforts seek will not necessarily result in any greater effectiveness in securing the prohibition against transnational bribery. There are, it is argued, many important obstacles to effective convergence in the regulation of transnational bribery, which relate to the structure of the legal systems within which those prohibitions are supposed to operate.

14 See Wurmnest, W [2005]: 'Foreign Private Plaintiffs, Global Conspiracies, and the Extraterritorial Application of U.S. Antitrust Law', in Vol. 28, *Hastings International and Comparative Law Review*, 205, at 216, where he notes that developing nations often lack credible deterrence power to control the predatory conduct of multinational corporations.

The second constraint concerns the limits of the current liability regime for the regulation of transnational bribery by corporations. The administration and enforcement of international agreements is strongly linked to domestic institutional capacity. A component, critical to the effective regulation of the prohibitions against transnational bribery by national legal systems, is the imposition of effective sanctions. There are nevertheless significant shortcomings in the ability of states to impose effective sanctions. Modern transnational corporations have evolved into complex institutions, and the design of rules to alter their behaviour must be based on a more thorough understanding of how these corporations will respond to these rules. There are two broad methods that may underpin any regulatory strategy, and these two methods are also applicable to the efforts to curb transnational bribery by corporations. First, the law may impose obligatory commands on corporations to refrain from engaging in transnational bribery backed up by a system of deterrence including the sanctioning of non-compliance. Second, the law may analyse the nature of the corporation and then design rules to alter the behaviour of the corporations based on their anticipated responses to the rules. The creation of rules to alter the behaviour of corporations is particularly dependent on knowing more about the behaviour of these corporations.

Unfortunately, at present the deterrence model in the current regime for the regulation of transnational bribery allows the decision-makers within these corporations to shield themselves from liability. For instance, the legal principle that a corporation is a separate legal entity and therefore deserving of limited liability even if it is part of a corporate group is at odds with the fact that many corporate groups operate as a single entity, largely because of the economic benefits that result from the integration of activities. In the context of transnational bribery by corporations, the reason for constraining limited liability for corporations is even more compelling. This particular legal principle allows transnational corporations to shield themselves from liability for transnational bribery. These avenues for the evasion of liability for transnational bribery by corporations are therefore likely to produce troubling results with respect to some critical aspects of the regulation of transnational bribery.

Overview of Chapters

Although its initial point of departure is international law, the book nonetheless makes overtures to the disciplines of corporate and criminal law. Following the introduction, the book is divided into six additional chapters that examine the problem, response, and shortcomings of the response to transnational bribery. Chapter 2 examines the contemporary debate on corruption by incorporating the social science discourse of corruption into the mainstream legal discourse. Finding corruption to be a euphemism for a host of illicit activities, the analysis delimits the scope of the study by focusing on the problem of transnational bribery. Chapter 3 surveys the response of the selected domestic legal systems to the problems associated with the regulation of bribery and introduces the problems associated with the regulation of transnational bribery in particular. Specifically, this chapter examines the national response to the problem of transnational bribery by examining the scope and effectiveness of the FCPA.

Recognising that the regulation of transnational bribery cannot be divorced from its international context, an appraisal of the international responses to transnational bribery is the subject of Chapter 4. This chapter, in evaluating the current multilateral regime to regulate transnational bribery, lauds the current multilateral efforts to regulate transnational bribery, but suggests that the prospects for the success of these efforts are bleak. In Chapter 5, using the Oil for Food Programme as a case study, the book highlights some of the major challenges presented by the current framework governing the regulation of transnational bribery. At a minimum, this analysis suggests that the shortcomings of the current multilateral efforts to regulate transnational bribery stem from structural problems not with the prohibitions themselves, but with their interaction with the underlying legal systems, and these structural problems are therefore likely to produce troubling results with respect to some critical aspects of the regulation of transnational bribery.

Given the host of challenges identified with the regulation of transnational bribery, one unexplored area is the liability regime for transnational corporations. In Chapter 6, the book uses the liability regime for corporations to illustrate this unexplored shortcoming of the multilateral regime regulating transnational bribery. Chapter 7 lays out the foundation for a new liability framework for corporations. Chapter 8 summarizes and concludes the study.

Chapter 2
Corruption: The General Debate

The discussion of corruption, while long the subject of theoretical interest and debate, has finally emerged as a matter of significant practical importance. This emergence is timeous given the challenges that have been a hallmark of the debate over the last 30 years. Many developing countries, which are at the site of and bear a disproportionate impact of the burden of corruption, face significant challenges in delivering a wide range of public services essential for development. These developing countries are not all similar to countries where governments are barely able to provide services on one side of the spectrum to governments where institutions are doing well by most development measures at the other end. In between both ends of this spectrum, there remain many countries that are doing well on many of the development indices, but where corruption still remains a rampant problem. The core challenge inevitably boils down to this question: How to ensure that corruption does not roll back the developmental gains? Unfortunately, the core of the debate manifests itself in widespread disagreement over the precise contours of the word *corruption*, its effect, and the appropriate strategies to tackle the phenomenon. Given the fundamental nature of the disagreements, it is important to determine whether the points of contention can be resolved, or whether instead we should be seeking new ways of understanding the problem of corruption.

In the last 20 years, we have come a long way with respect to our knowledge base about the impact of corruption and the link with economic development. Initial reliance had been placed on conventional wisdom that suggested that countries were supposed to get less corrupt as their economies developed. We have, however, come to realize that simple causality between economic development and corruption simply does not exist and that the relationship appears to be more complex. We can categorically state that corruption limits economic growth by diverting resources away from productive activities. Researchers have, however, been documenting the fact that corruption also appears to be influenced by levels of development. This two-way causality accords with empirical evidence that countries at similar stages of development can display varying degrees of corruption.

The academic debate on corruption is marked by a sizeable literature.[1] This chapter seeks to provide a basis for understanding the phenomenon of corruption

1 Some of the influential writings on corruption include the following: Alam, M [1991]: 'Some Economic Costs of Corruption in LDCs', in Vol. 27, *Journal of*

by carrying out a cross-disciplinary analysis of the issue of corruption. The study of corruption carries with it particular problems that go beyond the definitional challenges. Most notable of these problems is the dearth of empirical literature on corruption. For instance, with several notable exceptions, such as Dittons's analysis of fiddling within the bakery firm in which he was employed, few are prepared to run the physical risks required to study illegal dealing from the inside.[2] The general reluctance to study corruption from the inside has ensured that there is a dearth of empirical studies on corruption and that most analysis of the subject

---

Development Studies, 89; Alam, M [1995]: 'A Theory of Limits on Corruption and Some Applications', in Vol. 48, *Kyklos*: *International Review for Social Science*, 419; Alatas, S [1990]: *Corruption: Its Nature, Causes and Functions* (Aldershot: Ashgate); Bhagwati, J [1982]: 'Directly Unproductive, Profit-seeking (DUP) Activities', in Vol. 90, *Journal of Political Economy*, 988; Bliss, C & Rafael, D [1997]: 'Does Competition Kill Corruption?', in Vol. 105, *Journal of Political Economy*, 1001; Buscaglia, E [2001]: 'An Analysis of Judicial Corruption and Its Causes: An Objective Governing-Based Approach', in Vol. 21, *International Review of Law and Economics*, 233; Glynn, P, Stephen K & Moisés, N [1997]: 'The Globalization of Corruption', in Kimberly Ann Elliott, (ed.) [1996]: *Corruption and the Global Economy* (Washington D.C.: Institute for International Economics), 7; Heimann, F [1997]: 'Combating International Corruption: The Role of the Business Community', in Kimberly Ann Elliott (ed.) [1996]: *Corruption and the Global Economy* (Washington D.C.: Institute for International Economics), 147; Johnston, M [1996]: 'The Search for Definitions: The Vitality of Politics and the Issue of Corruption', in Vol. 149, *International Social Science Journal*, 321; Johnston, M [1997]: 'Public Officials, Private Interests, and Sustainable Democracy: When Politics and Corruption Meet', in Kimberly Ann Elliott, (ed.) [1996]: *Corruption and the Global Economy* (Washington D.C.: Institute for International Economics), 61; Kaufmann, D & Paul S [1995]: 'Privatization and Corruption in Transition Economies', in Vol. 50, *Journal of International Affairs*, 419; Krueger, A [1993b]: 'Virtuous and Vicious Circles in Economic Development', in Vol. 83, *American Economic Review*, 351; Krueger, A [1993a]: *Political Economy of Policy Reform in Developing Countries* (Cambridge: MIT Press); Leys, C [1965]: 'What Is the Problem About Corruption?', in Vol. 3, *The Journal of Modern African Studies*, 215; Mauro, P [1995]: 'Corruption and Growth', in Vol. 106, *Quarterly Journal of Economics*, 681; Murphy, K, Schleifer, A & Vishny, R [1993]: 'Why is Rent-Seeking So Costly to Growth?', in Vol. 83, *The American Economic Review*, 409; Rose-Ackerman, S [1996]: 'Democracy and "Grand" Corruption', in Vol. 48, No. 149, *International Social Science Journal: Corruption in Western Democracies*, 365; Rose-Ackerman, S [1997]: 'The Political Economy of Corruption', in Kimberly Ann Elliott, (ed.) [1996]: *Corruption and the Global Economy* (Washington D.C.: Institute for International Economics), 31; Williams, R [1999]: 'The New Politics of Corruption', in Vol. 20, *Third World Quarterly*, 487; Kofele-Kale, N [2006]: 'Change or the Illusion of Change: The War Against Official Corruption in Africa', in Vol. 38, *George Washington International Law Review*, 697; Johnston, M, (ed.) [2005]: *Civil Society and Corruption: Mobilizing for Reform* (Lanham: University Press of America).

2 See Ditton, J [1977, May]: 'Alibis and Aliases: Some Notes on the "Mmotives" of Fiddling Bread salesmen', in Vol. 11, No. 2, *Sociology*, 233.

is assembled from source material and fieldwork that had some other object as the focus of its analysis.[3]

The first section of this chapter reflects on the various attempts to define corruption and the inherent difficulties encountered therein. The second section briefly evaluates the now sterile debate on the plausible benefits of corruption and locates the effects of corruption on a continuum between conduct having deleterious effects and those that serve a particular benefit. The various types of corruption and some of the reasons advanced for their occurrence highlight the complexity involved in trying to conceive of corruption as a single unified phenomenon. The cursory survey indicates that there are many forms of corruption, differing in participants, settings, stakes, techniques, and cultural legitimacy. Finding corruption to be a euphemism for a host of illicit activities, the third section focuses the debate by delimiting the boundaries of the phenomenon of corruption by focusing on a particular type of corruption (bribery). Section four considers the transnational dimension of bribery.

Difficulties in Defining Corruption

Anthropologists, economists, sociologists, and political scientists have remarkably different ways of viewing corruption. The anthropological literature on corruption in general has focused on the values concerned in corruption transactions. For instance, the anthropological literature has analysed bribery in the context of traditional gift-giving practices.[4] Studies by economists tend to focus on corruption as a function of scarcity.[5] For instance, one economist has described bribery as a situation where the benefit (to a corrupt agent) of acting against the expectation of a principal outweighs the cost; or where a public good, service, or office is sold for

---

3 See Buscaglia, E & Dakolias, M [1999]: 'An Analysis of the Causes of Corruption in the Judiciary', in Vol. 30, *Law and Policy in International Business Law and Policy in International Business*, 95, at 98–9, explaining the need for empirical studies on the causes of corruption and noting that no such empirical work exists. Ohnesorge, J [1999] criticises the lack of empirical historical research on corruption in 'Ratcheting Up the Anti-Corruption Drive: Could a Look at Recent History Cure a Case of Theory-Determinism?', in Vol. 14, *Connecticut Journal of International Law*, 467.

4 See Scott, J [1979]: 'The Analysis of Corruption in Developing Nations', in Ekpo, M, (ed.) [1979]: *Bureaucratic Corruption in Sub-Saharan Africa: Toward a Search for Causes and Consequences* (Washington D.C.: University Press of America), 29, at 29–30 for an analysis of corruption as a gift giving practice.

5 See Rose-Ackerman, S. [1999] *Corruption and Government: Causes, Consequences and Reform* (Cambridge: Cambridge University Press), at xi, where she states, '[e]conomics is a powerful tool for the analysis of corruption. Cultural differences and morality provide nuance and subtlety, but an economic approach is fundamental to understanding where corrupt incentives are the greatest and have the biggest impact'.

personal gain.[6] These economists have argued that because the demand for goods is greater than the supply, there is tendency for these goods to rise over and above their official price.[7] The sociological approach views corruption as a function of power-status relationships represented in the violation of socially accepted norms of duty and welfare. These sociologists argue that the institutionalized system of unequal rewards is the very basis for the commission of acts of corruption.[8] Political science commentators view the presence of corruption within a society as a symptom of more deeply rooted problems in the society's structure related in particular to the means of attaining and maintaining power.[9] This particular approach to corruption suggests that bureaucratic corruption, for instance, is an informal means of exerting influence at the enforcement stage of the political process.[10]

Constructing an all-encompassing definition of a nebulous occurrence such as corruption is a dispiriting task.[11] In the course of examining the various attempts at defining corruption, it is important to note that the various definitions employed tend to direct attention to different lines of enquiry. This is because, whether corruption is defined in terms of illegality, immorality or some other standard, the choice of definition reflects the focus of each analyst and reflects the kind of questions he hopes to provide answers for in his study. The purpose of this section is simply to provide a general review of the explanatory directions taken by various studies and to note their most striking features.

---

6 See Tilman, R [1979]: 'Emergence of Black-Market Bureaucracy: Administration, Development, and Corruption in the New States', in Ekpo, M, (ed.) [1979]: *Bureaucratic Corruption in Sub-Saharan Africa: Toward a Search for Causes and Consequences* (Washington D.C.: University Press of America), 341, at 341–3, who describes corruption in transaction terms.

7 For a description of corruption in the context of a market transaction, see Klitgaard, R [1988]: *Controlling Corruption* (Los Angeles: University of California Press) at 22; and Schleifer, A & Vishny, R [1993]: 'Corruption', in Vol. 108, *Quarterly Journal of Economics*, 599 at 599.

8 See Defleur, M [1995]: 'Corruption, Law and Justice', in Vol. 23, *Journal of Criminal Law and Justice*, 243 at 243. He defines corruption as a 'colonization of social relations in which two or more actors undertake an exchange relation by way of a successful transfer of the steering media of money or power, thereby sidestepping the legally prescribed procedure to regulate the relation'.

9 See Shihata, I [1997]: 'Corruption – A General Review with an Emphasis on the Role of the World Bank', in Vol. 15, Dickinson. *Journal of International Law*, 451, at 451 for a typical description of corruption in the political science context.

10 See Scott, J [1979]: 'Corruption, Machine Politics, and Political Change', in Ekpo, M, (ed.) [1979]: *Bureaucratic Corruption in Sub-Saharan Africa: Toward a Search for Causes and Consequences* (Washington D.C.: University Press of America), 101, at 101, for an interesting analysis of corruption as a form of interest articulation.

11 See Burger, E & Holland, M [2006]: 'Why the Private Sector is Likely to Lead the Next Stage in the Global Fight Against Corruption', in Vol. 30, *Fordham International Law Journal*, 45, at 48. They note the difficulties encountered by Member States in defining corruption in the UN Convention.

Corruption: A Mosaic of Activities

The host of illicit activities that have been grouped under the general heading of corruption is extensive. These actions range from conduct that included bribery, illegal political contributions, the sharing of confidential information, kickbacks, and fraud. With all these activities, a distinction was often drawn between 'political' and 'bureaucratic' corruption. Political corruption involved situations where lawmakers have improperly discharged their duties while acting in their role as creators of the rules and standards by which a polity operates.[12] Bureaucratic corruption, on the other hand, involves law administrators who improperly discharged their duties while acting in their capacity as those who put the law into practice.

Another distinction often drawn is between 'parochial' and 'market' corruption.[13] Parochial corruption refers to situations where public officials misuse their office for the benefit of their family, kin group, or equivalent. In this type of corruption, only ties of kinship, affection, caste, and so forth determine access to the favours of the power holders. Market corruption, on the other hand, occurs when an official misuses his office for monetary or equivalent gain. This type of corruption signifies an impersonal process in which the influence is accorded to those who can pay regardless of who they are. In practice, one is more likely to encounter mixed cases of both types of corruption.

The taxonomy of government corruption suggested by Alam and Mbaku identifies four different broad types of corruption.[14] The first, 'cost-reducing corruption', occurs when an official reduces the burden on an individual of interacting with the government, and thus lowers the cost or difficulty of conducting business or undertaking some other action.[15] A typical example might include granting a regulatory license in exchange for a bribe or waiving a tariff applicable to a product imported by a member of his family. They can both be classified as 'cost-reducing corruption', but the first example is also 'market' corruption while the second is 'parochial'. The second type of corruption in Alam and Mbaku's suggested taxonomy is the 'cost enhancing corruption'. Alam suggests that this sort of corruption usually arises in circumstances where the demand for a product or service provided by the government exceeds supply or in a situation where the government has a monopoly on the supply of the goods

12 Huntington, S [1979]: 'Modernization and Corruption', in Ekpo, M, (ed.) [1979]: *Bureaucratic Corruption in Sub-Saharan Africa: Toward a Search for Causes and Consequences* (Washington D.C.: University Press of America), 313, at 319.

13 See Scott, J [1979: 43–4].

14 See Alam, M [1989] 'Anatomy of Corruption: An Approach to the Political Economy of Underdevelopment', in Vol. 48, *American Journal of Economics and Sociology*, 441, at 443; and Mbaku, J [1994]: 'Bureaucratic Corruption and Policy Reform in Africa', in Vol. 19, *Journal of Social Political and Economic Studies*, 149, at 149.

15 Alam [1989: 442] and Mbaku [1994: 158] describe cost-reducing corruption.

or services. The government official can thus collect a rent by charging whatever personal fee the market will bear or collect the monopoly premium as a personal fee. The third category in this taxonomy of corruption is the 'benefit-enhancing corruption', which involves a transfer of benefits exceeding the amount permitted or authorized to the recipient of governmental services. Mbaku refers to this as collusive corruption, citing nepotism as a widespread example of this type of corruption.[16] The final category, 'benefit-reducing corruption', involves outright theft or appropriation of benefits.

Straightforward Definitions

Noonan, in his analysis of the different types of definitions of corruption suggests there are at least four different types of definitions of corruption:[17] the definition espoused by the advanced moralists, that of the law as written; that of the law as in any degree enforced, and that of common parlance. [18] *Webster's Dictionary* defines corruption as an:

> Inducement (as of a political official) by means of improper considerations (as bribery) to commit a violation of duty. The selling of political favours or other improper political or legal transactions or arrangements.[19]

In the preceding definition of corruption, the essence of the corrupt activity is located in some form of illicit, illegal, or otherwise improper transaction; or the relationship between someone performing a public duty and someone seeking an undue preference or advantage. In the *Oxford Dictionary* version of corruption, the transitive verb to 'corrupt' means:

> [t]o destroy or pervert the integrity or fidelity of (a person) in his discharge of duty; to induce to act dishonestly or unfaithfully; to make venal; to bribe.[20]

Both the Webster's and Oxford dictionary definitions of corruption explicitly include both the giving and receiving of bribes. These definitions however, are less specific about other forms of corruption; for instance, it would be difficult to include acts such as embezzlement within this definition.

---

16 See Mbaku [1994: 158].

17 See Noonan, J [1984]: *Bribes* (New York: Macmillan), at xii, who was referring to bribes in particular, but the statement is equally true of all forms of corruption.

18 The term *bribe* is used in this study as a specific example of corruption, and the relation between both terms is discussed in the section 'Bribery: A Specific Type of Corruption'.

19 *Webster's Third International Dictionary Unabridged*, June 2002.

20 *Oxford Dictionary of Current English*, March 2001.

Williams posits that corruption is a question of moral standards and values. He suggests that the standards adhered to by the community determine what practices are deemed as corrupt in that community.[21] Consonant with much of modern scholarship on corruption, the view taken here eschews the value-laden approach of the organic and moralist definitions of corruption. This is because despite the use of a general set of standards to condemn corrupt behaviour, these definitions do not offer a means of identifying and explaining specific instances of corruption in different societies. With particular relevance to transnational corruption, these definitions do not admit of the possibility that what is meant by corruption may vary from society to society.[22] Furthermore, in cases of differing standards, either within a particular society or between two independent societies, there currently exist no mechanisms for reconciling the different moral standards or deciding which moral standard should prevail. Once one accepts that corruption is a culturally laden phenomenon, as Heidenheimer notes, one must also accept that there are nevertheless certain commonalities within the different cultural formulations of corruption.[23]

Public Office and Public Interest Definitions

In a comparative study of writings on corruption, Heidenheimer identified various categories within which definitions of corruption generally fell. They included public office–centred definitions, market-centred definitions, and public interest–centred definitions. Heidenheimer observed that public office–centred definitions were concerned with the deviation of members of society from rules and formal duties, rather than with moral or physical decay of the society. The archetypal definition in this regard is that provided by Nye, who defined corruption as behaviour, which deviated from the normal duties of a public role because of private motivations, pecuniary, or status gains, or violated the rules against the exercise of certain types of private motivations.[24] The term behaviour utilized in Nye's definition encompasses improper action, inaction, and the wilful failure to act when and wherever required. This definition by Nye, however, contains certain possible ambiguities in that the definition excludes the activities of powerful lobbyists and

---

21 See Williams, R [1987]: *Political Corruption in Africa* (Aldershot: Gower Publication Inc.), at 13.

22 See, for instance, Ouzounov, N [2004]: 'Facing the Challenge Corruption, State Capture, and the Role of Multinational Businesses', in Vol. 37, *John Marshall Law Review*, 1181, at 1185, where he notes that perceptions of corruption vary depending on factors such as the industry where it is observed, the governing laws, and the local culture.

23 See Heidenheimer, A. [1970]: *Political Corruption: Readings in Comparative Analysis*, (New York: Holt, Rinehart, and Winston), at 4.

24 Nye, J [1979]: 'Corruption and Political Development: A Cost-Benefit Analysis', in Ekpo, M, (ed.) [1979]: *Bureaucratic Corruption in Sub-Saharan Africa: Toward a Search for Causes and Consequences* (Washington D.C.: University Press of America), 411, at 414.

private interest groups unless they seek to accomplish their ends through bribery or otherwise violate the rules governing the discharge of an official's public duty.

McMullan provides another public office–centred definition of corruption.[25] He states that corruption occurs when a public official accepts money or money's worth for doing something he is under a duty to do anyway or exercises a legitimate discretion for improper reasons. Along with Nye's definition, the definition of corruption espoused by McMullan also contains certain assumptions regarding the consequences of corruption, and both fail to address the issue of whether the behaviour defined as corrupt is perceived as corrupt in the particular society. On the other hand, the perception of society to the corrupt act is, in the view of Klich, central to the definition of corruption.[26] In her view, definitions that ignore the perception of society are flawed in that if the laws are unjust to begin with, breaking them, whatever the motivation, is hard to classify as corrupt. The shortcomings of infusing the public perception of corruption include the example of Nazi Germany, which had laws that mandated placing all Jews in concentration camps. According to the public office definition of corruption, any employee of the Nazi German government who would accept a bribe to help a Jew would be acting corruptly.[27] This example buttresses the previous argument regarding the influence of public perception both across different societies and across time on the definition of corruption.

The public interest–centred definitions of corruption, on the other hand, seek to fill the void left by the public office–centred definitions. Public interest definitions rely on the proposition that public institutions are public goods and thus exalt common interest over special interest. In this construct, activities are regarded as corrupt where public institutions are subverted to further private interests with or without detriment to the interest of the public. Friedrich provides one example of a public interest–centred definition of corruption in his analysis of corruption.[28] He posits that a pattern of corruption could be said to exist whenever a power holder is by monetary or other rewards not legally provided for, induced to take actions in favour of the provider, thereby doing damage to the public and its interest.

More pertinently, Rosgow and Laswell put the issue of the interest of the public at the heart of their definition of corruption.[29] They suggest that an act is corrupt when it violates the responsibility towards at least one system of public or civic order and is in fact incompatible with the system. The central tenet of these two

25 See McMullan, M [1961]: 'A Theory of Corruption', in Vol. 9, *Sociological Review*, 181, at 183–4.

26 Klich, A [1996]: 'Bribery in Economies in Transition: The Foreign Corrupt Practices Act', in Vol. 32, *Stanford Journal of International Law*, 121, at 127.

27 For a similar argument, see Green, S [2006]: *Lying, Cheating and Stealing – A Moral Theory of White Collar Crime* (Oxford: Oxford University Press), at 206–7.

28 Friedrich, C [1966]: 'Political Pathology', in Vol. 37, *Political Quarterly*, 70, at 74.

29 Rosgow, A & Laswell, H [1978]: 'The Definition of Corruption', in Heidenheimer, A, (ed.) [1978]: *Political Corruption: Readings in Comparative Analysis* (New Brunswick: Transaction Books) 54, at 54.

public interest–centred definitions is that corruption is characterized as being inimical to public interest by undermining the health of the society. The public interest definitions are disparaged by Williams, who proffers the opinion that the public interest approach to corruption amounts to an attempt to solve an essentially normative or ideological question by definition.[30] He further states that this line of reasoning is unjustifiable in that there is no consensus on what constitutes the interest of the public interest and therefore no agreeable criteria upon which one can determine whether certain forms of conduct undermine the interest of the public.

The essential distinction between the public office and public interest definitions of corruption is that the public interest–centred definitions advocate some kind of allowance for corruption where the laws are unjust. The advocates of the public office definitions, on the other hand, object to exonerating certain acts from being labelled corrupt on the basis that the substantive policy is in the interest of the public. The position taken in this study is distinct from public interest–centred definitions of corruption. The objection of this study to the public interest definitions is that the interest of the public is an amorphous and ambiguous concept, and thus susceptible to different interpretations and possible manipulation by conflicting interests in society. Therefore, the acceptance of a public interest definition of corruption would ensure that the determination of whether a particular policy influencing action is or is not corrupt would depend on whether the direction in which the corrupt act seeks to influence policy is, or is not, desirable. This would ensure not only that such judgements would nearly always be controversial but would also suggest that the end effectively justifies the means. The unintended effect, therefore, would be that what appears to be a legal wrong could be exonerated from the charge of corruption if the parties can argue convincingly that the substantive policy they are seeking to influence is in the interest of the public.[31]

Other significant problems with the public interest–centred definitions of corruption have been noted by Dunfee. For instance, under the public interest–centred analysis of corruption, other duties could mitigate one's engagement in a bribe transaction.[32] These could include duties such as feeding one's family, employing workers, or pursuing a worthwhile goal. Williams has rejected definitions of corruption cast in terms of morality or the public interest because of the difficulty in identifying precisely the public whose opinion is to be decisive.[33] He also rejects definitions cast in terms of descriptions of corrupt conduct that, whilst eschewing normative considerations, are too general to give operative significance to the term corruption.

---

30 See Williams [1987: 15].

31 For a similar view, see Johnston, M [1982]: *Political Corruption and Public Policy in America* (Monterey: Brooks/Cole Publishing Company), at 5–6.

32 See Dunfee, T [1999]: 'Social Contracts and Marketing Ethics', in Vol. 63, *Journal of Marketing*, 14, at 14.

33 Williams [1987: 19]. Johnston [1982: 7] also presents arguments against defining corruption by reference to public opinion.

Market-Centred and Normative-Based Definitions

Market-centred definitions, in contrast to the public-interest definitions of corruption, seek to locate the definition of corruption in the neutrality of economics. These market-centred definitions suggest that individuals use their position or authority to maximize personal gains by dispensing public benefits. An example of a market-centred definition of corruption is provided by Leff, who defines corruption as an extra-legal institution used by individuals to gain influence over the actions of bureaucracy.[34] In this formulation of corruption, the act of corruption is used by an individual or groups to get what they want from government, or prevent actions they do not want, often drawing upon many of the same resources as more conventional forms of influence. Leff further points out that the acts of corruption, when viewed neutrally, are only indicative that these individuals are participating in the decision-making process of the society. The crucial factor, however, remains that participation takes place at the enforcement stage rather than at the time before the decision is made. In this sense, corruption is a form of influence, albeit an illicit form of influence.

Tilman's market-centred definition suggests that acts of corruption invariably constitute a shift from a mandatory pricing model to a free market model.[35] He points out that individuals may decide that it is worthwhile to risk the known sanctions and pay the higher costs rather than to lose the benefit. When this occurs, bureaucracy ceases to be patterned after the mandatory market and takes on the characteristics of the free market. This particular characterization of corruption initially strikes conflicting sentiments in that Tilman's explanation would suggest that the free market model could only be achieved by permitting the market participants to engage in corrupt activities. This paradigm could thus be used as an excuse for eliminating a free market through the imposition of mandatory controls. This view, however, ignores a significant fact. The free market does not advocate the complete absence of controls. Mandates can be justified (using economic terminology) if they are demonstrably Pareto superior or, at least, Kaldor-Hicks efficient.[36] In contrast, a free market approach to corruption can be only justified without having to reach a firm conclusion on the efficiency issue if corruption is presumptively efficient. The two market-centred definitions of corruption thus adopt the standard

---

34 See Leff, N [1979]: 'Economic Development through Bureaucratic Corruption', in Ekpo, M, (ed.) [1979]: *Bureaucratic Corruption in Sub-Saharan Africa: Toward a Search for Causes and Consequences* (Washington D.C.: University Press of America), 8, at 8.

35 See Tilman [1979: 347].

36 Under Pareto efficiency, an outcome is more efficient if at least one person is made better off, and nobody is made worse off. Kaldor-Hicks efficiency suggests that an outcome is more efficient if those who are made better off could in theory compensate those who are made worse off and lead to a Pareto optimal outcome. Thus, a more efficient outcome can, in fact, leave some people worse off. See Posner, R [1998]: *Economic Analysis of Law* (5th ed.) (New York: Aspen Law and Business), at 14–17, for a background discussion on Pareto efficiency and explaining the relationship between Pareto and Kaldor-Hicks efficiency.

assumption of neo-classical economics that each individual seeks to maximize his preferences. Moreover, they generally assume that each individual acts in her own self-interest, with self-interest very narrowly defined. This approach presents a significant obstacle to the articulation of a cogent market-centred definition of corruption, as it leaves no scope for the normative aspect of law.

The denial of the normative aspect of law by the market-centred definitions, including norms that are fundamental to the law such as duty and rule, is supplemented by scholars such as Scott, who joins a number of economists in defining the normative element of corruption as a deviation from legal or formal norms of official conduct.[37] This view is echoed by Waterbury, who suggests that corruption may be defined in a legal or normative sense.[38] The distinction between corruption in the legal or normative sense, although controversial, is useful as it implies that we can attempt to use formal legal concepts to identify corruption in the legal sense while employing socio-cultural norms and judgements to identify corruption in the normative sense. The normative sense appeals to standards and values, while the legal meaning appeals to rules and laws. In the legal sense, self-regarding behaviour on the part of public functionaries directly violates legal restrictions on such behaviour. In most instances, an act satisfies the elements of both definitions, but it is possible for an act to be corrupt in one sense and not the other.

Normatively, a public functionary may be considered corrupt whether or not a law is being violated in the process. The perversion or destruction of integrity is crucial to both the legal and normative meanings. The legal sense is, however, distinguishable by its emphasis on the improper discharge of a public duty. The legal sense, in effect, relates corruption to the violation of a rule; and that notion is correspondingly related to a particular motive, improper advantage, or gain. A characteristic outcome of this relation is that legal rules are limited as they are confined to the administration of justice in situations where people are thought to have contravened rules or laws prohibiting corrupt behaviour. No reference is made to the society's perception of the significance of the actions of the individual. This perception, on the other hand, is crucial in the determination of corruption in the normative sense. Indeed, the contrasts between the formal rules and the social norms are intriguing in their own right. The legal definitions, however, have considerable merit in that laws offer some hope of consistency and are regularly subject to judicial interpretation and refinement. In this way, the illegality of behaviour is part of the contemporary notion of corruption; and the legal definition has an effect on the nature, scope, and consequence of such behaviour. The limitations and

---

37 See Scott [1979: 29]; Johnston [1998: 8]; Rose-Ackerman, S [1978]: *Corruption: A Study in Political Economy* (New York: Academic Press), at 7.

38 See Waterbury, J [1979]: 'Endemic and Planned Corruption in a Monarchical Regime', in Ekpo, M, (ed.) [1979]: *Bureaucratic Corruption in Sub-Saharan Africa: Toward a Search for Causes and Consequences* (Washington D.C.: University Press of America), 355, at 355.

inadequacy of legal definitions, however, are that the legislative process is often an arena for political competition and conflict in which the winners translate their victories into general rules binding on their political opponents. It is often possible for the politically powerful to legitimate their conduct by manipulating legislative and legal processes.

A Semantic Armistice

The previous discussion indicates that the literature on corruption is replete with definitions ranging from very broad formulations that encompass any behaviour on the part of individuals that deviates from accepted norms to more narrow definitions that focus on exchanges of money (bribery) that induce officials to break the law. Many of the previous commentators defined categories of behaviour as corrupt, with many relying on laws and other formal rules because of their relative precision to identify corrupt actions. This reliance on the law and formal rules is not without its critics, who suggest that in many societies, the law lacks legitimacy and consistent meaning, and that these legalisms tells us little about the social significance of behaviour and that public opinion or cultural standards are best for building definitions.[39] Still others dispute the behaviour classifying approach itself, regarding the moral health of society as the main issue in defining corruption.[40]

In general, even within the various factions of the scholars mentioned previously and the corruption discourse in general, ideological differences ensure that there is little agreement on what constitutes corruption, a consistent approach to the treatment, or an accepted definition of what exactly is corruption. The supposition is that the idea of corruption is being used to identify the subversion of norms of conduct that serve a particular social function. Therefore, corruption can only be defined at a particular place and under a system by certain established methods for classifying behaviour. This classification is generally achieved through the criminal law and its imposition of sanctions on certain actions. In defining and identifying those acts that are labelled corrupt, legislative isidecision-makers seek to reflect and mould social values concerning appropriate behaviour. The act of legislation not only serves to constrain the behaviour of social actors in conformity with the values in question but also the enculturation of these values more generally within society.

This raises the possibility that the word corruption is being used in many ways and more pertinently, not as an analytic claim but a semantic one. This hardly ends the inquiry, as these various conceptions of the corruption cannot be unrelated uses of the word. At best, the different uses of the word corruption would be more akin to alternative and possibly competing, definitions of the same word, which in turn, suggests a more serious set of concerns. Consider the multiple

---

39 See Peters, J & Welch, S [1978]: 'Political Corruption in America: A Search for Definitions and Theory', in Vol. 72, No. 3, *American Political Science Review*, 974 at 974–4.

40 See Thompson, D [1993]: 'Mediated Corruption: The Case of the Keating Five', in Vol. 87, No. 2, *American Political Science Review*, 369, at 369–81.

definitions of corruption highlighted previously. Many of the definitions overlap, but are not identical. Conduct could be classified as corrupt under, for instance, a public interest–centred definition but not an economic definition. That might be suggestive that the difference is only semantic. However, the line between genuinely contestable meaning and pure semantics is notoriously unclear. The distinct meanings of corruption come out of a history of real theoretical conflict or confusion. That the word is used in different ways and contexts is in part a semantic armistice to that conflict, which is hardly resolved by the differing uses of the word. This semantic use of the word has not proffered a solution to the definitional dilemma, but has endured as a symptom. Assuming this conflation of the semantic usage of the word corruption and prohibition of corruption as a legal standard to be true, the legal culture is prone to exacerbating the problems inherent in the regulation of corruption by merging the various meanings of the word.

The argument has thus far established that a universally agreed definition of corruption would be very difficult to achieve. Nevertheless, a universally agreed definition is not central to the main argument developed. This is because even if we were to adduce a common, universal, definition of corruption – if we could set aside the difficulties outlined previously – there are other profound difficulties with seeking to regulate corruption, as will be shown in the ensuing discussion. In that respect, the definitional debate is only important insofar as it helps to reveal the preconceived assumptions of particular commentators and their evaluation of the current efforts to combat transnational corruption.

There are however, other difficulties besides the semantic usage of the word corruption, which exacerbate the definitional dilemma encountered in the regulation of corruption. These difficulties have persisted and been articulated under the rubric of the debate about the harmful effects of corruption. Commentators trying to situate the debate in the value neutral terms of economics by using an efficiency perspective have sought to distinguish between welfare-maximizing and welfare-eroding practices. The idea is that a determination of whether a practice is welfare-maximizing or welfare-eroding should inform the decision regarding which set of practices to regulate or tolerate. The critical assumption being that the use of efficiency criteria ensures that one can distinguish, without turning to morality, between activities that tend to maximize the total welfare of state citizens and those that do not.

The difficulties associated with providing an all-encompassing definition of corruption discussed previously and the illustrative examples of definitions by various authors indicate that none of the attempts to define corruption has won sufficiently wide enough support to be accepted as providing the benchmark for defining corruption. The object of this section is not, however, to resolve the definitional problem or otherwise seek to define corruption in a way that avoids all such problems. Rather, the analytical approach taken is to delimit the boundaries of the study of the issue of corruption by examining a specific type of corruption – bribery – the concept of which is not innately contested. Before the argument examines the issue of bribery, the next section examines the debate on the consequences of corruption.

Harmful Effects of Corruption: A Cost-Benefit Analysis

Conventional Wisdom on the Effects of Corruption

The discussion in the literature outlining the harmful or beneficial effects of corruption is voluminous. Academics have lined up on both sides of the debate, arguing for and against the deleterious effects of corruption. Some of the writings of commentators ascribing negative effects to corruption have been speculative, while others have been based on empirical research, but generally, both have attempted to assign negative effects to corruption.[41] The main proponent of the harmful effects of corruption, Mauro, an International Monetary Fund (IMF) economist, found that corruption reduced private investment and thus the rate of economic growth.[42] Finding the negative association between corruption and private investment to be statistically and economically significant, he suggests that quantitatively, a decrease in existing corruption might raise the ratio of investment to Gross Domestic Product (GDP) by almost 4 percent and the annual growth of GDP per capita by almost 0.5 percent.[43]

Building on Mauro's observations, Wei's study examined the effect of corruption on Foreign Direct Investment (FDI) using two different survey data sources, including Transparency International's Corruption Perception Index (CPI).[44] He concluded that: (1) a rise in either host-country tax rate or corruption level reduced inward FDI flows; (2) corruption had the same effect on FDI into East Asian host countries as elsewhere; and (3) US investors, despite the FCPA, were no more averse to corruption in host countries than the average OECD investors were. Other commentators like Campos take a less concrete stand in suggesting that despite the fact that the negative effect of corruption on the economy is lessened if a corrupt government is predictable, there is still a negative effect.[45]

Nevertheless, a vast majority of the literature assigning negative effects to corruption have not been empirical in nature. The literature, in general, indicates that

41 See Snider, T & Kidane, W [2007]: 'Combating Corruption Through International Law in Africa: A Comparative Analysis', in Vol. 40, *Cornell International Law Journal*, 691, at 695.

42 See Mauro, P [1995: 700704].

43 See Mauro, P [1996]: 'The Effects of Corruption on Growth, Investment, and Government Expenditure: A Cross Country Analysis, in Corruption and the Global Economy', in Kimberly Ann Elliott, (ed.) [1996]: *Corruption and the Global Economy* (Washington D.C.: Institute for International Economics), 83, at 91.

44 See Wei, S [1997a]: '*How Taxing Is Corruption on International Investors?*' National Bureau of Economic Research, Working Paper No. 6030.

45 See Edgardo Campos, J et al. [1999]: 'The Impact of Corruption on Investment: Predictability Matters', in Vol. 27, *World Development*, 1059, at 1059.

corruption distorts economic decision making,[46] ensures that goods are of a lower quality,[47] imposes a form of taxation on the consumer,[48] and impedes international economic relations.[49] Still, other commentators suggest that corruption leads to inefficiency[50] and impedes transnational commercial relationships by decreasing market access, excluding competition, and in turn fostering monopolies.[51]

The classic study on the effects of corruption remains the study of corruption in the Irrigation Department of a state in Southern India. In this study, Wade observed the degradation of the bureaucratic system because of corruption.[52] In another study of the same system, Wade also found that senior officials raised money by selling government posts to junior officials, thus perpetuating the entry into bureaucratic service of dishonest and incapable persons.[53] Commentators have observed other effects of corruption on bureaucratic systems. Alam, for instance, indicates that resources are diverted and wasted to hide illicit activities, with bureaucrats holding back information and resources in order to extract larger bribes.[54]

---

46 Bader, M & Shaw, B [1983]: 'Amendment of the Foreign Corrupt Practices Act', in Vol. 15, *New York University Journal of International Law and Politics*, 627, at 627. They state that bribery alters economic decision-making in market economies. Rather than purchasing a good or service based on the price, quality, and fit of that good or service, the purchase is based on the size of the bribe.

47 Alam [1989: 448–52] suggests that manufacturers and providers have little incentive to produce high–quality, low–cost goods and services, and instead are rewarded when they divert money from production to the payment of bribes.

48 See Schleifer & Vishny [1993: 611–15], who state that corruption is more distortionary than heavy taxation because of the added imperative of secrecy. See also Wei [1997a], who finds empirically that *corruption* severely distorts economies.

49 Lacey, K & Crutchfield, B [2003]: 'Crackdown on Money Laundering: A Comparative Analysis of Feasibility and Effectiveness of Domestic and Multilateral Policy Reforms', in Vol. 23, *Northwestern Journal of International Law and Business*, 263, at 265.

50 See Gevurtz, F [1987]: 'Commercial Bribery and the Sherman Act: The Case for Per Se Illegality', in Vol. 42, *University of Miami Law Review*, 365, at 390–91. He outlines the inefficiencies created when firms bribe officials to create monopolies.

51 Abbott states that '[g]overnmental corruption and non-transparency are likely to benefit inefficient local operators over efficient multinational operators.' See Abbott, F [1997]: 'Foundation-Building for Western Hemispheric Integration', in Vol. 17, *Northwestern Journal of International Law and Business*, 900, at 914. Also see Hovenkamp, H [1989]: 'Antitrust's Protected Classes', in Vol. 88, *Michigan Law Review*, 1, at 16. He provides examples of how bribes are used to obtain or retain monopolies.

52 See Wade, R [1982a]: 'Irrigation Reform in Conditions of Populist Anarchy: An Indian Case', in Vol. 14, *Journal of Development Economics*, 285, at 285; and Wade, R [1982b]: 'The System of Administrative and Political Corruption: Canal Irrigation in South India', in Vol. 18, *Journal of Development Studies*, 287, at 291.

53 See Wade, R [1985]: 'The Market for Public Office: Why the Indian State Is Not Better at Development', in Vol. 13, *World Development*, 467, at 478–80.

54 Alam [1995: 431–49] states that bribery may impose costs because of the official's efforts to maximise the offer of bribes by creating false uncertainties.

Johnson has also suggested that corruption has a deleterious impact on the polity, ensuring that capable and honest people avoid corrupt bureaucracies.[55] The corrupt individuals, on the other hand, seek jobs that pay good bribes rather than jobs for which they are qualified and ultimately corrupt the honest individuals.[56] The impact of corruption on society has also been alluded to by Rose-Ackerman, who concludes that corruption undermines the legitimacy of government, leaving the impression that the government is for sale to the highest bidder.[57] Another commentator reiterating the negative impact of corruption on society, Boswell, suggests that the greatest casualty of corruption has been the erosion of public trust in public institutions and leaders, and the foundation of democracy.[58]

The Diminutive Dissent on the Harmful Consequences of Corruption

A thin strand in the literature challenges the speculation that corruption is a phenomenon with negative consequences only; arguing that in some circumstances corruption may be beneficial.[59] Some of these commentators suggest that the grey economy responds to most of the same market forces as the legitimate economy, stimulating growth by responding to market demand for products not legally available.[60] Huntington has gone as far as to argue that corruption may

---

55 See Johnson, O [1975]: 'An Economic Analysis of Corrupt Government, With Special Application to Less Developed Countries', in Vol. 28, *Kyklos*: *International Review for Social Science*, 47, at 57. He observes that capable and honest persons avoid government work for moral reasons when corruption is pervasive.

56 See Tanzi, V [1994]: *Corruption, Governmental Activities and Markets*, International Monetary Fund Working Paper No 94/99, at 26. Also see Thoumi, who observes that over time an honest individual in a corrupt system adapts and becomes more dishonest. Thoumi, F [1987]: 'Some Implications of the Growth of the Underground Economy in Columbia', in Vol. 29, *Journal of International Studies and World Affairs*, 35, at 44.

57 See Rose-Ackerman [1978: 44]. Also see Werlin, H [1973]: 'The Consequences of Corruption: The Ghanaian Experience', in Vol. 88, *Political Science Quarterly*, 71, at 79. He states that the effect of corruption is to generate an atmosphere of distrust that pervades all levels of administration.

58 See Boswell, N [1996]: 'Combating Corruption: Focus on Latin America', in Vol. 3, *South-Western Journal of Law and Trade in the Americas*, 179, at 184. See also Cragg, A [1998]: 'Business, Globalization, and the Logic and Ethics of Corruption', in Vol. 53, *International Journal*, 643, at 654, who notes that respect for law and legal institutions is a casualty of bribery. See also Lambsdorff, J [2007]: *The Institutional Economics of Corruption and Reform: Theory, Evidence and Policy* (Cambridge: Cambridge University Press), 53–134, where he discusses the empirical research that evidences the harm that corruption imparts on society.

59 Shihata [1997: 454] describes the pro-corruption arguments in the literature to include capital formation, predictability in government relationships, and efficient escape from burdensome regulations.

60 For a general exposition of this argument, see Brooks, M & Heijdra, B, [1991]: *Dividing the Spoils*, Policy Paper No. 20. Australian Institute for Public Policy.

well serve as a yardstick for measuring the level of modernization and political development of a society.[61] He acknowledges that although corruption tends to weaken or perpetuate the weakness of government, it helps to integrate groups into the political system. In concluding that corruption may sometimes have beneficial effects, he suggests that the corruption produced by the expansion of governmental regulation may help to stimulate economic development.

For Huntington, corruption could serve to overcome excessive bureaucratic inflexibility, thus reducing long-term costs. In his final analysis, he posits that corruption is rampant in societies that lack effective political parties, basing his argument on the idea put forward by Henry Ford that partisanship and corruption are in reality antagonistic principles. Ford stated that:

> [p]artisanship tends to establish a connection based upon an avowed public obligation, while corruption consults private and individual interests which secrete themselves from view and avoid accountability of any kind. The weakness of party organisation is the opportunity of corruption.[62]

Another writer assigning a positive function to corruption is Leff.[63] In his view, corruption serves as an extra-legal institution used by individuals or groups to gain influence over the actions of the bureaucracy.[64] As such, the existence of corruption indicates only that these groups participate in the decision-making process more often than would otherwise be the case. In this view, corruption represents an important means for influencing policy at the enforcement stage and may thus work important changes on government policy.[65] Hence, an analysis of legislative influence that focuses on the legislative process alone thus runs the risk of distorting the actual pattern of influence in the society. Leff further points out that, for instance, if business groups are otherwise at a disadvantage in articulating their interests to the government, and if these groups are more likely to promote growth than is the government, then their enhanced participation in policy formulation can help development.

---

61 See Huntington, S [1968]: *Political Order in Changing Societies* (New Haven, CT: Yale University Press), at 321.

62 Ford, H [1958]: *The Rise and Growth of American Politics* (New York: Macmillan), at 322.

63 See Leff [1979: 325].

64 This view is contested by Salbu [1999b: 49]; he states that the once-popular functionalist view of bribery, under which corruption purportedly yields benefits of allocative efficiency and optimal capital formation, retains little favour among today's academics.

65 A sizable number of individual and group demands in developing nations reach the political system, not before laws are passed, but rather at the enforcement stage. This form of corruption has seldom been treated as an alternative means of interest articulation. Those individuals who engage in corruption in this manner are as surely influencing the outcome of policy just as if they formed a group to pressure the government to change its policy. See Scott [1979: 101].

This position taken by Leff stems from a public interest–centred definition of corruption. In support of this line of argument, Scott suggests that corruption can often be seen as one of the many processes of political influence rather than simply as the misuse of office in violation of community norms.[66] A sizable number of individual and group demands in less-developed nations reach the political system, not at the legislative stage, but rather at the enforcement stage. Influence before legislation is passed is generally called pressure group politics, and influence at the enforcement stage often involves corruption. This form of corruption has seldom been treated as an alternative means of interest articulation. Those individuals who engage in corruption in this manner are as surely influencing the outcome of policy just as if they formed a group to pressure the government to change its policy.

Nye joins Leff in emphasizing the positive function of corruption on economic development.[67] He emphasizes that it is not only necessary for economic development but it also serves as an integrative function, reducing inter-elite conflict and bridging the gap between the groups based on power and those based on wealth. Similarly, Huntington bases his argument that corruption might be good for economic development on the premise that there is confusion between bureaucratic corruption and bureaucratic inefficiency.[68] In his analysis, corruption refers to extra-legal influence on policy, while inefficiency refers to the economy of means used by the bureaucracy in achieving specified policy objectives. Empirically, they may both appear together, but it is important for analytical purposes to understand that they could be independent of each other. The point being that it is bureaucratic inefficiency and not corruption *per se* that undermines economic development.

The central premise of Huntington's argument is one that is difficult to refute. It, however, remains inconclusive as evidence of the benefits of corruption to economic development.[69] An alternate argument for the benefits of corruption is proposed by Scott in his analysis, which draws on the main points of some of the various writers ascribing positive consequences to corruption.[70] Scott suggests three circumstances in which corruption could minimize costs and improve efficiency. First, where the narrowness of loyalties or the scarcity of organizational skills inhibits the formation of interests groups. Second, corruption could minimize costs in circumstances where the administration of law is so loose and erratic that

66 See Scott [1979: 101–2]; he suggests that corruption can often be seen as one of the many processes of political influence rather than simply the misuse of office in violation of community norms.

67 See Nye [1979: 415–18].

68 Huntington [1979: 319].

69 In fact, a recent survey of more than 150 high-ranking public officials and key members of civil society from more than 60 developing countries ranked public sector corruption as the most severe impediment to development and growth in their countries. See Chanda, P [2004]: 'The Effectiveness of the World Bank's Anti-Corruption Efforts: Current Legal and Structural Obstacles and Uncertainties', in Vol. 32, *Denver Journal of International Law and Policy*, 315, at 315.

70 See Scott [1979: 40–41].

the existing law bears little relation to administrative behaviour. Third, where a minority is discriminated against, and corruption serves to protect their interest.

The arguments by the preceding commentators who ascribe positive functions to corruption can be criticized for being empirically irrelevant[71] and myopically selective.[72] Illustrations of these two criticisms of commentators attributing positive functions to corruption become readily obvious when one examines these arguments in detail.[73] Klitgaard classifies the arguments that corruption may play a positive role into three categories: those made by economists, political scientists, and the catchall group.[74] The first is the economists who argue that corrupt payments introduce a kind of market mechanism ensuring that goods are allocated based on willingness to pay rather than politics, random selection, or merit. Corruption therefore puts goods in the hands of those who value them the most and who would use them more effectively. The assumption in this argument is that where the market is not used to distribute goods and services, corruption will creep in as an illicit market substitute.

Even if one was to accept this line of reasoning, the argument still suffers from fundamental flaws. Although corruption may lead to some market efficiency, it would do so at the cost of the benefits of the reduction of the levels of corruption sought to be achieved by the introduction of the rules. In addition, an occasional act of corruption may be efficient; however, once systematized and deeply ingrained, it never is.[75] These flaws make the argument myopically selective because the arguments fail to incorporate the benefit of the rules and the effects of corruption on the system as a whole. This is depicted by Rashid's study on bribes to obtain telephone service in India.[76] In his original premise, he expected that bribes would help to differentiate customers in a system that otherwise was completely egalitarian, and thus bribes would allow for Pareto optimalization. Rashid, however, found that while this may have been the case at first, over time bureaucrats came to expect bribes and created inefficiencies in order to extract

71 Empirical irrelevance occurs when the logical connection between an independent variable and a dependent variable depends on intervening conditions that are highly unlikely to exist in empirical reality.

72 While myopic selectivity occurs when a claim of functionality based on logic fails to take into account possible concomitant costs and alternative means.

73 Ekpo, M [1979]: 'Gift-Giving and Bureaucratic Corruption in Nigeria'. In Ekpo, M, (ed.) [1979]: *Bureaucratic Corruption in Sub-Saharan Africa: Toward a Search for Causes and Consequences* (Washington D.C.: University Press of America), 161, at 170.

74 See Klitgaard [1988: 32].

75 See Shihata [1997: 454], who notes the consensus among scholars that the long-term damage done by corruption far outweighs any immediate benefits.

76 See Rashid, S [1981]: 'Public Utilities in Egalitarian LDC's: The Role of Bribery in Achieving Pareto Efficiency', in Vol. 34, *Kyklos: International Review for the Social Sciences*, 448, at 448-55.

more and larger bribes; rather than contributing to Pareto optimality, corruption degraded the system.[77]

The second category, as suggested by Klitgaard, is the political scientists who argue that politicians may use corruption to foster political integration, which may in turn lead to political harmony.[78] In addition, writers who have been inspired by the structural-functional schools in sociology and anthropology view corruption as fulfilling positive functions, particularly with respect to social integration.[79] They further contend that corruption could be a mechanism for political participation and influence, particularly ethnic minorities and foreign corporations.[80] The third category is a catchall group for organizations who argue that they benefit by their employee's circumvention of the rules where bureaucratic rules are constraining the organization. However, in these circumstances, although corruption may serve organizational interests, especially when it circumvents unnecessary bureaucratic red tape, it more commonly has disastrous effects on merit systems, allocation of resources, and pursuit of an organization's mission.

The Consequences of Corruption as a Continuum

The empirical studies, economic theories, and literature on corruption in general reveals many counteracting mechanisms concerning the relationship between corruption and its various effects, without any hint as to which effects might be dominant. The two viewpoints regarding the benefits or detriments of corruption are not diametrically opposed. The impact of conduct such as corruption on society is not fixed. It is not hard to imagine corruption serving particular benefits while at the same time causing harm. The dichotomy between corrupt conduct with deleterious effects on society and certain conduct labelled as corrupt but performing essential functions is just convenient shorthand for a far more complicated continuum. There is a constantly shifting equilibrium regarding the relative impact of the cost of corruption on society as the effects of corruption differ depending on the particular conduct, system, or time within a particular society.

In view of the assertion that the impact of corruption is neither fixed nor easily quantifiable, the question raised in relation to the central argument of this study

77 Paying bribes engenders a reputation that leads to greater bribe demands. See Earle, B & Cava, A [2009]: 'Are Anti-Corruption Efforts Paying Off? International and National Measures in the Asia-Pacific Region and Their Impact on India and Multinational Corporations', in Vol. 31, *University of Hawaii Law Review*, 59, at 84.

78 See Scheppele, K [1999]: 'The Inevitable Corruption of Transition', in Vol. 14, *Connecticut Journal of International Law*, 509, at 515–18, who describes in detail how people adapted to the Soviet system with behaviour that would be considered corrupt in other systems.

79 See Ekpo [1979: 168].

80 See Ohnesorge [1999: 473], who notes that in repressive politics, corruption opens the door for desired consumer goods.

pertains to how regulators choose to deal with specific instances of corruption based on their consequences. Unless the regulators know the differential impact of conduct, it is difficult to devise a rule that enhances the general welfare of the system. The fundamental difficulty facing regulators is thus the incommensurability of the stakes. If the regulators err by condemning a beneficial practice, the benefits may be lost for good. If, on the other hand, the regulators err by permitting a deleterious practice, the welfare losses of these deleterious practices decrease over time. This is because society internalizes these practices and makes corrections accordingly. True, this long run may be a long time coming, with loss to society in the interim. This should not, however, obscure the point that regulatory errors that tolerate corrupt practices tend to be self-correcting, while erroneous condemnations are not. The question therefore raised is this: in which direction should the particular rule prohibiting conduct as corrupt err? For a number of reasons, it is arguable that errors on the side of not excusing questionable corrupt practices are preferable. This is because most forms of corruption are harmful; excusing a particular practice about which we are ill-informed is less likely to be harmful. However, the costs of searching for these desirable examples are high, and the system corrects regulatory errors that tolerate corrupt practices more readily than it corrects erroneous condemnations.

Bribery: A Specific Type of Corruption

Corruption encompasses a variety of behaviour, of which bribery is only one of them.[81] As Bayley noted, bribery and corruption are intimately linked but separable. A person bribed is a person corrupt; but a man may be corrupt who does not take bribes.[82] The notion that bribery is the most obvious instance of corrupt conduct is widespread. In this common conception, the crime of bribery is at the epicentre of a series of concentric circles representing the various degrees of corrupt conduct. Unlike most other forms of corruption, bribery is widely regarded as having fixed boundaries. The challenge to successfully curbing bribery relates to the difficulties in detection and enforcement rather than uncertainty about its definition.

A bribe is a transaction that occurs in an extra-legal setting. In this transaction, the bribe-giver transfers a benefit, consisting of anything of value to the bribe-taker, as *quid pro quo* for preferential treatment by the bribe-taker.[83] The preferential

81 See Nichols, P [2012b]: 'The Business Case for Complying with Bribery Laws', in Vol. 49, *American Business Law Journal*, 325, at 330, where he notes that the literature conflates the terms *bribery* and *corruption.*

82 Bayley, D [1966]: 'The Effects of Corruption in a Developing Nation', In Vol. 19, *Western Political Quarterly*, at 719.

83 *Quid pro quo* is a vital element of any definition of bribery. See Sorauf, F [1994]: 'Politics, Experience and the First Amendment: The Case of American Campaign Finance', in Vol. 94, *Columbia Law Review*, 1348, at 1350. Also see Tanzi [1994: 24], who states that the benefit derived must be seen as a direct *quid pro quo* for the specific act of corruption.

treatment by the bribe-taker constitutes the abuse or misuse of power identified as central to the definition of the transaction as corrupt.[84] Nichols stresses the importance of the position of the bribe-taker by defining bribery as a transaction in which an official misuses his or her office because of considerations of personal gain, which need not be monetary.[85] A wider notion of bribery would suggest that bribery occurs when one person (the bribe-giver) provides an inducement to another person (the bribe-taker) that is intended to be in exchange for the bribe-taker doing, or not doing, something that would favour the briber and be contrary to the bribe-taker's positional duty.[86] This definition includes not only governmental bribe taking, but also a great deal of activity within the private sector.[87]

The sort of actions required to be undertaken by the party receiving the benefit plays a key role in determining how a bribe transaction is characterized. The actions undertaken by the bribe-taker for the bribe-giver have been divided into two categories.[88] The 'according to rule benefits' involve extra-legal payments for actions that the recipient of the bribe is already required to undertake by a pre-existing obligation. This type of corruption has acquired several names, including facilitating or grease payment, speed money, or petty corruption. It is often treated less harshly than other forms of corruption because of a sense that it is extremely difficult to combat. It is also treated less harshly because it is perceived that the result would be the same without the illegal payment and it is difficult to distinguish these bribes form gratuities. The second category, 'against the rule benefits', involves a situation where the bribe taker acts in a way that is prohibited by the rules that create the office. The benefit that is conferred by the bribe-giver may be anything of value to the briber and is made in expectation that the bribe-taker will alter his position for the benefit of the briber.[89] This alteration of position confers a benefit in the form of control, however slight, over the bribe-taker's office.

There have been several studies conducted that have provided significant insights into the effects of bribery and sought to analyse the causes and effects of bribery on society. Wade conducted one of the most comprehensive observational studies of bribery in his analysis of the Irrigation Department in a Southern

84 This simple definition of bribery comports with most statutory definitions of the crime of bribery. See Lindgren, J [1993]: 'The Theory, History, and Practice of the Bribery-Extortion Distinction', in Vol. 141, *University of Pennsylvania Law Review*, 1695, at 1725, who looks at statutory definitions and concludes that the central kind of bribery is that given to pervert official decision-making.

85 See Nichols [1999b: 258].

86 See Dunfee [1999: 22].

87 For a discussion of the distinctions between tips, bribes, and gifts, see Rose-Ackerman [1999: 91–110].

88 See Oldenburg, P [1987]: 'Middlemen in Third-World Corruption: Implications of an Indian Case', in Vol. 39, *World Politics*, 508, at 523.

89 See Lindgren, J [1988]: 'The Elusive Distinction Between Bribery and Extortion: From the Common Law to the Hobbs Act', in Vol. 35, *University of California Los Angeles Law Review*, 815, at 823, noting that a bribe is given in exchange for preferential treatment.

Indian state.[90] In this classic study of bribery, Wade described an agency plagued by problems of corruption where officials demanded bribes from villages in exchange for irrigation services. Sometimes the farmers paid the engineers to gain assurance that the water to which they had a right would be forthcoming. In other instances, the farmers paid the engineers to furnish water to which they would otherwise have no right.[91] The study focused on how bribes affected the system and noted that the basic causes of corruption in the system included excessive bureaucratic control and declining real salaries in the public sector.[92]

In another influential study, although it was on corruption but with notable reference to bribery, Rose-Ackerman discussed the causes and consequences of corruption principally from an economic perspective.[93] Rose-Ackerman suggested that corruption was a type of rent-seeking behaviour, in which private producers and politicians gained an advantage in dividing the benefits of economic activity. These observations by Rose-Ackerman are amply demonstrated by Wade's study, in which he observed that officials demanded bribes from villages for the supply of water. However, in order for the officials to be posted to positions where they could demand bribes, they would need to make payoffs to a superior.[94] This system subsisted in a chain of bribery that reached to the level of local politicians who had influence over bureaucratic postings and needed the bribe money for campaign finance. Rose-Ackerman's study is also interesting in that it divides the causes of corruption into economic, cultural, and political factors.[95]

From the perspective of an economist, Rose-Ackerman argues that bribery arises for the same reason payments are made in private markets. The reason being that government officials have something to sell for which private citizens are willing to pay. In making her goal the suppression of all corruption, not just economically deleterious corruption, Rose-Ackerman clearly disagrees with other economists who would approach the subject in standard cost-benefit terms.[96] Rose-Ackerman concedes that several analysts believe that bribes have desirable incentive properties. She, however, dismisses such claims at the outset and maintains that not all payments to government officials are bribes, as some payments are merely gifts.[97] Rose-Ackerman uses the distinction between gifts and

---

90 See Wade [1982b: 287].

91 *Ibid.*, at 299.

92 *Ibid.*, at 289–303. See Nichols, P [2011]: 'The Perverse Effect of Campaign Contribution Limits: Reducing the Allowable Amount Increases the Likelihood of Corruption in the Federal Legislature', in Vol. 48, *American Business Law Journal* 77, at 100–13, describing factors considered by a public official contemplating a bribe, including criminal penalties, social costs, and psychic costs.

93 See Rose-Ackerman [1999].

94 See Wade [1982b: 303–4].

95 See Rose-Ackerman [1999: 3–4].

96 She recognises that the analysis of corruption should consider more than the standard cost benefit analysis utilised by economists. *Ibid.*, at 16–26.

97 *Ibid.*, at 110.

bribes as a convenient segue to suggest that that the distinction between bribes and gifts is a cultural construct. Rose-Ackerman further suggests that since corruption has different meanings in different societies, and because culture is dynamic and constantly changing, what constitutes corruption must be, as well.[98]

Problem of Transnational Bribery

The relationship, if any, between corruption and culture has invariably affected the arguments regarding the justification for the regulation of corruption in the transnational context.[99] In recent years, the issue of transnational bribery has received considerable attention as a problem in the relationship between the developed and developing countries.[100] Lawmakers and legal scholars have recognized bribery as a serious problem in international business transactions, and this concern has grown as improved communication has exposed an increasing number of abuses.[101] The apparent result of this concern is a voluminous literature on bribery of foreign government officials.[102]

---

98 The view that corruption is defined by culture is disputed by commentators who argue that this view has no empirical basis. See Marong, A [2002]: 'Toward a Normative Consensus Against Corruption: Legal Effects of the Principles to Combat Corruption in Africa', in Vol. 30, *Denver Journal of International Law and Policy*, 99, at 105.

99 See Delaney, P [2006]: 'Transnational Corruption: Regulation Across Borders', in Vol. 47, *Virginia Journal of International Law* 413, at 417–19 for an exploration of the contours of the problem of transnational corruption.

100 Bribery is seen as the most significant problem, particularly, though not exclusively, in trade between North and South. See Wood, G [1995]: 'Ethics at the Purchasing/Sales Interface: An International Perspective', in Vol. 4, *International Marketing Review*, 7, at 7.

101 *See* Vogl, F [1998]: '*The Supply Side of Global Bribery*', in Vol. 35, *World Bank Finance & Development*, 30, at 30, noting increased press and television coverage of global corruption.

102 Many of these books and articles are cited throughout this article and include Greanias, G & Windsor, D [1982]: *The Foreign Corrupt Practices Act: Anatomy of a statute* (Lexington: Lexington Books); Bliss, J & Spak, G [1989]: 'The Foreign Corrupt Practices Act of 1988: Clarification or Evisceration?', in Vol. 20, *Law and Policy in International Business*, 441; Crutchfield, B & Dundas, M [1980a]: 'Responsibilities of Domestic Corporate Management Under the Foreign Corrupt Practices Act', in Vol. 31, *Syracuse Law Review*, 865; Kim, J & Kim, J [1997]: 'Cultural Differences in the Crusade Against International Bribery: Rice-Cake Expenses in Korea and the Foreign Corrupt Practices Act', in Vol. 6, *Pacific Rim Law and Policy Journal*, 549; Rossbacher, H & Young, T [1997]: 'The Foreign Corrupt Practices Act Within the American Response to Domestic Corruption', in Vol. 15, *Dickenson Journal of International Law*, 509; Timmeny, W [1982]: 'An Overview of the FCPA', in Vol. 9, *Syracuse Journal of International Law and Commerce*, 235; Windsor, D & Getz, K [1999]: 'Regional Market Integration and the Development of Global Norms for Enterprise Conduct', in Vol. 38, *Business and Society*, 415; Windsor, D & Getz, K [2000]:

Transnational bribery occurs when a person (legal or juristic) from one country bribes a public official of another country. It is impossible to determine the precise level of transnational bribery that occurs. It is therefore debatable whether the recent awareness about transnational bribery reflects an increase in the incidence of transnational bribery or is a reflection of the growing awareness of a situation that already existed. Notwithstanding, a 1997 World Bank estimate placed the total corruption involved in international trade at about $80 billion per year.[103] A more recent estimate by the World Bank of the amount of bribes paid suggested a figure of more than $1 trillion dollars (US$1,000 billion) each year.[104] Another survey conducted by the World Bank of 3600 firms in 69 countries found that 40 percent of the surveyed businesses pay bribes.[105] For example, a commentator has estimated that German corporations pay more than $3 billion per year in bribes to obtain business contracts abroad.[106]

'Multilateral Cooperation to Combat Corruption: Normative Regimes Despite Mixed Motives and Diverse Values', in Vol. 33, *Cornell International Law Journal*, 731; Brown, H [1994]: 'The Foreign Corrupt Practices Act Redux: The Anti-Bribery Provisions of the Foreign Corrupt Practices Act', in Vol. 12, *International Tax & Business Law*, 279; Brown, H [1998]: 'Parent-Subsidiary Liability Under the Foreign Corrupt Practices Act', in Vol. 50, *Baylor Law Review*, 1; Brown, H [1999]: 'The Extraterritorial Reach of the US Government's Campaign Against International Bribery', in Vol. 22, *Hastings International and Comparative Law Review*, 407; Brown, H [2001]: 'Extraterritorial Jurisdiction Under the 1998 Amendments to the Foreign Corrupt Practices Act: Does the Government's Reach Now Exceed Its Grasp?', in Vol. 26, *North Carolina Journal of International Law & Commercial Regulation*, 239; Elliot, K [1998]: 'The Problem of Corruption: A Tale of Two Countries', in Vol. 18, *Journal of International Law & Business*, 524; Hendrix, S [2005]: 'New Approaches to Addressing Corruption in the Context of U.S. Foreign Assistance With Examples From Latin America and the Caribbean', in Vol. 12, *Southwestern Journal of Law and Trade in the Americas*, 1; Freeman, J [2006]: 'The Razor's Edge in Cafta's Bribery Provision: Is the U.S. Really Concerned About Eliminating Corruption?', in Vol. 13, *Southwestern Journal of Law and Trade in the Americas*, 189; Zervos, A [2006]: 'Amending the Foreign Corrupt Practices Act: Repealing the Exemption for "Routine Government Action" Payments', in Vol. 25, *Penn State International Law Review*, 251; Opara, I [2007]: 'Nigerian Anti-Corruption Initiatives', in Vol. 6, *Journal of International Business and Law*, 65.

103 Walsh states that the World Bank estimate is based on the assumption that bribery makes up 5 percent of all foreign direct investment and imports into countries with high levels of corruption. See Walsh, J [1998]: 'A World War on Bribery', in *Time International*, 22 June 1998, at 16.

104 See World Bank Press release, 8 April 2004. Available at http://web.worldbank.org/WBSITE/EXTERNAL/NEWS/0,,contentMDK:20190187%7EmenuPK:34457%7EpagePK:34370%7EpiPK:34424%7EtheSitePK:4607,00.html. Last visited 4 March 2013.

105 See Brunetti, A Kisunko, G & Weder, B [1997]: 'Institutional Obstacles for Doing Business Data Description and Methodology of a Worldwide Private Sector Survey', 1759 World Bank Policy Research Working Paper, at 31.

106 Guggenheim, K [1996]: 'Corruption, Not Revolutions or Coups, Topples Governments These Days', in *Los Angeles Times*, 6 Oct. 1996, at A4.

A 1999 survey conducted by Transparency International and Gallup International of almost 800 business executives in 14 emerging market economies requested participants to rank the likelihood of corporations from the 19 largest exporting countries paying bribes.[107] The results of this survey created the Bribe Payers Index (BPI), and some of the highlights are worth mentioning. In the BPI, Sweden, Australia, and Canada were perceived to have the corporations least likely to pay bribes. China, South Korea, Taiwan, and Italy were perceived to have corporations that were most likely to pay bribes. The US ranked in the middle of the perceived bribe payers index. Comparing the results of the BPI with the CPI is an interesting exercise in buttressing the geographic morality argument discussed in Section C of Chapter 4. Some countries appear to have a double standard for bribery, discouraging it at home, but tolerating the actions of their nationals engaged in bribery abroad.[108] Conversely, certain countries do not actively enforce their prohibitions against the bribery of foreign public officials, yet their corporations are perceived as less likely to pay bribes in foreign countries. Most importantly, the US, expected to rank highly on the BPI, because, until the OECD Convention was adopted, it was the only country to criminalize bribery, ranked in the middle of both indexes. The US tied with Germany on the BPI, a country that until recently allowed tax deductions for bribes.[109] These comparisons are offered with the caveat that since both indexes are based on perceptions, they may merely be reflecting opinions rather than actual levels of transnational bribery.

Notwithstanding the difficulties in quantifying the precise levels of transnational bribery, there is consensus on the fact that it is a problem that requires some form of regulation. This, however, is the extent of the consensus, and the arguments justifying the regulation of corruption vary with some commentators attempting to justify the regulation of corruption by arguing that corruption is morally wrong and causes harm to others and the society as a whole. By contrast, others argue that there is no requirement to demonstrate harm because corruption conflicts with societal norms of fair play. Further, it is precisely because of the conflict between corruption and these societal norms that the criminal law is used to enforce societal standards by prohibiting corruption. What, however, happens when the incidences of corruption transcend societal barriers with differing standards, as is the case with transnational bribery by corporations?

---

107 See Transparency International: *The Transparency International Bribe Payers Index*. Available at http://www.transparency.org/research/bpi/bpi_1999. Last visited 4 March 2013.

108 See Hess, D & Dunfee, T [2000]: 'Symposium Fighting International Corruption & Bribery in the 21st Century: Fighting Corruption: A Principled Approach; The C2 Principles (Combating Corruption)', in Vol. 33, *Cornell International Law Journal*, 593, at 595.

109 See Report by the OECD Committee on International Investment and Multinational Enterprises (CIME), 26 May 1997. Available at http://www.oecd.org/investment/anti-bribery/anti-briberyconvention/2087917.pdf. Last visited 4 March 2013.

Within this context of the efforts to regulate transnational bribery in general has been an informative debate about the relationship between domestic morality and transnational policy. This debate centres around the curbing of transnational bribery whilst ensuring that transnational legal prescriptions are not imposed on developing countries. Salbu and Nichols have each articulated extremes of the controversy over global moral community building.[110]

Salbu cautions against the imposition of values through extra-territorial prescriptions against transnational bribery because these prescriptions seek to make judgements regarding the appropriateness of gift-giving in various cultures.[111] Salbu's argument is predicated on what he styles the premature attempt to create a global community, which evokes the kind of virtue-inculcating lessons that inspire a person to refrain from accepting or offering bribes. This premature attempt, he cautions, risks moral imperialism. Salbu accepts that a unified agenda and value convergence in the regulation of transnational bribery could emerge in the future, but argues that multilateral policies or extra-territorial application of unilateral policy should not precede such convergence. His general condition is that when laws are imposed across borders, there should be considerable transnational value consensus. Otherwise, the imposition threatens to deny respect for legitimate regional value variance.

---

110 The debate spans several articles cited in this book. For example, see Salbu, R [1999a]: 'Battling Global Corruption in the New Millennium', in Vol. 31, *Law & Policy in International Business*, 47; Salbu, S [1997]: 'Bribery in the Global Market: A Critical Analysis of the Foreign Corrupt Practices Act', in Vol. 54, *Washington & Lee Law Review*, 229; Salbu, S [1999b]: 'The Foreign Corrupt Practices Act as a Threat to Global Harmony', in Vol. 20, *Michigan Journal of International Law*, 419; Salbu, S [2000]: 'A Delicate Balance: Legislation, Institutional Change, and Transnational Bribery', in Vol. 33, *Cornell Journal of International Law*, 657; Salbu, S [2001]: 'Information Technology in the War Against International Bribery and Corruption: The Next Frontier of Institutional Reform', in Vol. 38, *Harvard Journal on Legislation*, 67; Salbu, S [2001]: 'Transnational Bribery: The Big Questions', in Vol. 21, *Journal of International Law & Business*, 435; Salbu, S. [1999c]: 'Extraterritorial Restriction of Bribery: A Premature Evocation of the Normative Global Village', in Vol. 24, *Yale Journal of International Law*, 223. For the articles authored by Nichols, see Nichols, P [1997]: 'Outlawing Transnational Bribery Through the World Trade Organization', in Vol. 28, *Law & Policy in International Business*, 305; Nichols, P [1999a]: 'Are Extraterritorial Restrictions on Bribery a Viable and Desirable International Policy Goal Under the Global Conditions of the Late Twentieth Century?', in Vol. 20, *Michigan Journal of International Law*, 451; Nichols, P [2000]: 'The Myth of Anti-Bribery Laws as Transnational Intrusion', in Vol. 33, *Cornell International Law Journal*, 627; Nichols, P [2001]: 'The Fit Between Changes to the International Corruption Regime and Indigenous Perceptions of Corruption in Kazakhstan', in Vol. 22, *University of Pennsylvania Journal of International Economic Law*, 863; Nichols, P. [1999b]: 'Regulating Transnational Bribery in Times of Globalization and Fragmentation', in Vol. 24, *Yale Journal of International Law*, 257; Nichols, P [2004]: 'Corruption as an Assurance Problem', in Vol. 19, *American University International Law Review*, 1307.

111 Salbu [1999c: 223].

While Salbu's critical appraisal of the premature attempt to evoke a normative global village might ring true, he, however, fails to mention when or how the value convergence on the regulation of transnational bribery should take place. More importantly, he fails to signify how one would appreciate that the value convergence has occurred. Nichols, on the other hand, notes that all countries prohibit bribery of their public officials and that all cultures condemn the practice both legally and religiously, ensuring that the risks of imperialism cautioned by Salbu are virtually non-existent.[112] In a recent study, Nichols uses qualitative methods to study corruption, utilizing the opportunities presented by the similarities and differences in Singapore and Malaysia.[113] He argues that the differences in the degree to which each group internalizes corruption laws suggests differences in the psychic costs that members of each group contemplates when considering whether or not to act corruptly. He concludes that actors consider a variety of costs and benefits when determining whether to violate corruption laws. Nichols skilfully uses the fact that all countries prohibit bribery and that it is in the degree of internalization that differences exist to emphasize the argument that the value convergence alluded to by Salbu does, in fact, exist. Nichols concludes that given such cross-cultural agreement and the fact that national legal systems determine whether a particular transaction constitutes bribery, the extra-territorial and transnational prohibition of the practice of bribery is the logical step in the regulation of transnational bribery.

This study recognizes the necessity for the transnational regulation of bribery, but cautions that the justification for the extra-territorial regulation of transnational bribery needs to be excised from its foundations in morality and based instead on notions of the overall benefits to society. This cautionary note is echoed by Kennedy, who has characterized arguments such as Nichols' call for the transnational regulation of bribery using extra-territorial prohibitions, as the foundation for the anti-corruption campaign currently being waged by the international community.[114] Kennedy's analysis seeks to answer the question whether one should, in the end, favour or oppose the campaign against corruption currently being waged by the assortment of institutions, policy-makers, and intellectuals.

In response to this question, Kennedy points to the lack of clear arguments among those who oppose the anti-corruption campaign and attributes this to the fact that opposition to the anti-corruption campaign might easily be construed as support for corruption. Likening the opposition to corruption to the opposition to terrorism, Kennedy maintains that to oppose any of these practices places one uneasily outside the common sense of the international community. He posits

112 See Nichols [1999b: 298–302].

113 Nichols, P [2012a]: 'The Psychic Costs of Violating Corruption Laws', in Vol. 45, *Vanderbilt Journal of Transnational Law*, 145.

114 See Kennedy, D. [1999]: 'The International Anti-Corruption Campaign', in Vol. 14, *Connecticut Journal of International Law*, 455.

that although it is widely recognized that 'one person's terrorist is another's freedom fighter', one is not permitted to speak in favour of terrorism, and likewise, despite the difficulty in defining corruption, in polite society one must be opposed to it.[115] Kennedy, in his analysis has rightly recast the question whether one should or should not have an anti-corruption campaign into the different question: whether a campaign against corruption could have procedural or definitional excesses.

In Kennedy's view, the anti-corruption campaign may have gone too far, for instance by disrupting too much of the local economic fabric of developing countries too quickly. With respect to definitional limitations, the anti-corruption campaign may have overextended definitional boundaries by being extended to the point that it is no longer plausible to claim that the practices being opposed are corrupt. Despite the poignancy of Kennedy's observation, he does not make much of the underlying ideological struggle that characterizes the current anti-corruption campaign. Such ideological concerns of necessity often mar many promising initiatives as well as provide creative tensions that underpin the pursuit of these anti-corruption campaigns. Kennedy does, however, observe that the current anti-corruption campaign clearly taps into a widespread sense of illegitimacy. However, when one begins to define the object of this quite general condemnation not just in moral terms, but also in terms of the rule of law, and to specify its link to retarded economic development, quite familiar difficulties emerge.[116]

Kennedy rightly surmises that these familiar difficulties relate to the fact that the efforts to battle corruption suddenly become an effort to stigmatize some economic policies and some legal regimes at the expense of others precisely without analyzing their distributional or social consequences in any specific detail.[117] It is in this sense, Kennedy maintains, that the anti-corruption campaign, even at its most reasonable core, remains an ideological project, an effort to leverage the rhetorical advantages of a shared moral opprobrium for a series of specific legal or institutional changes without having to specify who will win and who will lose as a consequence.[118]

The deeper issue in the debate betrays the danger of stereotyping complex phenomena such as corruption through the emphasis on one particular aspect at the cost of a fuller understanding of the whole phenomenon. More importantly, the rhetoric of the anti-corruption campaign casts the problem of corruption as a domestic problem in which developing countries bear the cost of the corruption

115 *Ibid.*, at 455–6.

116 *Ibid.*, at 465.

117 As an example, some commentators have argued that anti-corruption campaigns may also inadvertently threaten democratic institutions in countries with politically active militaries by weakening civilian leaders while leaving the military largely unscathed. See Robinson, N & Sattar, N [2012]: 'When Corruption Is an Emergency: "Good Governance" Coups and Bangladesh', in Vol. 35, *Fordham International Law Journal*, 737, at 740.

118 *Ibid.*

through stunted development.[119] The rhetoric ignores the fact that corruption owes its current salience in the international arena to the concerns regarding the effects of corruption on foreign investors. Once the anti-corruption campaign is viewed in the context of its impact on foreign investors, the arguments against corruption lose their retardation of development rationale and become primarily a question of redistribution between foreign and local investors.

Conclusion

This chapter examined the attempts by commentators to provide an all-embracing definition of the phenomenon of corruption, and found that the definitions tended to obfuscate a proper analysis of the issue of corruption. Noting that the prime importance of definitions of corruption lay in the tendency to reveal the focus of the particular analyst, the chapter nonetheless found that the assembled definitions of corruption were more replete in their tendency to reveal the preconceived assumptions of particular commentators rather than provide a theoretical framework for the analysis of corruption. The examination of the various definitions was, however, important in highlighting some of the difficulties associated when attempts are made to regulate corruption across states with different normative principles.

The chapter noted that corruption is a complex, multifaceted phenomenon deeply rooted in the social, political, and economic systems of a country. In terms of the consequences of corruption, there was a surprising lack of consensus on the effects of corruption. The chapter examined the studies that challenge the speculation that corruption is a phenomenon with negative consequences only; arguing that in some circumstances corruption may be beneficial. Notwithstanding, the literature in general indicated that corruption distorts economic decision-making, ensures that goods are of a lower quality, and imposes a form of taxation on the consumer, leads to inefficiency and impedes transnational commercial relationships by decreasing market access, excluding competition and in turn fostering monopolies. The chapter surmised that corruption results in costs to society such as in terms of foregone investment and growth opportunities, as well as in terms of equity and fairness.

In view of the multifaceted and complex nature of the phenomenon of corruption, the suggested framework for tackling corruption would be defined, by necessity, by how one conceptualizes corruption as a problem. An irrevocable choice on the definition of corruption is not, however, necessary for the development of a framework to tackle the problem. The analytical approach adopted by the chapter

119 See Spalding, A [2010]: 'Unwitting Sanctions: Understanding Anti-Bribery Legislations as Economic Sanctions Against Emerging Markets', in Vol. 62, *Florida Law Review*, 351, at 358–61. He argues that the FCPA was passed to address a foreign-policy problem rather than purely as a means to address domestic concerns.

to circumvent the definitional problem of corruption was to focus on examining a specific type of corruption – bribery. The chapter demonstrated that even in the types of corruption where there appeared to be a consensus, the issue of bribery for instance, there was still considerable disagreement on the precise contours and the strategies to tackle the problem. The chapter noted the recognition of bribery as a serious problem in international business transactions, a problem that invariably highlights the relationship between corruption and culture on the one hand, and the interaction between developed and developing countries on the other.

The issue here concerns the instances when the incidences of corruption transcend societal barriers with differing standards, as is the case with transnational bribery. The chapter argued that the debate highlights the danger of stereotyping complex phenomena such as corruption without a full understanding of the phenomenon. More pertinently, viewing the problem of corruption as a domestic problem in which developing countries bear the cost of the corruption through stunted development ignores the fact that corruption owes its current salience in the international arena to the concerns regarding the effects of corruption on foreign investors. Changing the terms of the debate to view the issue of corruption as a question of redistribution between foreign and local investors therefore suggests that the efforts by developed countries to curb the problem of corruption are equally as important as the efforts by developing countries.

Chapter 3
Regulating Bribery

The framework established by states for the regulation of domestic bribery plays an important role in the efforts to build a transnational regulatory framework. Although the debates around regulation of bribery in the domestic arena took place alongside the development of a transnational framework for regulating bribery, it was within the context of the transnational regulation of bribery that the dilemmas around the challenges associated with controlling bribery have been sharply accentuated. The regulation of transnational bribery replicates a regulatory framework that is already theoretically present at the domestic level. The resort to a transnational framework does not arise because domestic law does not make provision for the regulation of bribery. Rather, the reliance on a transnational framework often results from dissatisfaction with the scope of domestic law and the expectation of a more effective framework under the transnational regime. Thus, the inability of domestic institutions to enforce existing bribery laws through the effective deployment of sanctions was in many respects the precursor to the development of a transnational framework for the regulation of bribery.

The development of domestic and transnational bribery regulation influences and reinforces each other. The interaction and overlap between the domestic and transnational regime is in many respects necessary, given that in some jurisdictions the transnational enforcement regime may be the only effective response to bribery. The failure of domestic regimes invariably puts some pressure on the transnational framework to offer a comprehensive framework for tackling bribery. In principle, the ideal would be the encouragement of the development of transnational principles on the regulation of bribery, while permitting national tailoring that mirrors the principles developed in the international oversight framework.

Understanding the connection between domestic and the transnational regulation of bribery is important. On a superficial level, the regulations of domestic and transnational bribery are inexorably linked. The evolution of the regulation of domestic bribery and its transnational counterpart has not occurred in completely separate spheres. Understanding the nature of their interaction, whether they are mutually reinforcing, and if so, whether this mutual reinforcement is exclusive, may serve to build more effective systems. Nonetheless, it may be that the nature of their interaction underscores a deliberate tension between both spheres. The two spheres demonstrate basic features such as cooperation, competition, and conflicts, basic behaviours that are associated with interaction between two or more complex systems. What occurs in the domestic sphere affects transnational sphere and in turn what occurs in other national systems.

Viewing the relationship of both frameworks on each other as parts of a general framework of interaction suggests that the strength of any one framework strand depends, in part, upon the strength of the others, and that each particular thread deserves attention. This interrelationship also intimates that improving the response to domestic capacity in one arena has collateral consequences that may have a significant impact on the transnational framework as well as other domestic fora. This view is at odds with notions that advocate the perception that the regulation of bribery is only possible at the national level, or requires a form of state or sovereignty that, tragically, the transnational legal regime cannot provide. Examining the sources of cooperation, competition, and conflict between the domestic and international regime and developing approaches that acknowledge both the separateness and connection that both regimes present can achieve the development of a more effective regulatory framework.

Given the conclusions in Chapter 2 with respect to the multifaceted nature of corruption and the analytical approach adopted to circumvent the definitional problem of corruption by focusing on bribery, this chapter compares and examines the legal framework for the regulation of both domestic and transnational bribery in the US and the UK.[1] Until the passage of the UK Bribery Act 2010, the law on bribery was drawn from a range of common law and statutory sources, creating a complex and ambiguous regulatory framework that fell short of international obligations acceded to by the UK.[2] The choice of the US FCPA as a focus for analysis in this chapter is predicated on the fact that the statute was the first national statute criminalizing transnational bribery of foreign officials. Enacted in 1977, the FCPA provides almost 30 years of operational outcomes to review in estimating the effectiveness of the statute. More importantly, the FCPA is the legislation on which the various multilateral anti-bribery initiatives are modelled and thus potentially offers valuable lessons for the implementation of the various multilateral conventions.

The first section of this chapter examines the regulatory framework for domestic bribery in the UK and US. The first part of this section examines specific anti-bribery legislation and highlights the physical and mental elements required to establish an allegation of bribery. The second part examines, particularly in the US, the broader array of legislative prohibitions that may be imposed on persons engaging in bribe transactions. The second section of this chapter focuses on the domestic regulatory framework for transnational bribery. Given the rich history of material from 30 years of operation of the FCPA, the focus of this

1 See Ryznar, M & Korkor, S [2011]: 'Anti-Bribery Legislation in the United States and United Kingdom: A Comparative Analysis of Scope and Sentencing', in Vol. 76, *Missouri Law Review*, 415, at 443–53, where they chart the scope of the US and UK anti-bribery schemes, including their respective sentencing components.

2 Bonneau, J [2011]: 'Combating Foreign Bribery: Legislative Reform in the United Kingdom and Prospects for Increased Global Enforcement', in Vol. 49, *Columbia Journal of Transnational Law*, 365, at 369–76, outlines the state of the UK bribery laws prior to the passage of the act and discusses the impetus for reform.

section is on the US law with respect to transnational bribery. The first part of this section discusses the legislative history and scope of the anti-bribery provisions of the FCPA. The second part of this section examines the enforcement of the FCPA by examining its enforcement and the sanctions that have been imposed for the violation of the anti-bribery provisions. The chapter notes that making comparisons between transnational bribery levels with or without legislation prohibiting transnational bribery is practically impossible. This ensures that making generalizations on the effectiveness of legislation prohibiting bribery, such as the FCPA, is notoriously difficult.

Domestic Regulation of Bribery

Anti-Bribery Legislation in the US and UK

Prior to the passage of the UK Bribery Act 2010, the UK law on bribery was drawn from a multiplicity of statutory sources.[3] The statutory offences on corruption were contained in four different criminal statutes.[4] The Public Bodies Corrupt Practices Act 1889 in Section 1, makes it an offence to "corruptly solicit or receive, or agree to receive, for himself, or for any other person, any gift, loan, fee, reward, or advantage whatever as an inducement to, or reward for, or otherwise on account of any member, officer, or servant of a public body". This section applies to passive bribery and a similarly worded Section 2 applies to active bribery. As originally enacted, the 1889 Act applies only to public bodies in the UK.[5] The Prevention of Corruption Acts 1906 extended the scope of the 1889 Act to include all corrupt solicitations whether in the public or private sector. Section 1(1) provides in part that any agent who corruptly accepts or agrees to accept from any person, for himself any gift or consideration as an inducement or reward for doing or forbearing to do any act in relation to his principal's shall be guilty of an offence. The 1906 Act defined an agent as including "any person employed by or acting for another" and a person serving under the Crown or public authority.[6]

---

3 According to Swanson, T [2007]: 'Greasing the Wheels: British Deficiencies in Relation to American Clarity in International Anti-Corruption Law', in Vol. 35, *Georgia Journal of International and Comparative Law*, 397, at 401, the British law on bribery was a piecemeal mix of various statutes and common law precedents.

4 The Public Bodies Corrupt Practices Act 1889, the Prevention of Corruption Act 1906 and the Prevention of Corruption Act 1916 (collectively called the Prevention of Corruption Acts 1889 to 1916); and The Anti-Terrorism, Crime and Security Act 2001.

5 Section 7 provides that the expression public body does not include any public body existing elsewhere than in the UK.

6 See 1906 Act, Section 1(2) and Section 1(3). Also see Section 1(3), as amended by 1916 Act, Sections 4(2), (3).

The 1916 Act broadened the definition of a public body and introduced the presumption of corruption. Section 2 of the 1916 Act provided that in "proceedings against a person for an offence under the Prevention of Corruption Act 1906, or the Public Bodies Corrupt Practices Act 1889, it is proved that any money, gift, or other consideration has been paid or given to or received by a person, the money, gift, or consideration shall be deemed to have been paid or given and received corruptly as such inducement or reward as is mentioned in such Act unless the contrary is proven". The effect of this presumption was to shift the burden of proof to the defendant to show on the balance of probabilities that the payment received was not corrupt.[7] In *R v Braithwaite*, the defendant was charged with corruption for having corruptly received from a company a gift or consideration as a reward for showing favour to the company.[8] The defendant admitted to having received goods or services from the company, but alleged that he had paid for or intended to pay for them. The court held that the receipt of goods or services from the company amounted to the receipt of consideration, and therefore the burden of proof lay on the defendant to prove on the balance of probabilities that the consideration had not been paid and received corruptly.

The Anti-Terrorism, Crime and Security Act 2001 was enacted in response to the events of 11 September 2001 and includes legislation on bribery and corruption. Part 12 of the Anti-Terrorism, Crime and Security Act 2001 extends the scope of the UK law on bribery to 'foreign' bribery. It provides that the existing bribery offences are also offences if they are committed outside the UK. This is the case even if they involve foreign agents or principals having no connection to the UK, or holders of a foreign public office, or officials of foreign bodies or authorities, which are the equivalent in the country concerned of those covered by the domestic offence. In other respects, the Anti-Terrorism, Crime and Security Act 2001 left the elements of the bribery offence unchanged. The act made it clear, however, that the existing presumption of corruption in respect of the statutory offences did not extend to the foreign bribery offence.[9]

There were several problems associated with the prescribed statutory offences of bribery. First, there was an arbitrary distinction made between public and private sector recipients of bribes.[10] The 1889 Act relates to the public sector, while the 1906 Act extends its provisions to agents irrespective of whether they are in the public or private sector. Commentators have suggested that given the blurring of the distinction between public and private sector entities, this arbitrary distinction

7 *Carr-Briant* [1943] K.B. 607.

8 [1983] 2 All E.R. 87.

9 There have not been any cases of bribery brought under the act.

10 The Law Commission Consultation Paper No 185, 'Reforming Bribery: A Consultation Paper', 2007, at 3. Available at http://lawcommission.justice.gov.uk/docs/cp185_Reforming_Bribery_consultation.pdf (*Reforming Bribery Consultation*). Last visited 4 March 2013.

makes it difficult to define the scope of the offence with sufficient clarity.[11] This issue is partially illustrated by the case of *R v Natchi*, where the plaintiff was convicted under the 1889 Act for bribing an official of the Immigration and Nationality Department.[12] The conviction was reversed on appeal on grounds that the 1889 Act applied to members, officers, and servants of public bodies, but did not apply to employees of government departments.

Second, there was a certain degree of inconsistency with respect to the terminology employed and scope of the various statutory provisions.[13] For instance, the 1889 Act covers situations where the benefit of the bribe is conferred on a third party. In contrast, the 1906 Act requires that the recipient of the bribe is also the public officer. Another inconsistency relates to the nexus between the benefit being conferred. The 1889 Act requires that the benefit is connected to the particular transaction where the public officer exercises his function, while the 1906 Act does not require such a nexus. There are additional problems associated with the requisite *mens rea*, and these issues are discussed further in the following text.

There were extensive discussions to amend and update the corruption laws in the UK.[14] The Law Commission published a report in 1998 that included a draft bill.[15] In the report, the Law Commission recommended the streamlining of the corruption offences into a single bill that would remove the distinction between public and non-public bodies, abolish the presumption of corruption in the 1916 Act, and remove the requirement of the consent of a law officer before prosecution could be undertaken.[16] With respect to the scope of offences, the report recommended the creation of five separate offences of corruption, and a definition of corruptly that encompassed acting primarily in return for the conferring of an advantage.[17] In response to the recommendations of the Law Commission, the UK government agreed with the proposal to abolish the distinction between public/non-public bodies, the definition of corruptly, and the presumption of corruption in the 1916 Act.[18] However, the UK government questioned the removal of the requirement of consent before a prosecution could be undertaken.

---

11 Nicholls, C, Daniel, T, Polaine, M & Hatchard, J [2006]: *Corruption and Misuse of Public Office* (New York: Oxford University Press), para 5.83, at 197.

12 [2002] 2 Cr.AppR 20.

13 *Reforming Bribery Consultation*, at 6.

14 For an in-depth discussion on the efforts to reform the UK law, see Nicholls, C, Daniel, T, Polaine, M & Hatchard, J [2006: 171–222].

15 The Law Commission Report No 248 'Legislating the Criminal Code: Corruption', 1998 Law Commission No 248. Available at http://lawcommission.justice.gov.uk/docs/lc248_Legislating_the_Criminal_Code_Corruption.pdf. Last visited 4 March 2013.

16 *Ibid.*, at 29–50 and 105–13.

17 *Ibid.*, at 67–8 and 78–9.

18 UK Home Office [2000]: 'Raising Standards and Upholding Integrity: the Prevention of Corruption'. Cm 4759, at Chapter 6. Available at http://www.archive.official-documents.co.uk/document/cm47/4759/4759-fw.htm. Last visited 4 March 2013.

In 2003, the UK government submitted a Corruption Bill to Parliament. The Joint Committee of both Houses considered the draft bill and produced its report on 17 July 2003.[19] The report of the Joint Committee was critical of the complex language of the bill, the failure to clearly define corrupt conduct sufficiently,[20] the limited scope of the bill with respect to the conduct covered,[21] and the limitation provided by focusing on the principal/agent relationship.[22] Following the publication of the Joint Committee report, the bill was withdrawn from Parliament. The UK government accepted some of the recommendations proposed by the Joint Committee, notably the suggestion that Director of Public Prosecutions should be allowed to give consent to prosecution. The UK government nonetheless maintained that the concept of principal/agent should form the basis of the corruption offence.[23]

In an attempt to seek a new consensus on the way forward, the UK government published a consultation paper in December 2005.[24] Prior to the conclusion of the consultation, in November 2006, an updated and amended Corruption Bill was put forward to the House of Lords as a Private Member's Bill. The Corruption Bill proposed abolishing the existing common law offence of bribery together with the statutory corruption offences. Three new statutory offences would be created, which include corruptly conferring an advantage, corruptly obtaining an advantage, and performing functions as an agent corruptly.[25] The Corruption Bill defined bribery by reference to the improper conduct that results from a bribe and included a number of modern features of anti-corruption laws, such as explicit offences of bribing foreign public officials; of foreign bid-rigging; and of fixing sporting events.[26] It included a requirement for UK companies to take steps to ensure that their foreign subsidiaries and associated companies did not commit corruption offences; and a duty to report suspicions of corrupt behaviour in the public sector.[27]

---

19 House of Lords and House of Commons Joint Committee on the Draft Corruption Bill, Draft Corruption Bill: Report and Evidence, 2002–03, H.L. 157. Available at http://www.publications.parliament.uk/pa/jt/jtcorr.htm. Last visited 4 March 2013.

20 *Ibid.*, at 14–15.

21 *Ibid.*, at 31.

22 *Ibid.*, at 30.

23 Home Office [2003]: 'The Government Reply to the Report from the Joint Committee on the Draft Corruption Bill' Cm 6086, at 5–7. Available at http://www.archive2.official-documents.co.uk/document/cm60/6086/6086.pdf. Last visited 4 March 2013.

24 Home Office Consultation Paper [2005] 'Bribery Reform of the Prevention of Corruption Acts and SFO Powers in Cases of Bribery of Foreign Officials: A Consultation Paper'. Available at http://www.homeoffice.gov.uk/documents/cons-2005-bribery/cons-bribery-response-0307?view=Binary. Last visited 4 March 2013

25 Corruption Bill, Sections 1(1), (2), and 2. Available at http://www.publications.parliament.uk/pa/ld200607/ldbills/018/2007018.pdf. Last visited 4 March 2013.

26 *Ibid.* Sections 3, 4, and 5.

27 *Ibid.* Sections 8 and 11.

The response to the 2005 government consultation was published in March 2007.[28] The consultation revealed that there was broad support for reform of the existing law but no consensus as to how it could be best achieved. The government was of the view that the terminology should refer to an offence of bribery rather than corruption.[29] Regarding the definition of corruptly, the view taken was that a detailed definition would be preferable to leaving the issue to be determined by the jury and requested that the Law Commission address the definition of corruptly.[30] Concerning a definition of the central harm that should be addressed, the government considered several options that included definitions that focused on the issue of corrupt intention,[31] the conferral of an improper advantage,[32] the breach of a duty,[33] and the subversion of markets.[34] The government once again maintained its preference for the principal/agent model and acknowledged the need for stricter rules for the public sector than the private sector. The UK government was, however, opposed to the introduction of a separate offence related to the bribing of sportsmen, bid-rigging, sports fixing, and the expanded liability of UK corporations for the acts of their subsidiaries operating abroad.

In November 2007, responding to a request from the UK government, the Law Commission published its consultation on reforming the law of bribery. The Law Commission focused on the issue of bribery to delineate the distinction between the narrow offence of bribery rather than corruption in the wider sense.[35] The consultation paper recommended abolishing the distinction the that law draws between public and private sector bribery,[36] the repeal of the current statutory and common law offences,[37] clarification on the fault elements of the offence of bribery,[38] the creation of a discrete offence of bribery of a foreign public official,[39] and the assertion of jurisdiction over UK residents or nationals for bribery committed abroad.[40] The Law Commission also recommended the creation of the

28 Home Office [2007]: 'Consultation on Bribery: Reform of the Prevention of Corruption Acts and SFO Powers in Cases of Bribery of Foreign Officials: Summary of Responses and Next Steps'. Available at http://www.homeoffice.gov.uk/documents/cons-2005-bribery/cons-bribery-response-0307?view=Binary. Last visited 4 March 2013.

29 *Ibid.,* at 3.

30 *Ibid.*, at 5.

31 Proposed by Simmons and Simmons, *ibid.*, at 5.

32 Proposed by the Joint Committee, *ibid.,* at 6.

33 Proposed by Transparency International, *ibid.*, at 6.

34 Proposed by Professor Alldridge, *ibid.*, at 7.

35 Reforming Bribery Consultation at 1.

36 *Ibid.*, at 4–5.

37 *Ibid.*, at 9.

38 *Ibid.*, at 10.

39 *Ibid.*, at 321–2.

40 *Ibid.*, at 7.

defences of duress and reasonable belief that the payment was legally required,[41] but proposed that there should be no exception for facilitating payments.[42]

Regarding prosecutions, the Law Commission proposed a requirement for the consent of the Director of Public Prosecutions for a prosecution for the general offence of bribery and the consent of the Attorney General for offences with an extra-territorial element.[43] With respect to the issue of corporate liability, the consultation paper noted the criticisms of the existing law and identified several options that could increase the effectiveness of corporate convictions, including the creation of offences such as inadequate supervision of a foreign subsidiary company, the consent or connivance of a high-ranking employee to the making of a bribe, and the negligent supervision of others employed by the corporation. The Law Commission did not submit proposals that would impose liability on corporations that failed to adequately supervise their foreign subsidiaries. The Law Commission proposed a deferral of the consideration of the law relating to liability of corporations to a wider review of the issue.[44]

The UK Bribery Act 2010 came into force on 1 July 2011 and took into account many of the criticisms and suggestions that were highlighted in the consultative process.[45] The new law replaces the patchwork of old common law and statutory scheme laws that governed the offence of bribery in the UK. The act makes it an offence to give or offer a bribe to foreign public officials; criminalizes the giving or offering of bribes to private individuals; and also makes it an offence for any person, whether public official or private citizen, to solicit or receive a bribe.

In Section 1, the UK Bribery Act 2010 creates the general offence of offering, promising, or giving a financial or other advantage in any of the three following circumstances. First, to induce a person to improperly perform a relevant function or duty. Second, to reward a person for such improper activity. Third, to know or believe that the acceptance of the advantage would itself be an improper performance of a function or duty. In Section 2, the act prohibits the act of being bribed by prohibiting the requesting, agreeing to receive, or accepting a financial or other advantage while consequently intending that a relevant function or activity be performed improperly. In Section 6, the act criminalizes the bribery of foreign officials with the intention of influencing the foreign official in his or her capacity as a foreign public official in order to obtain or retain either business or an advantage in the conduct of the business.

41 *Ibid.*, at 10.

42 *Ibid.*, at 297.

43 *Ibid.*, at 10.

44 *Ibid.*, at 135.

45 For a discussion of the new UK Act, see Jordan, J [2011a]: 'Recent Developments in the Foreign Corrupt Practices Act and the New UK Bribery Act: A Global Trend Towards Greater Accountability in the Prevention of Foreign Bribery', in Vol. 7, *New York University Journal of Law & Business*, 845, at 863–8.

The UK Bribery ACT 2010 introduced a new strict liability offence that makes it a crime for a corporation to fail to prevent bribery. Section 7 of the act provides that a commercial 'organization' violates the law when a person 'associated' with the organization bribes another person intending to obtain or retain business or a business advantage for the organization. The act goes on in Section 8 to define someone 'associated' with a commercial organization as 'a person who performs services for or on behalf of' the commercial organization. The corporation may defend itself from the corporate offence by establishing adequate procedures to prevent or detect the giving or receiving of bribes by such associated person.[46]

The jurisdictional reach of the act is very broad. The act applies to all United Kingdom companies, citizens, and residents, regardless of where the bribery occurred.[47] The provisions also apply to any individual or company, irrespective of their nationality, if the relevant acts of the violation take place in the United Kingdom.[48] This provision applies to any company that partially conducts its business in the UK regardless of any other nexus to the United Kingdom.[49] The act prescribes liability for violation by individuals with imprisonment for a term of up to 10 years. Individuals and corporations violating the act face a penalty fine of an unlimited amount.[50]

The existing statutes concerned with bribery in the US have been streamlined into a single comprehensive section of the Criminal Code.[51] The bribery provision is Section 201(b), and it covers both active bribery and passive bribery.[52] The elements of the offence require that a thing of value was given, offered, or promised to or accepted by a present or future public official with corrupt intent (intent to influence or be influenced in the performance of an official act) for the commission of a fraud against the US, or any act in violation of lawful duty. The act of an official is defined broadly and includes issues for action or decision by the official and requiring the official to act in his official capacity.[53] The prohibition applies to

---

46 Section 7 of the UK Bribery Act 2010. See Jordan, J [2011b]: 'The Adequate Procedures Defense Under the UK Bribery Act: A British Idea for the Foreign Corrupt Practices Act', in Vol. 17, *Stanford Journal of Law, Business & Finance*, 25, at 29–37, where he explains the adequate procedures defence, and recent guidance on the defence provided by the UK government.

47 Section 12(4) of the UK Bribery Act 2010.

48 Section 12(1) of the UK Bribery Act 2010.

49 Sections 7, 12(5)–(6) of the UK Bribery Act 2010.

50 Section 11 of the UK Bribery Act 2010.

51 Pub. L. No. 87–849, 76 Stat. 1119 (codified as amended at 18 U.S.C. § 201 (2000)).

52 Section 201(b)(1) sets forth the elements of a bribery offense applicable to the bribe giver, and § 201(b)(2) sets forth the elements applicable to the bribe recipient.

53 § 201(a)(3) provides that the term 'official act' means any decision or action on any question, matter, cause, suit, proceeding or controversy that may at any time be pending; or that law may be brought before any public official, in such official's capacity, or in such official's place of trust or profit.

government employees, members of congress even if they have not yet assumed authority and have only been selected.[54]

In both the UK and US, the physical elements required to establish the offence of bribery are pretty straightforward in comparison to the requisite state of mind. The issue of the requisite standard for the state of mind in both the common law and statutory offences of bribery in the UK was very unclear. The common law required that the act is 'contrary to the known rules of honesty and integrity', and the statutory offence required that the bribe is given or received corruptly. Regarding the common law, the case law did not appear to support the position that the briber should intend the bribee to commit a breach of his duty. In the case of *R v Gurney*, for instance, the defendant was charged with attempting to bribe a justice of the peace. In the instructions to the jury, the court directed the jury to ignore whether or not the defendant had an intention to produce any effect on the justice's decision, thereby removing the requirement that the briber intend for the bribee to act contrary to the known rules of honesty and integrity.[55] There are clearer provisions in Section 1(2)(b)(1) of the UK Bribery Act 2010, which stipulate that the person offering the bribe must intend to induce a person to perform improperly a relevant function or activity, have resolved these issues.

In another instructive case, *R v Parker*, the appellant was the chairman of a district council planning committee and granted planning permission to a building firm.[56] The appellant admitted that he had received a sum of money from the applicant after the grant of the application. He denied, however, that he had acted improperly because his conduct had not in any way been influenced by the money received. The court, in dismissing the appeal, held that corruption included the receipt of money for a past favour without any prior agreement. The offence under Section 1 of the Public Bodies Corrupt Practices Act 1889 lay not in showing favour to the application, but in accepting a reward for doing so; and accordingly, the councillor was guilty as soon as he accepted the payment.

The requisite state of mind is similarly an issue in the statutory offences of bribery. The statutory provisions do not define the term corruptly, and the courts have construed the term inconsistently. In the case of *Cooper v Slade*, the House of Lords described the term corruptly as 'purposely doing an act which the law forbids as tending to corrupt.'[57] In another case, the court stated that the word corruptly was analogous to having an evil mind.[58] Further, the defendant must have dishonestly intended to weaken the loyalty of servants to their master and to transfer that loyalty to himself.[59] The equation of corruptly with dishonestly was in a later case disapproved by the courts. In the case of *R v Wellburn*, Lord Justice

54 § 201(a)(1)–(2)
55 [1867] 10 Cox CC 550.
56 [1985] Crim LR 589.
57 [1856] 10 E.R. 1488, at 1499 per Wills J.
58 *Per* Martin B in *Bradford Election Case (No 2)* [1869] 19 LT 723, at 728.
59 *Lindley* [1957] Crim LR 321, followed in *Calland* [1967] Crim LR 236.

Lawton, giving the judgment of the Court, approved a direction given by the trial judge, in the following terms:

> 'Corruptly' is a simple English adverb and I am not going to explain it to you except to say that it does not mean dishonestly. It is a different word, it means purposefully doing an act which the law forbids as tending to corrupt.[60]

The *dicta* in the UK cases clearly indicate that all the prosecution needs to prove is that the accused purposely did an act that the law forbids as corrupt. If it is proven that a payment was made, the offence of bribery is established. The issues of who is responsible for initiating the request of the payment or the timing of the payment are of itself irrelevant to guilt. Where a bribe is paid and received, the issue of whether it is solicited or proffered is irrelevant. In either event, both payer and payee are guilty; for each has purposely done an act that the law forbids as corrupt. This position is affirmed by the UK Bribery Act 2010, which creates separate offences for bribing in Section 1 and being bribed in Section 2.

Similar to the UK, the US bribery offence requires a corrupt intent to influence or be influenced in an official act. The US Supreme Court, in the case of *US v Sun Diamond Growers*, construed this to mean that there must be proof of a specific intent to give or receive something of value in exchange for an official act.[61] In this context, a vague expectation of some future benefit will not constitute the offence of bribery under the statute. The case also addressed the issue of the nexus between the gift and the decision of the public official. The theory presented by the prosecution asserted that the gifts were provided to curry favour with an official wielding substantial authority over the defendant's business. The Court rejected the government's theory that the statute prohibits gifts designed solely to gain favour with the recipient, without proof of a nexus between the gift and a particular future decision of the official.[62]

Other Domestic Statutes Regulating Bribery

Bribery is never as simple, or necessarily as brazen, as the offer and receipt of a payment in exchange for official action. Both the UK and US statutes on bribery contain an amorphous definition of the term corruptly. In most cases of bribery, the link between the benefit and the act of the official is often very difficult to establish, making the prosecution of bribery very difficult. Given the political nature of corruption charges (as they may be used, for example, to attack political foes), there is a tendency for statutes to employ precise terms to define the offence of bribery. However, actions on the penumbra of bribe transactions and the evidential burden of establishing the offence of bribery will be difficult to incorporate into even the most carefully drafted statute.

---

60 [1979] 69 Cr.App.Rep 254, at 264.

61 526 U.S. 398 (1999), at 404–5.

62 *Ibid.*, at 405.

The US courts have responded to some of the difficulties in prosecuting bribery by using other statutes that require proof of much more simple elements than required by the bribery statutes. One such statute is the Mail Fraud statute.[63] The Mail Fraud statute was adopted in 1872 to prevent individuals from using the post office to perpetrate frauds on unsuspecting victims.[64] The statute prohibits any scheme or artifice to defraud, or for obtaining money or property by means of false or fraudulent pretences, representations, or promises by which the defendant uses the post office or a commercial delivery service as a means to execute the fraudulent scheme. The statute does not define what constitutes a 'scheme or artifice to defraud', and the courts have construed the statute to encompass bribery of public officials. The courts broadly interpreted the fraud element of the offence, largely by failing to render a conclusive definition of the term 'scheme to defraud'.

The Mail Fraud statute has been used to prosecute a wide range of fraudulent schemes, both in the private and public sectors. In the public sector, public officials who fail to provide honest services are said to defraud the citizens and the state of their right to receive such services from those officials.[65] The basis of the application of the statute to prosecute public officials for bribery is that the acceptance of a bribe by a public official deprives the citizenry of its right to honest and faithful service from those who exercise government authority.[66] The deprivation was of an intangible right, as opposed to a property right, in violation of the official's duty to put the public interest before his own personal interest.[67] Congress, despite its initial origins from decisions of the federal courts

---

63 18 U.S.C § 1341 (2000). A companion provision, the Wire Fraud statute, 18 U.S.C. § 1343 (2000), applies the same analysis to fraudulent schemes involving the use of interstate wire, radio, or television transmissions. See *Carpenter v US*, 484 U.S. 19, 25 (1987).

64 See Henning, P [1995]: 'Maybe It Should Just Be Called Federal Fraud: The Changing Nature of the Mail Fraud Statute', in Vol. 36, *British Columbia Law Review*, 435, at 442.

65 There are numerous examples of public official prosecuted under the Mail Fraud Statute. For instance in *US v Holzer*, 816 F.2d 304, 307–10 (7th Cir. 1987), a county judge was prosecuted for concealing loans made or arranged by lawyers with matters before his court. In *US v Silvano*, 812 F.2d 754, 755, 758–60 (1st Cir. 1987) the acting budget director for the City of Boston was convicted for using his position to extort funds from a contractor and failing to disclose his friend's interest in a city contract. In *US v Barber*, 668 F.2d 778, 780, 784–5 (4th Cir. 1982), the former West Virginia Alcoholic Beverage Control commissioner was convicted for accepting illegal cash and liquor payments. In *US v Rauhoff*, 525 F.2d 1170, 1175–6 (7th Cir. 1975), an individual was convicted for attempting to bribe the Secretary of State of Illinois. In *US v Isaacs*, 493 F.2d 1124, 1149–52 (7th Cir. 1974) a former governor of Illinois and a former director of the Illinois State Department of Revenue were convicted for bribery.

66 See *US v Sawyer* 85 F.3d 713 (1st Cir. 1996) at 724, explaining that bribed officials breach their duty of honest services when decisions are the result of payment.

67 See Henning [1995: 461].

of appeals, eventually codified the intangible rights doctrine.[68] The doctrine is based on the belief that certain individuals are entitled to the honest and faithful services of another.[69]

The Mail Fraud statute is also used in the private context to prosecute private fiduciaries. In the private context, most situations involve a fiduciary, employee, or agent who owes the intangible right of honest and faithful services to a beneficiary, employer, or principal.[70] Under the intangible rights doctrine, a fiduciary, agent, or employee can be prosecuted under the statute for material deception or for failing to disclose, and a politician can be prosecuted for breaching his duty of honesty and loyalty owed to the public. The intangible rights theory provided a means to reach misconduct by public officials, especially in the instances where the case is difficult to prove.

Two cases typify the broad scope of the Mail Fraud statute through the liberal construction of the intangible rights doctrine in the public and private sectors. In *US v Margiotta*, the court affirmed the mail fraud conviction of a former local party chairman.[71] The chairman was indicted for devising a scheme to defraud the citizens of the town of the right to have the affairs of the town conducted honestly and free from corruption and of the right to his honest participation in governmental affairs. In *US v Bronston*, the court affirmed the mail fraud conviction of a New York lawyer and state senator who had personally represented a client whose interests were in direct conflict with a client of the lawyer's firm.[72] The court concluded that the jury was given evidence that Bronston owed a fiduciary duty and breached that duty, had specific intent to defraud, that he concealed a material fact, intended to cause actual economic harm to the victim, and used the mail in furtherance of the scheme to defraud. Both *Margiota* and *Bronston* marked important developments in mail fraud prosecutions. In *Margiota*, although the defendant was not a public official, the court permitted his mail fraud prosecution for failure to uphold the fiduciary duties of a public official. The court in the *Bronston* case similarly

68 See 18 U.S.C. 1346, which provides that the term 'scheme or artifice to defraud' includes a scheme or artifice to deprive another of the intangible right of honest services.

69 See Moohr, G [1994]: 'Mail Fraud and the Intangible Rights Doctrine: Someone to Watch Over Us', in Vol. 31, *Harvard Journal on Legislation*, 153, at 155. She states that a public official violates his fiduciary obligations to the public by depriving the public of honest services merely by failing to disclose material information.

70 There are numerous cases in the private context. For instance, in *US v Weiss*, 752 F.2d 777, 784–5 (2d Cir. 1985), a corporate officer was convicted for secretly creating an illegal securities cash fund. In *US v Barta*, 635 F.2d 999, 1001–3 (2d Cir. 1980), a bond trader who abused his employer's trust by concealing information was convicted on the grounds that he defrauded his employer of its right to honest and faithful services. In *US v Bryza*, 522 F.2d 414, 422 (7th Cir. 1975), the court upheld the mail fraud conviction of a buyer because he deprived his employer of his honest and faithful services by failing to disclose kickbacks received from suppliers.

71 688 F.2d 108 (2d Cir. 1982).

72 658 F.2d 920 (2d Cir. 1981).

expanded the scope of mail fraud in the private sector because the decision was based only on the fact that *Bronston* case failed to disclose the conflict.

The Supreme Court sought to limit the broad ambit of the Mail Fraud statute; the limitation was, however, curtailed by the US Congress, which intervened and restored the scope of the statute. In the case of *McNally v US*, several individuals were convicted for concocting a scheme to defraud the citizens and government of Kentucky of various intangible rights, including the right to conduct state affairs honestly.[73] The Supreme Court reversed the conviction because the Mail Fraud statute was intended only to protect the government's interest in property rights. The reasoning of the court was that the term 'to defraud' implied a deprivation of something of value, thereby excluding from protection the intangible right to honest services by state and local officials. Congress reacted to this decision by enacting 18 U.S.C. 1346, which states that the term scheme or artifice to defraud includes a scheme or artifice to deprive another of the intangible right of honest services.[74]

The scope of the Mail Fraud statute in the US, following the enactment by congress, was clarified in the case of *US v Sawyer*.[75] The defendant was an insurance company lobbyist who had entertained Massachusetts state legislators with golf outings and meals. As a private citizen, Sawyer did not owe fiduciary duties to the state or its citizens. The defendant was however charged with causing state legislators to deprive citizens of their right to legislator's honest services. The court noted that honest services fraud typically involves either bribery or a failure to disclose a conflict of interest.[76] The court explained that the public is deprived of an official's honest services when an official with decision-making power does not make disinterested decisions or fully disclose the motive for the official act.

Another means of imposing liability on individuals engaging in bribery in the US is through the Racketeer Influenced and Corrupt Organization (RICO) Act.[77] RICO provides both civil and criminal sanctions against persons engaged in 'enterprise criminality'.[78] Enterprise criminality has been defined to include all types of organized criminal behaviour including simple political corruption and sophisticated white-collar criminal schemes.[79] Although individuals can be prosecuted under the RICO statute, the focus of the statute is upon enterprises. The definition of an enterprise is broad and has been interpreted to include:

> … a group of persons associated together for a common purpose of engaging in a course of conduct. … The … [enterprise] is proved by evidence of an ongoing

73 483 U.S. 350 (1987).

74 18 U.S.C. 1346 (1994).

75 85 F.3d 713 (1st Cir. 1996).

76 See *ibid.*, at 724.

77 18 U.S.C. 1961–1968 (1988).

78 Section 1963 provides for criminal penalties, including imprisonment, fines, and forfeiture of property. Section 1964 provides for civil remedies.

79 See *US v Cauble*, 706 F.2d 1322, 1330 (5th Cir. 1983).

> organization, formal or informal, and by evidence that the various associates function as a continuing unit.[80]

The RICO statute, in its definition of an enterprise, expressly provides that a corporation would be considered an enterprise.[81] The RICO statute is broad and can reach every activity in which an enterprise may be used to promote a crime. This broad prohibition is achieved through provisions that prohibit four types of activity. First, the investment of income derived from a pattern of racketeering activity in an interstate enterprise.[82] Second, acquiring or maintaining an interest in an enterprise through a pattern of racketeering activity.[83] Third, conducting the affairs of an enterprise through a pattern of racketeering activity.[84] Fourth, conspiring to violate any of the preceding sections.[85] Racketeering within the context of the RICO statute encompasses violent acts, the provision of illegal goods and services, corruption among public officials, and commercial and other forms of fraud.[86]

The statute confers a private right of action on any person injured in his business or property and confers civil liability for the violation of the statute.[87] The case of *Environmental Tectonics Corp., Int'l v W. S. Kirkpatrick & Co., Inc* illustrates the scope of the private action under the RICO statute and its application to transnational bribery transactions.[88] In this case, Kirkpatrick's Chairman and CEO permitted Kirkpatrick to pay out commissions totalling over $1.7 million to various Nigerian officials to secure contracts with the Nigerian government. The plaintiff, Environmental Tectonics Corporation International, after the rejection of its lower bid on the same project, investigated and discovered that Kirkpatrick had paid secret commissions to obtain the contract. The corporation, Kirkpatrick, and the CEO were both convicted under the FCPA and fined substantially.[89] The Court also held that allegations of bribes paid to foreign government officials in order to obtain military contracts are sufficient to allege a pattern of racketeering under RICO.

---

80 *US v Turkette,* 452 U.S. 576 (1981) at 583.

81 18 U.S.C. § 1961(4) (1982) provides that the definition of enterprise includes 'any individual, partnership, corporation, association, or other legal entity, and any union or group of individuals associated in fact although not a legal entity'.

82 Section 1962(a).

83 Section 1962(b).

84 Section 1962(c).

85 Section 1962(d).

86 See Blakey, R [1983]: '*The RICO Civil Fraud Action in Context: Reflection on Bennett v. Berg*', in Vol. 58, *Notre Dame Law Review*. 237, at 300–306.

87 18 U.S.C. 1964(c).

88 847 F.2d 1052, 1063 (3d Cir. 1988), aff'd sub nom, *W.S. Kirkpatrick & Co. v Environmental Tectonics Corp.*, 493 U.S. 400 (1990).

89 See website of the Department of Justice. Available at http://www.usdoj.gov/criminal/fraud/fcpa/append/appendixa.html. Last visited 23 October 2007.

Private parties whose businesses have been affected by the bribes paid by their competitors have also sought to use other legal remedies to seek redress and to expose the conduct of their competitors. One statute that has been used by these plaintiffs is the Robinson-Patman Act.[90] The Robinson-Patman Act in Section 2(c) prohibits the payment of brokerage fees, commissions, and other illegitimate compensation to agents in connection with the sale of goods.[91] Although this provision primarily applies to price discrimination, courts have held that Section 2(c) does prohibit commercial bribery.[92] In *Environmental Tectonics*, the court held that the passing of payments from seller to buyer was a clear violation of Section 2(c).

Similarly, in the case of *Municipality of Anchorage v Hitachi Cable, Ltd.*, Hitachi Cable's bribery of two employees of the municipality of Anchorage led to various charges, including violations of the Robinson-Patman Act.[93] In this case, Hitachi argued that the municipality lacked standing to sue, based on the argument that when a seller bribes a buyer's agent, only competitors of the seller suffer competitive injury. The court expressly rejected this narrow reading of the standing requirement of Section 2(c), holding that when commercial bribes are paid to a company's employees to obtain contracts for the sale of goods, the company has standing to sue. These two cases illustrate the potential use of Section 2(c) of the Robinson-Patman Act against competitors engaging in illicit payments.

Another statute that has been used by private plaintiffs is the Sherman Act.[94] Section 1 of the Sherman Act prohibits contracts, combination in the form of trust or otherwise, or conspiracy, in restraint of trade or commerce among the several states or with foreign nations. Liability for violation is established by Section 2, which provides that every person who shall monopolize, or attempt to monopolize, or combine or conspire with any other person or persons to monopolize any part of the trade or commerce shall be deemed guilty of a felony.[95] Private plaintiffs have sought to broaden these provisions of the Sherman Act to cover bribery. The traditional scope of Section 1 of the Sherman Act prohibits unreasonable restraints of trade such as anti-competitive agreements among competitors in the form of price fixing, sharing of price information, or prohibitions on competitive bidding by members of a commercial organization.[96] Some commentators have argued that in certain situations, bribery could be monopolistic and thus a restraint on trade

---

90 15 U.S.C. 13a, 13b, 21a (1996).

91 *Ibid.*

92 See *Environmental Tectonics v W.S. Kirkpatrick, Inc.*, 847 F.2d 1052, 1066 (3rd Cir. 1988).

93 547 F. Supp. 633 (D. Alaska 1982).

94 Sherman Act 15 U.S.C. 1–7 (1988). 15 U.S.C. 1 (1988).

95 15 U.S.C. 2 (1988).

96 The classic rule formulation can be found in *Standard Oil Co. of New Jersey v US*, 221 U.S. 1, 31 S.Ct. 502 (1911). See also *Interstate Circuit, Inc. v US*, 306 U.S. 208 (1939), which held that licenses to theatres that required a minimum price of admission and other restraints was a violation of the Sherman Act.

in violation of the Sherman Act.[97] These commentators argue that bribery in this context can be exclusionary for the purposes of the Sherman Act because it has an impact on the competitiveness of the rival.

Recently the Sherman Act also has been used to address bribe transactions. The rationale for the extension of the Sherman Act to bribery rests on the argument that bribery, like other anti-competitive arrangements, is a restraint of trade.[98] This approach appears to have been followed by the court in *Associated Radio Service Co. v Page Airways, Inc.*[99] The court, in assessing the exclusionary tactics of the defendants, noted that the payment of the bribes coupled with the fact that Page had paid $10,000 over the next highest bid constituted an exclusionary practice in violation of Section 2 of the Sherman Act. The prospects of using the Sherman Act for private actions against bribery are limited by the inconsistent application of the act to bribery transactions. For instance, in *Parmelee Transportation Co. v Keeshin*, the court concluded that commercial bribery was not a classic restraint to trade and therefore was beyond the scope of the Sherman Act.[100] This line of reasoning was also followed in the *Municipality of Anchorage* case discussed previously, where the court concluded that bribery in international business transactions were in themselves insufficient to sustain an action under the Sherman Act.

Section 201, discussed previously, only applies to federal officers and employees and does not extend to state or local government officials in the US. The Hobbs Act was adopted by congress as a successor to an earlier law, the Anti-Racketeering Act of 1934, which was designed to combat extortion and violence perpetrated by criminal organizations against private individuals.[101] The Hobbs Act prohibits robbery and extortion to obtain property, and it defines two types of extortion: physical coercion ('wrongful use of actual or threatened force, violence, or fear') and the use of public office ('under colour of official right').[102] Federal prosecutors in the US have successfully used the extortion 'under color of official right' provision of the Hobbs Act to prosecute the receipt of bribes by state and local officials.[103] The act was used in the case of *United States v Kenny* to prosecute

---

97 Areeda, P & Turner, D [2000]: *Antitrust Law: An Analysis of Principles and their Application* (New York: Aspen Law and Business), 167.

98 Areeda, P & Turner, D [2000: 167–72] assess the situations under which bribery can be punished as an unreasonable restraint of trade.

99 624 F.2d 1342 (5th Cir. 1980).

100 292 F.2d 794 (7th Cir. 1961). This formal reading of the Sherman Act was followed by the US District Court for the District of Idaho in *Sterling Nelson & Sons, Inc. v Rangen, Inc.*, 235 F. Supp. 393 (N. Idaho 1964), as well as by the Ninth Circuit in *Calnetics Corp. v Volkswagen of America*, 532 F.2d 674 (9th Cir. 1976).

101 Act of June 18, 1934, ch. 569, 48 Stat. 979 (superseded by the Hobbs Act in 1946).

102 18 U.S.C. § 1951(a) (2000).

103 For an in-depth discussion of the parameters of the 'under color of official right', see Gayed, J [2003]: '"Corruptly": Why Corrupt State of Mind Is an Essential Element for Hobbs Act Extortion Under Color of Official Right', in Vol. 78, *Notre Dame Law Review*, 1731.

a local official who required that a percentage of all government contracts be paid to him for the privilege of doing business with local governments.[104] Although, there was no overt use of force or a threat to obtain the payment, the court upheld the conviction on the basis that either evidence of a threat could establish the extortion or that the defendant obtained the money because of their position of official authority.[105]

The court's ruling and subsequent interpretations have made it unnecessary to establish that the official in any way threatened the payer of the money, or indeed that there was any overt discussion of the reason for the payment. In *Evans v United States*, the court held that the proof that the defendant had the authority to affect the outcome of an exercise of governmental authority and acceptance of a bribe met the requirements for a conviction under 'colour of official right'.[106] The limitation of the Hobbs Act with respect to the offence of bribery is that it only applies to passive bribery, imposing a sanction on the public official extorting the bribe, but not the person who pays the bribe.

In summary, the domestic regulation of bribery, as highlighted above, is characterized by large areas of uncertainty concerning the scope and application of the offence. Both the US and UK do not have a coherent set of domestic laws regulating the offence of bribery, although this has been somewhat addressed by the passage of the new legislation in the UK. Prior to the passage, the law on corruption was described as 'an area of law riddled by logical inconsistency and historical hangovers'.[107] Another commentator, specifically on UK bribery framework, stated that the law on bribery was in 'impressive disarray'.[108] Similarly, the US law on domestic bribery is also not coherent. One provision of federal law regulates bribery to federal officials, while a different one addresses corruption connected to state and local programs that receive federal funds.[109] The US Congress is yet to enact a statute dealing specifically with the problem of public corruption and the extent to which the federal power should be applied to the corrupt acts of state and local officials.

Another problem associated with the current US law concerns the precise mental element that has to be proved before a person can be found guilty of corruption. Under the current law in the US, the prosecution is required to prove

104 462 F.2d 1205, 1210 (3d Cir. 1972).

105 *Ibid.*, at 1229.

106 504 U.S. 255, 266 (1992).

107 Alldridge, P [2000]: 'Reforming the Criminal Law of Corruption', in Vol. 11, *Criminal Law Forum*, 287, at 287.

108 Lanham, D [1987]: 'Bribery and Corruption', in *Essays in Honour of J C Smith*, Consultation Paper No 145, para 4.15, 92, 104.

109 18 U.S.C. § 201 (2000) regulates bribery of federal officials and 18 U.S.C. § 666 (2000) regulates state and local programs that receive federal funds. See Henning, P [2001]: 'Public Corruption: A Comparative Analysis of International Corruption Conventions and United States Law', in Vol. 18, *Arizona Journal of International and Comparative Law*, 793, at 798–9.

that the defendant acted 'corruptly' – a word that is not defined. The uncertainty of the meaning of the word corruptly remains one of the most important defects in the present law. Furthermore, prosecutions for bribery often fail even though there is evidence that a public official acted in breach of his or her duty because of the difficulties associated with proving that a bribe was paid or even agreed.

Domestic Regulation of Transnational Bribery: The US FCPA

The FCPA was the first national statute criminalizing transnational bribery of foreign officials. The statute was enacted in 1977 and was in part a reaction to the Watergate scandal.[110] The Watergate Special Prosecutor, while probing the illegal corporate contributions to the 1972 Nixon presidential campaign, discovered numerous corporate political slush funds that had evaded accounting controls.[111] Following up on the disclosures by the Watergate Special Prosecutor of these overseas slush funds used by US corporations to make illegal campaign contributions in the US and corrupt payments to foreign officials, the Securities and Exchange Commission (SEC) undertook its own broad-ranging investigation.[112] The SEC investigations, originally directed at corporate nondisclosure of funds used for illegal political campaign contributions in the US, revealed that over 300 American companies had also made questionable payments to foreign officials.[113]

In 1975, the SEC sued four major companies: Gulf Oil Corporation, Phillips Petroleum Company, Northrop Corporation, and Ashland Oil, Inc. The SEC alleged that the establishment of secret slush funds for unaccountable distribution of moneys abroad violated US securities law requiring that public companies file accurate financial statements.[114] The SEC also initiated court proceedings against a fifth Company, United Brands Corporation. The employees of United Brands Corporation had informed the SEC that the chairperson had agreed to pay $2.5 million to senior officials of the Honduran government.[115] This payment was made in exchange for the repeal of a recently enacted tax on bananas. United Brands was charged with securities fraud for failing to report the payment of a bribe. The SEC

110 See Schroth, P [2002]: 'The United States and the International Bribery Conventions', in Vol. 50, *American Journal of Comparative Law*, 593, at 593–6.

111 See Dundas, M & Crutchfield B [1980]: 'Historical Analysis of the Accounting Standards of the Foreign Corrupt Practices Act', in Vol. 10, *Memphis State Law Review*, 499, at 499–500.

112 See Brown [1998: 3].

113 See Deberardine, V [1984]: 'Foreign Corrupt Practices: Creating an Exception to the Act of State Doctrine', in Vol. 34, *American University Law Review*, 203, at 221.

114 See 'The Activities of American Multinational Corporations Abroad', Hearings Before the Subcomm. on International Economic Policy of the House Comm. on International Relations, 94th Cong. 37 (1975), microformed on CIS No. 76-H461-15.

115 See Posadas, A [2000]: 'Combating Corruption Under International Law' in Vol. 10, *Duke Journal of Comparative & International Law*, 345, at 349.

held that this payment was a materially relevant fact for reporting purposes and should have been disclosed to the investing public.[116]

To ascertain the extent to which US corporations engaged in such actions, the SEC indicated that it would refrain from taking enforcement action against US companies that voluntarily disclosed having made any such questionable payments.[117] In a subsequent report published by the SEC in 1976, it was disclosed that over 400 US companies, including 177 Fortune 500 companies, admitted through voluntary disclosure sessions to having made 'questionable payments' to foreign officials.[118] The far-reaching extent of the number of companies that had made questionable payments shocked congress, which was still reeling from the Watergate scandal.[119]

Both the US House of Representatives and Senate comprehensively reviewed the issue of questionable foreign payments. With the benefit of the report by the SEC, congress conducted its own fact-finding exercise, which revealed widespread incidents of international bribery involving corrupt payments of hundreds of millions of dollars.[120] The House Committee on International Relations and the Senate Committees on Foreign Relations and Banking, Housing, and Urban Affairs held extensive hearings on the matter.[121] During the hearings, the chairman of Lockheed testified to the fact that about $20 million, 15 percent of the commissions paid to foreign agents, were paid to foreign officials.[122] Also acknowledged by the Lockheed chairman was the payment of over $100 million to agents in connection with sales in Saudi Arabia.[123] The testimony of the Lockheed chairman indicated that Lockheed paid bribes of more than $1 million to Prince Bernhard, the husband of Queen Juliana of the Netherlands; $1.7 million to the former premier of Japan, Kakeui Tanaka; over $7 million to politically connected, right–wing Japanese militarist Yoshio Kodama; $2 million to Italian officials; and scores of lesser amounts to about eight different countries, including Germany, Mexico, Spain, and Greece. The disclosures of payments by Lockheed and other

116 *Ibid.*, at 349–50.

117 See Pines, D [1994]: 'Comment, Amending the Foreign Corrupt Practices Act to Include a Private Right of Action', in Vol. 82, *California Law Review*, 185, at 187.

118 See 'Report of the Securities and Exchange Commission on Questionable and Illegal Corporate Payments and Practices Submitted to the Senate Comm. on Banking, Housing, and Urban Affairs', reprinted in 353 *Sec. Reg. & L. Rep.* 36–41 (1976).

119 See Senate Report No. 105–277, at 1 (1998).

120 See Brown [1998: 3].

121 See Posadas [2000: 348–58] for details regarding the congressional hearings on these corrupt practices.

122 See 'Lockheed Bribery', Hearings Before the Comm. on Banking, Housing, and Urban Affairs', 94th Cong. (1975), at 40.

123 See 'Multinational Corps. and U.S. Foreign Policy', Hearings Before the Subcomm. on Multinational Corps. of the Comm. on Foreign Relations, 94th Cong. (1975), at 352–3.

companies provided the motivation for congress and the SEC to fully examine the scope of illicit payments.[124]

Despite evidence of widespread questionable overseas payments, opinions differed substantially as to how the problem of overseas corruption should be addressed. Some advocated public disclosure as the most appropriate means of inhibiting questionable payments. Others advocated criminalization.[125] On March 31, 1976, President Ford instituted a Cabinet-level task force, the Task Force on Questionable Foreign Payments Abroad, to review the problem of questionable payments and propose remedial legislation. In its final report, the Task Force concluded that a disclosure approach was preferable to a criminalization approach.[126] In the end, congress concluded that criminalization was a more effective deterrent than simply requiring disclosure. The Senate Committee on Banking, Housing, and Urban Affairs reached a similar conclusion.

Legislative History and Amendments to the FCPA

The principal motivation for the passage of the FCPA was moral indignation against what appeared to be widespread incidents of corporations engaging in transnational bribery. Since the FCPA's passage, there have been several amendments to strengthen the provisions of the legislation. Before the enactment of the FCPA, US corporations that bribed foreign officials abroad could only be prosecuted through indirect means such as under the US securities law. The broad disclosure requirements mandated by the SEC meant that payments made to secure business abroad were a required in the SEC filings of corporations. Interestingly, the SEC disclosure requirements only required the disclosure of bribes and did not prohibit the payment of bribes.[127] However, such indirect means of preventing foreign bribery were ineffective; the FCPA was meant to be a more direct and effective means of enforcement.[128]

The FCPA is isecomposed of two parts, each designed to prevent such corrupt payments. The first part sets strict accounting and record-keeping requirements. The second part prohibits bribery of foreign officials. The FCPA has been amended twice since its passage in 1976.[129] In 1988, congress amended the FCPA

---

124 See Lacey, K & George, B [1998]: 'Expansion of Sec Authority into Internal Corporate Governance: The Accounting Provisions of the Foreign Corrupt Practices Act (a Twentieth Anniversary Review)', in Vol. 7, *Journal of Transnational Law & Policy*, 119, at 128.

125 See Brown [1999: 428].

126 *Ibid.*, at 428–9.

127 Noonan [1984: 676].

128 See Pines [1994: 188].

129 See Crutchfield, B & Lacey, K [2006]: 'The Changing Face of White-Collar Crime: Investigation of Halliburton Co./Tskj's Nigerian Business Practices: Model for Analysis of the Current Anti-Corruption Environment on Foreign Corrupt Practices Act

as part of a broad legislative effort to strengthen the global competitiveness of American businesses. These measures were enacted as part of the Omnibus Trade and Competitiveness Act of 1988.[130] The amendments were aimed at reaffirming congressional commitment to stemming transnational corporate corruption, while limiting the exposure of US businesses to violations of the FCPA by clarifying certain areas of the act. The FCPA was again amended through the International Anti-Bribery and Fair Competition Act of 1998.[131] The intent of the 1998 amendments was to bring the FCPA in line with the international law obligations mandated by the OECD Convention.

The anti-bribery provisions of the FCPA hold US corporations and nationals accountable for payments made to foreign government officials that influenced any such officials to confer an improper economic advantage to a US corporation or national.[132] Though the jurisdictional scope of the 1977 FCPA was extra-territorial, liability was limited to corporations registered or principally acting in the US and to US citizens.[133] Further, the 1977 FCPA set a reason to know standard for the attachment of vicarious liability. The 1977 FCPA required that the party have a reason to know of questionable actions undertaken by its agents to be vicariously liable.[134] The 1977 FCPA also included a corruptly provision that emphasized the view of congress concerning the immoral nature of an illegal payment under the FCPA.[135]

From the instant the FCPA was implemented, American corporations complained about the FCPA's provisions, and clamoured for its amendment.[136] Criticism of the 1977 Act fell into two categories. First, critics complained that the statute's provisions were extremely vague and it was therefore difficult for corporations to know whether they were complying or not with the requirements of the statute. Second, critics complained that the FCPA's provisions covered such a broad scope that the FCPA threatened to unduly impair the conduct of US business abroad.[137] Corporations claimed that uncertainty over potential FCPA liability stemming from foreign business partners was leading to major corporate losses to foreign business competitors, many of whom were not subject

Enforcement', in Vol. 96, *Journal of Criminal Law & Criminology*, 503, at 514–15. They review the amendments to the FCPA.

130 Congress enacted the Patent Process Amendments Act as part of the Omnibus Trade and Competitiveness Act of 1988, Pub. L. No. 100-418, Title IX, 102 Stat. § 9003, 1107, 1563 (1988).

131 International Anti-Bribery and Fair Competition Act of 1998, Pub. L. No. 105-306, 112 Stat. 3302.

132 Foreign Corrupt Practices Act of 1977, Pub. L. No. 95-213, §§ 103-04, 91 Stat. 1494 (1977) §§ 103(a), 104(a).

133 §§ 103(a), 104(a).

134 104(a)(3).

135 See Senate Report No. 105-277, at 1 (1998).

136 See Pines [1994: 189].

137 See *Ibid.*, at 190 for a vociferous criticism of the FCPA.

to extra-territorial anti-corruption laws.[138] According to US corporations, these losses came in the absence of the economic benefits stemming from a restoration of popular confidence in the integrity of American businesses, the reciprocal gain that congress promised when it passed the 1977 FCPA. Further criticisms revolved around the uncertain vicarious liability provisions of the 1977 FCPA. In response, congress attempted to ease the burden on US businesses by amending the FCPA in 1988.

The new FCPA amendments made several major changes that affected the anti-bribery provisions of the act. First, the requisite state of mind for third-party payments was changed from a broad 'reason to know standard' to the more narrow 'knowing standard'.[139] A person is deemed to know that a payment to a third party will be used to bribe a foreign official if the person is aware or has a firm belief that the third party is engaging in such conduct or that such a result is substantially certain to occur.[140] congress may have modified the standard with the intent of limiting vicarious liability to actions by foreign business associates, of which American businesses had actual knowledge, thereby eliminating liability for those actions of which the American business should reasonably have known.

The second major change that the amendments made was the exemption of several types of payments from the scope of the FCPA.[141] Grease payments, or facilitating payments, were excluded as long as the purpose of the payment was to expedite or to secure the performance of a routine governmental action. This replaced the 1977 exemption for duties by officials who were essentially ministerial or clerical. These additions were intended to aid corporations by exempting small and genuinely innocent payments. It has been noted, however, that difficulties in retroactively demonstrating the innocence of questionable transactions makes reliance on these safety provisions tenuous at best.[142] The exception allows small payments to lower-level foreign government officials to secure performance of duties that these officials would have eventually performed or were bound to perform anyway. In this context, small bribes would not give rise to liability under the FCPA. The reality that American corporate competitiveness would be severely hampered if they were not allowed to grant these small payments made the exception popular initially, especially for its potential use in foreign nations where

---

138 *Ibid.*

139 15 U.S.C. 78m(b), 78dd-1, 78dd-2, 78ff (1988) (originally enacted as Pub. L. No. 95-213, 91 Stat. 1494 (1977), and amended by Foreign Corrupt Practices Act Amendments of 1988, Pub. L. No. 100-418, 5001-5003, 102 Stat. 1107, 1415–25)._15 U.S.C. 78dd-1(a)(3), -2(a)(3).

140 15 U.S.C. 78dd-1(f)(2), -2(h)(3) (defining knowing for the purposes of the FCPA in general).

141 Under 15 U.S.C. 78dd-1(b), -2(b), a routine governmental action refers only to actions that are ordinarily and commonly performed by a foreign official.

142 See Bialos, J & Husisian G [1997]: *The Foreign Corrupt Practices Act: Coping with Corruption in Transitional Economies* (New York: Oceana Publications), at 42–9.

lower government officials regularly requested such payments to supplement their own income.[143]

The limited practicable use of the Facilitating Payments exception, however, eventually led US business interests to criticize the exception.[144] In response to the criticisms, the US Department of Justice (DOJ) modified its interpretation of the Facilitating Payments exception. The DOJ interpretation of the 1988 amendments distinguished between lower-level and higher-level officials as the determining factor in establishing whether a particular payment fell within the exception. In the modified interpretation, the focus was on the action requested and the amount of the payment, rather than the level of the official accepting the bribe.[145] The current DOJ interpretation of the FCPA exempts any facilitating or expediting payment, for expediting or to secure the performance of a routine governmental action. This exception was narrowly tailored, and the DOJ has used the value of the payment conferred as its central criteria for prosecution. The DOJ uses the value of the payment because of the complexity involved in assessing the specific circumstances of particular transactions made abroad.

The third major change brought by the 1988 FPCA amendment was the introduction of an affirmative defence where the payment was lawful in the country of the public official where it was made.[146] The availability of this defence, however, is perhaps even more tenuous than that of the facilitating payments exception for two reasons. First, not only is the burden of proof substantial but a foreign country would also rarely sanction payments to their officials through written public law. In addition, especially in transitional economies, it is risky to rely on constantly changing and uncertain local laws. Another defence is that if the payment was a reasonable and bona fide expense, similar to the costs of travel and lodging, incurred to promote or demonstrate a product, or perform a contract with a foreign government.[147]

The fourth change made by the 1988 amendments altered the enforcement provisions of the act. The Attorney General was allowed to determine whether a system of guidelines or general precautionary procedures would help businesses comply with the FCPA. In addition, the act essentially codified prior DOJ procedure by requiring the DOJ to provide opinions regarding the legality of actions upon request by any US business. An opinion issued by the DOJ that an action conforms to FCPA provisions creates a presumption that such conduct is legal under the FCPA. Fifth, the amendments stipulated that the President should

143 Bialos & Husisian [1997: 42].

144 See Duncan [2000: 29].

145 Low, L [1998]: 'The Foreign Corrupt Practices Act: How to Comply Under the New Amendments and the OECD Convention', in American Bar Association Center for Continuing Legal Education. Available at http://www.abanet.org/cle/. Last visited 23 October 2007.

146 Omnibus Trade and Competitiveness Act of 1988 §§ 5003(a), 5003(c).

147 *Ibid.*

pursue international agreement among the members of the OECD to create FCPA-like legislation in the countries that are members of that body.[148] The President was required to submit to congress a report on these negotiations, as well as other international developments in the field.

The third sets of amendments to the FCPA were carried out in 1998. In order to comply with the OECD Convention, the US government sought approval for the ratification of the OECD Convention and its key legislative proposals to implement the provisions of the Convention.[149] Both houses of the US Congress held hearings concerning the proposed legislation.[150] On October 20, 1998, the House unanimously adopted the International Anti-Bribery and Fair Competition Act, which amended the Securities Exchange Act of 1934 and the FCPA of 1977.[151] The Senate also unanimously passed the legislation on October 21, 1998.[152] The FCPA, though in most areas was consistent with the provisions of the OECD Convention, still required several amendments. The amendments in incorporating the OECD Convention, while significant, did not alter the basic scheme of the FCPA. The 1998 amendments extended the reach of the FCPA both substantively and jurisdictionally.

Substantively, the 1998 amendments enlarged the proscribed purposes for corrupt payments to include payments made in order to obtain an improper advantage in obtaining or retaining business, a broader definition than previously covered. The 1998 amendments incorporate the OECD Convention language in reference to criminalizing payments made to secure 'any improper advantage' as opposed to the FCPA language of 'inducing him to do or omit to do any act'. The FCPA prior to the amendment covered payments to influence the acts or decision of an official, to induce the official to violate his lawful duty, and to induce the official to use his influence to affect a government decision. In effect, the FCPA adopted the broadened OECD Convention definition of bribery, which prohibits payments to foreign officials to obtain or retain business or to secure any improper advantage.

Another substantive amendment incorporating the provisions of the OECD enlarged the definition of persons considered 'foreign officials' to include persons employed by international organizations. The OECD definition of foreign officials was more comprehensive than the provision in the FCPA. Like the FCPA, the definition of 'foreign public official' includes 'any person holding a legislative, administrative or judicial office of a foreign country, whether appointed or elected' as well as 'any person exercising a public function for a foreign country, including

---

148 15 U.S.C. 78dd-1.

149 See Letters from Ann M. Harkins, Acting Assistant Attorney General, to the Hon. Newt Gingrich and the Hon. Albert Gore, Jr. Available at http://www.justice.gov/criminal/fraud/fcpa/docs/transltrs.pdf (4 May 1998). Last visited 4 March 2013.

150 'The International Anti-Bribery Act of 1998', Comm. on Banking, Housing, and Urban Affairs, S. Rep. No. 105-277, (1998) and Com. Comm., Report to Accompany H.R. 4353, H.R. Rep. No.105-802, at 10 (1998).

151 See 144 Cong. Rec. H11670-72 (Oct. 20, 1998).

152 See 144 Cong. Rec. S12973-74 (Oct. 21, 1998).

for a public agency or public enterprise'.[153] However, in contrast to the FCPA, the OECD Convention also includes within the definition of 'foreign public official,' officials or agents of 'a public international organization'. These amendments to the FCPA were critical for the successful prosecution of two World Bank staff members involved in transnational bribe transactions. In the cases of *US v Basu* and *US v Sengupta,* the two former World Bank staff members pleaded guilty to FCPA violations for receiving and facilitating bribes to a Kenyan government official.[154]

The jurisdictional amendments substantially enlarged the reach of the FCPA and broadened the jurisdiction of the FCPA to match the basis for the assertion of jurisdiction provided by the OECD Convention. The jurisdictional limits of the FCPA prior to the 1988 amendments were limited. Although the FCPA provided for nationality-based jurisdiction, the assertion of nationality-based jurisdiction was limited by the requirement that an instrument of inter-state commerce, such as a phone call, was utilized in the bribery transaction. The Securities Exchange Act of 1934, of which the FCPA is a part, establishes the same basis of jurisdiction for actions brought under its Section 10.[155] Thus, decisions under Section 10 are instructive as to the jurisdictional reach of the FCPA. The use of communications in furtherance of the fraudulent scheme are sufficient to establish federal jurisdiction under Section 10.[156] The amendments broadened the jurisdictional reach of the FCPA to US nationals without the need for a territorial nexus.

The case of *US v Mead* illustrates the broad jurisdictional reach of the FCPA.[157] In this case, Saybolt Incorporated (Saybolt) and Saybolt North America, Inc., both subsidiaries of a Dutch corporation, were charged with violating the anti-bribery provisions of the FCPA. Saybolt's president, a British citizen with US resident alien status, was arrested and charged with violating the FCPA. The Chairman of the board of directors, a Dutch national and resident, was indicted *in absentia* on identical charges. The corporations, Saybolt and Saybolt North America, both pled guilty and pursuant to the plea were fined $4.9 million, received five years of probation, and agreed to cooperate in the investigation and prosecution of the individuals involved. The chairman of Saybolt's board appears to be the first non-resident foreign national to be indicted for violating the FCPA. This jurisdictional expansion was justified by his position and relationship with the two corporations subject to US jurisdiction.

The basis for the assertion of jurisdiction under the FCPA now encompasses acts of US corporations and nationals that have no territorial link to the US in

---

153 OECD Convention, Article 4.

154 *US v Sengupta*, No. 1:02CR00040 (D.D.C. 2002) and *US v Basu* (D.D.C. 2002).

155 Section 10 of the Securities Exchange Act of 1934.

156 See the case of *Harrison v Equitable Life Assurance Society of the U.S.*, 435 F. Supp. 281, 284-85, (W.D. Mich. 1977), where the court found that a communication sent from the defendant by telephone arranging meetings to complete the sale of securities was sufficient to establish jurisdiction.

157 3 FCPA Rep. 699.533 (D.N.J. 1998).

furtherance of unlawful payments that take place outside of the US. These amendments also extended US territorial jurisdiction to reach violations of the FCPA by foreign nationals, both individuals and entities, solely predicated on an act in furtherance of the violation having been committed within the territorial US. The FCPA prior to the amendment only covered issuers of securities that were registered under the 1934 SEA. The OECD Convention, however, called on signatory nations to establish jurisdiction both based on territoriality and nationality. The FCPA was thus extended to cover 'any person', extending the reach of the FCPA to include all foreign persons who commit an act furthering a corrupt activity while in the US. Furthermore, the 1998 amendments extended jurisdictional reach of the US to its nationals outside US territory. The FCPA now makes provision for the assertion of jurisdiction over US nationals for bribery committed outside its territory.[158]

Notwithstanding the amendments incorporating the obligations acceded to by the US through the OECD Convention, the evaluation conducted by the OECD Working Group on Bribery identified several shortcomings with respect to the implementation of the OECD Convention.[159] Notably, although the Working Group on Bribery recommended that the US develop specific guidance with respect to facilitation payments and the defence of reasonable and bona fide expenditure, the US authorities were of the opinion that the FCPA definition provided sufficient guidance.[160] Another recommendation proposed by the Working Group on Bribery concerned the extension of the books and records provisions of the FCPA to non-issuers based on the level of foreign transactions so as to improve the level of deterrence. The US authorities rejected the recommendation to expand the coverage of the FCPA to non-issuers on the basis that other laws including those governing bank and tax fraud were sufficient to cover non-issuers.[161] The recommendation proposed by the Working Group on Bribery requesting the amendment of the FCPA to incorporate the language of the OECD Convention that stipulates that it is an offence to offer, promise, or give a bribe 'in order to obtain or retain business or other improper advantage in the conduct of international business' was also declined by the US. The US authorities were of the opinion that the legislative history of the amendments to the FCPA as well as the case law indicate that the existing language of the statute encompasses obtaining an 'improper advantage'.[162]

---

158 See 15 U.S.C. §§ 78 dd-1(g)(2), -2(i).

159 'United States: Phase 2 Follow-Up Report on the Implementation of the Phase 2 Recommendations on the Application of the Convention and the 1997 Recommendation on Combating Bribery of Foreign Public Officials in International Business Transactions'. Available at the OECD website: http://www.oecd.org/investment/anti-bribery/anti-briberyconvention/1962084.pdf. Last visited 4 March 2013.

160 *Ibid.*, at 9.

161 *Ibid.*, at 10.

162 *Ibid.*, at 14.

Scope of the Anti-Bribery Provisions of the FCPA

The anti-bribery provisions of the FCPA are set forth in two substantively identical sections. One was directed at issuers of registered securities, and the other was directed at all other US business concerns.[163] The required elements of the offence are the use of an instrumentality of inter-state commerce, in furtherance of a payment or offer to pay something of value to a foreign official, political party, or political candidate for the corrupt purpose of inducing the official to act or refrain from acting to assist the company in obtaining, retaining, or directing business.[164] The prohibition applies against making bribes directly, and the payment of bribes through intermediaries or third parties. The FCPA forbids making payments to third parties 'knowing' that the payments will be used for bribery purposes.[165] This standard is intended to discourage a conscious disregard or wilful blindness approach to the commission of the offence of bribery.

The level of knowledge required for the imposition of liability is vague, despite the extensive discussion in both the statute and the report by the Committee.[166] The 1988 amendments replaced the even more problematic 'reason to know' standard with a 'knowing' requirement. The legislative history clarifies what constitutes 'knowing' and expressly excludes wilful blindness.[167] The legislative history provides that the 'knowing' requirement is satisfied if the defendant acts with reckless disregard [with respect to the occurrence of bribery] and with a conscious purpose to avoid learning the truth unless the defendant believed that the conduct was not bribery. It is debatable whether the 'knowing' requirement changed the *mens rea* requirement from the 'reason to know' standard.[168] The prosecutions under the FCPA to date have not addressed the issue of the plaintiff's knowledge of the payment and thus the exact parameters of this standard are not known.

---

163 See 15 U.S.C. §§ 78dd-1 and 15 U.S.C. §§ 78dd-2.

164 15 U.S.C. §§ 78dd-1(a).

165 15 U.S.C. §§ 78dd-1(a)(3)(A) and (B).

166 For a discussion on the requisite level of knowledge, see Colare, J [2006]: 'The Evolving Domestic and International Law against Foreign Corruption: Some New and Old Dilemmas Facing the International Lawyer', in Vol. 5, *Washington University Global Studies Law Review*, 1, at 9–10.

167 ('If … a defendant acts with reckless disregard [with respect to the occurrence of bribery] and with a conscious purpose to avoid learning the truth, the requirement of knowledge would be satisfied unless the defendant actually believed [that such conduct is not bribery]'.) See. H.R. Rep. No. 576, 100th Cong., 2d Sess. 920 (1988), reprinted in 1988 U.S.C.C.A.N.

168 See Dale C. Turza, 'Remarks at The ABA/CLE Conference on the Foreign Corrupt Practices Act: How to Comply Under the New Amendments and the OECD Convention', in Marina del Rey, CA. (Feb. 19, 1999). Quoted in Duncan, C [2000]: 'The Foreign Corrupt Practices Act Amendments: Moral Empiricism or Moral Imperialism', in Vol. 1, *Asian Pacific Law & Policy Journal*, 16.1, at 16.14. He argues that the change is unlikely to forge a meaningful difference in the *mens rea* requirement for a violation.

The level of knowledge often makes it difficult to prosecute violations successfully. For instance, in the case of *US v American Totalisator Co.*, the American Totalisator Company (ATC) was accused of making payments to its Greek business agent knowing that all or a portion of those payments would be forwarded to a Greek official in violation of the FCPA.[169] The payments were allegedly made in exchange for the official assisting ATC in obtaining and retaining business with the Greek Horse Racing Administration. The DOJ declined to pursue criminal prosecution of ATC, presumably because of ATC's cooperation with the DOJ in building the case as well as a lack of evidence.

The prohibition under the FCPA not only includes actual transfers of money or gifts but also includes offers or promises to make such payments.[170] There is, however, a certain degree of ambiguity regarding when liability attaches. The ambiguity lies in how far a defendant must go to consummate the making of a payment to an official before violating the FCPA. The legislative history failed to stipulate whether a very preliminary act would violate the FCPA, merely stating that there is no requirement that the payment be fully consummated or successful in producing the desired outcome.[171]

The FCPA definition requires that payment or the offer of payment be made for inducing a foreign official to misuse his official capacity to assist in obtaining or retaining business.[172] The scope of the misuse of official capacity is illustrated by the case of *US v Vitusa Corp.*[173] In this case, Vitusa Corporation (Vitusa) contracted to sell powdered milk to the government of the Dominican Republic. After Vitusa made three deliveries of powdered milk, the government failed to pay its bill in full. A local Dominican government official informed a Vitusa business agent that he would use his influence to encourage the government to pay the outstanding balance to Vitusa in exchange for a service fee. The president of Vitusa decided to pay the fee. Vitusa, and its president individually, both pleaded guilty to a single count of making an unlawful payment to a foreign official in violation of the FCPA. The company was fined $20,000, while the president was fined $5,000 and sentenced to probation for two years.

The term corruptly emphasizes the illegal nature of the payment. The provisions of the FCPA define a foreign public official broadly to include any officer or employee of a foreign government or any department, agency, or instrumentality thereof, or any person acting in an official capacity for or on behalf of any such government, department, agency, or instrumentality.[174] There is no limit to foreign official by status level because the FCPA covers local and provincial as well as national government officials. The term could include military officers,

169 3 FCPA Rep. 699.067 (D. Md. 1993).
170 15 U.S.C. §§ 78dd-1(a)(3).
171 S. Rep. No. 95-114, at 10 (1977) reprinted in 1977 U.S.C.C.A.N., 4098 at 4108.
172 15 U.S.C. §§ 78dd-1(a)(1)(A) and (B).
173 3 FCPA Rep. 699.155 (D.N.J. 1994).
174 See 15 U.S.C. §§ 78dd-1(f)(1), 78dd-2(h)(2).

ambassadors, and members of the royal family or political party functionaries.[175] Clearly, the FPCA is broad and encompasses a wide variety of government officials. However, the definition in the FCPA, in contrast to the definition provided by the OECD Convention, does not include persons holding judicial office in a foreign country. Seemingly, this leaves open a loophole in the OECD Convention in that bribes paid to political parties, party officials, or candidates are not included within the scope of offences that signatories are required to prohibit.

Under the FCPA, US corporations are not liable for the FCPA violations of their subsidiaries.[176] Although the statute is ambiguous on this point, the legislative history and case law indicates that a US corporation is not liable for the FCPA violations of a foreign subsidiary acting on its own behalf.[177] However, the FCPA may apply, through the knowledge requirement, to foreign subsidiaries of US corporations that are subject to the actual control of the US parent corporation.[178] Therefore, the US parent would both have to have knowledge of the alleged violations and the ability to prevent them. An otherwise covered violation conceived and executed entirely by the foreign branch or subsidiary would itself not expose the US parent to liability, even if the subsidiary were 100 percent owned by the US corporation.[179] Demonstrating lack of knowledge under such circumstances, however, may prove difficult. In addition, any US national abroad is subject to the act, even if he or she is employed by a foreign-owned firm.[180]

Effectiveness of the FCPA: Enforcement and Sanctions

Commentators suggest that transnational bribery remains a widespread practice despite the efforts of these transnational legal prescriptions, but whether these levels have increased, remained stable, or decreased cannot be determined conclusively.[181] However, some reliable indicators may serve as proxy for the effectiveness of these transnational legal prescriptions in the absence of empirical evidence. One possible proxy is the level of enforcement of national legislation

---

175 15 U.S.C. §§ 78dd-3(h)(2)(A).

176 For a review of the liability of US corporations for violations of the FCPA see Marceau, J [2007]: 'A Little Less Conversation, a Little More Action: Evaluating and Forecasting the Trend of More Frequent and Severe Prosecutions Under The Foreign Corrupt Practices Act', in Vol. 12, *Fordham Journal of Corporate & Financial Law*, 285, at 296–309.

177 See H.R. CONF. REP. NO. 95-831, at 15 (1977), reprinted in 1977 U.S.C.C.A.N. 4098, 4126 and *Dooley v United Technologies Corp.*, 803 F. Supp. 428, 439 (D.D.C. 1992), holding that the legislative history excludes foreign subsidiaries from FCPA coverage.

178 15 U.S.C. §§ 78dd-3(f)(1).

179 15 U.S.C. §§ 78dd-3(f)(3)(A) and (B).

180 15 U.S.C. §§ 78dd-3(i)(1) and (2).

181 See Segal, P [2006]: 'Coming Clean on Dirty Dealing: Time for a Fact-Based Evaluation of the Foreign Corrupt Practices Act', in Vol. 18, *Florida Journal of International Law*, 169, at 171, for a review of the effectiveness of the FCPA and arguing that the FCPA has been totally ineffective.

through the number of successful prosecutions for transnational bribery.[182] The inference is that a high level of enforcement would have a deterrent effect and lead to lower levels of transnational bribery by corporations.

Two governmental agencies have the authority to enforce the FCPA. The Department of Justice has authority to prosecute criminal violations of the FCPA and has jurisdiction to bring civil actions to enjoin violations by other domestic concerns.[183] The SEC retains jurisdiction over 'issuers'. This retention was given on account of the general enforcement procedures of the federal securities laws, which give primary responsibility for issuers of US securities to the SEC.[184] The SEC may also bring civil actions against issuers of US securities for violations of the act, such as failure to keep detailed books or failure to maintain an adequate internal accounting system.[185] Initial SEC investigations into a corporation has often led to the discovery of criminal violations, such as altering accounting records to conceal bribes in the form of executive bonuses or salaries. The SEC's role with respect to criminal prosecution, however, terminates when it has compiled sufficient evidence of a potential violation.[186] The SEC must then refer the case to the Department of Justice for further investigation and prosecution.

The DOJ has primary authority over criminal enforcement of FCPA. The DOJ's Fraud Section initiates and conducts most prosecutions under the FCPA.[187] Due in large part to the severity of available penalties, the vast majority of DOJ prosecutions under the FCPA have resulted in voluntary disclosures by the suspected parties rather than a full trial. The SEC also has significant civil enforcement capabilities, which it usually uses to further its inherent interest in patrolling violations of the accounting provisions of the FCPA. SEC prosecutions are principally directed through the SEC's Division of Enforcement.[188] Thus, although the DOJ takes a dominant role in prosecuting the 1998 Amended FCPA's anti-bribery provisions, an individual or business entity could face multiple prosecutions for an alleged violation of the 1998 Amended FCPA.

To ensure that there is little ambiguity in terms of the consequences of FCPA violations, the DOJ established 'opinion procedures' in 1992. The opinion procedures provide a mechanism whereby US nationals could inform the DOJ of an imminent transaction and receive an opinion from the DOJ about the

182 See Bixby, M [2010]: 'The Lion Awakes: The Foreign Corrupt Practices Act—1977 to 2010', in Vol. 12, *San Diego International Law Journal*, 89, for a breakdown of cases brought by the DOJ and the SEC from the 1970s through 2010.

183 See the DOJ publication detailing policy with respect to enforcement of the FCPA: *Lay-Person's Guide to the FCPA Statute* (June 2001). Available at http://www.usdoj.gov/criminal/fraud/docs/dojdocb.html. Last visited 7 October 2007.

184 *Ibid.*

185 *Ibid.*

186 *Ibid.*

187 *Ibid.*

188 *Ibid.*

proposed transaction. The significance of these opinion procedures is that the company gives the DOJ an actual transaction, not a hypothetical situation, based on the full disclosure of all relevant facts. The corporation receives, within a period of 30 days, a written opinion from the Attorney General with specific regard to its situation. The opinion provided does not make a determination as to whether the conduct violates the FCPA. Rather, the DOJ opinion addresses the more narrow issue of whether the prospective conduct falls within the enforcement police of the anti-bribery provisions of the FCPA. There has not been a tremendous amount of use made of the opinion procedure. Despite the ease and potential benefits of the opinion procedures, between 1993 and 1998 there were only 12 requests for opinions submitted to the DOJ.[189]

The penalties for violation of the anti-bribery provisions of the act are substantial. Individuals who violate the act are subject to imprisonment for up to five years and may be fined up to $100,000.[190] Violators may also be subject to civil penalties of up to $10,000 for each violation.[191] The act prohibits the indemnification, directly or indirectly, of a fine or penalty imposed on an individual.[192] Corporations convicted of criminal violations of the FCPA may be fined up to $2 million.[193]

Not all payments to foreign officials are prohibited, however. As mentioned previously, payments that are solely intended to expedite or secure the performance of a routine governmental action by a foreign official are exempt from the anti-bribery prohibition.[194] Such payments are often referred to as 'facilitating payments' or 'grease payments'. The rationale is that unlike payments designed to induce preferential treatment, the purpose of facilitating payments is to provide an incentive to low-level foreign officials to carry out their duties efficiently. The exception for grease payments may thus relieve corporations of liability for payments to low-level officials made merely to accelerate administrative processes abroad.[195]

The FCPA recognizes an affirmative defence for reasonable and *bona fide* promotional expenses.[196] To constitute a reasonable and *bona fide* expenditure under the FCPA, the expenditure must be directly related to the promotion of products or services or to the execution of a contract with the foreign government or

---

189 *Ibid.*

190 15 U.S.C. §§ 78dd-3(g)(2)(A).

191 15 U.S.C. §§ 78dd-3(g)(2)(B).

192 15 U.S.C. §§ 78dd-3(g)(3).

193 15 U.S.C. §§ 78dd-3(g)(1)(A).

194 15 U.S.C. §§ 78dd-3(h)(4)(A) and (B).

195 However, see Koch, R [2005]: 'The Foreign Corrupt Practices Act: It's Time to Cut Back the Grease and Add Some Guidance', in Vol. 28, *Boston College International and Comparative Law Review*, 379 at 380, where she argues that that the interpretation of grease payments is not drawn narrowly enough.

196 15 U.S.C. §§ 78dd-2(c)(2).

agency.[197] The case of *U.S. v Metcalf & Eddy* illustrates the scope of the facilitating payments exception.[198] The DOJ interpreted the provision of airfare, travel expenses, and pocket money to an Egyptian official and his family during business trips to the US as exceeding the legitimate levels for *bona fide* promotional expenses.

Other payments are exempt from the anti-bribery provisions as well. Proof that a payment to a foreign official was lawful under the written laws of the foreign country could constitute an affirmative defence to an alleged violation of the FCPA.[199] Lack of knowledge may also be a defence, although it is, of course, a question of fact.

Despite the existence of formal mechanisms, there have been fewer than expected successful prosecutions for violation of the FCPA.[200] Since the inception of the FCPA, the DOJ has instituted 56 separate prosecutions for violations of the anti-bribery provisions of the FCPA. Between 2002 and 2007, the DOJ instituted 74 investigations into violations of the anti-bribery provisions. Most of the convictions under the FCPA were based on the defendants entering a guilty plea. In one of the cases, the court granted a motion for judgment of acquittal at the close of the government's case.[201] Of the 56 prosecutions, 58 were against individuals and 40 against corporations. A conviction, after a trial of the defendants, is the less common outcome of the cases, with a majority of the cases being resolved through plea agreements. Of the 71 cases against both individuals and corporations since 1990, 43 were resolved through plea agreements, and only four resulted in convictions after a trial. In 1990 alone, seven of the cases were dismissed and since then only one other case has resulted in a dismissal. In five cases between 1990 and 1991, the defendants were acquitted after the trial. Similar to the dismissals, there have not been any acquittals after trial since then.

The number of reported investigations by either the DOJ or the SEC (or both) into potential violations of the FCPA has increased significantly over the last four years.[202] In 2002, both the DOJ and SEC instituted seven investigations. The number rose to 11 in 2003 and to 18 in 2004. The number of investigations in 2005 did not follow the trend of the previous four years because only four new investigations were disclosed. In 2006, there was a dramatic increase with fourteen investigations disclosed. One important trend concerns the number of

---

197 15 U.S.C. §§ 78dd-1(c)(2); 78dd-2(c)(2).

198 3 FCPA Rep. 699.749 (D. Ma. 1999).

199 15 U.S.C. §§ 78dd-2(c)(1).

200 See Koehler, M [2010]: 'The Facade of FCPA Enforcement', in Vol. 41, *Georgetown Journal of International Law*, 907, at 1009, where he makes reference to a façade of FCPA enforcement and argues for greater judicial scrutiny through defendants challenging enforcement actions.

201 *U.S. v Harris Corporation, John D. Iacobucci and Ronald L. Schultz* (Cr. No. 90-0456), N.D. Cal., 1990.

202 See Low, L [2003]: "The Anti-Corruption Laws of the United States and Mexico", in Vol. 11, *United States-Mexico Law Journal*, 149, at 152.

prosecutions against corporations. Major corporations such as General Electric, Goodyear, IBM, Baker Hughes, Halliburton, and Lockheed have all been the subject of criminal prosecution under the FCPA. Between 1998 and 2003, only two of the prosecutions were against corporations. This trend reversed dramatically starting in 2004. The 18 new investigations instigated in 2004 were all investigations concerning corporations. Fourteen were US corporations, and the other four were foreign corporations. Clearly, the focus of prosecutions is on corporations engaging in transnational bribery. There is, however, very little information by which the effectiveness of the FCPA in deterring bribery can be measured. The prosecution of cases can be assumed to provide some sort of deterrence to corporations, but measuring the number of bribes in transnational business transactions is impossible.

Another limited proxy for measuring the effectiveness of the FCPA is the BPI developed by Transparency International (TI) with the assistance of Gallup International Association, which measures the sources of international corruption. More than 770 executives at major corporations, chambers of commerce, commercial banks, and law firms in 15 countries answered detailed questionnaires about their perceptions of which countries are home to multinational corporations that are paying bribes. In the BPI, TI, and Gallup selected those emerging markets where there is a reasonable spread of international competition and difficulties with bribery in international business transactions.

The BPI ranks exporting nations on a 1 to 10 scale, where 10 represents a very low perceived level of bribery, and 1 indicates a very high level of bribery. Australia had the best score, 8.4. It is interesting to note that despite a two-decade history since the adoption of the FCPA, the US had a score of 5.3 in the 2002 BPI, placing thirteenth out of the 21 countries listed on the BPI. Furthermore, research conducted on the behaviour of corporations from OECD countries in transitional states indicated that US corporations were no less likely to engage in the payment of procurement bribes than corporations from other countries were.[203] Taken together, the paucity of effective prosecutions and the low ranking on the BPI is a relatively poor result given that the FCPA has been in operation for close to 30 years. Beyond the paucity of investigations and a low ranking on the BPI, it is not possible to determine how effective the FCPA has been as a policy tool to curb transnational bribery for the following reasons. First, it is not possible to establish how US corporations would have behaved without the FCPA. Second, estimating the number of transnational bribe payments after the passage of the FCPA is not feasible.

Two main problems have been identified with the apparent lack of effectiveness of the FCPA.[204] The first concerns the limited enforcement of the act, which has been attributed to the ineffectiveness of the agencies charged with maintaining the

203 Hellman, J, Jones, G & Kaufmann, D [2000]: 'Beyond the "Grabbing Hand" of Government in Transition: Facing up to "State Capture by the Corporate Sector", in Vol. 11, No. 2, *Transition: The Newsletter about Reforming Economies*, 8 at 9.

204 See Pines [1994: 192].

FCPA provisions and their failure to cooperate.[205] The second concerns difficulties in prosecuting foreign bribery cases, and a possible lack of political support for certain prosecutions. According to Pines, in an interview with a former federal prosecutor, the prosecutor described an investigation involving alleged bribes paid by the Olin Corporation to South African officials to facilitate an arms sale to the country. The prosecutor stated that in addition to discovery problems, the South African government refused to permit interviews of their nationals.[206]

Another factor affecting the effectiveness of the FCPA concerns the absence of a private cause of action. A commentator has argued for the inclusion of a private right of action to the FCPA. The proposal advocates the adoption of a restricted right of action to a group of potential plaintiffs who believe that a competing US business engaged in the bribing of a foreign official.[207] He suggests that a private right of action will bring more FCPA suits to courts and ensure that the precedents created help to clarify some of the vague provisions of the FCPA. In essence, a private right of action would serve to mitigate two of the major criticisms, vagueness and under enforcement, of the FCPA.

The courts in the case of *Lamb v Phillip Morris, Inc.* specifically rejected the possibility of a private right of action.[208] In this case, subsidiaries of Phillip Morris donated $12.5 million to The Children's Foundation of Venezuela, an organization chaired by the Venezuelan president's wife. In return, Phillip Morris gained price controls on Venezuelan tobacco, assurances that existing tax rates applicable to tobacco companies would not be raised, and other benefits. The plaintiffs brought an action against Philip Morris for violation of the FCPA. The Sixth Circuit dismissed the action because the FCPA does not provide for a private cause of action. This case illustrates a very limiting feature in the coverage of the FCPA.

Conclusion

The chapter focused on the domestic regulation of both national and transnational bribery, using the UK and US as exemplary jurisdictions. Given the long history of the FCPA, a significant amount of the material in this chapter was based on the experience of the FCPA, and the chapter concluded that the effectiveness of the FCPA to curb transnational bribery by corporations had been limited. There is very

205 *Ibid.*, at 193.

206 *Ibid.*, at 194–5.

207 *Ibid.*, at 216. See Jatto, L [2010]: 'Africa's Approach to the International War On Corruption: A Critical Appraisal of the African Union Convention on Preventing and Combating Corruption', in Vol. 10, *Asper Review of International Business and Trade Law*, 79, at 94–5. He proposes an amendment to the African Union Convention permitting victims of corruption to seek and obtain compensation in the form of civil remedies over and above the penal sanctions prescribed under domestic anti-corruption legislation.

208 915 F.2d 1024 (6th Cir. 1990).

little authoritative or official guidance on the scope of the FCPA as there are very few litigated cases, prosecutions, and civil enforcements dealing with the difficult issues surrounding the more controversial aspects of the statute. The paucity of prosecutions and the lack of reliable statistics or other information showing the number of allegations received; and investigations commenced, terminated, or abandoned also makes it difficult to draw definitive conclusions about the effectiveness of the FCPA.

The pertinent question raised is this: what accounts for the failure of the FCPA to curb the prevalence of transnational bribery by corporations? The answer to the question is particularly important to the regulation of transnational bribery by corporations because the similarity of the legislative provisions adopted by the signatories to the corruption conventions is likely to ensure that these enactments have the same lacklustre effect as the FCPA on the occurrence of transnational bribery by corporations. In many respects, the debate over why transnational bribery remains commonplace despite the ubiquity of transnational bribery legislation revolves around not just differences in moral values but also differences in what are considered the appropriate legal strategies and in the ultimate policy outcomes desired. These differences have implications for whether and to what extent current multilateral efforts to regulate transnational bribery are likely to curb transnational bribery.

Chapter 4
Multilateral Regulation of Transnational Bribery

The level of cooperation by states to address common problems has burgeoned in the decades since the Second World War. The level of cooperation among states has displaced many of the fundamental premises that defined international cooperation. Some of the displaced premises include fundamental tenets like the ultimate sovereignty of states and several related traditional doctrines that formed the conceptual foundations of the international law. We have also seen international cooperation extended to domains previously reserved for nation states. Nation states have even come to accept that there are certain principles that are universally binding even without consent and sometimes over their objections.

One area in which there has been noticeable cooperation has been in the efforts by states to control corruption. Over the last decade, international collaboration to control corruption has intensified particularly through a process of articulation of the shared norms on corruption. This process of articulation by the international community has brought about some consensus by the transnational community on the appropriate mechanisms for tackling transnational corruption. For an international community comprising diverse legal cultures and histories, reaching broad agreement on such fundamental issues was difficult. However, the rapid development of these shared norms on the issue of corruption attests to a possible convergence in perspectives towards the regulation of the practice. The convergence of these perspectives could be attributed in part to the fact that in the regulation of corruption, shared problems often engender collaborative solutions. The development of transnational standards thus offers both a process for the articulation and enforcement of these shared norms.

The principal arguments regarding the lack of effectiveness of the current multilateral initiatives to curb transnational corruption has engendered a lively debate about the relationship between domestic morality, transnational policy, economic efficiency, and the effectiveness of legislation. This debate has taken place under the rubric of the desirability of the extraterritorial prohibition of transnational bribery as an international policy goal. In many respects, the debate on why transnational corruption remains commonplace despite the ubiquity of transnational legislation revolves around not only differences in moral values but also differences as to what are considered the appropriate legal strategies and the ultimate policy outcomes desired. The answer to this question thus has implications for whether and to what extent current multilateral efforts to regulate transnational corruption are likely to curb these practices. In promoting future policy coordination, the regulation of transnational corruption provides a mechanism to observe the critical dimensions of the interaction between the norms in various domestic communities and the transnational context of these interactions.

Translating the shared norms and shared lofty ethical principles into efficacious laws in the domestic realm is a difficult endeavour. There is an implicit assumption that compliance by signatories with the multilateral initiatives to combat corruption can lead to a reduction in the levels of transnational corruption. Indeed, the principles regarding regulation of transnational corruption have already achieved a remarkable degree of worldwide convergence as evidenced through the levels of accession to the multilateral initiatives. The high levels of compliance with the norms to regulate transnational corruption would suggest that evaluating effectiveness within the context of the corruption conventions would be conceptually straightforward. However, effectiveness can be, and often is, independent of the level of compliance, being dependent on a myriad of norms and practices that shape the response of a particular legal system to the problem of transnational corruption. The array of norms and practices that can shape the effectiveness of a legal system makes ascertaining why the multilateral initiatives have not been effective a more challenging endeavour. The pertinent question remains why, against the background forces for global convergence as evidenced by the harmonization of regulations prohibiting transnational bribery, do the signatories differ markedly in their capacity to regulate transnational bribery by corporations.[1] What explains these differences? And should they be expected to persist or to disappear? Although there are several multilateral initiatives that touch on corruption, notably, the convention on the fight against corruption involving officials of the European Communities or officials of the EU member states, and the African Union Convention on Preventing and Combating Corruption,[2] the analysis is limited to three conventions that serve to illustrate the central argument.

Multilateral Initiatives to Regulate Transnational Bribery

The United Nations Convention on Corruption

The earliest attempt by the United Nations (UN) to tackle the issue of corruption was a very ambitious project.[3] On December 15, 1975, the UN General Assembly (GA) passed Resolution 3514 on 'Measures Against Corrupt Practices of Transnational

1 For a discussion on the challenges associated with enforcing anti-corruption conventions, see Carrington, P [2010]: 'Enforcing International Corrupt Practices Law', in Vol. 32, *Michigan Journal of International Law*, 129, at 142–9.

2 See Robinson, M [2012]: 'Global Approach to Anti-Bribery and Corruption, An Overview: Much Done, But a Lot More to Do…', in Vol. 37, *Thurgood Marshall Law Review*, 303. Discusses the various conventions. See Jatto [2010: 82–94] for an in-depth analysis of the anti-corruption mechanism put in place by the African Union Convention.

3 Posadas provides a general description of the early UN efforts to combat corruption. See Posadas [2000: 365–75].

and Other Corporations, Their Intermediaries and Others Involved'.[4] Resolution 3514 condemned all corrupt practices, including bribery, and reaffirmed the rights of member countries to enforce laws against corporations involved in corrupt practices.[5] The UN GA also called on member countries to adopt legislation to prevent corruption. It also invited the UN Commission on Transnational Corporations to prepare recommendations that would help to eliminate corrupt practices, including bribery.[6] Despite the resolution's virtual lack of substance, it was the first truly international acknowledgement that corruption in international business transactions was an issue that required addressing.

The call by the GA was subsequently supported by the formation of an *Ad Hoc* Intergovernmental Working Group on Corrupt Practices. The group was charged with formulating an international agreement to prevent and eliminate illicit payments.[7] The group completed its work with the issuance of a proposal in 1978.[8] Based on the proposal of the group, a UN committee, the Committee on International Agreement on Illicit Payments, drafted a convention focusing on illicit payments.[9] The convention sought to criminalize the offering, promising, or giving of illicit payments to public officials in connection with international commercial transactions.[10] It is interesting to note that in this draft convention the issue of the liability of corporations for corruption was already at the forefront of the debate. Article 1(2) did not make it mandatory for states to impose criminal liability on corporations for bribery; rather it made allowances for states that did not impose criminal liability on legal persons to take appropriate measures according to its national law to achieve comparable deterrent effects. The deference to national legislation was, in effect, tacit acceptance of the fact that the convention could not compel states to implement legislation that was incompatible with the principles of their legal system and instead urged these states to find alternative means of achieving similar deterrent effects. This draft convention was adopted by the UN Economic and Social Council and sent to the GA for consideration in 1980.[11]

4 G.A. Res. 3514, U.N. GAOR, 30th Sess., Supp. No. 34, at 69 (1976) U.N. Doc. A/10034.

5 See *ibid.*, para 2.

6 See *ibid.*, para 6. See also the UN ESCOR, 61st Sess., Ag. Item 13, addendum (1976), U.N. Doc. E/5838/Add.1 (containing a survey of aspects of national legislation on corrupt practices and an analysis of governments' views and proposals to further deal with the problems of corrupt practices).

7 See Posadas [2000: 367]. UN ESCOR, 6th Sess. Supp No. 10 (1980), U.N. Doc. E/1980/40.

8 E.S.C. Res. 2041 (LXI), U.N. ESCOR, 61st Sess., 2032 mtg. (1976), U.N. Doc. E/5883.

9 E.S.C. Res. 1978/71, U.N. ESCOR, 2d Sess., 38 mtg. (1978), U.N. Doc E/1978/133.

10 Report of the Committee on an International Agreement on Illicit Payments on its first and second sessions. U.N. Doc. E/1979/104.

11 See Posadas [2000: 368].

The GA, largely for political reasons, did not adopt the draft convention. At about the same time the draft convention was sent to the GA for consideration, the group of 77 developing countries also introduced a draft decision entitled 'Transnational Corporations'.[12] The draft decision on Transnational Corporations introduced a precondition that the conference on an International Agreement on Illicit Payments, which would have adopted the draft convention, could only be convened after the closure of the UN Conference on a Code of Conduct on Transnational Corporations.[13] The UN Conference on a Code of Conduct on Transnational Corporations did not produce a final code agreeable to all parties. The main source of conflict concerned the status of the code under international law and more specifically, whether the Code of Conduct on Transnational Corporations would be mandatory under international law. Other issues that made it difficult to reach an agreement concerned the standard of treatment and compensation for expropriating transnational corporations and whether a minimum international legal standard existed or national standards would be sufficient.[14] The fundamental disagreement and deep opposition to the adoption of the Code of Conduct on Transnational Corporations resulted in neither the draft convention nor the Code of Conduct on Transnational Corporations being adopted.

Fifteen years passed before the GA once again seriously considered the issue of corruption. In 1996, the GA passed Resolution 51/59 (Action Against Corruption),[15] with an international code of conduct for public officials, and adopted the UN Declaration Against Corruption and Bribery in International Commercial Transactions.[16] In 1997, the Economic and Social Council of the UN recommended that the GA, adopt a draft resolution entitled International Cooperation Against Corruption and Bribery in International Commercial Transactions.[17] This was followed in 1998 by a call to the Secretary-General to ask the Secretariat of the UN to update the UN manual on *Practice Measures Against Corruption* by incorporating recent developments and the impact of recent multilateral initiatives.[18]

The initiatives by the UN continued to gather momentum. In 2001, through Resolution 55/61, the GA requested that the Secretary-General convene an intergovernmental open-ended expert group to examine and prepare draft terms

12 Transnational Corporations, India: Draft Decision, UN ESCOR, 2nd Sess., Ag. Item, 12 (1980) I, UN Doc E/1980/C.1/L.22.

13 See UN ESCOR, 6th Sess. Supp No. 10 (1980), U.N. Doc. E/1980/40.

14 See Posadas [2000: 368–9].

15 G.A. Res. 51/59, U.N. GAOR 3d Comm., 51st Sess., 82d plen. mtg., annex (1997), U.N. Doc. A/RES/51/59.

16 G.A. Res. 51/191, U.N. GAOR 2d Comm., 51st Sess., 86th plen. mtg., pmbl. (1997) U.N. Doc. A/RES/51/191.

17 E.S.C. Res. 1997/25, U.N. ESCOR, 36th pln. mtg. (1997), U.N. Doc. E/CN.15/1997.3; G.A. Res. 52/87, U.N. GAOR, 52d Sess., 70th pln. mtg. (1998), U.N. Doc. A/RES/52/87.

18 Action Against Corruption, E.S.C. Res. 1998/16, U.N. ESCOR, 44th plen. mtg., para. 1, (1998), U.N. Doc. E/INF/1998/INF/3/add.2).

of reference for the negotiation of a future legal instrument against corruption.[19] The 'Intergovernmental Open-Ended Expert Group to Prepare Draft Terms of Reference for the Negotiation of a Future Legal Instrument against Corruption', was convened pursuant to GA resolution 55/61 and met in Vienna from 30 July to 3 August 2001.[20] The group recommended to the GA, through the Commission on Crime Prevention and Criminal Justice and the Economic and Social Council, the adoption of a draft resolution on the terms of reference for the negotiation of an international legal instrument against corruption. In response to the recommendation, the GA in resolution 56/260, directed the '*Ad Hoc* Committee for the Negotiation of a Convention against Corruption' to negotiate a broad and effective convention.[21] The Informal Preparatory Meeting of the '*Ad Hoc* Committee for the Negotiation of a Convention against Corruption' was held in Buenos Aires from 4 to 7 December 2001. The text of the UN Convention Against Corruption was negotiated during seven sessions of the '*Ad Hoc* Committee for the Negotiation of the Convention Against Corruption', held between 21 January 2002 and 1 October 2003. The convention was approved by the *ad hoc* committee and adopted by the GA by resolution 58/4 of 31 October 2003.[22]

UNCAC, adopted by the GA in its resolution 58/4 of 31 October 2003, entered into force on 14 December 2005, pursuant to Article 68 of the convention, which provided for its entry into force on the 90th day after the date of deposit of the 30th instrument of ratification, acceptance, approval or accession. The road leading to the adoption of the UNCAC was long and tortuous. Despite its adoption, it is uncertain whether broad and effective compliance can be achieved. Nonetheless, the adoption of the UNCAC is remarkable in that it represents the broadest consensus that one is likely to see with regard to the issue of corruption. With the broad composition of developed and developing states signatory to the UNCAC, the convention, unlike others, has the potential to create and disseminate a truly global message on corruption.

Scope of the United Nations Convention against Corruption

The UNCAC is an elaborate instrument comprising eight chapters with 71 articles.[23] The convention's central elements relate to prevention, criminalization,

---

19 G.A. Res. 55/61, U.N. GAOR 3d Comm., 55th Sess., 81st plen. mtg., annex (2001), U.N. Doc. A/RES/55/61.

20 Report of the Meeting of the Intergovernmental Open-Ended Expert Group to Prepare Draft Terms of Reference for the Negotiation of an International Legal Instrument against Corruption. U.N. Doc A/56/402-E/2001/105.

21 G.A. Res. 56/26, U.N. GAOR 3d Comm., 56th Sess., 93rd plen. mtg., annex (2002), U.N. Doc. A/RES/56/260.

22 G.A. Res. 5/4, U.N. GAOR 3d Comm., 58th Sess., 51st plen. mtg., annex (2003), U.N. Doc. A/RES/56/260.

23 For a review of the broad provisions of the UNCAC, see Snider & Kidane [2007: 706–11].

international cooperation, and asset recovery. The UNCAC recognizes the importance of the prevention of corruption by requiring the establishment of anti-corruption bodies and enhanced transparency in the financing of election campaigns and political parties.[24] The UNCAC similarly mandates signatories to promote the involvement of non-governmental organizations (NGOs) and community-based groups, as well as other elements of civil society, and to raise public awareness of corruption.[25]

The UNCAC sets forth in detail a variety of measures that states are obligated to take to strengthen international efforts to fight corruption of public officials, whether in the form of bribery, embezzlement, money laundering, or related acts. The convention is organized into seven substantive chapters that deal with general provisions, preventive measures, criminalization and law enforcement, international cooperation, asset recovery, technical assistance and information exchange, and mechanisms for implementation. Articles 15 to 42 of the UNCAC require parties to criminalize embezzlement, money laundering, and the bribing of their own and foreign government officials in relation to the conduct of international business. These articles also encourage states to adopt laws criminalizing offences such as trading in influence, the abuse of functions, illicit enrichment, and bribery in the private sector. The issue of international cooperation is the subject of Articles 43 to 50 and covers extradition and procedures for mutual legal assistance. Articles 51 to 59 on asset recovery establish a system whereby assets recovered in one jurisdiction can be returned to the beneficial owners located in another

Chapter II of the UNCAC, in Articles 5–14, contains a compendium of preventive measures to combat corruption. This chapter includes provisions for the development of anti-corruption policies and the establishment of preventive anti-corruption bodies with specific measures for the public sector.[26] These measures include provisions to enhance transparency in the funding of candidatures for elected public office and the funding of political parties.[27] Also provided for in the preventive measures are provisions for the establishment of appropriate systems of procurement based on transparency, competition, and objective criteria in decision-making.[28] Signatories are required to take measure to strengthen the capacity of the judiciary and prosecution services to combat corruption.[29] The preventive measures

24 In Articles 5 to 14, the convention sets forth a series of preventive measures that states must undertake, including the adoption of anti-corruption policies and practices, and the use of a body (or bodies) to ensure implementation of those policies and practices.

25 Article 13 of the convention requires state parties to take appropriate measures to promote the active participation of individuals and groups outside the public sector, such as civil society, non-governmental organisations, and community-based organisations, in the prevention of and the fight against corruption; and to raise public awareness regarding the existence, causes, and gravity of and the threat posed by corruption.

26 UNCAC, Articles 5 and 6.

27 UNCAC, Articles 7 and 8.

28 UNCAC, Article 9.

29 UNCAC, Article 11.

extend to preventing corruption involving the private sector and the participation of civil society in measures to prevent corruption.[30]

In addition to the preventive measures outlined previously and in recognition of the primary significance of criminalization in combating corruption, the UNCAC, in Articles 15–44, requires signatories to criminalize a broad range of activities that fall under the rubric of corruption. Article 15 requires signatories to establish the bribery of national public officials as a criminal offence. Article 16 contains the foreign equivalent of Article 15, requiring signatories to criminalize the bribery of foreign public officials. The definition of bribery of a foreign public official is the

> promise, offering or giving to a foreign public official or an official of a public international organization, directly or indirectly, of an undue advantage, for the official himself or herself or another person or entity, in order that the official act or refrain from acting in the exercise of his or her official duties, in order to obtain or retain business or other undue advantage in relation to the conduct of international business.[31]

Other activities required by signatories to be established as criminal offences include the embezzlement, misappropriation or other of any property entrusted to the public official by virtue of his or her position; abuse of functions; trading in influence; illicit enrichment; laundering the proceeds of crime; concealment; and the obstruction of justice.[32]

Chapter IV contains a series of measures that deal with international cooperation including the extradition of offenders, mutual legal assistance, and cooperation in the course of investigations and other law-enforcement activities. In Article 43, signatories are required to 'consider assisting each other in investigations of and proceedings in civil and administrative matters relating to corruption'.[33] Given the broad range of offences outlined in Chapter III of the convention and the fact that the obligation to criminalize some of these activities was optional, particular difficulties with the issue of the dual criminality requirements are raised. Given that not all the countries will be able to criminalize all the acts of corruption, on account of conflicts with their constitutional provisions, there was a need to broaden the dual criminality requirements of the convention. The approach adopted was to expand, to the extent possible within the fundamental legal requirements of each signatory state, the dual criminality requirements of the convention. Specifically, under the convention, offenders may be extradited without the dual criminality where this is permitted by the law of the requested state party.[34]

---

30 UNCAC, Articles 12 and 13.
31 UNCAC, Article 16(1).
32 UNCAC, Articles 17, 18, 19, 20, 23, 24, and 25.
33 UNCAC, Article 43(1).
34 UNCAC, Article 44(2).

The theme underlying the dual criminality requirement is that where dual-criminality is required, it must be based on the fact that the relevant signatories have criminalized the conduct underlying an offence, and not whether the actual provisions of the offence in both states are identical.[35] This theme also pervades the provisions on extradition and the transfer of sentenced persons. Article 44 provides for cooperation between signatories for the extradition of offenders. The convention provides that the article shall apply to the offences established in accordance with the convention where the person who is the subject of the request for extradition is present in the territory of the requested state party, provided that the offence for which extradition is sought is punishable under the domestic law of both the requesting state party and the requested state party.[36] Article 45 provides for the transfer of sentenced persons and encourages signatories to enter into bilateral or multilateral agreements or arrangements on the transfer to their territory of persons sentenced to imprisonment or other forms of deprivation of liberty in order that they may complete their sentences there.

While the UNCAC requires signatories to take specific steps in various areas, the language is often notably vague in many areas. For instance, the UNCAC does not contain a specific definition of *corruption*; rather the convention focused on specific acts of corruption. Nonetheless, with regard to the criminalization of corruption, the UNCAC requires countries to establish criminal and other offences across the wide range of corrupt acts mentioned previously. In fact, the UNCAC included many new elements, such as funding of political parties[37] and electoral processes,[38] and the use of electronic means in asset recovery and investigations, which had previously not been agreed by states in a multilateral framework.[39]

Although the focus of the UNCAC was primarily on corruption in the public sector, the convention nonetheless made provision for corruption in the private sector. Unfortunately, the provision for the criminalization of private bribery (between companies in the private sector) was made non-mandatory. The discretion given to signatories in how (and whether) to apply particular provisions may ultimately undermine the effectiveness of the convention. Most notable among the self-imposed limitations in the convention is the requirement that 'State Parties shall carry out their obligations under the Convention in a manner consistent with the principles of sovereign equality and territorial integrity of States and that of non-intervention in the domestic affairs of other States'.[40] In fact, Article 4(2) explicitly prohibits 'the exercise of jurisdiction and performance of functions that are reserved exclusively for the authorities of that other state by its domestic law'. The language of the convention thus leaves it to the individual signatory to limit the extra-territorial reach of other signatories and even arguably, inconsistent international agreements. The phrase 'in accordance with the fundamental principles of its legal

35 UNCAC, Article 43(2).
36 UNCAC, Article 44(1).
37 UNCAC, Article 7(3).
38 UNCAC, Article 7(2).
39 UNCAC, Article 51.
40 UNCAC, Article 4(1).

system' is found in many of the convention's articles including the provisions that relate to preventive anti-corruption policies and practices, preventive anti-corruption bodies, and the public sector and public sector reporting.

The convention was adopted by the GA of the UN on 31 October 2003 and was open to signature until 9 December 2005.[41] The convention was also open for signature to regional economic integration organizations if at least one member state of the organization had signed the convention.[42] As of 17 October 2007, 140 countries had signed up to the convention, and 103 countries had ratified the convention. Notable among the countries that are yet to ratify the convention include Switzerland, Germany, Italy, and Japan.[43]

Monitoring is not provided for in the text of the convention itself. Rather, responsibility for reviewing implementation of the convention lies with the Conference of State Parties.[44] The Conference of State Parties, at its first meeting in December 2006 established an Open-ended Intergovernmental Working Group to make recommendations to the Conference of the State Parties at its second session on the appropriate mechanisms or bodies for reviewing the implementation of the convention and on the terms of reference of such mechanisms or bodies.[45] The Open-ended Intergovernmental Working Group on Review of the Implementation of the UN Convention against Corruption held its first meeting in Vienna from 29–31 August 2007.[46] The working group will be making a recommendation on the framework of the review mechanism to the Conference of State Parties at its second session in January 2008. Given the absence of an operational review mechanism, there is little or no information with respect to the compliance by state parties with the provisions of the convention.

The OECD Convention

The OECD is an association of developed country states comprising 30 member countries. The organization provides a forum where these nations discuss issues

41 UNCAC, Article 67(1).

42 UNCAC, Article 67(2).

43 See http://www.unodc.org/unodc/en/treaties/CAC/signatories.html. Last visited 4 March 2013.

44 UNCAC, Article 63, which establishes a Conference of State Parties 'to improve the capacity of and cooperation between States Parties to achieve the objectives set forth in this Convention and to promote and review its implementation'.

45 Report of the Conference of the States Parties to the United Nations Convention against Corruption on its first session, held in Amman from 10–14 December 2006. Report available at http://www.unodc.org/pdf/crime/convention_corruption/cosp/session1/V0659563e.pdf. Last visited 5 March 2013.

46 Report on the meeting of the Open-ended Intergovernmental Working Group on Review of the Implementation of the United Nations Convention against Corruption held in Vienna from 29–31 August 2007. Report available at http://www.unodc.org/unodc/en/treaties/CAC/working-group1.html. Last visited 5 March 2013.

on the development, harmonization, and cooperation in the areas of economic and social policy.

The OECD played a pivotal role in the development of the current multilateral campaign against corruption. As early as 1976, the OECD members adopted a 'Declaration on International Investment and Multinational Enterprises'. This declaration included guidelines on bribery attached to the declaration as an annex.[47] The OECD guidelines specifically addressed the issue of bribery. However, due to a lack of consensus amongst the signatories, the OECD guidelines were silent on the more politicized issue of the criminalization of bribery of foreign public officials. In 1988, complying with a mandate in the FCPA, the US began to facilitate an international bribery agreement among OECD members. This effort was initially resisted by members of the OECD on the basis that it would require extra-territorial application of criminal laws.

Significant progress towards the adoption of a convention was achieved in 1994, when the OECD adopted a Recommendation on Bribery in International business Transactions.[48] The Recommendation called upon member countries to take effective measures to deter, prevent, and combat bribery of foreign public officials in connection with international business transactions. The OECD iseCIME and its Working Group on Bribery in International Business Transactions (the Working Group) were directed by the Recommendation to monitor the implementation of the Recommendation. The Recommendation isolated the non-criminality of foreign bribery and tax deductibility of bribes as issues requiring further examination. In 1996, the OECD Council adopted a specific Recommendation on the Tax Deductibility of Bribes.[49]

In May 1997, the OECD met to review the steps taken by its member states pursuant to the 1994 recommendations. This included a review of the implementation of the tax deductibility recommendation. CIME proposed, and the OECD adopted, a Revised Recommendation at this meeting.[50] The Revised Recommendation reaffirmed the OECD commitment to criminalize bribery and stated that a convention, rather than a model code, was the appropriate instrument to achieve that goal. The OECD ministers decided to promptly open negotiations on a convention, and after six months of negotiations, all 29 members and 5 non-members agreed in

47 Declaration on International Investment and Multinational Enterprises, 21 June, 1976, 15 International Legal Materials, at 967.

48 Recommendation of the Council of the OECD on Bribery in International Business Transactions, OECD Doc. SG/PRESS (94)36 (1994).

49 See OECD website http://www.oecd.org/document/46/0,2340,en_2649_34859_2048174_1_1_1_1,00.html. *Implementing the 1996 OECD Recommendation on the Tax Deductibility of Bribes to Foreign Public Officials*, OECD (May 26, 1997) (Report by the Committee on Fiscal Affairs to the OECD Council at Ministerial Level). Last visited 4 March 2013.

50 *Revised Recommendation of the Council on Combating Bribery in International Business Transactions*, 1997. See OECD website at https://www.kpk-rs.si/upload/datoteke/Revised_OECD_R_CBIBT_01.pdf. Last visited 4 March 2013.

Paris to sign the Convention on Combating Bribery of Foreign Public Officials in International Business Transactions on 17 December 1997.[51]

The OECD convention entered into force on 15 February 1999. All 30 OECD countries signed the convention as well as four non-members (Argentina, Brazil, Bulgaria, and Chile). Slovenia became the fifth non-member to join the convention, depositing its instrument of accession with the Secretary-General in September 2001. With Slovenia's accession, there were 35 contracting parties to the convention in total. Ratification of the convention and incorporation into the national law of signatory countries is almost complete.

Scope of the OECD Convention on Corruption

The provisions of the OECD convention, though modest, represented a monumental step in the efforts to coordinate a disparate set of legal systems towards adopting minimum standards to prohibit transnational bribery.[52] The OECD convention mandated signatories to enact legislation prohibiting the bribery of a foreign public official.[53]

The OECD convention requires that each signatory prohibit the intentional offer, promise, or giving of any undue pecuniary or other advantage, whether directly or through intermediaries, to a foreign public official, for that official or for a third party, in order that the official act or refrain from acting in relation to the performance of official duties, in order to obtain or retain business or other improper advantage in the conduct of international business. A foreign public official is defined as '[a]ny person holding a legislative, administrative or judicial office of a foreign country, whether appointed or elected; any person exercising a public function for a foreign country, including for a public agency or public enterprise; and any official or agent of a public international organization'.[54]

The convention also mandates that signatories criminalize complicity, attempt, and conspiracy to commit such bribery.[55] What constitutes either an attempt or conspiracy is not clearly defined in the OECD Convention. The OECD Convention nevertheless directs signatories to incorporate their relevant concepts of attempt, complicity, and conspiracy. Although the OECD Convention required that the implementing legislation prohibit the offering or giving of bribes, the signatories were not obliged to adopt legislation prohibiting the soliciting or

51 This convention was negotiated in the framework of the OECD, but is not an official OECD document. For further information, see http://www.oecd.org/document/21/0,2340,en_2649_34859_2017813_1_1_1_1,00.html. Last visited 4 March 2013.

52 For an in-depth review of the provisions of the OECD convention, see Pieth, M, Low, L & Cullen, P, (eds.) [2007]: *The OECD Convention on Bribery: A Commentary* (Cambridge: Cambridge University Press).

53 Article 1 defines the offence of bribery of a foreign public official and provides definitions for terms used throughout the convention.

54 OECD Convention, Article 1(4)(a).

55 OECD Convention, Article 1(2).

receiving of bribes. The convention mandated that corporations and other legal entities should be held responsible to the same extent as corporate officials.[56]

The OECD Convention also directs signatories to establish accounting standards that would encumber parties engaging in bribery of foreign public officials in their attempts to hide their activities. Signatories are required to impose sanctions on the violation of accounting practices that violate these standards.[57] The provisions of the OECD Convention require that signatories establish 'effective, proportionate and dissuasive' sanctions.[58] Signatories are also required to adopt measures that assure that the bribe and the proceeds of bribery are subject to confiscation, or alternatively are offset by a fine of equal or greater value.[59] Signatories who have implemented money laundering legislation are directed to extend such classification to include the bribery of foreign officials.[60]

A program of systematic monitoring of the implementation of the treaty is provided for in Article 12 with specific responsibility granted to the OECD Working Group on Bribery.[61] The convention tasked the OECD Working Group on Bribery with receiving information from signatories to the convention, organizing regular reviews on progress towards implementation, examining and highlighting issues of concern, and providing information to the public.[62] The OECD Working Group's review of the implementation was conducted in two phases. In Phase 1, the OECD Working Group reviewed each signatory country's implementing legislation and case law to determine the level of compliance with the implementing legislation.[63]

In Phase 2, the OECD Working Group studied the structures put in place to enforce the laws and rules implementing the convention and the application of the legislative framework in practice.[64] In 2000, the OECD Working Group concluded

---

56 Article 2 of the convention requires each party to establish the liability of legal persons for the bribery of a foreign public official.

57 OECD Convention, Articles 8(1) and (2).

58 OECD Convention, Article 3(1).

59 OECD Convention, Article 3(3).

60 OECD Convention, Article 7.

61 See Tyler, A [2011]: 'Enforcing Enforcement: Is The OECD Anti-Bribery Convention's Peer Review Effective?', in Vol. 43, *George Washington International Law Review*, 137. He evaluates the implementation and effective application of the anti-bribery provisions of the OECD Convention and argues that the convention boasts significant successes in implementation through its peer-review process, but that there are considerable challenges remaining to achieving full compliance.

62 See Article 34, 'Commentaries on the OECD Convention'. Available at the OECD website at http://www.oecd.org/document/1/0,2340,en_2649_34859_2048129_1_1_1_1,00.html. Last visited 23 October 2007.

63 See 'OECD Anti-Bribery Convention: Procedure of Self- and Mutual Evaluation – Phase 1'. Available at the OECD website at http://www.oecd.org/document/21/0,2340,en_2649_34855_2022613_1_1_1_1,00.html. Last visited 4 March 2013.

64 See 'OECD Anti-Bribery Convention: Procedure of Self- and Mutual Evaluation – Phase 2'. Available at the OECD website at http://www.oecd.org/document/27/0,2340,en_2649_34855_2022939_1_1_1_1,00.html. Last visited 4 March 2013.

its Phase 1 review and noted that in general, countries had made laudable efforts to ensure that national implementing legislation satisfy the obligations of the convention. The OECD Working Group, on the basis of the review of national implementing legislation, concluded that 'there [wa]s overall compliance with the Convention's obligations in the great majority of countries'.[65] The specific details of compliance with respect to individual countries are discussed in the following text.

The OAS Convention

The OAS was formed in 1951 by the nations of North and South America as a regional agency within the UN under Article 52 of the UN Charter.[66] The organization is encompassed of Western Hemisphere independent states and currently has 35 participating members.[67] The OAS Charter mandates collective action by its member states in the areas of economic development and international cooperation.[68]

The OAS publicly recognized the need to combat corruption on 11 December 1994 at the Summit of the Americas in Miami, Florida in a document entitled 'Summit of the Americas Declaration of Principles (Summit Declaration)'.[69] In an accompanying document entitled 'Summit of the Americas Plan of Action (Summit Plan of Action)', the OAS set forth a separate series of proposals devoted to attacking corruption.[70] The Summit Plan of Action proposed several cooperative measures to promote the adoption of similar measures by other non–Western Hemisphere states with citizens transacting in the Western Hemisphere. The Summit Plan of Action also called for the development of a closer relationship with the OECD; the development of methods of cooperation to enable rapid investigations; and the development of a regional, coordinated approach to combating corruption in the form of an international agreement.

---

65 Report by the CIME: 'Implementation of the Convention on Bribery in International Business Transactions and the 1997 Revised Recommendation', 3. Available at the OECD website at http://www.oecd.org/dataoecd/63/39/2378254.pdf. Last visited 4 March 2013.

66 OAS Charter Art. 1. The charter was opened for signature in 1948 and entered into force in 1951 pursuant to its provisions on ratification and entry into force.

67 'Organization of American States, Member States'. Available at http://www.oas.org/en/member_states/default.asp. Last visited 4 March 2013.

68 OAS Charter, Articles 29–32, 34–51.

69 'Summit of the Americas: Declaration of Principles and Plan of Action', in Vol. 34. *International Legal Materials*, 808, 808–38 [1994].

70 Although the Summit Plan of Action did not specifically detail how to achieve the anti-corruption measures it advocated, the Appendix to it does state that the OAS, as well as public and private sector partnerships, play important roles in connection with combating corruption, in Vol. 34, *International Legal Materials*, 818–19, 835–6, 838, [1994]. The Appendix also states that the Summit Plan of Action envisages roles for the Inter-American Development Bank and its affiliates in combating corruption. *Ibid.*, at 837.

In 1996, the OAS approved the Inter-American Convention Against Corruption, which established the first international legal framework aimed at tackling bribery and corruption of government officials.[71] Thirty-one members had signed the convention as of September 2003. To bolster the convention, the Secretary General of the OAS prepared a working document, entitled 'A Plan of Action Against Corruption (Working Plan)', in an effort to develop further its collective measures approach.[72] The Working Plan called for the OAS to establish information services, in the form of a database of the measures that parties had taken in furtherance of the Inter-American Convention Against Corruption mandates, in order to facilitate a coordinated approach to combating corruption.

Scope of the OAS Convention on Corruption

The provisions of the OAS Convention are far-reaching.[73] The OAS Convention provides for the criminalization of transnational bribery and illicit enrichment. Under Article III of the convention, signatories agreed to consider preventive measures to create, maintain, and strengthen their domestic laws to combat corruption. These measures, which go beyond criminalizing certain conduct as offences, fall into three primary areas: transparency and accountability in government, ethical standards for government officials, and measures applicable to private concerns. The mandatory provisions of the convention in Article VI identify a number of activities that it categorized as acts of corruption. These included solicitation or acceptance of a bribe, offering or granting of a bribe, improper acts or omissions by public officials, fraudulent use or concealment of property, and conspiracy.[74]

The OAS Convention requirement, which mandates that signatories prohibit transnational bribery, is contained in Article VIII. The article mandates states to prohibit the offering by its nationals and domiciled businesses any article of monetary value or benefit in connection with any economic transaction in exchange for any act or omission in performance of that public official's function.[75]

In addition to these binding articles, the OAS Convention provides for other aspirational objectives. The OAS Convention enumerates four additional acts of

---

71 Inter-American Convention Against Corruption, Mar. 29, 1996, OEA/Ser.K/XXXIV.1 CICOR/doc.14/96 rev.2,: in Vol. 35 International Legal Materials, 724 (1996).

72 The Working Plan calls for the organisation of workshops, seminars, and conferences with participation of experts that can help the governments train officials responsible for preventing and punishing crimes of corruption. Office of the Secretary General of the Organization of American States. 'A Plan of Action Against Corruption', 24 May 1996. See the OAS website at http://www.oas.org. Last visited 23 October 2007.

73 See Morrissey, D [2007]: 'The Fight Against Corruption by International Organizations', in Vol. 39, *George Washington International Law Review*, 165, at 169–79 for an in-depth discussion of the OAS Convention.

74 OAS Convention, Article VI(1)(a)–(e).

75 This provision is, however, subject to the Constitution and fundamental principles of the legal systems of the state parties.

corruption that the signatories agreed to consider criminalizing under domestic law in order to promote uniformity among the member states and to further the purposes of the OAS Convention. These acts, which are subject to progressive development, included the improper use of information by government officials, the improper use of property by a government official, the attempt by any person to obtain illicit benefits, and the diversion of state property.[76] The OAS Convention also encourages mutual legal assistance and promotes the use of preventive measures such as codes of conduct for public officials. The OAS Convention encourages signatories to take steps to promote transparency in procurement, disclosure of assets, and public access to information.

In 2001, the OAS GA adopted the 'Report of Buenos Aires on the Mechanism for Follow-up on Implementation of the Inter-American Convention Against Corruption'.[77] The follow-up mechanism operates under a voluntary peer review system where each country will provide a self-assessment of improvement through a questionnaire, which is then analyzed by other state parties.[78] A Committee of Experts is responsible for the technical analysis of implementation of the OAS Convention. As of 2007, the Committee of Experts met on 10 occasions and reviewed implementing measures by Argentina, Paraguay, Colombia, Nicaragua, Uruguay, Panama, Ecuador, Chile, Bolivia, Peru, Costa Rica, Venezuela, Mexico, Trinidad & Tobago, Honduras, El Salvador, Dominican Republic, and the Bahamas.[79] The methodology adopted by the committee for reviewing the implementation of the provisions of the convention selected for the first round was limited. The review examined the existence in each state party of the legal framework and other measures for the enforcement of the provision of the OAS Convention.[80] The review did not extend to the provisions of Article VI, which deal specifically with the bribery of foreign public officials.

Comparing the Conventions

The three conventions principally aim to develop common standards concerning certain corruption offences. Though they do not provide a uniform definition of corruption, the OAS and UNCAC provide for the criminalization of a wide variety

76 OAS Convention, Article XI(1)(a)–(d).

77 In 2001, the OAS GA adopted the 'Report of Buenos Aires on the Mechanism for Follow-up on Implementation of the Inter-American Convention Against Corruption'.

78 See De Michele, R [2004]: 'The Follow-Up Mechanism of the Inter-American Convention Against Corruption, A Preliminary Assessment: Is the Glass Half Empty?', in Vol. 10, *Southwestern Journal of Law and Trade in the Americas* 295, at 306 for a review of the assessment mechanism of the convention.

79 See http://www.oas.org/juridico/english/mesicic_com_experts.htm. Last visited 4 March 2013.

80 The text of this methodology can be found at: www.oas.org/juridico/english/followup_method.htm. Last visited 4 March 2013.

of offences. The three conventions include provisions to criminalize the bribery of foreign public officials. All three conventions opted for broad definitions for the bribery of foreign public officials, leaving it to states to define as long as all the elements outlined in the conventions are contained in the national implementing legislation. Granted, the broad definitions contained in the conventions are unlikely to match the definitions in the disparate legal systems precisely; a broad definition does, however, have the added advantage of not restricting the scope of national offences to narrow confines.

The OECD Convention deals specifically with the issue of the bribery of foreign public officials and addresses the issue in seven of its 17 articles. In contrast, the OAS Convention deals with bribery in only one of its 28 articles, setting as its goal the broader task of combating corruption in governmental affairs. The scope of the domestic offences under the OAS Convention is set out in Article VI, which requires signatories to criminalize acts of corruption that include the solicitation, acceptance, offer, or delivery of improper payments. Other offences include the illicit use of a position of authority for the official's own benefit; the fraudulent use or concealment of property derived from that position of authority; and participation in any of these acts as accomplice, collaborator, or conspirator. Similar to the OAS Convention, the UNCAC provides for a broad range of offences including money laundering, bribery of national and foreign public officials, embezzlement, and misappropriation of public property, trading in influence, abuse of functions, and laundering the proceeds of crime.

The three conventions require their signatories to provide for complicity, conspiracy, and attempt to bribe a foreign public official.[81] Their definitions of a public official are similar even though the OECD and UNCAC include the officials of international organizations. The definition of officials of international organizations and the international organizations within the scope of the definition is unclear. The definition makes no distinction, for instance, between officials and other contracted staff of a temporary nature. Neither does the definition make provision for staff members seconded to these international organizations. The wording of the UNCAC and OECD conventions regarding the purpose for which the bribe is paid are more limited in scope than the wording of the OAS Convention. The UNCAC and OECD conventions both provide that bribes must be given 'to obtain or retain business or other improper advantage in the conduct of international business'.[82] In contrast, the motive for which the bribe may be paid is broader in the OAS Convention, only requiring that the bribery be in connection with any economic or commercial transaction.[83]

The UNCAC and OAS conventions, in addition to their provisions on bribery, direct signatories to establish illicit enrichment as an offence.[84] The language of

81 UNCAC, Article 27.

82 UNCAC, Article 16; OECD Convention, Article 1.

83 OAS Convention, Article VIII.

84 UNCAC Article 21; OAS Convention, Article IX.

the provisions on transnational bribery and illicit payments in the UNCAC and OAS conventions contain the proviso that the offences are to be established subject to the constitution and fundamental legal principles of each state party.[85] Here, both conventions aspire to be inclusive and accommodating of the differing principles within the signatory states. Both conventions in this regard offer a set of general guidelines that mandate broad outcomes by setting minimum standards for legislation that allow each signatory the flexibility to adopt measures compatible with its own existing legal principles. This provision is not contained in the articles requiring states to criminalize acts of domestic corruption under both the UNCAC and OAS conventions. The effect of this proviso is that on entry into force of the treaty, states that have failed to criminalize domestic bribery will immediately be in contravention of the UNCAC and OAS conventions.

On the other hand, states that fail to enact transnational bribery and illicit enrichment offences will not be contravening the conventions. In contrast, the provision for the establishment of the offence of transnational bribery provides an unqualified obligation on the signatories to the OECD Convention to adopt measures as may be necessary to establish transnational bribery as a criminal offence. The obligation of the signatories is nonetheless flexible enough to take into account the differences in national legal systems. The Commentaries to the OECD Convention indicate that the drafters believed that signatories were entitled to adopt a 'functional equivalence' approach. The Commentaries to the OECD Convention provide that 'this Convention seeks to assure a functional equivalence among the measures taken by the Parties to sanction bribery of foreign public officials, without requiring uniformity or changes in fundamental principles of a Party's legal system'.[86] In effect, the OECD Convention does not provide the language to be adopted by the signatories. Rather, the signatories are required to ensure that their enacting legislation provides similar results even if the language of their implementing legislation is not similar to that provided by the OECD Convention.

There are several provisions in the OECD Convention that are absent from the OAS Convention. The OECD Commentaries provide affirmative defences where the payments are 'small facilitation payments' or is 'permitted or required by the by the written law or regulation of the foreign public official's country, including case law'.[87] The UNCAC and OAS Conventions, in contrast, are less tolerant and provide for neither of these affirmative defences. The OECD Convention establishes guidelines for sanctions and requires the statutes of limitations imposed

85 OAS Convention, Article VII, contains a proviso that conditions the adoption of the transnational bribery offence stating that: 'Subject to its Constitution and the fundamental principles of its legal system, each State Party shall prohibit and punish …'

86 Commentaries on the Convention on Combating Bribery of Foreign Public Officials in International Business Transactions, cmt. 2, OECD Doc. DAFFE/IME/BR(97)20 (1998) (Commentaries).

87 Commentaries, Article 1, 1.

by signatories to be reasonable. The OECD Convention also contains a provision that requires signatories to refrain from being influenced by consideration of national economic interest in the pursuit of prosecutions.[88] These provisions do not have any equivalent in the OAS Convention.

Another provision present in both the UNCAC and OECD Conventions that is absent from the OAS Convention is the provision for the liability of legal persons.[89] Both the UNCAC and OECD Conventions recognize that legal persons are often involved in corruption offences and that severe constraints exist with the capacity of domestic legal systems to prosecute natural persons acting on behalf of the legal persons. The size and complexity of legal persons makes it difficult to identify the natural persons who may be held responsible. Legal persons are thus able to escape liability due to their complexity, while continuing the acts of corruption after sanctions are imposed on natural persons because the legal person as a whole is not deterred by individual sanctions. Both conventions recognise that not all states provide criminal sanctions for legal persons and thus permit the signatories to provide administrative or civil sanctions, provided the sanctions are effective, proportionate, and dissuasive.

The three conventions contain provisions that establish a series of criteria under which signatories have to establish their jurisdiction over the criminal offences enumerated in conventions. The bases required for the assertion of jurisdiction are on the grounds of territoriality and nationality in all three conventions. The territoriality principle, as envisaged by the conventions, is interpreted broadly and there is no requirement that the whole offence is committed exclusively on the territory of the state that is asserting jurisdiction.[90] The UNCAC further provides for the assertion of jurisdiction on the effects principle, allowing a state to assert jurisdiction when the offence is committed against the state (effects jurisdiction).[91] The assertion of jurisdiction on this basis is subject to Article 4 of the UNCAC, which stipulates that none of the provisions in the convention is intended to encroach on the state sovereignty.

The three conventions also provide for the assertion of jurisdiction based on the principle of nationality. The conventions recognize that under the terms of general international law, nationals of a state are still obliged to comply with the domestic law of the state of nationality even when they are acting outside its territory. All three conventions further provide that the signatories will either extradite or prosecute the accused within their territories.[92] If a signatory country refuses to

88 OECD Convention, Article 5.

89 Article 26 of the UNCAC and Article 2 of the OECD Convention require states to establish, in accordance with their own laws, the liability of legal persons for the bribery of a foreign public official.

90 This issue is discussed at length in Chapter 5.

91 UNCAC, Article 42(2)(d).

92 UNCAC, Article 42(4); OECD Convention, Article 10; and OAS Convention, Article XIII.

extradite one of its own nationals accused by another signatory of making a bribe, the refusing signatory must submit the case to its own authorities for prosecution.

One issue constraining the regulation of corruption concerns the means and channels of international cooperation between states. The potential contentiousness of regulating transnational bribery ensures that procedural and sometimes political obstacles delay or prevent the prosecution of the offenders. The three conventions deal with substantive and procedural law matters, which closely relate to these corruption offences and seek to improve international cooperation. All three conventions attempt to foster cooperation among signatories in the investigation, prosecution, and punishment of offences under the conventions.[93] The OECD and OAS Conventions contain a broad reference outlining the guiding principle that the states undertake to develop to the widest possible extent international cooperation in all areas of the fight against corruption and transnational bribery.

In contrast, the UNCAC contains substantial and detailed sections covering a host of areas concerning international cooperation in criminal matters. Chapter IV of the UNCAC is devoted to the issue of international cooperation and makes elaborate provision for extradition, the transfer of sentenced persons, mutual legal assistance, and the transfer of criminal proceedings, law enforcement cooperation, and joint investigations.[94] The elaborate framework provided by the UNCAC should facilitate international cooperation, as the provisions on international cooperation are likely to serve as the legal basis for the cooperation requested by other state signatories. Unfortunately, Article 43(1) provides that the general duty of a signatory to cooperate apply only when consistent with its domestic legal system. The reference to the domestic legal system means that the extent of the duty to cooperate is to be determined by the domestic law of the state from whom cooperation is being sought. Furthermore, the provision does not carry an obligation to modify those domestic legal systems to facilitate cooperation.

The three conventions provide for mutual legal assistance and extradition.[95] The provisions in the UN and OECD Conventions go further and impose an obligation on states to cooperate in non-criminal proceedings brought by a state against a legal person within the scope of the convention.[96] They also provide that the conventions themselves can serve as a legal basis for extradition for signatories that make extradition conditional upon the existence of a treaty. States that refuse to grant an extradition request either on grounds that it had no extradition treaty with the requesting state or because the existing treaty would not cover the request, may use the convention themselves as a basis for surrendering the person requested. They also contain provisions that preclude signatories

93 See UNCAC, Article 38; OAS Convention, Article XIV; and OECD Convention, Article 9.

94 UNCAC, Articles 43, 44, 45, 46, 47, 48, and 49.

95 See OAS Convention, Article XIII; and OECD Convention, Article 10.

96 UNCAC, Article 42(1); OECD Convention, Article 9.

from denying requests for assistance on the grounds of bank secrecy.[97] The UN and OECD Conventions additionally establish that whenever dual criminality is considered a requirement for international cooperation, the requirement would be deemed fulfilled irrespective of the categorization of the offence by the state.[98] One important advantage of harmonizing the elements of the offence of transnational bribery is to lower the threshold for satisfying the dual criminality requirement.

State parties have received the three conventions rather differently. The speed at which the OECD convention was enacted was notable. It took only four years for the OECD to pass the convention from the adoption of the anti-bribery recommendation. The speed of ratification and entering into force of the convention attests to the political will existing in relation to the issue of transnational bribery. The degree of overall compliance with the standards set by the OECD Convention has been very high. Three years after the entry into force of the OECD Convention, all except three of the signatories to the OECD Convention had enacted the necessary implementing legislation. The OECD Working Group on Bribery conducted a review of the implementing legislation of all the signatories to the convention and in most cases only suggested slight improvements to the existing national laws.[99]

On the other hand, the OAS Convention has fared much worse in relation to compliance by signatories compared to OECD. The OAS Convention, like the OECD Convention, is not self-executing; it is subject to ratification and implementation by the signatory parties. However, progress in ratification by all of the countries that signed the OAS Convention has been slow. To date, although 26 countries signed the OAS Convention, only 17 countries have deposited their instruments of ratification with the OAS. Despite the major achievement in the adoption of the OAS Convention, implementation has faced significant hurdles. The OAS Convention has not been implemented by any of the states that have ratified it. This low level of compliance with the enactment of implementation national legislation persists despite the fact that 21 of the 35 OAS member states signed the convention, which took effect on 6 March 1997.[100] Compliance was high for the OECD Convention, but low for the OAS Convention. What explains the disparate levels of implementation between both conventions and what is likely to be the level of compliance with the UNCAC?

---

97 UNCAC, Article 40.

98 UNCAC, Article 43(2); OECD Convention, Articles 9(2), 9(3); and OAS Convention, Article XVI.

99 2002 Report by The Committee on International Investment and Multinational Enterprises. 'Implementation of the Convention on Combating Bribery of Foreign Public Officials in International Business Transactions and the 1997 Recommendation', 3–4. Available at the OECD website: http://www.oecd.org/dataoecd/52/59/2087917.pdf. Last visited 4 March 2013.

100 Under the convention, the ratification of only two countries was necessary for the convention to enter into force. The convention met this standard within a year of its adoption.

Two possible tentative explanations for the low level of compliance with the OAS Convention are herein offered. First, the OAS Convention proposes a broad and ambitious framework to regulate corruption. The OAS Convention set itself the broader objective of fighting corruption in governmental affairs and deals with the passive and active aspects of bribery. For instance, the OAS Convention directly treats transnational bribery in only one of its 28 articles. The other articles are devoted to other types of corruption. The major theme pervading the OAS Convention is governmental corruption with a focus on the demand side of the bribery transaction. The OECD Convention, on the other hand, is more narrowly focused and only deals with the supply side of bribery. Specifically, the OECD Convention deals with the issue of bribery of foreign public officials and requires signatories to penalize the offerers and payers of bribes. The main objective of the OECD Convention is to address active bribery in international business transactions and deals directly with this offence in seven of its 17 articles. The low level of compliance with the OAS Convention is in part a result of the fact that the OAS Convention's broad focus would require significant changes in national legislation of the signatory parties.

A second tentative explanation for the low level of compliance with the OAS Convention is the lack of a comprehensive process for monitoring the implementation of the convention by the signatories. Unlike the OECD Convention, the OAS Convention contains no deadline for implementation, and the mechanism for monitoring the national legislation of the signatories to ensure compliance with the OAS Convention only became operational five years after the OAS Convention came into force. The lack of an adequate monitoring mechanism may have affected the level of compliance.

These two tentative explanations for the low level of compliance with the OAS Convention may lead to similarly low levels of compliance with the UNCAC for two reasons. First, similar to the OAS Convention, the UNCAC has an even broader mandate than both the OECD and OAS Conventions. As noted previously, reaching a consensus on a convention on corruption among the disparate member states of the UN was a slow and arduous process. The lack of agreement was in part due to the fact that the UN comprises not only disparate states with very dissimilar legal systems but also states at varying levels of economic development. Similar to the OAS Convention, the UNCAC has set far-reaching goals that would require significant amendments to national legislation by most of the signatories to the UNCAC.[101] Second, another factor that suggests that there may be low levels of

101 This has caused some commentators to suggest that the UNCAC may have been enacted without any real intention of being implemented. See Webb, P [2005]: 'The United Nations Convention Against Corruption: Global Achievement or Missed Opportunity?', in Vol. 8, *Journal of International Economic Law*, 191, at 229. For a detailed criticism of the UNCAC, see Schroth, P [2005]: 'The United Nations Convention against Doing Anything Serious about Corruption', in Vol. 12, *Journal of Legal Studies in Business*, 1.

compliance with the UNCAC is that the convention also lacks an effective process for monitoring compliance.

Effectiveness of Cooperation and Compliance with the OECD Convention

The proclivity of countries to pursue investigations and prosecutions for the bribery of foreign public officials varies widely with no discernible pattern accounting for the differences.[102] On the one extreme, you have countries like Japan that appear to have taken very little initiative in investigating or prosecuting allegations of bribery of foreign public officials.[103] The review of Japan's implementation of the OECD Convention, conducted by the Working Group on Bribery under Phase 2, indicated that it appeared that no case of bribing a foreign public official had been decided by the courts, referred to the police, filed as an accusation, or filed by prosecution authorities. In fact, there was no evidence that any case had be filed and subsequently closed despite widespread media reports detailing allegations of Japanese corporations paying bribes abroad. The failure to pursue allegations for the bribery of foreign public officials was in marked contrast to the statistics on the number of prosecutions and convictions for domestic bribery and against corporations in general. In 1998 alone, there were 98 convictions for domestic bribery and other economic offences. Between 1998 and 2002, there were on the average about 1747 prosecutions and 259 convictions for all criminal offences against corporations in each year.[104]

The lack of active investigation of the bribery of foreign public officials by Japanese authorities, set alongside Japan's implementation of the OECD Convention is instructive on the relationship between compliance and effectiveness. Japan enacted implementing legislation in the form of amendments to the Unfair Competition Prevention Law, which came into force on February 15, 1999. Japan was a clear model of a compliant signatory to the OECD Convention. In fact, the Phase 1 review of Japan's implementation of the OECD Convention conducted by the OECD Working Group on Bribery commended Japan on its significant progress, especially in responding to the recommendations made

102 See Coffee, J [2007]: 'Law and the Market: The Impact of Enforcement', in Vol. 156, *University of Pennsylvania Law Review*, 229, at 258, where he observes that the effectiveness of enforcement is difficult to measure by inputs because objective data can be misleading in either direction.

103 See Heifetz, D [2002]: 'Japan's Implementation of the OECD Anti-Bribery Convention: Weaker and Less Effective Than the U.S. Foreign Corrupt Practices Act', in Vol. 11, *Pacific Rim Law and Policy Journal*, 209, at 209.

104 'Japan: Phase 2 Report on the Application of the Convention on Combating Bribery of Foreign Public Officials in International Business Transactions and the 1997 Recommendation on Combating Bribery in International Business Transactions', at 6, 45. Available at the OECD website at http://www.oecd.org/dataoecd/34/7/34554382.pdf. Last visited 4 March 2013.

by the Working Group.[105] Despite the high level of compliance with the OECD Convention, the level of effectiveness of the efforts to curb transnational bribery by the Japanese authorities was very low.

In contrast to the lacklustre effectiveness of Japan's efforts, the government of Korea has made encouraging progress both in implementing new laws to comply with the OECD Convention and successfully prosecuting and securing convictions for two high-profile cases of the bribery of foreign public officials.[106] In one of the cases, both the corporation and the individuals involved were convicted, and in the second case, although the corporation was prosecuted, a conviction was not secured because the corporation was not a legal person. The Phase 1 review of Korea's implementation of the OECD Convention conducted by the OECD Working Group on Bribery had identified significant shortcomings and loopholes in the legislative provisions prohibiting the bribery of foreign public officials.[107] For instance, the FBPA does not explicitly state whether the payment must be for the benefit of a foreign public official or a third party in order to constitute bribery. In addition, the FBPA does not explicitly state whether the payment must be made directly or through intermediaries. The FBPA also contains an explicit requirement that prosecutors must establish that the payment is made in order to obtain or retain business or other improper advantage in the conduct of business. Therefore, a payment to a foreign judge in order to influence the judge's decision and obtain an acquittal will not be considered a bribe.[108]

Some countries do not have significant investigations, prosecutions, and convictions for bribery similar to Japan but for clearly very different reasons. Although the corporations in Iceland have been subject to criminal liability since the early 1970s, most of the corporations that have been held criminally liable for crimes were convicted for tax offences. There has not been a single case where a corporation has been prosecuted for bribery. In fact, bribery cases are so rare that

105 See 'General Reports to Ministers on the Implementation of the Convention and the Revised Recommendation 2002', at 7. Available at the OECD website at http://www.oecd.org/dataoecd/52/59/2087917.pdf Last visited 0\4 March 2013. Also see 'Japan, Review of Implementation of the Convention and 1997 Recommendation, 21 May 2002' at the OECD website at http://www.oecd.org/dataoecd/15/21/2387870.pdf . Last visited 4 March 2013.

106 'Korea: Phase 2 Report on the Application of the Convention on Combating Bribery of Foreign Public Officials in International Business Transactions and the 1997 Recommendation on Combating Bribery in International Business Transactions', at 7. (Korea: Phase 2) at the OECD website at http://www.oecd.org/dataoecd/17/13/33910834.pdf. Last visited 4 March 2013.

107 'Korea, Review of Implementation of the Convention and 1997 Recommendation, July 1999' at the OECD website at http://www.oecd.org/dataoecd/15/6/2388296.pdf. Last visited 4 March 2013.

108 Kim, J [1999]: 'Korean Implementation of the OECD Bribery Convention: Implications for Global Efforts to Fight Corruption', in Vol. 17, *University of California Pacific Basin Law Journal*, 245, at 265–6.

only four have been recorded, and only two of the four resulted in convictions. Three of the cases were prosecuted before 1946, and two of them involved individuals under the influence of alcohol offering bribes to police officer.[109]

While the lack of prosecutions and convictions in Iceland may be explained by the paucity of bribery, the lack of convictions of corporations in the UK cannot be so easily accounted for. Despite the longstanding existence of bribery offences and criminal liability for corporations in the UK, there is no known conviction of a corporation for either domestic or foreign bribery.[110] There is also scant evidence of any prosecution of corporations for bribery offences. One exception was a case in 1972 where the UK authorities unsuccessfully prosecuted a corporation for domestic bribery.[111] The conviction was overturned on a technicality because the judge wrongly instructed the jury on the applicable legal test. With respect to prosecuting the bribery of foreign public officials, one commentator has remarked that the request by the UK government to the Serious Fraud Office to stop the investigation into allegations of the bribery of a foreign official is 'symptomatic of a continuing lack of willingness on the part of many OECD members to enforce the convention'.[112]

In contrast to the broad applicability of criminal liability for corporations in the UK, under federal law in Mexico, there are only two offences imposing criminal sanctions on corporations, and the bribery of a foreign public official is one of them.[113] Interestingly, despite the application of criminal sanctions to corporations for the bribery of a foreign public official, these sanctions do not apply to domestic corruption, money laundering, or accounting offences. Despite these differences, Mexico is similar to the UK in that there have not been any cases where a corporation has been charged with a bribery offence.[114]

---

109 'Iceland: Phase 2 Report on the Application of the Convention on Combating Bribery of Foreign Public Officials in International Business Transactions and the 1997 Recommendation on Combating Bribery in International Business Transactions', at 21. Available at the OECD website at http://www.oecd.org/dataoecd/12/8/2498248.pdf. Last visited 4 March 2013.

110 See Spiegelberger, W [2006]: 'Russian Roulette: Doing Business in Russia in Compliance With Anti-Bribery Laws and Treaties', in Vol. 2, *New York University Journal of Law & Business*, 819, at 825–41, for a comparison of the level implementation of the OECD Convention by the US, UK, and Canada.

111 See *R. v Andrews-Weatherfoil Ltd* [1972], 1. All E.R. 65 (C.A.).

112 Hatchard, J [2007]: 'Countering Corruption and Enhancing Human Rights: Responsibilities of the Corporate Sector in the African Context'. Paper presented at the Business, Accountability and Human Rights Conference, 16–17 January 2007, Johannesburg, South Africa, at 3. Available at http://www.fhr.org.za/article.php?a_id=10. Last visited 4 March 2013.

113 At the federal level, Mexico introduced criminal sanctions for legal persons in 1999 for offences expressly providing for their application (Article 11 of the FCC58). The offences include bribery of foreign public officials (Article 222 bis FCC59) and acts or omissions seriously affecting national consumption (Article 253 FCC).

114 'Mexico: Phase 2 Report on the Application of the Convention on Combating Bribery of Foreign Public Officials in International Business Transactions and the 1997

Similarly, in Canada, there has been no documented conviction of a corporation for the bribery of a domestic or foreign public official. As at March 2004, proceedings were ongoing with respect to one corporation charged with bribing a US immigration official.[115] Since the entry into force of the implementing legislation in Norway in January 1999, there has also been no recorded conviction for bribery of a foreign public official. However, Norway has one conviction for acts of bribery of a foreign public official committed before the entry into force of the implementing legislation, under the alternative offence of breach of trust.[116]

Sweden is another country showing considerable progress in aggressively investigating and prosecuting allegations of bribery. Sweden has managed to secure convictions for the offence of bribery of a foreign public official in a high-profile case involving Word Bank staff members discussed earlier. On 12 January 2004, the Huddinge District Court convicted a Swedish consultant and his accountant for paying kickbacks to two officials of the World Bank in 1998. According to the court judgement, the officials awarded three contracts for projects in Africa to the defendants. As of September 2005, six other proceedings were ongoing (including five at a very early stage of investigation). The Swedish authorities had also investigated four cases that did not result in any prosecutions.[117]

Even in countries that have implemented legislation criminalizing the bribery of foreign public officials but do not establish criminal liability for corporations, and instead impose administrative sanctions, there is scant evidence of aggressive prosecution of corporations for foreign bribery. Germany, for instance, does not recognize criminal liability for corporations, instead relying on a system of administrative fines. These administrative fines are, however, rarely imposed on corporations for offences involving corruption. The failure to impose these sanctions does not rest on a general reluctance to mete out administrative sanctions,

---

Recommendation on Combating Bribery in International Business Transactions', at 18. Available at the OECD website at http://www.oecd.org/dataoecd/53/31/33746033.pdf. Last visited 4 March 2013.

115 'Canada: Phase 2 Report on the Application of the Convention on Combating Bribery of Foreign Public Officials in International Business Transactions and the 1997 Recommendation on Combating Bribery in International Business Transactions', at 6. Available at the OECD website at http://www.oecd.org/dataoecd/20/50/31643002.pdf. Last visited 4 March 2013.

116 'Norway: Phase 2 Report on the Application of the Convention on Combating Bribery of Foreign Public Officials in International Business Transactions and the 1997 Recommendation on Combating Bribery in International Business Transactions', at 44. Available at the OECD website at http://www.oecd.org/dataoecd/3/28/31568595.pdf. Last visited 4 March 2013.

117 'Sweden: Phase 2 Report on the Application of the Convention on Combating Bribery of Foreign Public Officials in International Business Transactions and the 1997 Recommendation on Combating Bribery in International Business Transactions', at 10. Available at the OECD website at http://www.oecd.org/dataoecd/20/8/35394676.pdf. Last visited 4 March 2013.

as these sanctions are frequently imposed on corporations in areas such as anti-trust, tax evasion, and environmental crimes.[118] This negates the inference that the failure to pursue convictions for corporations aggressively is based on a general reluctance to hold corporations liable for criminal actions.

In fact, the countries recording high rates of criminal convictions for corporations have been in offences in the tax, environmental, and labour areas of the law. For instance, in Belgium there have been over 400 corporations convicted for crimes since the passage of legislation establishing criminal liability for corporations in 1999. Despite the high number of corporate convictions, all the convictions concerned non-intentional violations of labour and environmental laws. There was only one minor case involving the receipt of bribe proceeds by civil servants in the Belgian police service. No corporation has been convicted for the bribery of a domestic or foreign public official.[119] The situation in Finland is similar to that in Belgium. Since the imposition of criminal liability for corporations in 1995, five corporations have been convicted for crimes. The convictions were for the violation of environmental statutes and none concerned bribery.[120]

In contrast, some countries demonstrated a significantly high rate of convictions for the offence of bribery, but interestingly no convictions for either transnational bribery or corporations. In France, only individuals have been held responsible of the offence of bribing public officials.[121] Despite the fact that there were over a thousand convictions for bribery between 1994 and 2001, none of the convictions was against a corporation.[122] Most interestingly, the passage of the legislation imposing criminal liability on corporations appeared to have no discernible effect on the liability regime for corporations. There have been over

118 'Germany: Phase 2 Report on the Application of the Convention on Combating Bribery of Foreign Public Officials in International Business Transactions and the 1997 Recommendation on Combating Bribery in International Business Transactions', at 28–9. Available at the OECD website at http://www.oecd.org/dataoecd/52/9/2958732.pdf. Last visited 4 March 2013.

119 'Belgium: Phase 2 Report on the Application of the Convention on Combating Bribery of Foreign Public Officials in International Business Transactions and the 1997 Recommendation on Combating Bribery in International Business Transactions', at 37–8. Available at the OECD website at http://www.oecd.org/dataoecd/59/8/35461651.pdf. Last visited 4 March 2013.

120 'Finland: Phase 2 Report on the Application of the Convention on Combating Bribery of Foreign Public Officials in International Business Transactions and the 1997 Recommendation on Combating Bribery in International Business Transactions', at 18. (Finland: Phase 2). Available at the OECD website at http://www.oecd.org/dataoecd/52/0/2088239.pdf. Last visited 4 March 2013.

121 *Ibid.*, at 47.

122 'France: Phase 2 Report on the Application of the Convention on Combating Bribery of Foreign Public Officials in International Business Transactions and the 1997 Recommendation on Combating Bribery in International Business Transactions', at 46. Available at the OECD website at http://www.oecd.org/dataoecd/36/36/26242055.pdf. Last visited 4 March 2013.

3,600 criminal convictions for economic and financial offences. Of these, over a hundred were convictions for bribery. Although the number of convictions has remained constant, the number of convictions for corruption offences has doubled.

The French authorities suggest that this increase is due to an improvement in the prosecution of such offences, rather than an increase in corruption itself.[123] Since the adoption by France of Act No. 2000-595 of 30 June 2000, amending the Criminal Code and the Code of Criminal Procedure to prohibit transnational bribery, there have not been any convictions for the bribery of a foreign public official. The high level of prosecution for domestic bribery by France cannot be used as proxy for a similar determination to prosecute the bribery of foreign public officials because the interest of states and the policy objectives sought in the prosecution of domestic as opposed to foreign bribery cases are very different.

In June 2007, allegations surfaced suggesting that the British arms manufacturer BAE Systems had paid more than $2 billion in bribes to a Saudi Arabian public official over a 22-year period.[124] The payments were allegedly associated with contracts for the purchase of military equipment by the government of Saudi Arabia from the UK. The formal Memorandum of Understanding (MOU) between both governments was signed in 1985, and there have been two subsequent agreements worth over $40 billion in additional arms deliveries. The agreement was structured as a barter arrangement wherein the UK was paid in oil in exchange for fighter jets. In addition, the Saudis agreed to pay for certain services and infrastructure construction in cash, part of which is alleged to have been utilized to pay for consulting fees to the Saudi public official by BAE Systems. The allegations further suggested that the UK Ministry of Defense (MOD) was complicit in the payment as the MOD officials processed quarterly invoices from the Saudi official by handing them over to BAE, which would then transfer the money into the Saudi official's accounts in the Riggs Bank in Washington, D.C.

The investigation by the UK Serious Fraud Office (SFO) into allegations of bribery and false accounting by BAE Systems was instigated by reports made by a former BAE employer in 2001. Despite the notification in 2001, no action was taken by the SFO until September 2003, following the leak of the allegations to the media. In November 2004, the SFO made two arrests as part of the investigation.[125] In December 2005, the Attorney General invited comments on the public interest issues arising from this investigation from the Foreign and Commonwealth Office, Ministry of Defence, Department of Trade and Industry, Home Office, HM

---

123 *Ibid.*, at 6.

124 Steinberg, J [2007]: 'Executive Intelligence Review, 22 June 2007'. Available at http://www.larouchepub.com/other/2007/3425scandal_of_cntry.html. Last visited 4 March 2013.

125 See http://news.bbc.co.uk/2/hi/business/3978703.stm. Last visited 4 March 2013. For an in-depth discussion of the BAE case, see Stevenson, D & Wagoner, N [2011]: 'FCPA Sanctions: Too Big to Debar?', in Vol. 80, *Fordham Law Review*, 775, at 798–802.

Treasury, and the Prime Minister's Office.[126] Based on the responses received, the Director of the SFO took the view that 'the balance of the public interest was in favour of continuing the investigation'.[127] Similar to the Director of the SFO, the Attorney General also formed the view that the investigation should continue. Seven months after the decision to continue the investigation, the Attorney General and Director of the SFO, in a series of meetings, received further representations from the Cabinet Secretary and the Saudi Ambassador regarding the risk that Saudi Arabia would withdraw its cooperation with the UK on counterterrorism if the investigation continued.

In December 2006, the Prime Minister wrote to the Attorney General and expressed the view that the continuation of the investigation would give rise to a risk of a collapse in UK/Saudi cooperation resulting in negative consequences for the UK public interest in terms of both national security and the UK's highest-priority foreign policy objectives in the Middle East. According to the brief submitted by the UK government, the Director of the SFO concluded that it would not be in the public interest to continue with the investigation because of the risk to national and international security and the risk that lives would be endangered. The decision to drop the investigation was announced by the SFO shortly afterward, on 14 December 2006.[128]

Two organizations, the Campaign Against Arms Trade (CAAT) and The Corner House, sought a judicial review in the High Court against the UK government's decision to discontinue the investigation.[129] The bases for the challenge were that first, the decision was based on considerations of potential damage to relations with another state, a consideration prohibited by Article 5 of the OECD Convention. Second, the Prime Minister in his advice to the Attorney General improperly took into account considerations of damage to diplomatic relations. Third, the actions of the Prime Minister amounted to unlawful interference with the independence of prosecutors under domestic and international law.[130]

With respect to the assertion that the UK violated its obligations under the OECD Convention, the claimants argued that although the OECD Convention did not contain a derogation provision with respect to threats to national security or permit any limitation based on national security, the convention nonetheless

126 'Skeleton Argument on Behalf of the Director of the Serious Fraud Office', at 2. (SFO Brief). Available at http://www.thecornerhouse.org.uk/pdf/document/SkelPerHearGOVT.pdf. Last visited 4 March 2013.

127 *Ibid.*, at 3.

128 *Ibid.*, at 4–5.

129 For a full discussion of the deficiencies in the ruling provided by the UK Court, see Rose, C [2012]: 'The Corner House Case and the Incomplete Incorporation of the OECD Anti-Bribery Convention in the United Kingdom', in Vol. 20, *Tulane Journal of International and Comparative Law*, 351, at 354–83.

130 'Skeleton Argument on Behalf of the Corner House Research and Campaign Against Arms Trade', at 2–4. Available at http://www.thecornerhouse.org.uk/pdf/document/SkeletonPerHearCHCAAT.pdf. Last visited 4 March 2013/

contained an implied prohibition against derogation on grounds of national security.[131] The crux of the claimant's argument turned on the interpretation of Article 5 of the OECD Convention which provides that:

> Investigation and prosecution of the bribery of a foreign public official shall be subject to the applicable rules and principles of each Party. They shall not be influenced by considerations of national economic interest, the potential effect upon relations with another State or the identity of the natural or legal persons involved.[132]

The claimants further argued that Article 5 expressly prohibits the taking into account of the effects of relations with another state when making investigation and prosecution decisions. These are precisely the matters relied upon by the Director in the decision to stop the investigation.

In addition to challenging the jurisdiction of the court to rule on the meaning of the OECD Convention, the UK government argued that the decision to discontinue the investigation did not put the UK in breach of its international obligations under Article 5 of the OECD Convention for the following reasons. First, the threat to national and international security was such that, even if consideration of those matters had been contrary to OECD Convention, the threat was of such compelling weight that the UK government would have been permitted to act in contravention of the convention.[133] The UK government further argued that the OECD Convention was not directed to limiting the ability of a contracting state to take steps it judged necessary for protection of national security or the right to life. Second, the ordinary meaning of Article 5 recognizes that national authorities should continue to have their usual wide investigative and prosecutorial discretion, subject only to the three limitations set out. So a wide range of factors relevant to prosecutorial and investigative decisions (including many factors of considerably less weight than national security and the right to life) may, according to the ordinary meaning of Article 5, legitimately be taken into account as the basis for a decision to discontinue an investigation. The core of the UK government's argument turned on the question of whether Article 5 should be interpreted so as to include an implied term that prohibits or limits the exercise of prosecutorial discretion further than the items enumerated in the text of the convention.

In the judgement delivered by the High Court in April 2008, the court sidestepped the crucial issue of the interpretation of Article 5 of the OECD Convention and instead based its decision on the very narrow ground that the government and the Director of the SFO erred in their decision to discontinue the investigation when

131 For a similar argument, see Cullen, P [2007]: 'Article 5 – Enforcement', in Pieth, M, Low, L & Cullen, P (eds.) [2007]: *The OECD Convention on Bribery: A Commentary* (Cambridge: Cambridge University Press), at 289.

132 OECD Convention, Article 5.

133 SFO Brief, at 7–8.

they submitted to a threat from a foreign nation.[134] The court acknowledged the wide discretion afforded to the Director to discontinue an investigation, which enabled him to take into account risk to life and to national security in deciding whether to continue an investigation.[135] The court carefully sidestepped the possible intrusion by the judiciary on the foreign policy remit of the executive branch on the basis that the threat uttered by the representative of Saudi Arabia was not simply directed at the UK's commercial, diplomatic and security interests, but was aimed at its legal system.[136] The court opined that when a 'threat involves the criminal jurisdiction of this country, then the issue is no longer a matter only for the government, the courts are bound to consider what steps they must take to preserve the integrity of the criminal justice system'.[137] In holding that the Director abdicated his responsibility by submitting to the threat, the court held that the Director ceased to exercise the power to make the independent judgment conferred on him by Parliament.[138]

On the more controversial issue of the interpretation of Article 5, the court reaffirmed the principle that municipal courts were precluded from adjudicating upon or enforcing the rights arising out of the international obligations of sovereign states.[139] The court further acknowledged that the absence of a domestic obligation requiring the Director to take account of Article 5 meant that whether or not Article 5 was a relevant consideration was at the discretion of the Director.[140] The court was, however, entitled under the principles of public law to determine the lawfulness of a self-direction on which a decision is based. Furthermore, where the self-direction turns on the interpretation of an international law instrument, the court is entitled to review the legality of the decision under domestic law.[141] The court opined that the fact that the Director chose to justify the decision by invoking compatibility with the convention entitled the court to review the legality of the decision under ordinary domestic law principles.[142]

Having dealt with the issue of the ability of the court to decide on the issue, the Court turned to the decision of the Director and agreed with the argument put forward by the UK government with respect to the fact that national security was not a prohibited consideration.[143] This is the main ground upon which the decision of the court deserves criticism. The criticism rests on the fact that the contracting parties to convention would not have entered into an agreement containing a

134 *R (Corner House Research and Campaign Against Arms Trade) v Director of the Serious Fraud Office* [2008], EWHC 714 (Admin) at pars 57–60.

135 *Ibid.*, at 54.

136 *Ibid.*, at 58.

137 *Ibid.*, at 57

138 *Ibid.*, at 68.

139 *Ibid.*, at 107.

140 *Ibid.*, at 112.

141 *Ibid.*, at 118.

142 *Ibid.*, at 119.

143 *Ibid.*, at 128.

detailed set of standards and procedures for accomplishing a certain result if it were contemplated that the same result could be achieved by other means. The court nonetheless recognized the arbitrary distinction between national security, which was permitted, and potential effects on relations with another state, which was not, and concluded that the case before them illustrated the difficulty in distinguishing between both contexts.[144] The court acknowledged that unless a sensible distinction was drawn and applied in a consistent manner by the contracting parties to the OECD Convention, Article 5 would be deprived of any sensible effect and the convention would not achieve its objective.[145]

The court underscored the importance of uniformity in the interpretation of the convention and with the objective of achieving uniformity, and on this basis refrained from making a pronouncement on the scope of Article 5. The court stated that 'we must recall that we are a national court exercising jurisdiction in relation to a domestic decision. If each of the Contracting Parties draws a line between that which is a permitted consideration and that which is forbidden, the objective of uniform discipline cannot be achieved'.[146]

While the arguments put forward by the claimants make a compelling case for interpreting the OECD Convention to extend the grounds enumerated in the text with respect to the grounds upon which prosecutorial discretion should not be influenced, this argument unfortunately cannot be extended to the interpretation of treaties. The theoretical issue raised by the ambiguity of Article 5 relates to the methodology that should be employed by the courts in resolving the ambiguity. The standard rules of statutory interpretation are inherently objective. In this formulation, the text to be interpreted has ordinary meanings and the task of the court is to determine the understanding that neutral third parties would apply. In the context of treaty interpretation, the objective is somewhat different. The interpretation of treaties, being contracts, is a subjective task because the interpretation should be guided by expectations of the contracting parties because the treaty exists only to the extent that there is a common agreement between the parties.

With respect to the broader implications of the actions of the UK government, while the position taken by the UK government may serve to uphold a national policy that is beneficial to the UK, it creates the potential for similar action by other state parties to the OECD Convention.[147] In fact, the UK government's interpretation may very well have already influenced the reaction of other state parties and will certainly provide a precedent for other states faced with similar choices. For instance, the South African government, in November 2007, followed the approach adopted by the UK government. According to a former member of the

144 *Ibid.*, at 140.

145 *Ibid.*, at 130.

146 *Ibid.*, at 150.

147 See Rose-Ackerman, S & Billa, B [2007]: 'Treaties and National Security'. In John M. Olin Center for Studies in Law, Economics, and Public Policy, Research Paper No. 351, at 13–14. Available at http://ssrn.com/abstract=1001460. Last visited 4 March 2013.

South African Parliament, the government blocked an inquiry by the Director of Public Prosecutions into whether bribes were paid to South African public officials by BAE Systems.[148] Andrew Feinstein, a former ANC member of Parliament's Public Accounts Committee, stated that the presidency killed off its investigation, pressured the Auditor General to change a report criticizing the R21-billion deal to buy planes from BAE as 'flawed', and stymied an inquiry by the national director of public prosecutions into whether the ANC accepted bribes to fund its election campaigns. Furthermore, the position taken by the UK government will preclude any protests against actions taken by other state parties, regardless of the extent to which the actions contravene any of the provisions of the OECD Convention.

Shortcomings of the Multilateral Initiatives: An Inconclusive Debate

There are several dimensions to the debate concerning the appropriate strategy for tackling transnational bribery. The first level of the debate concerns whether transnational bribery should be tackled on the demand- or supply side. The position advocated concedes that a mixed strategy tackling both the demand- and supply side would be appropriate. The second and more salient debate relating to the problem of transnational bribery by corporations concerns the appropriate strategy for tackling the supply side of transnational bribery. The question as framed by this debate is whether the supply side of transnational bribery should be tackled through extra-territorial prohibition or through host state regulation alone. Commentators on the supply side of the debate and commentators on the demand side of the debate have argued for and against multilateral efforts to combat the supply side of transnational bribery, but the debate is presently stalemated and inconclusive.

From the perspective of some critics, the current multilateral initiatives are ill conceived and the initiatives are responsible for the failure to curb transnational bribery. Some of the proponents of the current multilateral initiatives, in contrast, laud the current multilateral initiatives. They argue essentially that transnational bribery damages the quality of transnational relationships, thus endangering global security and locate the inefficacy of the current multilateral initiatives in the level of enforcement of these initiatives. The relevance of this debate to the argument is that in seeking to answer the central question of this debate, both sides have proffered reasons for the failure of the current efforts to curb the prevalence of transnational bribery. Why the current multilateral efforts to regulate transnational bribery have failed to achieve this purpose is a central question with important ramifications for the international regulatory regime. The importance lies in the fact that without an adequate understanding of the reasons for the inefficacy of a particular transnational legal regime, it would be impossible to devise useful international regulatory regimes.

---

148 Guardian Newspaper Report, 13 November 2007. Available at http://www.guardian.co.uk/world/2007/nov/13/bae.southafrica. Last visited 4 March 2013.

The Traditional Non-Consensus on the Regulation of Transnational Bribery

On an intuitive view, the regulation of transnational bribery would be best served by supply side multilateral efforts to combat transnational bribery using extra-territorial legal prescriptions. Salbu, the main opponent of the current multilateral efforts, makes two related provocative critiques of the current multilateral efforts to curb transnational bribery.[149] He argues that global attitudes about what comprises bribery are so varied that the extra-territorial application of anti-bribery laws creates both moral and political perils. The moral perils concern the danger associated with moral imperialism from the extra-territorial application of domestic laws. In this view, the imposition of laws across borders should be preceded by considerable transnational value consensus. Otherwise, the imposition threatens to deny respect for legitimate regional value variance.[150]

In Salbu's view, cultures should be brought to convergence, if at all, by persuasion, rather than by fiat, and any form of extra-territorial anti-bribery legislation, even the most perfectly conceived, must be considered imprudent under current global conditions. More pertinently, Salbu argues that while the ideal of a normative village may be enticing, the current condition is one of culturally pluralistic nations. Therefore, the ubiquitous transnational application of any one set of laws is dangerous. The peril of extra-territorial application is the risk of inflicting incongruent or discordant values on others in instances where legitimate, nuanced moral differences are supportable.[151]

Nichols, a proponent of the current multilateral efforts to regulate transnational bribery, describes Salbu's claim as unsupportable because it grossly misconstrues the nature of prohibitions against transnational bribery.[152] Nichols finds the moral imperialism argument proffered by Salbu troubling, and in particular, a subterfuge for perpetuating entrenched vested interests. He offers two arguments by way of rebuttal of the moral imperialism arguments proffered by Salbu. First, Nichols counters the moral imperialism charge against the extra-territorial prohibitions by observing that if a specific act is legal in the country in which it occurs, it cannot be prosecuted under the current multilateral prohibitions against transnational bribery. Second, given the general condemnation of bribery, respect for cultural differences should not be equated with respect for the corrupt practices of the minority that engages in bribery in a particular society.[153]

---

149 See Salbu [1999c: 226–7].

150 *Ibid.*, at 227. Also see Dalton, M [2006]: 'Efficiency v. Morality: The Codification of Cultural Norms in the Foreign Corrupt Practices Act', in Vol. 2, *New York University Journal of Law & Business*, 583, at 606–8, for a discussion of the problems associated with the application of corruption legislation across different cultural norms.

151 *Ibid.*, at 231.

152 See Nichols [1999a: 471].

153 *Ibid.*, at 472–3.

Despite the intuitive appeal of these arguments, Nichols misses the thrust of Salbu's argument. Whilst most countries prohibit bribery, there is an enormous amount of discretion exercised by a state in the decision to prosecute a particular allegation of bribery. Unfortunately, the extra-territorial prohibition of transnational bribery impinges upon the host state's discretionary authority to prosecute particular allegations of transnational bribery. Nevertheless, this flaw in the Nichols argument does not imply that the broad proposition put forward by Salbu is correct.

Salbu's second argument, relating to political perils, questions whether the growing consensus on the harmful effects of transnational bribery is enough to justify the adoption of extra-territorial restraints.[154] His concern is that regardless of how many countries eventually join in the present multilateral efforts, the attempts of one sovereign to moderate activity within the borders of another will always pose the risk of disagreements, resentment, and conflict. In this view, current multilateral efforts are too seriously flawed to be considered prudent legislation as they not only attempt to criminalize the acts of foreigners in foreign countries but also attempt to monitor transactions that occur within foreign boundaries, which host countries are likely to want to control themselves.

Nichols counters that there is no evidence to suggest that extra-territorial control of transnational bribery leads to global disharmony or decreases the level of commerce among states.[155] This is because the criminalization of transnational bribery neither presents a new set of laws nor regulates the conduct of host country governments. Further, the criminalization of transnational bribery neither dictates the behaviour of foreign government officials nor other foreign entities. The prohibition applies to citizens of states enacting the legislation, an exercise of the nationality principle, well established and uncontroversial under international law.

This view is again contested by Salbu who locates potential tension in the fact that signatory countries are outlawing extra-territorial bribes throughout the world, and not just in their own countries.[156] Salbu argues that the rest of the world, on the other hand, has not agreed to the intrusion but is nevertheless subjected to it. Nichols concludes that Salbu's view has little room for communities not coincident with political borders, and has little consideration for the myriad of threats that are not the product of state interaction.[157] Salbu surmises that global pluralism undermines efforts to successfully regulate transnational bribery and that the current multilateral efforts cannot avoid moral imperialism simply by virtue of their multilateralism.

Ala'i also ascribes morality, albeit geographic morality, to the inefficacy of the current multilateral attempts to curb transnational bribery.[158] This notion

154 Salbu [1999c: 226–7].

155 Nichols [1999a: 454].

156 Salbu [1999c: 253].

157 Nichols [1999a: 457].

158 See Ala'i, P [2000]: 'The Legacy of Geographical Morality and Colonialism: A Historical Assessment of the Current Crusade Against Corruption', in Vol. 33, *Vanderbilt*

of geographical morality is defined by Ala'i as the norm by which citizens of developed states are permitted to engage in acts of corruption in developing states without the attachment of moral condemnation. Ala'i attributes the past failures of multilateral or transnational initiatives to curb bribery to the legacy of colonialism and geographical morality, which have sown the seeds of distrust between the North and the South and concludes that the current anti-corruption initiative cannot escape the legacy of geographical morality. The moralists used this principle of geographical morality during the colonial era to justify acts of corruption in the colonies. In the post-colonial era, justification for corruption was based on the revisionist discourse on corruption, which cited development and tolerance for local cultures and values as the basis for continued acts of corruption. The amorality of the revisionist approach to corruption allowed transnational corporations and others to hide behind cultural relativism in order to justify their involvement in corrupt acts, including bribery of public officials in the former colonies.[159]

In Ala'i's view, the recent rejection through multilateral initiatives of cultural relativism has failed to unseat the deep-rooted distrust created and sustained by the historical link between the topic of corruption, including anti-corruption discourse and the exploitation of developing countries. Ala'i concludes that current multilateral efforts are destined to fail since they perpetuate the legacy of the rule of geographical morality by adhering to its divisive view.

Deconstructing the Traditional Non-Consensus

The question for policy-makers as framed by this debate is whether the use of multilateral initiatives to combat transnational bribery is likely to bring about a reduction in the incidents of transnational bribery. Both the proponents and opponents of the current multilateral efforts have opposing views, which share fundamental assumptions about the desirability of curbing transnational bribery. The two views differ only in their assessment of the cause of the inefficacy of the current multilateral regime and therefore in the preferred policy approach to regulating transnational bribery. The position taken here is that neither explanatory model convincingly demonstrates the reasons for the failure of the current multilateral efforts to regulate transnational bribery.

The rationale of the opponents of the current multilateral efforts is based on a model of state interaction that presumes that this interaction is characterized by competition among the various states over regulatory capacity. According to this paradigm, states are engaged in a continual process of competition over the legitimate exercise of regulatory capacity over transnational bribery. The position taken is not diametrically opposed to this view in that it recognizes the significance

---

Journal of Transnational Law, 877, at 881.

159 For a general discussion on the cross-cultural moral implications of corruption control in the law and ethics literature, see Spahn, E [2009]: 'International Bribery: The Moral Imperialism Critiques', in Vol. 18, *Minnesota Journal of International Law*, 155.

of the domestic regulatory regime and the predictions regarding the efficacy of the current multilateral efforts, in line with the opponents of the current multilateral efforts, but disagrees with the reasons advanced for the inefficacy of the current multilateral regime. The point of departure lies in the assertion that the lack of effectiveness of the current multilateral framework is caused by the attempts by developed countries to impose their moral values on developing countries through extra-territorial anti-bribery laws.

The leap made by the opponents of the current multilateral efforts from highlighting the dangers of moral imperialism, a legitimate concern, to a reinforcement of the state sovereignty paradigm as the flaw in the current multilateral efforts is unjustified. It is one thing to critique the current state of regulation; it is quite another to demonstrate that a different system will prove superior. Salbu attempts to explain why host state regulation would be more effective. First, he identifies the critical question, as to whether host state regulation would be more effective than the current multilateral efforts to regulate transnational bribery, and answers the question in the negative. Salbu's analysis thus misses an important point. First, he misidentifies the critical question, which should not focus on whether the host state regulation would be better, but whether the multilateral efforts would be worse than host state regulation. His analysis completely ignores the significant and analytically crucial possibility that host state regulation and multilateral efforts may interact and that multilateral efforts may actually strengthen host state regulation.

Second, Salbu's main critique of the current multilateral efforts can be described as a criticism based on a lack of consensus on the normative foundation for regulating transnational bribery. In this norm-driven criticism, Salbu sees a lack of shared ideas on corruption between the developed and the developing countries as the reason for the inefficacy of the multilateral efforts. This view is invalid because the focus on the lack of shared ideas in essence ignores the very important social function played by norms in the process of regulating transnational bribery. In this view, legitimacy and its perception should not be understood as a bar to effectiveness, but rather, legitimacy is a norm or value that influences the compliance and in turn the effectiveness of the transnational legal prescriptions against bribery. Absent the internalization of these norms, there is very little hope of these norms becoming embedded in domestic legal systems, a process critical to the effectiveness of these transnational prescriptions.

More importantly, even in instances where there is consensus on shared ideas, evidenced by states complying with multilateral legal prescriptions, overt compliance tells us very little about the level to which the norms have been nternalized. As argued previously, the level of compliance with the multilateral conventions prohibiting bribery tells us very little about the effectiveness of these transnational prescriptions and therefore offers little guidance in terms of the goal of reducing the prevalence of transnational bribery. In this regard, any meaningful effort to curb the prevalence will have to perform a deeper analysis of the causal relationship between the underlying legal system and the level of effectiveness of the bribery conventions.

In direct repudiation of Salbu's assertions, international cooperation in the regulation of transnational bribery by states differs from other more traditional areas of cooperation amongst states. In other more typical areas of cooperation, reciprocal action on the part of some states may induce or sustain compliance by other states with the commitments over time. Although this marked reciprocity might sustain cooperation between developed states in terms of enforcing these transnational prescriptions, the incentives for reciprocity do not extend to the developing countries that are the site of most cases of transnational bribery. This ensures that commitments by developing countries to curb transnational bribery and their violations cannot be effectively deterred by the threat of retributive violation by developed countries.

There are also problems associated with cooperation even among the developed states. Some problems requiring international cooperation are more transparent than others and are therefore capable of being monitored, making the monitoring of effectiveness easier. Transnational bribery, however, is not one of those problems. This ensures that one of the central variables to valuable monitoring of the effectiveness of transnational legal prescriptions, reputational concerns, is absent. Another variable in determining the level of effectiveness concerns the relational gains among the various signatories to the transnational prescription. States in which the adequate regulation of transnational bribery would require pervasive and costly domestic regulatory activity are less likely to be less successful in their efforts to curb transnational bribery.

In many respects, the debate is inconclusive. The opponents of the multilateral initiatives tend to overstate the problem: The multilateral initiatives alone cannot be the cause of the inefficacy. Given the increase in the level of cooperation through the various multilateral efforts to curb corruption, the theory of state interaction in the transnational arena has evolved from the model of competition reflected in the approach of the proponents of the multilateral efforts to curb the problem of transnational bribery. The opponents of the multilateral initiatives also tend to overplay their preferred solution of strengthening domestic capacity: Strengthening domestic capacity alone will not increase the efficacy of the regulatory regime.

As highlighted previously, the last 20 years have witnessed an intensification of the articulation of a shared vision on the appropriate economic, political, and legal strategy for the transnational community in the regulation of corruption. The intensification represents tacit acceptance that given the transnational nature of modern business transactions, stemming corruption cannot be the preserve of domestic legal systems alone. Given that the domestic legal systems that are the site of these corrupt practices are often experiencing periods of transition, the peculiar cross-jurisdictional problems associated with the regulation of transnational bribery puts an additional strain on the already weak capacity of the domestic legal systems capacity to respond to corruption.

The proponents of the current multilateral initiative, on the other hand, tend to understate the problem: They advocate a transnational regulatory regime without fully exploring its relational and process characteristics. The proponents also tend to avoid sustained consideration of solutions by failing to spell out the essential characteristics of how the proposed transnational regulatory regime would work in practice. To address the shortcomings of this state competition model expounded by the opponents of the multilateral initiatives, the proponents of the current multilateral efforts posit, based on a game theoretical approach, that the rational pursuit of self-interest is a key determinant in shaping the enforcement of the current multilateral initiatives. In this view, states as rational strategic, interdependent, decision-making actors determine the level of compliance in any area of cooperation.[160] These states, as rational actors, choose their level of compliance with the multilateral efforts to curb transnational bribery.

Although the game theory approach, advocated by the proponents of the current multilateral efforts, was developed to address the shortcomings of the state competition model, accepting this model would constitute a conceptual step backwards. As a descriptive model, characterizing states as rational actors who determine their own levels of compliance and enforcement of transnational bribery prescriptions fails to capture the essence of observable phenomena in the regulation of transnational bribery. For instance, there is no indication that there is any difference between the numbers of bribes paid by either US or Japanese corporations or changes in the levels of bribes paid despite the very different enforcement strategies of these two states. This is because the regulation of transnational bribery presents regulatory challenges that are not purely administrative or cost-based.

The regulation of transnational bribery is largely about domestic regulation and regulatory structures and the differences among states in their understanding of the standards set in the multilateral initiatives. This argument pursued in this book suggests that the vociferous exchanges over the use of multilateral initiatives in the regulation of transnational bribery have produced a polarized set of alternatives that fail to capture the essence, much less the complexity of the problem. Consequently, the following two chapters illustrate some of the more complex challenges in the regulation of transnational bribery. Chapter 5 uses the Oil-for-Food Programme as a case study to examine the selective enforcement of transnational bribery prescriptions by states. Chapter 6 focuses on an area of significant importance to the regulation of transnational bribery: the liability of corporations for transnational bribery.

---

160 See Davis, K [1999]: 'Self-Interest and Altruism in the Deterrence of Transnational Bribery', in Olin Working Paper No. 99-22, 1–56 at 48. See also Davis, K [2012]: 'Why Does The United States Regulate Foreign Bribery: Moralism, Self-Interest, or Altruism?', in Vol. 67, *New York University Annual Survey of American Law*, 497, at 498.

Conclusion

This chapter focused on some of the multilateral responses to the problem of the transnational bribery and examined three main multilateral initiatives adopted by states to curb transnational bribery by corporations. The three conventions require the signatories to criminalize the transnational bribery of foreign public officials by corporations. The chapter noted varying levels of compliance with the conventions, but suggested that the level of compliance by signatory parties says very little about the effects of these multilateral initiatives on curbing transnational bribery. The argument developed in the chapter established a simple but important point. As an analytical endeavour into the effectiveness of the current efforts to curb transnational bribery by corporations, the level of compliance with the multilateral initiatives does not provide definitive information on the effectiveness of the efforts to curb transnational bribery. An inquiry into the effectiveness of these transnational prohibitions on the other hand would therefore need to measure the correlation between the particular legal prescription and the incidences of transnational bribery.

The chapter also examined the principal arguments regarding the lack of effectiveness of the current multilateral initiatives to curb transnational bribery. The discussion concerning the efficacy of these initiatives has engendered a lively debate about the relationship between domestic morality, transnational policy, economic efficiency, and the effectiveness of legislation in curtailing transnational bribery. This discussion has taken place under the rubric of the desirability of the extra-territorial prohibition of transnational bribery as an international policy goal. The main condemnation of the current efforts to regulate transnational bribery relates to the prevalence of transnational bribery despite extensive legal devices to control the practice. In these criticisms, domestic regimes seem too weak to pursue adequate regulation of their own while being ensconced in notions of sovereignty and jurisdiction, which hamper efforts to respond adequately to the cross-jurisdictional cooperation requisite to the effective regulation of transnational bribery.

The chapter evaluated the primary explanations that have been put forward to explain the failure of the current multilateral initiatives to regulate transnational bribery by corporations. First, it found the principal premise of the opponents of the current multilateral efforts who argue that the multilateral initiatives are ineffective because of the risk moral imperialism engendered by the extra-territorial application of domestic laws and the attempt to impose transnational value convergence where none exists to be incomplete. The chapter also found the argument that the current multilateral initiatives are ineffective due to the lack of enforcement insufficient to explain the shortcomings of these initiatives. The limitations of the explanatory models of both the proponents and opponents of the multilateral initiatives at a minimum imply that we disentangle the semantics of the debate by critically analysing the underlying causes for the failure of current multilateral efforts to stem the incidents of transnational bribery.

Chapter 5
Selected Challenges in the Regulation of Transnational Bribery: A Case Study of the OFFP

The transactions occurring under the Oil-for-Food Programme (OFFP) provide interesting context in which to analyse some of the difficult issues presented in the regulation of transnational bribery. Since almost all states have outlawed bribery, the underlying substantive cause of action, in theory, should be common to the legal systems involved. For this reason, there is a presumption that the prosecution of misconduct by participants in the OFFP by a foreign state would not violate the substantive policy of the foreign state, but would further the substantive policies of both states.

Unfortunately, states may use their prohibitions against transnational bribery to their advantage or to the advantage of their nationals either by limiting the scope of prohibitions or through selective enforcement. Limiting the scope of the transnational bribery prohibitions is more visible than selective enforcement as the various conventions on corruption provide processes for monitoring the level of compliance by signatories. The adoption, failure to adopt, or implement any of the corruption conventions is clearly visible to other signatories to the convention. Selective enforcement, on the other hand, is less visible and provides many opportunities for states to conceal the extent of their commitment to curbing transnational bribery.

This chapter, using the OFFP as a case study, examines some of the challenges posed by the problem of transnational bribery to the multilateral efforts to curb the practice.[1] The first section provides context by describing the salient features of the OFFP and the structure of the transactions that could be regarded as constituting transnational bribe transactions. The second section examines whether states that have signed up to the OECD Convention, and thus assert that they have criminalized transnational bribery within their legal systems, would characterize the transactions as the bribery of a foreign public official. Given the strong emphasis in transnational bribery prescriptions on the importance of the local jurisdiction classifying the conduct as criminal, the third section, using the US and UK as examples,

1 The information concerning the OFFP is drawn from the reports provided by the Independent Inquiry Committee, 'Report on the Manipulation of the Oil-for-Food Programme'. These reports are available at the committee website at http://www.iic-offp.org/documents.htm. Last visited 4 March 2013.

examines the attitude of the courts to foreign law. Given the penchant for selective enforcement in the regulation of bribery, the fourth section examines the issue of jurisdiction over the bribery of foreign public officials. The fifth section examines the difficulties in obtaining evidence for the prosecution of transnational bribery.

The Oil-for-Food Programme

In 1990, following Iraq's invasion of Kuwait, Security Council (SC) Resolution 661 imposed broad sanctions on Iraq.[2] These sanctions required UN member states to refrain from purchasing oil and other goods from Iraq, and to cease the export of non-humanitarian goods to Iraq.[3] The comprehensive sanctions imposed by the SC lead to critical shortages of food and medicines in Iraq.[4]

To alleviate the humanitarian situation in Iraq, the SC permitted Iraq to sell oil in exchange for humanitarian supplies through the UN. In deference to Iraq's sovereignty, Iraq was permitted to choose both its oil purchasers and humanitarian suppliers. This concession gave Iraq the opportunity to influence the foreign policy of states and garner high-profile supporters for its cause. In selecting oil purchasers and humanitarian suppliers, Iraq gave special preference to companies in countries that were members of the SC that it perceived as sympathetic to the lifting of the sanctions.[5] Companies from Russia, France, and China significantly benefited from the OFFP).[6] A similar pattern of preference prevailed for Iraq's choice of suppliers of humanitarian goods.[7] In contrast, oil purchases by US and UK companies were minimal.[8]

Background: Sanctions, the Oil-for-Food Programme, and the Security Council

In 1995, the SC, responding to reports of an imminent humanitarian crisis in Iraq, passed Resolution 986, which established the framework for the

2 Security Council Resolution 661 S/RES/661 (7 August, 1991).

3 Resolution 661.

4 Working Group Report.

5 Independent Inquiry Committee, Report on the Manipulation of the Oil-for-Food Programme (Management Report I). Chapter I: 'Summary of the Report on Manipulation', 27 October 2005, at 2.

6 Russian companies purchased over $9.3 billion worth of oil from Iraq, nearly one-third of all oil sales under the OFFP and four times more than any other country. French companies purchased over $4.4 billion and Chinese over $4.9 billion worth of oil from Iraq.

7 Russian companies sold the highest number with $3.8 billion of supplies. French companies sold $3 billion worth of supplies, and Chinese companies sold $1.7 billion. Together, the US and UK had a combined sale of $406.5 million.

8 Independent Inquiry Committee, Report on the Management of the Oil-for-Food Programme. (Management Report II). Volume II: 'Report of Investigation: Programme Background', 7 September 2005, at 30.

Oil-for-Food Programme.[9] The framework provided by Resolution 986 required that proceeds from the sale of Iraq oil would be deposited in an escrow account established by the Secretary-General.[10] The funds were intended to be used to purchase medicine, health supplies, foodstuffs, and essential civilian needs for the Iraqi people.[11] The first shipment of oil under the Oil-for-Food Programme, took place in December 1996, and the first batch of humanitarian goods purchased from the proceeds of the oil sales arrived in Iraq in March 1997.[12]

The framework within which the OFFP operated dictated that Iraq selected both the purchasers of oil and suppliers of humanitarian goods. The procedures established for the sale of oil required companies to negotiate and enter into a contract with Iraq's State Oil Marketing Organisation (SOMO). Approval for the contract was then sought from the UN. The procedures also required that approval was contingent on the company registering with the UN through the diplomatic mission of its home country. Once approved by the UN, the oil was lifted from one of two approved port terminals in Iraq. Independent inspectors employed by the UN supervized the lifting of the oil. The company was required to pay the full contract price by means of a letter of credit in favour of the escrow account set up by the UN before lifting the oil.[13]

Similarly, a company wishing to sell humanitarian goods would contract with the relevant domestic ministry of the government of Iraq (GoI). These goods were required to have been identified in advance in a distribution plan that the Secretary-General of the UN had approved. The contract was forwarded through the company's home country mission to the UN for a review of its pricing and value. On approval by the UN, the contract was sent to the committee set up by the SC to administer the sanctions regime for approval.[14]

After the passage of resolution 661, the SC created a special sanctions committee, the 661 Committee, to provide oversight over the Iraq sanctions regime. The 661 Committee mirrored the composition of all 15 members of the SC. Shortly after its creation, the 661 Committee adopted its procedures and chose to make decisions only by means of unanimous consent among all 15 of its members.[15] Significantly, the SC itself does not require consensus for its decisions.[16] The chair of the committee was held by the permanent representative of the country chosen to

9 Security Council Resolution 986 S/RES/986 (14 April, 1995).

10 Resolution 986, para 10.

11 Resolution 986, para 8(a).

12 Independent Inquiry Committee, 'Interim Report', 3 February 2005, at 4.

13 Management Report I, at 25.

14 *Ibid.*, at 26.

15 Management Report II, at 19.

16 Provisional record of the 661 Committee meeting, S/AC.25/SR.2, 1 (Aug. 17, 1990). The United Nations Charter provides that '[d]ecisions of the Security Council on procedural matters shall be made by an affirmative vote of nine members including the concurring votes of the permanent members.' United Nations Charter, Chapter V, Articles. 27(2)(3).

head the 661 Committee by the members of the SC. The remaining representatives were ordinarily lower-level diplomats from the remaining SC countries. The SC generally selected a Western European country that did not have a permanent seat on the council to chair the 661 Committee. Despite the high rank of the chairman, he wielded very little authority because of the degree to which the committee was polarised and dominated by the P-5 members.[17]

Manipulation of the OFFP: Oil Allocations and Humanitarian Contracts

Despite the restrictions imposed by the sanctions regime, the GoI was successful in obtaining revenues outside the OFFP in violation of the sanctions regime. The GoI obtained these revenues through payments levied on humanitarian contracts, oil allocations, and through the smuggling of oil to neighbouring countries.

Under the OFFP, the GoI sold $64.2 billion of oil to 248 companies.[18] Comparatively, the revenues derived from the levies on oil allocations in breach of the sanctions regime were minimal. The GoI, however, utilized its power of selection to advance its broader interest in overturning the sanctions regime. Iraq selected oil recipients in order to influence foreign policy and international public opinion in its favour giving preference to companies from countries that it perceived sympathetic to lifting sanctions, especially Russia, France and China.[19] The levy on humanitarian goods was the largest source of income obtained by the GoI in breach of the SC-imposed sanctions. Under the OFFP, 3,614 companies sold *$34.5* billion of humanitarian goods to Iraq.[20] Iraq derived more than *$1.5* billion in income from levies paid by companies selected to receive contracts for humanitarian goods under the OFFP.[21]

Levies Paid for Oil Allocations

Soon after the OFFP commenced, the GoI imposed a requirement on all its oil buyers to make payments of 10 cents per barrel in addition to their required payments to the escrow account.[22] The GoI sought approval for the imposition of this requirement in a letter from Iraq's Minister of Oil, Amer Rashid, to the Secretary-General, which requested that the UN amend its letters of credit under the OFFP to include the payment and for the remittance of the payment into a special account designated by Iraq's SOMO. The 661 Committee considered the request and clarified that any payment to Iraq outside the escrow account would

17 Management Report II, at 20.
18 Management Report I, at 1.
19 *Ibid.*, at 2.
20 *Ibid.*, at 1.
21 *Ibid.*, at 4–5.
22 Management Report II, at 32.

contravene the sanctions regime.[23] Nevertheless, the GoI continued to collect surcharges from its oil.

Over the two years that these levies were imposed, SOMO collected between 10 and 30 cents per barrel from the buyers of Iraqi oil. Every contracting customer was advised of the requirement and paid despite the fact that they were notified by the UN that these payments were in breach of the sanctions regime.[24] The oil purchasers often disguised the payments by funnelling them through offshore bank accounts or labelling them as legitimate oil-related expenses. For example, one company was advised by a bank official to change the references on payments from 'commissions' to 'loading fees'.[25]

By far the largest number of payments was from Russian companies (including many state-owned companies) to Iraq's embassy in Moscow – more than $52 million from March 2001 to December 2002.[26] Generally, lower-level Russian company representatives came on a regular basis to the Moscow embassy to drop off cash owed for surcharge payments. From time to time, Iraqi diplomats took charter flights from Moscow to Baghdad with the cash in diplomatic pouches for delivery to the Iraqi Ministry for Foreign Affairs. The cash was deposited later into a SOMO account at the Rafidain Bank in Baghdad and then periodically transferred to the Ministry of Finance's account at the Central Bank of Iraq.[27]

Humanitarian Contracts

Similar to the levies imposed on purchasers of oil, the GoI imposed a requirement, in contravention of the sanctions regime, requiring all suppliers of commodities to make payments outside the framework of the OFFP. In August 2000, following instructions from Saddam Hussein, the Vice President of Iraq circulated a memorandum to all ministries ordering the collection of side payments on all contracts signed by suppliers of commodities under the OFFP. The requirement was ostensibly mandated by the GoI as the memo was followed by an announcement by the Minister of Trade at a meeting at which all Iraqi Ministers were present.[28] The GoI diligently instituted the requirement, and by the end of 2000, did not approve bids by prospective suppliers of goods to Iraq, who refused to make the side payments approved by the ministries.

The suppliers were notified of the side payment requirement after they had submitted a bid and been selected by the ministry. If the supplier agreed to make the side payment, the contract was inflated to allow the supplier a margin for the

23 *Ibid.*, at 32.
24 Management Report I, at 3.
25 *Ibid.*, at 4.
26 *Ibid.*, at 33.
27 *Ibid.*, at 34
28 *Ibid.*, at 35.

side payment prior to submission to the UN for approval.[29] A variation on the inflation of the contract prices was to disguise the side payment as an 'after-sales-service fee' performance bond, or training expense. The contractor would later pay this inflated percentage back to the GoI.[30]

Initially, side payments were set at 2 to 5 percent for medication and food contracts, and 5 to 10 percent for all other goods. By the end of 2000, the side payments in all instances were set at 10 percent and occasionally went as high as 30 percent. In many instances, suppliers were asked to sign 'side letters' with the contracting ministry guaranteeing the payment of the kickback within a certain timeframe.[31] Each ministry was required to submit regular letters to the Ministry of Trade indicating the anticipated and received payments imposed on contracts.[32] The payments were made in connection with the contracts of more than 2,200 companies. Most of the suppliers either willingly complied with the requirement directly or made the payments through third parties or agents.[33] Initially, the Ministry of Finance collated the payments centrally. The responsibility for collection was subsequently transferred to the Central Bank of Iraq.[34]

The scope for selective enforcement with respect to prosecuting the companies involved is evident from the lack of a significant number of prosecutions initiated by national authorities. The reactions of the prosecutorial authorities in the countries whose corporations have been implicated in transactions occurring under the OFFP have been mixed. Australia launched a government inquiry soon after the report of the Independent Inquiry Committee was released.[35] After a full year of deliberation, the inquiry released its findings on the alleged $220 million in bribes that was paid by the Australian Wheat Board to the Iraqi regime. The report recommended that criminal prosecutions be pursued against 12 individuals connected with the Australian Wheat Board.[36] The Australian Securities and Investment Commission is suing high-ranking officials including the former managing director of the Australian Wheat Board.

In the US, several individuals have been tried and convicted for violations of the FCPA or acting as agents for the Iraqi regime. In 2006, a Korean businessman, Tongsun Park, was convicted for acting as an agent for the Iraqi regime and sentenced

---

29 *Ibid.*

30 *Ibid.*

31 *Ibid.*, at 36.

32 *Ibid.*

33 Management Report I, at 4–5.

34 *Ibid.*

35 See Villalta, P [2007]: 'Unethical Conduct in the Performance of International Government Contracts: AWB Ltd. and the United Nations Oil-for-Food Programme', in Vol. 37, *Public Contract Law Journal*, 59, at 60.

36 'Report of the Inquiry into certain Australian companies in relation to the UN Oil-for-Food Programme'. Available at http://www.oilforfoodinquiry.gov.au/agd/WWW/unoilforfoodinquiry.nsf/Page/Report.html. Last visited 4 March 2013.

to five years in jail.[37] Samir Vincent, an Iraqi, was fined $300,000 and sentenced to probation after providing substantial assistance to the justice department. The head of Bayoil, David Chalmers, was sentenced to two years in jail and ordered to repay $9 million in fines and restitution. Oscar Wyatt was jailed for one year and ordered to pay $11 million. The US authorities have taken several companies to court, including Chevron, El Paso, Ingersoll-Rand, Textron, York International, Vitol, and Akzo Nobel. The numbers of companies to settle FCPA charges arising from US enforcement actions are in excess of 18. Some examples of these settlements include the resolution of criminal and civil charges by ABB, a Swiss company, filed by the DOJ and SEC. Similarly, GE settled civil charges brought by the SEC alleging violations of the FCPA's accounting provisions arising from the participation of certain foreign subsidiaries in the Oil-for-Food Programme. GE and its subsidiaries consented to the entry of a permanent injunction against future violations of the books-and-records and internal controls provisions of the FCPA. GE and its subsidiaries paid a civil penalty of $23.5 million.

France had the second largest number of contracts under the OFFP. The French authorities have not, however, been able to secure any conviction for violations of the OFFP. Charges were brought in 2006 against 14 people including senior officials such as Christophe de Margerie, the head of Total, France's biggest oil company; Jean-Bernard Mérimée, a former French ambassador to the UN and adviser to Kofi Annan; Serge Boidevaix, a former head of France's foreign ministry; and Bernard Guillet, ex-diplomatic adviser to Senator Charles Pasqua, a former Gaullist interior minister.[38] A French criminal investigation into the involvement of executives from Total and other figures in the program was opened in 2002 and completed five years later. In 2006, Christophe de Margerie, Total's current chief executive, was held for questioning. A magistrate subsequently picked up the inquiry, but the prosecutor's office recommended that the case be dismissed on procedural grounds. The case was reopened in 2012 and it is likely that a new trial will take place.[39] In 2007, the UK Serious Fraud Office announced that it had launched an investigation into UK-based firms that paid bribes during the OFFP. The firms being targeted include the drug giants GlaxoSmithKline (GSK), AstraZeneca, Eli Lilly and UK bridge-builders Mabey and Johnson.[40] In 2011, two former directors of Mabey & Johnson were found guilty.[41] The company, which admitted breaching UN sanctions, had been fined £5 million in 2009.

37 Turner, M [2006, December]: 'Most Iraq oil-for-food scandal perpetrators go unpunished', in *Financial Times*.

38 Available at http://www.economist.com/node/10853611.

39 Available at http://www.english.rfi.fr/economy/20110803-total-be-tried-oil-food-corruption-saddams-iraq. Last visited 4 March 2013.

40 Available at http://www.guardian.co.uk/business/2007/feb/14/iraq.oilandpetrol. Last visited 4 March 2013.

41 Available at http://www.bbc.co.uk/news/uk-12416655. Last visited 4 March 2013.

Despite these actions, most of the countries whose corporations were named in the report have failed to take significant action. The Volcker report named over 52 countries whose companies had been involved in allegedly paying bribes, but very few of them have investigated or prosecuted the individuals and corporations involved. The failure by prosecutorial authorities institute actions are related to the difficulties in fitting the transactions occurring under the OFFP under the traditional rubric of bribery discussed in the following section.

Characterizing Transactions as Transnational Bribery under the OFFP

The transactions occurring under the OFFP provide an interesting context in which to analyse some of the difficult issues presented in the regulation of transnational bribery. Given the apparent international consensus on the prohibition of transnational bribery, the question of whether the payments made by the either the purchasers of oil and suppliers of humanitarian goods under the OFFP could be characterized as transnational bribes may appear trite. The characterization of the payments is nonetheless controversial with very little consistency in laws of states that have implemented the OECD Convention.

The elements of the offence mandated by the OECD Convention requires signatories to make it a criminal offence for 1) any person to intentionally offer, promise, or give 2) any undue pecuniary or other advantage, whether directly or through intermediaries 3) to a foreign public official 4) for that official or a third party to act or refrain from acting in relation to the performance of official duties 5) to obtain or retain business or other improper advantage in the conduct of international business.[42] Based on the perception of the legality of the payments, one would be either shocked or relieved to discover that the payments made under the Oil-for-Food Programme qualify as transnational bribery as set out by the elements of the OECD Convention.

For the purchasers of Iraqi oil under the OFFP, the records kept by the Iraqi officials clearly indicate that SOMO ran a highly organized system to collect payments. Every contracting customer was advised of the need to make the payments and most of the payments were made directly by cash deposits to the accounts of Iraqi officials. The requirements that the official was acting in relation to the performance of his official duties is satisfied and so is the element requiring that the payment be made to obtain or retain business. In fact, with the exception of high-ranking officials who may have granted a company a dispensation, SOMO prohibited future loadings if an entity owed surcharges on its oil allocations.

The elements required for the offence are similarly satisfied for the humanitarian contracts transactions. Over 2,220 companies participating in the OFFP made payments to the GoI. These companies were informed prior to the bidding process

42 Article 1 establishes a standard to be met by Parties, but does not require them to utilise its precise terms in defining the offence under their domestic laws.

for the contracts that they would be required to make these additional payments. The suppliers who agreed to the terms would have their contract values inflated to reflect the additional payment. In most cases, the payments had to be made before the goods in question reached the Iraqi border. A failure to make the payment would result either in the rejection of the delivery of their goods or in the cancellation of the contract. The payments for oil made by oil purchasers and payment by suppliers of humanitarian goods under the OFFP clearly fall within the framework of the offence of bribery of a foreign public official as set out by the OECD Convention.

In the same way as meeting the requirements for the offence under the OECD Convention, both the oil and humanitarian payments meet the requirements for offence in most national legislation. Under the implementation legislation in some states, however, whether domestic law prohibits the previously mentioned payments is less clear. For instance, under the FCPA, the problematic element for the payments under the OFFP concerns the requirement under the FCPA that an individual must have acted 'corruptly'.[43] To satisfy the requirement under the FCPA that the individual must have acted in a corrupt manner, the payment in question need only be intended to influence the recipient to misuse his official position to direct or obtain business wrongfully.[44] The meaning of the word 'corruptly', although clear, raises significant problems when applied to the payments made under the OFFP. The use of the word imports a moral dimension into the definition and requires that the payments were made knowing that they were bad from a US perspective.

Similar to the US, Ireland's legislation implementing the OECD Convention contains a requirement that the payment was made 'corruptly'. Ireland's implementing legislation, the Prevention of Corruption (Amendment) Act 2001, amended the meaning of the term 'agent' previously limited to 'any person employed by or acting for another' in Section 1(2) of the 1906 Act to categories of office holders and officials, both national and foreign, not previously covered.[45] The term 'corruptly' was adapted from the existing domestic offence of bribery, which has been interpreted by Irish courts to mean that the person making the offer does so deliberately and with the intention that the person to whom it is addressed should enter into a corrupt bargain.[46] The Irish authorities have clarified that the corrupt requirement does not necessarily mean dishonesty and encompasses doing an act that the law forbids.[47] Although there are no other reported cases commenting on the meaning of the term 'corruptly', it has been suggested that

43 The use of mails or any other means of interstate commerce is satisfied because the processing of the contracts was done at the UN in New York. All the parties entering contracts with the GoI were required to fax a copy to the UN office in New York for approval.

44 H.R. REP. No. 640, at 7–8 (1998).

45 'Ireland: Phase 1 Review of the Implementation of the Convention and the 1997 Recommendation', at 7. (Ireland: Phase 1). Available at the OECD website at http://www.oecd.org/dataoecd/26/39/2495019.pdf. Last visited 4 March 2013.

46 *R v Smith* [1960], Vol. 2, Q.B. 423 (CA).

47 Ireland: Phase 1, at 5.

the requirement would be satisfied where an official uses his public position in such a way that a reward or favour, not part of the ordinary or open remuneration of such post, is offered or taken.[48] Accordingly, cases brought under the OFFP in Irish courts would require that the payments made under the OFFP were utilized to benefit the Iraqi public officials.

New Zealand implemented the convention by the passage of the Crimes (Bribery of Foreign Public Officials) Amendment Act 2001 in May 2001.[49] The Crimes (Bribery of Foreign Public Officials) Amendment Act 2001 amended the Crimes Act 1961 by adding sections 105 C, 105 D, and 105 E. The sections criminalize the bribery of a foreign public official in business transactions. The case law in New Zealand is similar to that of Ireland and the term 'corruptly' does not necessarily mean dishonest, but deliberately knowing that the act is not for a lawful purpose, with the intention that the person to whom the bribe is intended should be influenced to enter into a corrupt bargain.[50] There is nevertheless little clarity on whether the 'law' in the Irish provision and 'lawful purpose' in New Zealand are referring to their respective laws, or whether it requires that the payments made be contrary to the laws of Iraq. If this were the case, the payments would not qualify as bribery because the GoI sanctioned the payments.

The fact that the payments can be characterized as bribes under the legislation of the state does not end the issue of whether or not the payments are transnational bribe transactions. The Commentary to the OECD Convention provides for an affirmative defence where the payment '…[is] permitted or required by the written law or regulation of the foreign public official's country, including case law'. Several countries have expressly enacted legislation stating that the acts of corruption would have to be contrary to the law in the foreign public official's country to constitute the offence of transnational bribery. For instance, Austria passed amendments to the Austrian Penal Code to implement the requirements of the Convention.[51] The amendments added a new subsection to Section 307 of the Austrian Penal Code, which extended the scope of the offence of bribery of domestic officials to include foreign public officials. The implementing legislation in Austria expressly provides that an act would not constitute the offence of bribery if the advantage is permitted or required by the law of the foreign public official's country.[52]

---

48 McDermott, C [1999]: *Criminal Law* (Dublin: Butterworths), at 42.

49 New Zealand: Phase 1, 'Review of the Application of the Convention on Combating Bribery of Foreign Public Officials in International Business Transactions and the 1997 Recommendation on Combating Bribery in International Business Transactions', at 1. (New Zealand: Phase 1). Available at the OECD website at http://www.oecd.org/dataoecd/51/62/2088257.pdf. Last visited 4 March 2013.

50 *R v McDonald* [1993]: Vol. 3, *New Zealand Law Reports*, 354.

51 Bundesgesetz vom 23. Jänner 1974 über die mit gerichtlicher Strafe bedrohten Handlungen (Strafgesetzbuch - StGB), BGBl. 1974/60 in der Fassung BGBl. I 1998/153.

52 Austria: Phase 1, 'Review of the Implementation of the Convention and the 1997 Recommendation', at 4. (Austria: Phase 1). Available at the OECD website at http://www.oecd.org/dataoecd/2/45/2380506.pdf. Last 4 March 2013.

Similarly, under Brazilian law, the payment will not be considered an offence if it is permitted by the law of the public official. Brazil implemented its obligations under the Convention by amending its Penal Code and Law No. 9,613, of March 3 1998 by enacting Law No. 10,467, of 11 June 2002.[53] This law added Section XI, Chapter II-A to the Penal Code and criminalizes the bribery of foreign public officials through an extension of the definition of a public official contained in the domestic legislation.[54] In both Austria and Brazil, the law of the official's country would be the point of reference for determining whether the payment is permitted. It is unclear whether this interpretation would apply if the payment is not expressly provided for or required by the law of the foreign official.

Canada implemented its commitments to the OECD Convention through the enactment of a new Act of Parliament, the Corruption of Foreign Public Officials Act.[55] The main offence of bribery of foreign public officials is set out in Section 3(1) of the Corruption of Public Officials Act. The Canadian legislation specifically excludes payments such as those made under the OFFP (made in conformity with domestic law).[56] The Canadian legislation excluded payments that are made for reasonable expenses incurred in good faith by or on behalf of the foreign public official that are directly related to the execution or performance of a contract between the person and the foreign state for which the official performs duties or functions. The interpretation given by the Canadian authorities to this provision is broad and encompasses all laws and regulations regardless of whether they are written or not.[57]

The requirements for the application of the defence in Australia, similar to the Canadian legislation, are not very strict and do not require that the conduct be expressly permitted. Legislation to implement the convention was passed by the Australian Parliament on June 17, 1999.[58] The amendments to the Australian Criminal Code Act 1995 (the Criminal Code Amendment Bribery of Foreign Officials Act 1999), include a codification of the offence of bribing a foreign

53 Brazil: Phase 1, 'Review of the Implementation of the Convention and the 1997 Recommendation', at 2. (Brazil: Phase 1). Available at the OECD website at http://www.oecd.org/dataoecd/52/46/33742137.pdf. Last visited 4 March 2013.

54 Section XI of the Penal Code (Decree Law No. 2,848 of 7 December 1940), Article 337-B Chapter II-A ('Crimes committed by individuals against a foreign public administration').

55 Canada: Phase 1, 'Review of the Implementation of the Convention and the 1997 Recommendation', at 1. (Canada: Phase 1). Available at the OECD website at http://www.oecd.org/dataoecd/13/35/2385703.pdf. Last visited 4 March 2013.

56 Section 3(3)(a) excludes from the purview of the offence a 'loan, reward, advantage or benefit' that is 'permitted or required under the laws of the relevant foreign state or public international organisation'.

57 Canada: Phase 1, at 3.

58 Australia: Phase 1, 'Review of the Implementation of the Convention and the 1997 Recommendation', at 1. (Australia: Phase 1). Available at the OECD website at http://www.oecd.org/dataoecd/13/35/2385703.pdf. Last visited 4 March 2013.

public official in Section 70.2. The Criminal Code Amendment Bribery of Foreign Officials Act 1999 in Subsection 70.2(2) clarifies the scope of the legitimacy of the benefit and provides that the benefit must not be legitimately due.

Interestingly, the prosecution bears the responsibility of proving that the benefit is not legitimately due and places three limitations on the applicability of the defence. The subsection provides that the fact that the benefit is customary, the value of the benefit, and official tolerance of the benefit are all factors to be disregarded in asserting the defence. Subsection 70.2(3) directly addresses the issue of the lawfulness of the conduct in the public officials state and expressly provides that in relation to all the categories of foreign public officials, an offence is not committed if the advantage is not prohibited under the law of the foreign public official. In contrast to the burden of proof concerning the legitimacy of the benefit, Subsection 70.2(3) provides that the defendant bears the evidential burden of proving the defense. The difference in the evidentiary burden in the two provisions is particularly confusing in that defendants, rather than argue that the payments are lawful, will suggest that the payments are legitimate, thus reversing the evidentiary burden of establishing the legitimacy of the payments.

In the countries mentioned previously, the companies that made payments under the OFFP are least entitled to raise the defence that the payments were either expressly permitted or at least not prohibited in Iraq. Some other countries have interesting twists particular to their legal systems that are worth mentioning. The Netherlands enacted two bills that came into force on February 1, 2001.[59] These bills were passed by Parliament in relation to the obligations under the OECD Convention. The Implementation Bill provides for several amendments to Dutch legislation in order to meet the obligations under the convention and other international instruments.[60] The amendments relevant to the obligations under the convention are contained in Article I and Article II of the Implementing Bill. The Dutch Penal Code provides a defence for payments where they are permitted by law.[61] This defence is, however, negated where the official order is issued without authority, except the order was assumed by the subordinate in good faith to have been issued with authority, and he complied with it in his capacity as a subordinate.[62] Interestingly, the standard of reference is Dutch law rather than the law of the foreign public official. In the case of the payments made under the OFFP, the defence would be available if Dutch law permitted the payments.

---

59 Netherlands: Phase 1, 'Review of the Implementation of the Convention and the 1997 Recommendation', at 1. (Netherlands: Phase 1). Available at the OECD website at http://www.oecd.org/dataoecd/39/43/2020264.pdf. Last visited 5 March 2013.

60 The amendments relevant to the other international obligations include corresponding amendments to the passive bribery offences (see Articles 362, 363, and 364 of the Penal Code) for the purpose of implementing the EU Corruption Protocol.

61 Article 43.1 of the Penal Code provides a defence where an offence is committed pursuant to an 'official order issued by a competent authority'.

62 See Article 43.2 of the Penal Code.

The second defence under Dutch law would be applicable where, for instance, the party is informed by a source with a sufficient degree of authority that the payment in question is required or permitted by the statutory regulations in force in the foreign public official's country.

In December 1998, Hungary enacted implementing legislation in the form of an amendment to the Hungarian Criminal Code, which came into force on 1 March 1999.[63] These amendments include the offence of bribing a foreign public official and a revised definition of 'foreign public official'. These have been placed under the new title 'Crimes against the Integrity of International Public Life'.[64] The foreign bribery offences were framed in conformity with the offences already in existence in the Criminal Code in respect of domestic officials.

The implementing legislation in Hungary provides a defence very different from the other signatories to the OECD Convention and is applicable to the payments made under the OFFP. The Hungarian legislation provides a defence where the benefit was given at the request of the foreign public official out of a fear of an unlawful disadvantage by the party.[65] 'Unlawful disadvantage' has been construed by the commentary on the Hungarian Criminal Code as a disadvantage that would not be suffered by the person paying the bribe if the foreign public official was to perform his functions legally.[66] Interestingly, although this defence on the face of it would be applicable to the payments made under the OFFP, it is arguable that the actions of the Iraqi public officials were lawful because the government sanctioned the actions.

Some countries expressly limit the application of this defence to the prosecution of the bribery of foreign public officials. Luxembourg approved and implemented the convention through a single piece of legislation.[67] The law came into force on 11 February 2001.[68] The implementing legislation amended both the Criminal Code and Code of Criminal Procedure. Luxembourg deliberately omitted the requirement of an undue benefit from its implementing legislation.[69] The scope of the offence in Luxembourg thus excludes small or facilitating payments from

---

63 Hungary: Phase 1, 'Review of the Implementation of the Convention and the 1997 Recommendation', at 1. (Hungary: Phase 1). Available at the OECD website at http://www.oecd.org/dataoecd/14/54/2386997.pdf. Last visited 5 March 2013.

64 Sections 258/B and F of the Hungarian Criminal Code.

65 Subsection 258/B(3) of the Hungarian Criminal Code.

66 Hungary: Phase 1, at 3.

67 Luxembourg: Phase 1, 'Review of the Implementation of the Convention and the 1997 Recommendation', at 1. (Luxembourg: Phase 1). Available at the OECD website http://www.oecd.org/dataoecd/39/40/2019732.pdf. Last visited 5 March 2013.

68 The Law of 15 January 2001, approving the Convention of the Organisation for Economic Co-operation and Development on Combating Bribery of Foreign Public Officials in International Business Transactions and relating to misappropriation, destruction of documents and securities, dishonest receipt of money by a public officer, unlawful taking of interests and bribery and amending other legal provisions.

69 Luxembourg: Phase 1, at 5.

the range of defences to the bribery offence. Interestingly, one of the elements of the offence is that the benefit is 'without right'. The interpretation of this phrase by the Luxembourg authorities is that the payment must be formally provided for by statute.[70] It is not clear whether written orders by the GoI would satisfy this requirement of being formally provided for by statute.

In other states, the requirement that the acts of the officials contravene the written law or regulations of foreign state is implicit in the implementing legislation. For instance, The Swedish Parliament passed the necessary amendments to Swedish legislation in order to be able to ratify and implement the convention on 1 July 1999.[71] The Swedish Penal Code was amended to add certain categories of foreign public officials to the list of persons to whom it was already an offence to give a bribe (e.g., certain domestic officials, employees, and certain persons who hold positions of trust), in addition to clarifying that the offence also applies where there is a third-party beneficiary. The implementing legislation requires that the public official receive an 'improper award'.[72] The interpretation of this phrase by the Swedish courts implies that the payments would not be an offence if the award is permitted or required by the written law or regulation of the public official's country.[73] Similarly, the Bulgarian implementing legislation requires that the offence applies to the giving of 'any undue pecuniary or other advantage'.[74] The Bulgarian case law interprets 'undue' to mean that the public official has no right to the payment in question. In both Bulgaria and Sweden, the availability of the written law defence turns on the interpretation of the phrase 'undue'. In these states, regardless of the validity of the acts and the laws of Iraq, liability is dependent on a finding that the payment is not due to the public official.

In other countries, the unavailability of the defence is implicit in the legislative enactment. For instance, Finland enacted its implementing legislation in November 1998, and this legislation came into force on 1 January 1999.[75] Through amendments to its Penal Code, the scope of application of the sections on bribery has been broadened to cover bribery of foreign public officials. The Finnish Penal Code does not contain an express requirement that the benefit is not due to the public official. The implication of the absence of the requirement is that even if the defendant was to establish that the benefit to the public official was due; this would

70 *Ibid.*, at 6.

71 Sweden: Phase 1, 'Review of the Implementation of the Convention and the 1997 Recommendation', at 1. (Sweden: Phase 1). Available at the OECD website at http://www.oecd.org/dataoecd/16/1/2389830.pdf. Last visited 4 March 2013.

72 *Ibid.*, at 3–4.

73 *Ibid.*, at 4.

74 Bulgaria: Phase 1, 'Review of the Implementation of the Convention and the 1997 Recommendation', at 3. (Bulgaria: Phase 1). Available at the OECD website at http://www.oecd.org/dataoecd/13/53/2385450.pdf. Last visited 5 March 2013.

75 Finland: Phase 1, 'Review of the Implementation of the Convention and the 1997 Recommendation', at 1. (Finland: Phase 1). Available at the OECD website at http://www.oecd.org/dataoecd/14/20/2386203.pdf. Last visited 5 March 2013.

still not be a defence to the offence. This would be the case even if the benefit was permitted or required by the law of Iraq. This interpretation is consistent with the interpretation that the Finnish authorities give to the penal code, which suggests that the penal code applies regardless of whether the benefit is undue, and even if due may still constitute the offence of bribery if the giver intended to affect a public official's actions in service.[76] The implementation legislation in Portugal also contains a requirement of an undue payment.[77] The interpretation given by Portuguese authorities is that a payment is regarded as undue if the benefit cannot be justified by other purposes. Nevertheless, once it is established that the benefit is undue, the payment would be an offence even where it is permitted or required by the written law of the public official's country.

What constitutes an 'undue' advantage will be of central importance in assessing the validity of the payments made to the GoI. A literal interpretation of the adjective 'undue' from the domestic legislation discussed previously suggests that it refers to things that the recipient is not lawfully entitled to accept or receive. The adjective was clearly included in the OECD Convention to exclude payments or benefits permitted by the law or by administrative rules as well as minimum gifts, gifts of very low value or socially acceptable gifts. The pertinent issue for addressing the validity of the payments therefore turns on the interpretation of the phrases 'written law' and 'regulations'.

Other issues raised also include whether or not a directive from the President, Vice President, or Ministers of Iraq would suffice as written laws and regulations. One interpretation is that the phrase 'written law' or 'regulations' refers specifically to laws promulgated by parliament. Another possible interpretation is that the phrase refers only to the written laws of legitimate states or democratically elected states. This construction is doubtful because even throughout the sanctions regime, the GoI was recognized both by the SC and the international community as a whole as the legitimate government of Iraq. Consequently, the issue of the validity of Iraqi law is discussed in the following section.

Judicial Interpretation of the Validity of Foreign Law

All parties doing business within a state reasonably expect that the laws of that state will regulate their activities. As Justice Holmes noted, the 'general and almost universal rule is that the character of an act as lawful or unlawful must be determined wholly by the law of the country where the act is done'.[78] An early

---

76 *Ibid.*, at 3.

77 Portugal: Phase 1, 'Review of the Implementation of the Convention and the 1997 Recommendation', at 5. (Portugal: Phase 1). Available at the OECD website at http://www.oecd.org/dataoecd/51/59/2088284.pdf. Last visited 4 March 2013.

78 *American Banana Co. v United Fruit Co.*, 213 U.S. 347 (1909), at 356. (*American Banana*).

illustration of the right of a state to determine the validity of acts within its territory is provided by the case of *Blad v Bamfield*.[79] Peter Blad, a Dane, was arrested in England for trespass and trover, arising from his seizure of defendants' goods in Iceland. Blad sought from the Court of Chancery a perpetual injunction restraining the actions against him because his seizure of the goods was justified by the terms of letters patent from the King of Denmark. The Defendants claimed that if the King of Denmark had granted any patents of privilege contrary to the freedom of trade, they were illegal and a breach of the treaty in question. The court granted the perpetual injunction. The Court refused to make a pronouncement on the validity of the King's letter.

The principle for the decision was derived from the early case of *Duke of Brunswick v King of Hanover*.[80] The House of Lords, giving judgment for the Duke, stated that:

> [A] foreign sovereign … cannot be made responsible [in England] for an act done in his sovereign character in his own country; … the courts of this country cannot sit in judgement upon an act of a sovereign … done in the exercise of his authority vested in him as sovereign.[81]

This decision by the House of Lords established that UK courts are precluded from questioning the validity of the acts of a foreign sovereign.

Similar to the UK, US courts recognize that the validity of an act is determined by the laws of the state where the act occurs and will not question the validity of the act of a foreign state.[82] In the case of *Underhill v Hernandez*, an American citizen alleged that a Venezuelan military commander refused to grant him a passport in an attempt to force him to remain in Venezuela.[83] The Court, finding for the defendant, stated that the Venezuelan general, as head of the de facto government, was not civilly responsible for his actions. Chief Justice Fuller noted in his dictum that every sovereign must respect the independence of all other sovereigns. The courts in one country should not judge governmental acts of another sovereign done within its own territory because adjudication would infringe upon the other nation's autonomy. The Court precluded domestic adjudication because the validity of a foreign sovereign's conduct within its own borders would have been challenged.

These principles enunciated by the US and UK courts preclude their national courts from challenging the validity of Iraqi law. Accordingly, these courts may

---

79 [1974] 3 Swans. 604.

80 [1848] 2 H.L. Cas. 1.

81 *Ibid.*, at 17, per Lord Cottenham.

82 For a recent discussion of the scope and parameters of the Act of State Doctrine, see Holt, J [2007]: 'The International Law Exception to the Act of State Doctrine: Redressing Human Rights Abuses in Papua New Guinea', in Vol. 16, *Pacific Rim Law & Policy Journal*, 459.

83 168 U.S. 250, 252 (1887).

adjudicate disputes that concern the acts of the Iraqi officials; the courts are, however, precluded from questioning the legality of the actions of the Iraqi official's. In this context, once the parties making the payments under the OFFP assert the existence of the Iraqi law authorizing the payments, the courts will be precluded from questioning the legality of the acts.

Although the principle that courts will not challenge the validity of the acts of a sovereign within its territory survives today as a general proposition, the operation of the principle has been weakened by the tendency of the courts to examine the acts to determine whether they constitute acts of the state. In the case of *Alfred Dunhill of London, Inc. v Republic of Cuba*, decided in 1976 by the US Supreme Court, the Cuban plaintiffs sued for trademark infringement and the value of cigars expropriated by the Cuban government and sold to the defendant.[84] The question was whether the Cuban agent's repudiation of this obligation constituted a public act. In a letter to the Court in *Dunhill*, the US Solicitor General argued that the court should not decline looking into the 'commercial' acts of the foreign sovereign.[85] The rationale for this argument was that a sovereign acting in a commercial capacity sheds its uniquely sovereign authority and takes on the characteristics of a private individual. The majority decided that commercial acts are not public acts and that the actions of the Cuban government in question did not qualify technically as an act of state because of Cuba's failure to demonstrate that it had been carried out with the requisite sovereign authority.

Similarly, the House of Lords in the case of *Nissan v Attorney General* demonstrated the limitations that the UK courts would accept on their ability to question the acts of a foreign sovereign.[86] In this case, the plaintiffs' hotel was seized for use as a British command headquarters. The court stated that

> Any ordinary governmental act is cognisable by an ordinary court of law (municipal not international). ... An act of state is something not cognisable by the court: if a claim is made in respect of it, the court will have to ascertain the facts but if it then appears that the act complained of was an act of state the court must refuse to adjudicate upon the claim.[87]

The statement by the court illustrates that the UK courts are willing to look into the acts in question to determine whether they constitute sovereign acts. However, once it is determined that the acts are the valid acts of a sovereign, the inquiry ceases.

The UK courts will also even go as far as examining the motivations behind the acts of the foreign state. The case of *Czarnikow v Rolimpex* involved a decree

---

84 425 U.S. 682 (1976).

85 These views were set forth in a letter to the Solicitor General reprinted as an appendix to the Opinion. (Letter from Monroe Leigh, Legal Adviser to Department of State, to Solicitor General (25 Nov 1975).

86 [1970] A.C. 179.

87 *Ibid.*, at 237F-H.

of the Polish government that prohibited further performance by the Polish state organization Rolimpex of a contract for the supply of sugar to an English corporation.[88] Although the case turned on how closely Rolimpex was connected with the Polish government, the Court expressed views on the relevance of the motives of the Polish government in passing the decree. These views varied, but no member of the House of Lords had any problems concerning the propriety of the court in examining the motives of the foreign government in passing the decree.[89]

Another illustrative case was *In re Claim by Helbert Wagg & Co.*, the court considered whether the court should honour measures taken under a law enacted by Germany in 1933.[90] The court stated that:

> In my judgment th[se] courts must recognize the right of every foreign state to protect its economy. … [T]his court is entitled to enquire what manner of legislation it really was, and for that purpose to see what was done under it.[91]

The statement of the courts suggests that they are willing to go further than looking at the act and will even inquire into the motivations of the state.

This decision stands in stark contrast to the view of the US Supreme Court in the case of *American Banana Co. v United Fruit* (‘*American Banana*’).[92] The case concerned the plaintiff's allegation under antitrust laws that the defendant conspired with a foreign government to ruin its banana plantations. The Costa Rican government, acting in its sovereign capacity, had seized the plaintiff's foreign lands. For the plaintiff's claim to succeed he had to prove the conspiracy element of his antitrust claim by inquiring into the motivations behind Costa Rican governmental actions. The Supreme Court, in an opinion by Justice Holmes, refused to question the foreign state's actions, arguing that a seizure by a state is not a thing that can be complained of elsewhere in the courts. The courts held that it was precluded from examining the motivations or factual circumstances surrounding a foreign sovereign's actions. The holding in this case was particularly limiting because the plaintiff did not even challenge the validity of a foreign government's actions, just the sovereign's motives.

As indicated previously, in the UK and the US, Iraqi laws will determine the validity of the payments as the acts occurred in Iraqi territory. Similarly, in both the US and UK, although the courts will not question the validity of the acts of a foreign sovereign, they will, however, frequently inquire into whether the act in question is a sovereign act. In the UK, the courts will go further and examine the motivations of the sovereign state, while in the US courts will not. Even though states may agree that the validity of the act is determined by the state in which the act occurs, there

88 [1978] 3 W.L.R. 274.
89 *Ibid.*, at 279.
90 [1956] 1 Ch. 323.
91 *Ibid.*, at 351–2.
92 213 U.S. 347, 356 (1909).

are variations to the extent to which states will recognize or challenge the validity of the acts. A determination that the acts are valid acts of a sovereign state does not oblige the state to enforce the act. Rather, considerations of conflict of laws immediately arise, in that the very act in question is a foreign law purporting to settle the case. Whether the law of the state should be applied, however, is for the municipal court to decide according to its own conflict-of-laws rules.

The UK case of *Dobree v Napier* is instructive in outlining the situation.[93] In this case, the defendant, an admiral of the Portuguese Navy had seized the plaintiff's ship for running a blockade. The question for the court was whether the defendant's service in the forces of a foreign power, illegal by English statute, gave the plaintiff a cause of action in tort. The court found that the validity of the seizure under Portuguese law meant that the plaintiff had not sustained any legal injury in the contemplation of the law. The underlying principle of this case is that an act authorized by a sovereign, even in breach of an English statute, would be a defence to a tort action.

Similarly, in the case of *Luther v Sagor*, the plaintiff had asked the court to refrain from enforcing the law of a sovereign state that was contrary to the principles of justice.[94] The case concerned a decree passed by the Soviet government of Russia declaring all mechanical sawmills to be the property of the republic. The decree, under which the plaintiff's mill had been seized, made no provision for compensation. The defendant had purchased a quantity of wood originating from the plaintiff's mill from the Russian government, and an action was now brought for a declaration that plaintiff was entitled to the wood. The plaintiff argued that the decree of confiscation was by its nature immoral, and contrary to the principles of justice as recognized by this country, that the courts of this country ought not to pay any attention to it. In rejecting the plaintiff's argument, the court stated that:

> [I]t appears a serious breach of international comity, if a state is recognised as a sovereign independent state, to postulate that its legislation is 'contrary to essential principles of justice and morality'. Such an allegation might well with a susceptible foreign government become a casus belli; and should in my view be the action of the Sovereign through his ministers, and not of the judges in reference to a state which their Sovereign has recognised.[95]

The US case of *Banco Nacional de Cuba v Sabbatino* illustrates that the US courts will also enforce a foreign decree even if it contravenes the principles of its legal system.[96] In this case, the financial agent of the Cuban government sued a US company for proceeds from a shipment of sugar. The US company had sold the shipment prior to the nationalization of all US sugar interests by the

93 [1836] 2 Bing. N.C. 781.
94 [1921] 3 K.B. 532.
95 *Ibid.*, at 558–9.
96 376 U.S. 398 (1964).

Cuban government. After passage of the expropriation decree, the US company entered into an identical contract with an instrumentality of the Cuban government, which in turn assigned the bills of lading to the plaintiff. The US company refused payment on the documents when tendered by the plaintiff. The proceeds from the sugar were paid over to the defendant under a New York statute authorizing receiverships for New York assets of nationalized foreign corporations. The Supreme Court held that it was barred from reviewing the validity of the Cuban act.

The decision is particularly interesting because the confiscated property or traceable proceeds were located in the jurisdiction of the US courts. The court enforced a decree whose discriminatory and confiscatory nature violated fundamental principles within the US legal system. In fact, the Cuban decree, if enacted by the US, would violate the due process and taking without just compensation clauses of the Constitution and be struck down by the courts.

Although the two UK cases of *Dobree v Napier* and *Luther v Sagor* set out a general principle, the situation in Iraq differs slightly because these cases did not challenge the validity of the either the Portuguese or Russian decrees. The decrees were challenged in reference to their conflict with English law or public policy. In the context of the Iraqi law permitting the payments, the challenge would not be that the payments are in conflict with English law or public policy. The challenge with respect to the Iraqi laws would be whether they are in conflict with international law as these laws were in conflict with several resolutions passed by the SC.

Although UK courts have been reluctant to encroach on what they deem to be the province of a foreign state when the foreign law contradicts either UK law or public policy, the courts have shown less reluctance when the claim is that the law violates international law. For instance, in the case of *Anglo-Iranian Oil Co. v Jaffrate [The Rose Mary]*, the court held that a nationalization decree was contrary to international law and refused to honour it.[97] Despite this holding, the position of the UK courts regarding the role of the court when faced with foreign law that contravenes international law is ambiguous.

There have been *dicta* in several cases suggesting that the UK courts will refuse to enforce the law of another state, which contravenes international law or UK public policy. For instance, in *Oppenheimer v Cattermole*, the validity of a German decree of 1941 that deprived Jews living outside Germany of their German citizenship and property was questioned.[98] Three members of the court were of the opinion that 'a law of this sort constitutes so grave an infringement of human rights that the courts of this country ought to refuse to recognize it as a law at all'.[99] The dissent disagreed with the majority in this point stating that a: '[F]oreign municipal law is not a question of law but of fact, and the only way

97 [1953] 1 W.L.R. 246.
98 [1975] 1 All E.R. 539 (H.L.).
99 *Ibid.*, at 567D-G.

known to English law of disregarding an unpleasant fact is to create the legal fiction that it does not exist'.[100]

In the US, the role of international law in determining the validity of the act of a sovereign within the territory of the state is similarly ambiguous. The lower courts, in the *Sabbatino* case, had held that US courts were not obliged to apply the law of a foreign state when the act violated international law.[101] The Supreme Court had to decide whether, as the defendants contended, the seizure of property violated substantive international norms. The majority did not relinquish the court's ability to apply international law to review the acts of a foreign state and in fact acknowledged the court's power to do so. The court stated that:

> The Judicial Branch will not examine the validity of a taking of property within its own territory by a foreign sovereign government, extant and recognized by this country at the time of suit, in the absence of a treaty or other unambiguous agreement regarding controlling legal principles, even if the complaint alleges that the taking violates customary international law.[102]

The review was, however, limited to the circumstances where international law would serve as part of rather than supersede the laws of the US.[103] The majority was explicit about the need for international consensus among states as a precondition for the courts to make a pronouncement. The absence of consensus would mean that the court was making ideological rather than legal choices.[104] In the absence of a clear treaty or other unambiguous legal principle governing whether the enactment of the Iraqi laws permitting the payments violated international law, it would be difficult to conclude that laws would be held to be invalid by the US courts.

Despite agreeing that the Court was not obliged to enforce the act of a foreign sovereign that was invalid under international law, they, however, differed in their opinions regarding the ability of international law to answer the precise question before the court. The majority, in a statement delivered by Justice Harlan, found the rule of substantive international law on expropriation of property unclear and outside the range of issues perceived to be judicially determinable.[105] Referring to the attempts to ascertain an international standard by which to measure the Cuban expropriation decree, the court stated that the area under international law:

---

100 *Ibid.*, at 555C.

101 *Sabbatino*, at 406.

102 *Ibid.*, at 423. Emphasis added.

103 *Ibid.*

104 Justice Harlan stated that '[i]t is difficult to imagine the courts of this country embarking on adjudication in an area which touches more sensitively the practical and ideological goals of the various members of the community of nations'. *Sabbatino*, at 430.

105 *Ibid.*

> [R]eflects an even more basic divergence between the national interests of capital importing and capital exporting nations and between the social ideologies of those countries that favor state control of a considerable portion of the means of production and those that adhere to a free enterprise system.[106]

The dissent, in a statement delivered by Justice White, expressed a contrary opinion about the ability of international law to provide a discernable set of standards stating that:

> [I]nternational law … provides an ascertainable standard for adjudicating the validity of some foreign acts, and courts are competent to apply this body of law.

The dissent was also certain with respect to the ability of the court to render a judgment stating that the determination of the governing rule of international law is itself part of 'the obligations of a court to dispense justice to the litigants before it'.[107] The minority clearly believed that all legitimate acts exercised by a sovereign were to be exercised consistently with the rules of international law for the US courts to recognize their validity.[108]

In contrast, for the majority in the *Sabbatino case*, the absence of consensus meant the absence of international law. In the OFFP, the absence of consensus was also a hallmark of the relations among the member states. Soon after the institution of the levies on oil purchases, media reports surfaced detailing the payments in contravention of the sanctions regime.[109] The UN Secretariat informed the 661 Committee that it had received information substantiating that oil purchasers were making payments to Iraq.[110] A proposal by the US delegate to the 661 Committee to issue a communication to all buyers indicating that the payments were in breach of sanctions was rejected by Russia. After successive discussions, the Russian delegate dropped his objection to the notice being sent out after the 661 Committee was informed that the UN Secretariat had sent out a notice.[111] The notice advised the oil buyers that payments outside the escrow account were a breach of the sanctions regime. In view of Russia's objections, the existence of a substantive international law rule for courts to interpret the acts of payments made under the OFFP are limited. In many respects, process dominates substance as in the international arena norms are derived from the acts of the states and not the other way around. The norms do not dictate the acts of the states.

The divisions among the member states over the OFFP went much deeper than objections by states to the characterization of the payments made under

106 *Ibid.*
107 *Ibid.*, at 456.
108 *Ibid.*, at 457.
109 Management Report II, at 134–5.
110 *Ibid.*, at 136.
111 *Ibid.*, at 137.

the OFFP. The discussions on the actions to take were equally contentious, and the 661 Committee was unable to reach a consensus. The lack of consensus and the unanimous consent rule adopted by the 661 Committee ensured that the Committee was unable to take the necessary steps to stop the levies imposed by the GoI.[112] The US and UK proposed the establishment of a screening procedure to ensure that the buyers of Iraqi oil were end-users and not middle men and the publication of additional warnings highlighting the prohibition against payments outside the escrow account. France, China, and Russia rejected these proposals. They maintained that the proposal went beyond the powers of the committee as the procedures of the committee did not provide for interference in the process by which Iraqi oil was traded.[113] A proposal to implement screening criteria for oil buyers, this time backed by France, was made by the UK to the SC directly. The proposal never reached a vote in the SC.[114] Another proposal to institute a pricing mechanism for Iraqi oil that would make it difficult for the GoI to levy payments was rejected by Russia and China.[115]

In light of the lack of agreement in the 661 Committee, the Chairman formally brought the issue to the attention of the SC. The issue was debated at length at a SC meeting, and still a consensus was not reached. Russia indicated that it would be willing to continue discussions, but objected to a decision being taken by the council. Accordingly, the SC took no decision on the proposals to stop the levies.[116] Following the inability of the SC to reach an agreement on the steps to prevent the collection of levies from purchasers of Iraqi oil, the US and UK took unilateral actions to stop the practice. Both states instituted a system of retroactive pricing of Iraqi oil, which had the effect of making it impossible for the GoI to manipulate the prices to collect levies from the oil purchasers. These unilateral steps were met by vehement protests from Russia and China.[117]

The SC, similar to the levies imposed on oil purchasers, was very well aware that the GoI had imposed side payments on contracts for humanitarian supplies. As early as November 1997, *Al-Hayat,* an Arabic newspaper based in London, reported that agents of Saddam Hussein had approached companies that were seeking to sell humanitarian goods through the OFFP and demanded side payments of up to 10 percent for facilitating such contracts.[118] US government officials have stated that it was 'fairly well known' that Iraqi authorities were attempting to abuse the OFFP by obtaining funds outside the escrow account.[119] Although the US raised the issue in a couple of 661 Committee meetings, there

---

112 *Ibid.*, at 140.
113 *Ibid.*, at 142.
114 *Ibid.*, at 143.
115 *Ibid.*, at 143.
116 *Ibid.*, at 145–6.
117 *Ibid.*, at 146.
118 *Ibid.*, at 157.
119 *Ibid.*, at 158.

were very limited discussions of the issue, and no proposals were considered to stem the practice.[120] The SC did not discuss the issue of humanitarian kickbacks in any of its meetings.[121]

The parameters of the deference given by national courts to the acts of a foreign state as a means of minimizing the conflicts that arise between states over the concurrent jurisdiction that international law grants to states illustrates the inherent tension in the assertion of sovereign rights by states. This tension is illustrated in the decision of the majority in *Sabbatino* case. Justice Harlan's opinion was that the prevailing norm among sovereign nations obliges the US Court in its interpretation of the acts of a foreign state.[122] At the same time, however, Justice Harlan opines clearly that the opposite is true, stating that '[t]he public law of nations can hardly dictate to a country which is in theory wronged how to treat that wrong within its domestic borders'.[123] International law on the one hand imposes obligations on states that are beyond mere courtesy to give deference to the acts of other sovereign states. On the other hand, the obligation is not an absolute obligation as international law recognizes the sovereign right of each state to be free from outside interference.

While the decisions of the courts provide evidence of restraint on the exercise of jurisdiction out of deference for the interests of other states, the parameters of such restraint are not sufficiently well established and the task of determining the level of deference falls to the individual discretion of each state. The domestic courts have indicated that they would be willing to follow established rules of customary international law. However, discerning the principles of customary international law is not always a straightforward exercise. The difficulty in discerning a crystallized rule of customary international law is illustrated by the divisions in the SC over the characterization of the payments. Given the lack of consensus among the members of the SC, it is unlikely that a domestic court would be able to discern any consistent state practice or the crystallization of any rule of customary international law on the validity of the payments made by the GoI under international law.

Jurisdiction

The exercise of extra-territorial jurisdiction by states over transnational bribery illustrates the tension when states exert their sovereignty rights. When a state enacts prohibitions against bribes within its territory, an inevitable consequence of the implementation of these prohibitions is a change in the distribution of wealth. As long as these prohibitions are within the state, the resulting changes in

120 *Ibid.*, at 175.
121 *Ibid.*, at 176.
122 *Sabbatino*, at 421.
123 *Ibid.*, at 423.

distribution of property rights affect only the state's own citizens, and the state's actions remain firmly within the legitimate reach of its sovereignty. When the bribe is in a different state and more so when the party involved is from a third state, the implementation of the transnational bribery prohibition affects the distribution of wealth and property rights in at least three states. The extra-territorial imposition of criminal sanctions on these transnational transactions sets forth a positive or descriptive assertion over conduct occurring within the territorial boundaries of another state. Normative implications over the conduct then flow from these positive assertions. These extra-territorial assertions therefore provide a standard for evaluating conduct within another state.

The extent to which these normative claims follow in a determinate way from the underlying positive assertion is controversial, but the ubiquity of these positive assertions over transnational conduct is common enough to justify assuming that there is a degree of rhetorical force behind it and raises two issues. The first issue is substantive and relates to differences that states may have over the normative content of the criminal law in question. Implicit in the current approach to international law is the notion that each state may pursue its own goals and values through the application of its laws and regulations. Under this paradigm, each state pursues the norms selected by its own political institutions. Given that norms vary across states, a state's application of its laws and the norms embodied in these laws to conduct outside the state and to the nationals of another state may serve to frustrate the norms of both the state where the conduct occurred and the state whose nationals are involved.

The second issue is procedural and relates to situations where normative differences already exist between states and the question turns to the permissible scope of a state's exercise of its extra-territorial criminal laws. Where two states share identical norms and laws, extra-territorial application of one state's law should further, rather than frustrate the policies of the other. However, when states have different normative policies the question remains as to what the permissible normative boundaries of each state and what mechanisms exist to prevent the encroachment by one state on the normative policies of another. On the one hand, each state may exercise restraint in the exercise of its extra-territorial criminal laws.

In areas where there is already consensus by states on the permissible scope of the application of extra-territorial criminal laws, international law may play a further mediating role in mitigating state conflicts. In the areas where is a lack of consensus, the potential for conflicts over the extra-territorial application of criminal laws are particularly problematic. These conflicts are in turn exacerbated where there are substantial differences in the norms and policy goals of the states. At the heart of the weaknesses in the efforts to regulate the abuses in the OFFP was the ambivalence that characterizes the relations between states in the international regime. In operation are what appear to be two conflicting norms under international law. The first norm is the international law norm of sovereignty, and the duty of every state to respect the independence of every other sovereign state.[124] The second conflict concerns the scope of international law to determine the manner in which one state will treat the acts of another state.

The issue of jurisdiction, even within the context of single legal systems, is complex because it touches on international law, and thus constitutional law, as well as conflict of law rules.[125] In the transnational context, the issue of jurisdiction takes on an added potency because analysis of the jurisdictional issues are often made even more problematic by the fact that national legal systems conceive and speak of jurisdiction in different ways with very little basis for comparison. The separate ambit of both international and conflict of law rules as they relate to the issue of jurisdiction have been identified by Mann.[126] The separate realms for international and conflict of law rules as identified by Mann suggests that international law sets down rules dealing with jurisdiction where two or more states are involved, while the principles of conflict of laws within a states establishes the applicable rules when there is a foreign element in a case. Given the separate realms within which the two areas of law operate, some commentators maintain that international law sets little or no limits on the jurisdiction that a state may appropriate to itself.[127]

The general pronouncement that international law places no limits on the powers of jurisdiction that a state may appropriate to itself has been severely criticized and it is increasingly being espoused that jurisdiction, where two more states are involved, is a limited concept.[128] There has been judicial confirmation of the limitations on

---

124 For a general discussion on sovereignty, see Jackson, J [2003]: 'Sovereignty-Modern: A New Approach to an Outdated Concept', in Vol. 97, *American Journal of International Law*, 782, at 789–90.

125 For a general discussion of the interplay between conflict of law rules and international law, see Trachtman, J [1994]: 'Conflict of Laws and Accuracy in the Allocation of Government Responsibility', in Vol. 26, *Vanderbilt Journal of Transnational Law*, 975, at 975–8. Also see Born, G [1992]: 'A Reappraisal of the Extraterritorial Reach of U.S. Law', in Vol. 24, *Law and Policy in International Business*, 1; Brilmayer, L [1987]: 'The Extraterritorial Application of American Law: A Methodological and Constitutional Appraisal', in Vol. 50, *Law and Contemporary Problems*, 311; Lowenfeld, A [1979]: 'Public Law in the International Arena: Conflict of Laws, International Law, and Some Suggestions for Their Interaction', in Vol. 163, *Recueil Des Cours*, 311. See Colangelo, A [2007]: 'Constitutional Limits on Extraterritorial Jurisdiction: Terrorism and the Intersection of National and International Law', in Vol. 48, *Harvard International Law Journal*, 121, at 126–6, for a review of extra-territorial jurisdiction in US and international law.

126 Mann, F [1973]: *Studies in International Law* (Oxford: Oxford University Press), at 28.

127 The ICJ in the Lotus Case stated that there is no restriction on the exercise of jurisdiction by any state unless the restriction can be shown by conclusive evidence to exist as a principle of international law. Furthermore, the onus rests on the claiming state to show that the exercise of jurisdiction was prohibited by international law. *Lotus* case: *S.S. Lotus (Fr. v Turk.)*, 1927 P.C.I.J. (ser. A) No. 9, at 25.

128 Fitzmaurice, G [1957]: 'The General Principles of International Law Considered from the Standpoint of the Rule of Law', Reprinted in Harris, D [1998]: *Cases and Materials on International Law* (London: Sweet and Maxwell), at 488–9.

the scope of the jurisdiction that a state may abrogate to itself where the interests of another state are implicated. For instance, in the *Anglo-Norwegian Fisheries* case, the court stressed that the delimitation of territorial waters, through a unilateral act, depends for its validity with regard to other states on international law.[129]

This principle was also noted in the *Nottebohm* case, where the court stated that while a state may formulate such rules as it wished regarding the acquisition of nationality, the exercise of diplomatic protection upon the basis of nationality was within the purview of international law.[130] Other arguments cited in support of the general principle that international law does set limits on the exercise of jurisdiction by states include the assertion that the law of international jurisdiction governed relations between states, an exercise of jurisdiction in violation of international norms violate the rights, if of anyone, of some other state.

Besides the interplay between jurisdiction under international law and conflict of law rules is also the interplay between civil and criminal jurisdiction. Commentators generally agree that customary international law does not prescribe any particular regulations regarding the restriction of courts' jurisdiction in civil matters.[131] As Shaw observes, the exercise of civil jurisdiction has been claimed by states on far wider grounds and the reaction of states more passive than has been the case in criminal matters.[132] Where criminal or more general public law issues are raised, the rules regarding jurisdiction in the international sense are implicated; and when civil or private law issues are raised, jurisdiction through the conflicts of law arena are implicated.[133]

Under the OFFP, for those corporations or individuals alleged to have paid bribes to the GoI, the exercise of jurisdiction by a state over its nationals is assumed without question. Jurisdiction over non-nationals is more problematic because the acts of bribery were committed in a foreign territory. The question that will be faced by many state courts will be whether they should apply assert extra-territorial jurisdiction over the foreign corporations implicated in the OFFP if doing so would appear to advance the goal of curbing transnational bribery and the amount of deference they should give to resolving conflicts of jurisdiction with other states. Viewed in its entirety, the possible prosecution of foreign corporations for bribes paid to the GoI raises issues that involve normative concerns where states prosecute transnational bribery, the proper constraints on states in the

129 *(U.K. v Nor.)*, 1951 I.C.J. 116, ICJ Reports, 1951, at 116.

130 *(Liecht. v Guat.)*, 1955 ICJ Reports, 4, 20–21.

131 See Akehurst, M [1972]: 'Jurisdiction in International Law', in Vol. 46, *British Yearbook of International Law*, 145, at 177; Mann [1973: 49–51], and Brownlie, I [1990]: *Principles of Public International Law* (4th ed.) (Oxford: Clarendon Press), at 299.

132 Shaw, M [1991]: *International Law* (3rd ed.) (Cambridge: Cambridge University Press), at 457.

133 Maier, H [1982]: 'Extraterritorial Jurisdiction at a Crossroads: An Intersection Between Public and Private International Law', in Vol. 76, *American Journal of International Law*, 280, at 281.

application of transnational bribery prohibitions, and the possible solutions to conflicts between states where they may arise.

Traditionally, the following bases for the exercise of criminal jurisdiction have been broadly accepted albeit with varying degrees of recognition. These include territoriality, nationality, effects, protective, and universal jurisdiction.[134] The first three bases are of direct relevance to the issue of transnational bribery. The territoriality principle is by far the most common basis for the exercise of jurisdiction over criminal activity and underpins the basis for the exercise of jurisdiction over cases of transnational bribery.[135] The principle of territoriality allows a state to subject parties or activities that occur in its territory to its regulations.[136] The UNCAC provides that 'each State Party shall adopt such measures as may be necessary to establish its jurisdiction over the offences established in accordance with this Convention when the offence is committed in the territory of that State Party'.[137]

Similarly, the OAS and OECD Conventions require signatories to adopt measures to assert jurisdiction based on territoriality for transnational bribery.[138] In response to its accession to the OECD Convention, Argentinean jurisdictional rules, which are set out in Article 1.1 of the Argentine Penal Code (APC), provide that the Act applies to offences (a) which are committed in the territory of Argentina or in the 'areas subject to its jurisdiction'; and (b) the effects of which will take place in the territory of Argentina or in the 'areas subject to its jurisdiction'.[139] The APC, however, does not expressly elaborate on the degree of the physical connection that is required to be able to establish territorial jurisdiction. Nevertheless, under Argentine law, territorial jurisdiction is triggered where the offence takes place 'partially' in Argentina. Furthermore, any action

134 Brownlie [1990: 300–304].

135 The territorial principle of jurisdiction has been described as the primary principle applied for the assertion of jurisdiction. See Lowenfeld, A [1989]: 'U.S. Law Enforcement Abroad: The Constitutional and International Law', in Vol. 83, *American Journal of International Law*, 880, at 883.

136 See the English case of *Compania Naviera Vascongado v Critina SS* [1938] A.C. 485.

137 See UNCAC, Article 42(1)a. The OECD Convention contains a similar provision in Article 5(1), (3).

138 Article 4(1) of the OECD Convention provides for jurisdiction on the basis of the principles of territoriality stating that 'Each Party shall take such measures as may be necessary to establish its jurisdiction over the bribery of a foreign public official when the offence is committed in whole or in part in its territory.' Similarly, Article V(1) of the OAS Convention provides that 'Each State Party shall adopt such measures as may be necessary to establish its jurisdiction over the offenses it has established in accordance with this Convention when the offense in question is committed in its territory.'

139 Argentina: Phase 1. 'Review of the Implementation of the Convention and the 1997 Recommendation', at 12. (Argentina: Phase 1). Available at the OECD website at http://www.oecd.org/dataoecd/31/50/2078382.pdf. Last visited 4 March 2013.

performed toward the accomplishment of the offence within Argentina would be sufficient to trigger territorial jurisdiction.[140]

Similarly, Canadian jurisdictional rules establish jurisdiction over the bribery of a foreign public official when the offence is committed in whole or in part in its territory. The leading Supreme Court of Canada decision on jurisdiction is *R v Libman*, in which the court stated that:

> [A]ll that is necessary to make an offence subject to the jurisdiction of our courts is that a significant portion of the activities constituting that offence took place in Canada. As it is put by modern academics, it is sufficient that there be a 'real and substantial link' between an offence and this country, a test well known in public and private international law.[141]

What determines a 'significant portion' or a 'real and substantial link' depends on the particular fact situation, but does not rely on an extensive physical connection between the offence and Canada. Three decisions in the Canadian courts serve to illustrate how particular fact situations are applied. In *Canada (Human Rights Commission) v Canadian Liberty Net*, a lower court had issued an injunction ordering Liberty to cease making racist messages available on its answering service.[142] Liberty changed its message to refer callers to a phone number in the US. Callers to this second number could then hear racist messages. The court held that as long as at least part of an offence has taken place in Canada, Canadian courts are competent to exert jurisdiction.

In *US of America v Lépine*, a group of co-conspirators in Canada agreed to purchase cocaine and fly it from Colombia to Canada with stops in the US.[143] The cocaine did not enter Canada because all the co-conspirators but one were arrested and the cocaine was seized at a US airport. The US sought extradition of one conspirator who had never left Canada. The court held that the facts of this case amply fulfil the 'real and substantial link' requirement articulated in *Libman* (in *R v Hammerbeck*).[144] In this case, the accused took his daughter to the US and kept her there for three weeks in violation of a child custody order. He was charged with abduction. The British Columbia Court of Appeal did not accept the argument that the offence had taken place outside of Canada. Instead, it held that Canadian courts had jurisdiction because the abduction started in Canada and the deprivation of the mother continued in Canada.

In contrast to the broad base for asserting territorial jurisdiction by Canada, Finland's exercise of territorial jurisdiction is somewhat narrower. Under the Penal

140 Argentina: Phase 1, at 13.
141 [1985] 2 S.C.R. 178, at 212–13.
142 [1998] 1 S.C.R. 626.
143 [1994] 1 S.C.R. 286.
144 [1993], R.F.L. (3d) 265, 26 B.C.A.C. 1.

Code, Finnish law applies to offences committed in Finland.[145] An offence is deemed to have been committed both where the criminal act was committed and where the consequence contained in the statutory definition of the offence became apparent.[146] The act of bribery is considered to be committed on Finnish territory if the act itself or its final result occurs in Finland. Nevertheless, territoriality underpins the basis for the exercise of jurisdiction over transnational bribery. The justification being that as a matter of convenience, criminal activities should be regulated by the state whose social order is most affected, the assumption being that this will be the state on whose territory the crimes are committed.[147]

Notwithstanding the Finish example of a restrictive view of territoriality, the right of a state to regulate the conduct of its citizens or nationals anywhere in the world is, like territorial jurisdiction, well established. The UNCAC provides for the exercise of jurisdiction by states over its nationals in article 42(2)b, which provides that state parties to the convention may establish jurisdiction over transnational bribery when the offence is committed by a national of that state party or a stateless person who has his or her habitual residence in its territory. The OAS and OECD Conventions also require signatories to adopt measures to assert jurisdiction based on nationality.[148] The nationality principle is applicable to juristic as well as to natural persons.

Not all states, however, recognize and have established nationality based jurisdiction for transnational bribery. Canada, for instance, rarely asserts extra-territorial jurisdiction, and has not established such jurisdiction with respect to the bribery of a foreign public official.[149] Although under its constitution, Canada has the ability to assert nationality based jurisdiction, it has chosen not to establish such jurisdiction with respect to transnational bribery. The Canadian authorities are of the opinion that the broad interpretation given by the courts to territorial

145 Chapter 1, Section 1 of the Penal Code (Rikoslaki [39/1889]. See Finland: Phase 1, at 1.

146 Chapter 1, Section 10, paragraph 1 of the Penal Code. *Ibid.*, at 9.

147 See 'Report of Sub-Committee of League of Nations Committee of Experts for the Progressive Codification of International Law on Criminal Competence of States' in respect of offences committed outside their territory. See 'First Session of the Committee of Experts for the Progressive Codification of International Law' [1926], in Vol. 20, *American Journal of International Law*, at 12–16.

148 Article 4(1) of the OECD Convention provides for jurisdiction on the basis of the principles of nationality stating that 'Each Party which has jurisdiction to prosecute its nationals for offences committed abroad shall take such measures as may be necessary to establish its jurisdiction to do so in respect of the bribery of a foreign public official, according to the same principles'. In contrast, the establishment of nationality based jurisdiction under the OAS Convention is not mandatory. Article V(1) states that '[e]ach State Party may adopt such measures as may be necessary to establish its jurisdiction over the offenses it has established in accordance with this Convention when the offense is committed by one of its nationals or by a person who habitually resides in its territory.'

149 Canada: Phase 1, at 13.

jurisdiction would be sufficiently effective.[150] The basis for this expansion already exists as Canadian courts have interpreted territorial jurisdiction very broadly and it is possible that the broad interpretation serves as an effective basis of jurisdiction. In the interim, though, this lack of assertion of extra-territorial jurisdiction based on nationality jurisdiction constitutes a major gap in the coverage of prohibitions of the bribery of foreign of public officials.

Similarly, Japan has not established nationality jurisdiction for transnational bribery. Under Article 4.3 of the Japanese Penal Code, extra-territorial jurisdiction is only applied to Japanese nationals who commit one of the following crimes: arson, forgery, rape, murder, bodily injury, kidnapping, larceny, robbery, fraud, extortion, or embezzlement in the conduct of business.[151] Some countries in establishing nationality jurisdiction went beyond the requirements of the OECD Convention. Australia extended nationality jurisdiction in relation to acts wholly outside Australia beyond nationals to residents because of the concern that long-term residents of Australia could evade prosecution if the country of their nationality did not prohibit transnational bribery. The Hungarian exercise of nationality jurisdiction is similarly expansive. Hungary will assert jurisdiction over a non-Hungarian who works for a Hungarian company who bribes a foreign public official abroad.[152]

The failure of the Canadian and Japanese authorities to establish nationality jurisdiction over the acts of their nationals for transnational bribery, in view of the fact that nationality based jurisdiction has been established for other criminal offences, appears to contravene the requirements of the provisions on jurisdiction of the OECD Convention. The OECD Convention provides that in the circumstances where a state provides for the assertion of extra-territorial jurisdiction over its national for other criminal offences, the state should extend these provisions to the bribery of foreign public officials in accordance with the principles of the state governing crimes committed abroad.[153]

Despite the almost widespread assertion of nationality based jurisdiction, there still remain curious anomalies even in some of the states that assert nationality based jurisdiction over transnational bribery. For instance, the Argentine APC does not establish nationality jurisdiction in general to offences committed abroad. However, Article 1(2) of the APC only applies to offences committed abroad where the offence is committed by 'agents or employees of Argentine authorities performing their duties'.[154] Therefore, Argentine law does not establish jurisdiction over its nationals who commit this offence abroad unless they are Argentine public officials.

---

150 *Ibid.*, at 14.

151 Japan: Phase 1. 'Review of the Implementation of the Convention and the 1997 Recommendation', at 13. (Japan: Phase 1). Available at the OECD website at http://www.oecd.org/dataoecd/15/21/2387870.pdf. Last visited 4 March 2013.

152 Hungary: Phase 1, at 11.

153 OECD Convention, Article 4(2).

154 Argentina: Phase 1. 'Review of the Implementation of the Convention and the 1997 Recommendation', at 13. Available at the OECD website at http://www.oecd.org/dataoecd/31/50/2078382.pdf. Last visited 5 March 2013.

In effect, there is a distinction in the application of its nationality jurisdiction between public officials and others as the scope of the Argentine jurisdictional rules in relation to transnational bribery are more stringent for its public officials as compared to its normal citizens. Interesting also is that the exercise of jurisdiction can lead to conflict between state parties as the same conduct can provide grounds for the assertion of jurisdiction by both the territorial state and the state of nationality. In the instances where two parties to the convention have prosecutorial jurisdiction over the same act of transnational bribery, the Convention counsels the two parties to consult, with a view to determining the most appropriate jurisdiction for prosecution.[155]

Whilst it is self-evident that state parties have the right to criminalize and enforce offences committed that fall under their jurisdiction by virtue of the territoriality or nationality principles, the exercise of jurisdiction under the effects principle is less clear. Many instances of transnational bribery may have very little connection with the state that seeks to prosecute. Recognition of this fact has led some states to adopt jurisdictional rules that permit them to exercise jurisdiction under the effects principle.[156] The effects principle is used when an act committed in one state causes injury in the territory of another state. Jurisdiction is grounded on the fact that the injurious effect, although not the act or omission itself, occurred in the territory of the state.[157] In the context of transnational bribery, this principle would apply in instances where the act of transnational bribery produces harmful consequences to the social or economic order inside the territory of a state. The exercise of this principle has been a major source of controversy in securities and antitrust cases where it has been invoked to support regulation of activities abroad by foreign nationals because of the economic impact of those activities in the regulating state.[158]

In the US, courts have traditionally allowed the assertion of jurisdiction over offences where the requisite conduct took place outside the territory of the US so long as the harmful effects or results occur within the territory of the US.[159] The effects doctrine developed primarily in the context of the extra-territorial application of US federal antitrust and securities laws.[160] The application of the effects principle has been a relatively recent development and prior to 1945, the

155 See Article 5, 'Commentaries on the OECD Convention'. Available at the OECD website at http://www.oecd.org/daf/anti-bribery/anti-briberyconvention/38028044.pdf. Last visited 4 March 2013.

156 The allowable scope of the application of 'effects' jurisdiction was debated in the US case of *Asahi Metal Indus. Co., Ltd. v Superior Court*, 107 S. Ct. 1026 (1987).

157 *US v Aluminum Co. of America*, 148 F.2d 416, 444 (2d Cir. 1945). (*Alcoa*).

158 See Casey, S [2005]: 'Balancing Deterrence, Comity Considerations, and Judicial Efficiency: The Use of the D.C. Circuit's Proximate Cause Standard for Determining Subject Matter Jurisdiction over Extraterritorial Antitrust Cases', in Vol. 55, *American University Law Review*, 585, for a discussion of extra-territorial jurisdiction in antitrust cases.

159 See the *dicta* of Judge Learned Hand's decision in *Alcoa* at 443, in which he stated that 'any state may impose liabilities, even upon persons not within its allegiance, for conduct outside its borders that has consequences within its borders which the state apprehends'.

160 The US Supreme Court in the case of *Hartford Fire Ins. Co. v Cal.*, 509 U.S. 764 (1993), at 795–6 stated that 'although the proposition was perhaps not always free from

US approach to the extra-territorial application of jurisdiction was grounded in the principle of territoriality developed by Justice Holmes in *American Banana*. This principle reasoned that when a statute was silent on the issue of extra-territorial jurisdiction, it should be construed to apply only to conduct within the territory of the US.[161]

A different approach was developed, the 'effects' approach, and adopted by Judge Learned Hand in *US v Aluminum Co. of America* ('*Alcoa*').[162] In this case, the court ruled that US antitrust laws could be applied to foreign corporations acting abroad if their conduct was intended to and had effects in the US. An approach distinct from the 'effects' approach proposes a 'balancing' exercise and was followed by Judge Choy in *Timberlane Lumber Co. v Bank of America* (*Timberlane*), in which a range of factors were weighed to determine 'whether the interests of, and links to, the United States ... are sufficiently strong, vis-a-vis those of other nations, to justify an assertion of extra-territorial authority'.[163]

The issue is, however, far from being settled law even though the US Supreme Court addressed the issue of the extra-territorial reach of US law in *Hartford Fire Ins. Co. v California*.[164] The nine Supreme Court justices rejected the territorial approach, but the court was narrowly split between the effects and balancing approaches. Five justices adopted the *Alcoa* effects approach, holding that 'the Sherman Act applies to foreign conduct that was meant to produce and did in fact produce some substantial effect in the United States'.[165] The remaining four justices, in dissent, argued for the balancing approach as set forth in *Timberlane*.[166]

In instances where acts of transnational bribery occur outside the US and these acts directly and substantially affect US interests, US courts would be permitted to exercise jurisdiction over the non-US parties even though they are absent from the territory under the effects doctrine. The potentially expansive application of US effects based jurisdiction is that a foreign competitor of a US national or corporation who pays a bribe that has the effect of preventing the US national from obtaining or retaining business would be sufficient enough basis for the assertion of jurisdiction over the foreign competitor. This assertion of jurisdiction is subject to the limitation of due process.[167] Due process considerations stipulate that before

---

doubt, it is well established by now that the Sherman Act applies to foreign conduct that was meant to produce and did in fact produce some substantial effect in the United States'.

161 *American Banana*, at 357.

162 148 F.2d 416, 444 (2d Cir. 1945).

163 549 F.2d 597, 613 (9th Cir. 1976).

164 509 U.S. 764 (1993).

165 *Ibid.*, at 796.

166 *Ibid.*, at 818–19 (Scalia, J., dissenting).

167 See Borchers, P [1990]: 'The Death of the Constitutional Law of Personal Jurisdiction: From Pennoyer to Burnham and Back Again', in Vol. 24, *University of California Davis Law Review*, 19, at 32–9, for a review of the historical evolution of the constitutional legal principles governing personal jurisdiction. See also Perdue, W [1987]: 'Sin, Scandal, and Substantive Due Process: Personal Jurisdiction and Pennoyer Reconsidered', in Vol. 62, *Washington Law Review*, 479, at 480–90, which traces the development of modern jurisdiction jurisprudence in the US.

a US court may adjudicate an alleged violation of the FCPA, that the assertion of personal jurisdiction over an absent defendant comport with traditional notions of fair play and substantial justice.[168] The test applied by court is whether the defendant purposefully established minimum contacts with the territory of the forum.[169]

Despite the due process limitation, the expansive assertion of jurisdiction based on the effects of extra-territorial conduct by the US courts has been the subject of criticism by several commentators who assert that it brings the US into conflict with other states.[170] In sum, the US courts have developed two approaches to the exercise of extra-territorial jurisdiction. One approach provides for application of US law whenever US domestic interests are implicated. The second approach requires that US law is applied only where US interests outweigh those of the other states. The former approach offers a bright-line rule, making it comparatively easy for courts to apply. The latter, while more cumbersome in application, potentially minimizes friction with foreign states.

The prosecution of foreigners for transnational bribery is by definition a domestic matter. However, this prosecution may not be normatively acceptable to another state. This is the case, even though each state defines the basis for asserting of jurisdiction over foreigners for engaging in transnational bribery by reference to its own normative principles and structural limitations.[171] The greater the similarity in the prohibitions against transnational bribery among a group of states, the less likely it is that the state's extra-territorial application of its bribery legislation will offend its fellow states. In theory, most states agree that transnational bribery should be prohibited and therefore the US prosecution of Russian nationals involved in the OFFP should not raise significant tension between both states. However, given the lack of general consensus on what constitutes corruption and other irreconcilable normative differences regarding its prohibition, conflicts are likely to arise between states.

---

168 See the cases of *McGee v Int'l Life Ins. Co.,* 355 U.S. 220, at 222 (1957); and *Milliken v Meyer*, 311 U.S. 457, at 463 (1940). US courts have generally applied the same basic due process standards developed in domestic cases to international cases. See Levin, M [1994]: 'Judicial Jurisdiction in International Civil Litigation', in Vol. 6, *International Quarterly*, 66, at 76.

169 See *Int'l Shoe Co. v State of Wash.*, 326 U.S. 310, at 316 (1945), where the Court stated that 'Due process requires … that in order to subject a defendant to a judgement in personam, if he be not present within the territory of the forum, he have certain minimum contacts with it such that the maintenance of the suit does not offend traditional notions of fair play and substantial justice'.

170 Gerber, for instance, states that the 'assertion of extraterritorial jurisdiction by the US has created, and continues to create, significant international conflicts. These conflicts often have damaged US foreign relations, especially with its allies, and they have even been held responsible for weakening the western alliance'. Gerber, D [1984]: 'Beyond Balancing: International Law Restraints on the Reach of National Laws', in Vol. 10, *Yale Journal of International Law*, 195, at 197.

171 See Lowenfeld, A [1989: 883], who argues that extra-territorial criminal statutes that go beyond the provisions of international law violate the due process provisions of the Constitution.

Unfortunately, the jurisdictional provisions of the UN, OECD, and OAS conventions do not address the issue of effects jurisdiction and therefore do not provide any guidance for state parties or specify which state party's interests should predominate in the event of a conflict. Thus, while accession to the corruption conventions provides a legitimate basis for states to exercise jurisdiction over transnational bribery, it leaves unanswered the challenging problem of resolving the conflicts that could arise when exercise of jurisdiction by two or more states overlap. In practice, therefore, the interpretation by each state of these provisions could lead to conflict among the states parties as to whose jurisdictional limits should apply. These conflicts over jurisdiction are more real than imagined.[172]

The gap in the conventions with respect to effects jurisdiction ensures that an internationally accepted framework to mediate conflicts between states over the regulation of transnational bribery that addresses both policy and procedural concerns remains to be established. By failing to develop and adhere to a consistent and effective approach to the interpretation of the domestic procedural rules that impact on the regulation of transnational bribery, the various national courts perpetuate and often worsen the problems of the approaches discussed above.

The international community has succeeded in fostering a consensus on the substantive aspect of transnational bribery, and this consensus is efficient and convenient to the goal of curbing transnational bribery. However, efficiency and convenience cannot be fostered in a vacuum. Procedure defines the process of litigation, while substantive law defines the rights and duties of persons in relations with each other. Substantive law is intended to provide the guidelines that govern behaviour by establishing standards by which disputes are resolved. Procedure is intended to provide a convenient and practical process by which substantive law is administered. Procedure is intended to administer substantive law fairly, efficiently, accurately, and at a minimum cost. The overriding purpose of procedure is to facilitate the administration of substantive law, not to supplant it or alter it. If the rules of procedure are intended only to facilitate the administration of substantive law, a defendant need not know which procedural laws govern until faced with a particular action. However, if substantive law is to serve its deterrent purpose, a defendant must be able to ascertain the applicable law prior to acting. Therefore, with respect to transnational bribery, one effect of the current system governing transnational bribery is that it nullifies the deterrent aspect of the law. In the circumstances where procedural rules are applied in such a manner as to eviscerate the substantive rules on the regulation of transnational bribery, these procedural rules need to be amended.

---

172 For instance, the British Protection of Trading Interests Act was enacted for the very purpose of safeguarding national interests from encroachment by foreign courts and administrative tribunals. See British Protection of Trading Interests Act (reprinted in [1982] Vol. 21, *International Legal Materials*, 834, at 839). See Riechenberg, K [1988]: 'The Recognition of Foreign Privileges in United States Discovery Proceedings', in Vol. 9, *Northwestern Journal of International Law & Business*, 81, at 131.

The principal argument that can be made in favour of states prosecuting foreign parties without recourse to the interest of other states or the home state of the party alleged to have paid bribes to the GoI is a pragmatic argument. A pragmatic approach suggests that aggressive prosecution by individual states may redress both the legislative and prosecutorial under enforcement that is characteristic of cases of transnational bribery. As the divisions in the SC over the correct policy approach towards Iraq illustrates, self-interested states may refrain from prosecuting their nationals involved in transnational bribery. The converse, which would entail deference to the jurisdictional claim of the party's state, entrusts prosecution of acts of transnational bribery with a state that may have very little or no incentive in prosecuting its own nationals.

There are possible pitfalls to aggressive prosecution by states because an inevitable by-product is that state courts will be entrusted with the responsibility of negotiating the terms of regulatory conflicts between states, a situation that has the potential to undermine the relationship between states and the multilateral solutions adopted to solve these conflicts. This issue is further explored in the next section in the context of gathering evidence for prosecuting transnational bribery.

Difficulties Obtaining Evidence for the Prosecution of Transnational Bribery

Similar to the exercise of jurisdiction, the gathering of evidence for use in litigating transnational bribery is another area of potential conflict between states. When the court of a state orders the discovery of information located outside its territory, it is employing state power extra-territorially to coerce conduct within a foreign territory. Such extra-territorial applications of the states' discovery rules may conflict with basic principles of justice in the state where the information is located, and may harm legally protected interests in that state.

Given the transnational nature of bribes involving foreign public officials, relevant litigants, witnesses, or documents may be located within the territory of a foreign state. Obtaining the testimony of witnesses or evidence located outside the territory of a state requires either the acquiescence or active cooperation of the state in which the witness or evidence is located. The exercise of the discovery order may conflict with the sovereign authority of the state in which the evidence is located. This conflict arises because of the traditional view of sovereignty that each state has exclusive control over the exercise of governmental power within its territory.

In anticipation of the potential for conflicts between states, the multilateral initiatives on corruption have proposed a broad framework to mediate international cooperation between state signatories. Article 9(1) of the OECD Convention requires signatories to provide, to 'the fullest extent possible under its laws', prompt and effective legal assistance for criminal investigations and proceedings for offences and non-criminal proceedings within the scope of the Convention. The OAS Convention also provides for international cooperation, albeit with stronger deference to the domestic laws of the signatory state. Article XIV provides that 'in accordance with their domestic laws' signatories shall afford one another the widest measure of mutual assistance by processing requests from authorities that 'in conformity with their domestic laws' have the power to investigate and prosecute corruption.

The UNCAC in Article 46 provides with language similar to the OAS Convention, that 'State Parties shall afford one another the widest measure of mutual legal assistance in investigations, prosecutions, and judicial proceedings in relation to the offences' covered by the Convention'. The article in the OAS Convention, in contrast to the OECD Convention, does not limit the assistance to criminal proceedings and non-criminal proceedings of legal persons. Article XIV provides for assistance and cooperation to 'facilitate legal proceedings and measures regarding the investigation or prosecution of acts of corruption'. Similarly, the UNCAC is similarly broad providing for assistance and cooperation for prosecutions and judicial proceedings. Article 43(1) provides that state parties, where appropriate and consistent with their domestic legal system, shall consider assisting each other in investigations of and proceedings in civil and administrative matters relating to corruption.

There are two particular issues that may give rise to conflicts between states in circumstances where courts seek to obtain evidence located within a foreign territory. The first issue concerns the methods governing the gathering of evidence, and the contentious point is whether the court requesting the evidence should require use of methods for obtaining evidence by the state where the evidence is located or discovery procedures available under its legal own system, which may be different. The UNCAC, in Article 46(3)(i), provides that the contravention of the domestic law of the state from whom cooperation is sought is a legitimate limit to the assistance and cooperation that may be provided by the state. The UNCAC, in Article 21, stipulates the grounds on which assistance may be refused and provides that a state may refuse to cooperate if the state considers that the execution would prejudice its sovereignty.

The second issue is whether, and under what circumstances, witnesses and custodians of property within the territory of a foreign state should be compelled to give evidence in a manner contrary to the laws and public policies of that state. The UNCAC professes to mediate these conflicts by according primacy to the domestic law of the state from whom cooperation is sought. Article 46(17) provides that requests for assistance shall be executed in accordance with and not contrary to the domestic law of the state from whom cooperation is sought. The article accords primacy to the domestic law of the requested state, stipulating that the request would only be provided in accordance with the procedures specified in the request where possible.

This principle of non-interference lays out the framework for the interaction between states and state courts must therefore be cognizant that extra-territorial discovery orders for obtaining evidence for use in transnational bribery proceedings may violate established norms of public international law. Well-established norms in international law include the fact that an agent of a state may not act on its behalf within the territory of another state without the authority of the state.[173] Similarly well-established is that a state may not send its agents onto foreign territory to seize documents for review nor may it order depositions within a foreign state.[174]

There are, however, many areas concerning the gathering of evidence in a foreign state that still remain controversial. For instance, it is unclear whether courts are prohibited from requiring that documents located within a foreign state are made available for inspection within the foreign territory, and whether persons or materials located in a foreign territory may be made available for inspection in the other state. Many foreign states would consider both these actions a violation of international law.[175] On the other hand, the US does not consider the inspection of documents or removal orders to be a violation of international law.[176]

States have differing views on the scope of discovery orders and these differences are not always compatible. The US, for instance, has one of the most liberal discovery procedures, in marked contrast to the European approach to discovery. In civil law countries like France, for instance, the investigatory process of discovery occurs exclusively under the aegis of the judge. The French reject the suggestion that such a critical function of the court be entrusted to the parties themselves.[177] Several states fiercely limit the scope of their discovery orders and liken the broad discovery permitted by the US to be a 'fishing expedition'.[178] Even the UK, with a common law system similar to that of the US, objects to

173 Brownlie [1990: 306–7].

174 See *Ings v Ferguson*, 282 F.2d 149, at 151 (2d Cir. 1960).

175 *Societe Nationale Industrielle Aerospatiale v US Dist. Court for the S. Dist. of Iowa*, 107 S.Ct. 2542 (1987). (*Aerospatiale*). Brief of Amicus Curiae, the Republic of France in Support of Petitioners at 12, *Aerospatiale* (No. 85-1695), reprinted in Vol. 25 *International Legal Materials*, 1526 (1986). Brief of the Government of Switzerland as Amicus Curiae in Support of Petitioners at 10, *Aerospatiale* (No. 85-1695), reprinted in Vol. 25 *International Legal Materials*, 1554 (1986). Brief of the Government of the UK of Great Britain and Northern Ireland as Amicus Curiae in Support of Petitioners at 14, *Aerospatiale* (No. 85-1695), reprinted in Vol. 25 *International Legal Materials*, 1564 (1986).

176 See Rosenthal, D & Yale-Loehr, S [1984]: 'Two Cheers for the ALI Restatement's Provisions on Foreign Discovery', in Vol. 16, *New York University Journal of International Law*, 1075, at 1075. They assert that the US may be the only nation that believes unilateral extraterritorial discovery does not violate international law.

177 Merryman, J [1985]: *The Civil Law Tradition* (Stanford: Stanford University Press), at 111–14.

178 Born, G & Westin D [1992]: *International Civil Litigation in United States Courts: Cases and Materials* (Cambridge MA: Kluwer Law and Taxation Publishers), at 411–47. See also Born, G & Hoing, S [1990]: 'Comity and the Lower Courts: Post-Aerospatiale Applications of the Hague Evidence Convention', in Vol. 24, *International Law*, 393, at 393.

the broad scope and intrusiveness of US discovery practice.[179] While there is room for cooperation between states, the lack of sufficiently well-established rules of customary international law and the differing views held by states on the permissible scope of discovery orders leaves significant potential for conflicts between states.

In the US, Rule 26(b) of the US Federal Rules of Civil Procedure permits parties to obtain discovery regarding any matter, not privileged, which is relevant to the subject matter involved in the case.[180] The rule was designed to be broad and permits a party to discover any information as long as it appears reasonably calculated to lead to the discovery of admissible evidence. As long as a US court has personal jurisdiction over a party, the court can force the party to produce documents in its possession or under its control, no matter where they are located.[181] The nationality of the party in control of the information is irrelevant as long as the court can establish personal jurisdiction over the entity. The US Courts temper the application of their broad assertion of jurisdiction by permitting the application of foreign discovery where, on balance, the interest of the US outweighs the interest of the foreign state. The test balances the vital and competing national interests at stake.

The UK equivalent to the US Federal Rules of Civil Procedure is contained in the Rules of the Supreme Court.[182] Compared to its US counterpart, the scope of discovery permitted is very limited. The UK practice of transnational discovery is tempered by Order 38, which mandates that discovery orders should be made where necessary for the purpose of justice and case law that establishes that the issuance of such orders lie primarily within the discretion of the courts.[183] The UK courts have specifically rejected the balancing analysis employed by US courts as an impossible task that invariably results in prejudice to foreign litigants, preferring instead to focus on principles of comity and fairness to the litigants.[184]

The multilateral treaty that purports to mediate the interaction between states with regard to transnational discovery, the Convention on Taking Evidence Abroad in Civil or Commercial Matters (The Hague Evidence Convention), is

179 Collins, J [1979]: '*Opportunities for and Obstacles to Obtaining Evidence in England for Use in Litigation in the United States*', in Vol. 13, *International Law* 27, at 28.

180 US Federal Rules of Civil Procedure Section 26. Rule 26 provides for the disclosure of all documents relevant to the subject matter. In addition, the information sought need not be admissible at trial as long as it appears reasonably calculated to lead to the discovery of admissible evidence.

181 See case of *In re Sarrio S. A.*, 1995 WL 598988 (S.D.N.Y. Oct. 11, 1995).

182 R.S.C. Ord. 24 r. 1-3 (Eng.).

183 McClean, D [1992]: *International Judicial Assistance* (Oxford: Clarendon Press), at 75.

184 See *MacKinnon v Donaldson Lufkin & Jenrette Securities Corp.* [1986] All E.R. 653, 662, where the potential for domestic favouritism in weighing foreign policies against national interests of sovereignty was noted.

of limited application to the gathering of evidence for transnational bribery.[185] The Hague Evidence Convention establishes the procedures for the courts of one state to obtain evidence in the territory of another state in civil or commercial matters. Article 1 of the Hague Evidence Convention explicitly refers to 'civil or commercial matters' and thus excludes penal and possibly other matters.[186] The relevance of the Hague Evidence Convention to the regulation of transnational bribery is thus very limited.

The procedures of the Hague Convention are, however, not the sole means for gathering evidence located in a foreign state. The Hague Convention itself does not state that it is the exclusive means of obtaining evidence located abroad and a state is therefore not limited to the Convention's procedures for securing evidence located abroad. The US Supreme Court in *Societe Nationale Industrielle Aerospatiale v U.S. District Court (S.D. Iowa)* made this point emphatically clear.[187] The specific issue was whether litigants in US courts were required to use the Hague Convention to obtain evidence located within signatory states. The Supreme Court held that the use of The Hague Convention was not mandatory and that US discovery rules could be used to obtain information located outside the state. The Court stated that the Convention itself neither stated nor implied that it was the exclusive means of obtaining foreign information; nor was there any other basis for finding such an obligation.

The wide ambit of US broad discovery rule and liberal application by the US courts of foreign discovery orders has led several states to enact nondisclosure laws designed to prohibit such discovery orders.[188] These nondisclosure laws fit into two general categories that include secrecy or confidentiality laws and blocking statutes. The first category comprises bank secrecy or confidentiality laws enacted by states that prohibit the disclosure of information. These states typically enact penal laws prohibiting the production of documents for use in foreign litigation. These confidentiality laws may be contained in penal statutes such as Article 273

185 23 U.S.T. 2555, T.I.A.S. No. 7444, 847 U.N.T.S. 231. *Opened for signature* 18 Mar. 1970.

186 The scope of the convention in respect to what constituted penal proceedings was the subject of a meeting at The Hague in 1978 of experts drawn from the governmental bureaux that had responsibility for applying the Convention. *See* 'Report on the Work of the Special Commission on the Operation of the Convention of 18 March 1970 on the Taking of Evidence Abroad in Civil or Commercial Matters', in Vol. 17, *International Legal Materials*, at 1425 (1978).

187 107 S.Ct. 2542 (1987).

188 A 1982 survey of blocking statutes cites discovery blocking statutes in the UK, Australia, Belgium, Canada, Ontario, Quebec, Denmark, Finland, France, the German Federal Republic, Italy, the Netherlands, New Zealand, Norway, the Philippines, South Africa, Sweden, and Switzerland. See Comment [1982]: '*Shortening the Long Arm of American Antitrust Jurisdiction: Extraterritoriality and the Foreign Blocking Statutes*', in Vol. 28, *Loyola Law Review*, 213, at 276–9.

of the Swiss Penal Code.[189] The statute penalizes a party for producing documents for use in foreign litigation and may be used as an excuse by the non-producing party to refuse production of documents.

The provision in the UNCAC on bank secrecy is limited to the domestic sphere. The provision requires signatories to ensure that there are appropriate mechanisms within their domestic legal system to overcome obstacles that may arise out of the application of bank secrecy laws.[190] This provision only applies to the invocation of bank secrecy to domestic criminal investigations. The provisions on bank secrecy in both the OECD and OAS Conventions are broader and preclude signatories from invoking bank secrecy as the basis for refusal to assist a request for information from a state.[191] The OAS Convention immediately qualifies this requirement stating that the '[r]equested State shall apply this article in accordance with its domestic law, its procedural provisions, or bilateral or multilateral agreements with the Requesting State'.[192]

The potential for conflict between states in the context of transnational discovery and bank secrecy laws concerns the extent to which these laws should be given recognition by a state that does not recognize the concept within its legal system. Considerable differences exist among the various foreign legal systems providing for protection of bank secrets. For instance, US law furnishes relatively little protection to bank records because no constitutional or other privilege exists with respect to the confidentiality of bank records.

The question therefore arises as to whether US courts should recognize the claim that bank records located abroad are privileged evidence under the foreign law and thereby immune from US discovery proceedings, and, if so, to what extent the privilege should be granted. The case of *Trade Dev. Bank v Continental Ins. Co.* concerned a civil action for the recovery of damages resulting from fraudulent investment activities.[193] The issue raised was whether the Swiss bank secrecy law would bar the disclosure of information in federal discovery proceedings. The Court acknowledged the principle that the privilege provisions contained in the Swiss law, if applicable, had to be recognized under US law.[194]

While the US courts have displayed a limited willingness to recognize foreign privileges in civil litigation, privilege claims in administrative, criminal, and grand jury investigations have been rejected. The US courts have refused to recognize foreign privilege claims against discovery orders by US law enforcement authorities in tax and securities investigations. In *Securities and Exchange Commission v Banca Della Svizzera Italiana*, the SEC sued a Swiss corporation for violating

189 'Recueil Systématique du Droit Fédéral' available at http://www.admin.ch/ch/f/rs/rs.html. Last visited 4 March 2013.

190 UNCAC, Article 40.

191 OAS Convention, Article XVI and OECD Convention Article 9(3).

192 OAS Convention, Article XVI.

193 469 F.2d 35 (2d Cir. 1972).

194 *Ibid.*, at 40.

insider-trading laws and sought to obtain the identity of the parties involved in the transactions.[195] Banca Della Svizzera Italiana (BSI) refused to disclose the requested information, asserting that compliance would violate the Swiss banking secrecy law. The Court stated that:

> [i]t would be a travesty of justice to permit a foreign company to invade American markets, violate American laws if they were indeed violated, withdraw profits and resist accountability for itself and its principals for the illegality by claiming their anonymity under foreign law.[196]

The Court decided that US interests overrode the confidentiality interests of the foreign state.

Similar to the US, UK courts have shown a high degree of deference to the confidentiality concerns of foreign states in civil proceedings. In *MacKinnon v Donaldson Lufkin & Jenrette Securities Corp.*, the London branch of a US bank was excused from producing documents held in its New York office.[197] The UK Court opined that it would be willing to grant a discovery order in situations where the suit concerned allegations of fraud.[198] The Court discussed the case of *London and County Securities v Caplan*, in which an English bank was ordered to procure documents relating to embezzlement charges from its foreign subsidiaries.[199] The Court suggested that the allegation of criminal fraud, coupled with the need for urgent relief to prevent the destruction of evidence and the fruits of the crime, constituted exceptional circumstances that could justify the imposition of discovery.

The procedural posture of the *Rio Tinto* case provides an interesting example of the differences between UK and US courts. In this case, the House of Lords addressed the issue of reverse privilege conflicts in international discovery proceedings, the admissibility in a state court of evidence obtained in a foreign state in violation of the state's laws.[200] In this case, the US Court issued letters rogatory to the English Court seeking confidential business information from an English corporation as well as from individuals. The requested information raised the issue of the privilege against self-incrimination. Under English law, both private individuals, and corporate bodies enjoy a right to refuse testimony if, because of such testimony, they would risk criminal prosecution and penalties.[201]

---

195 92 F.R.D. 111 (S.D.N.Y. 1981).

196 *Ibid.*, at 119.

197 [1986] 1 All E.R. 653.

198 *Ibid.*, at 661.

199 Cited *ibid., London and County Securities v Caplan* (26 May 1978, unreported).

200 Although the House of Lords declined the request by the US Court, the reason was because the action was directly linked to a criminal proceeding.

201 See Section 14(1) of the British Civil Evidence Act of 1968 in connection with Section 3(1)(b) of the Evidence (Proceedings in Other Jurisdictions) Act of 1975.

The comparable US privilege, based upon the Fifth Amendment of the Constitution, is limited to individuals, and does not apply to corporations.[202] The House of Lords ruled that since the claim was for a privilege under US law, its validity had to be determined as if it had been made in civil proceedings in the US.[203] The interesting aspect of the ruling was deference by the English Court to the US constitutional law even though the witnesses concerned were British subjects outside the US, and compliance with the evidentiary request was required exclusively in the UK. The US Court was faced with a similar situation and took the opposite approach in the *Societe Internationale pour Participations Industrielles et Commerciales, S.A. v Rogers* case.[204] Here, the plaintiff had asserted a Swiss banker-customer privilege, a privilege not available under US law. The court refused to grant the privilege, rejecting any suggestion that a foreign plaintiff could avail himself of rights not recognized under US laws.[205]

The second category of nondisclosure laws are blocking statutes enacted by states that create blanket protection for large categories of documents and vest relatively broad discretion over disclosure issues in government officials. These blocking statutes provide a strong deterrent to disclosure and, unlike the secrecy and confidentiality laws, represent the interests of the blocking state and not the interest of the individual parties. For instance, the British Protection of Trading Interests Act of 1980 (PTIA) gives the British government the power to block most types of discovery orders.[206] It authorizes the British Secretary of State to prohibit compliance with foreign court production orders that would infringe on either the sovereignty or the security of the UK.

Other types of blocking statute are more specific and an example is Canada's Uranium Information Security Regulations.[207] The law was passed with the intent of stifling US antitrust litigation concerning a worldwide uranium cartel. The law expressly forbade the production of any information relating to events that occurred over a specified period. Other Canadian statutes include the Ontario Business Records Protection Act,[208] Quebec Business Concerns Records Act,[209] and the Canadian Uranium Information Security Regulations.[210] The government

202 See *US v Morton Salt*, 338 U.S. 632, 652 (1950).

203 [1978] 1 All E.R. at 445.

204 357 U.S. 197 (1958).

205 *Ibid.*, at 443.

206 British Protection of Trading Interests Act (reprinted in [1982] in Vol. 21, *International Legal Materials* 834, at 839.

207 Prov. Can. Stat. 1976-2368, CAN. STAT. O. & REGS. 76-644 (21 Sept. 1976), *replaced by* Prov. Can. Stat. 1977-2923, CAN. STAT. O. & REGS. 77-836 (13 Oct. 1977), *in implementation of* Atomic Energy Control Act, 1970, sched. 9, CAN. REV. STAT. Chapter A-19.

208 Ont. Rev. Stat. Chapter 54 (1970).

209 Que. Rev. Stat. Chapter D-12 (1977).

210 Can. Consol. Regs. Vol. 3, ch. 366 (1978), promulgated under the Atomic Energy Control Act, § 9, Can. Rev. Stat. Chapter A-19 (1970).

of France has also enacted blocking statutes. The French legislation prohibits disclosure to a foreign entity of any information of an economic, commercial, industrial, financial, or technical nature that could impinge on French sovereignty and French economic or security interests.[211] Contravention of the law is subject to criminal sanctions including fines and imprisonment.

These blocking statutes often come into conflict with orders issued by a national court for the production of documents or witnesses located in the foreign state. The practice of states regarding balancing the conflict between discovery orders and intrusions on the sovereignty of foreign states differs considerably. Cases concerning the treatment of these blocking statutes in the UK and US illustrate the different approaches. In the US case of *Rogers* discussed previously, the government at the district court moved for an order requiring the plaintiff to produce documents in the possession of a Swiss banking company that the plaintiff controlled. The plaintiff failed to produce the documents, contending that disclosure of the requested bank records would violate the Swiss penal laws and might lead to the imposition of criminal sanctions. The district court dismissed the plaintiff's complaint and the court of appeals affirmed the dismissal.

The two questions for the Supreme Court were, first, whether the order to produce the documents was valid in view of the fact that compliance with the order would violate Swiss penal law. Second, whether the imposition of sanctions against the plaintiff for failure to comply was proper. The court held that the discovery order was validly issued even though compliance with the discovery by the plaintiff would violate Swiss penal law.[212] The reasoning of the court was that a broad preclusion of US courts from compelling the production documents based merely upon a plaintiff's fear of sanctions for violating a foreign law would undermine congressional policies.

Even within US courts, there is little consistency regarding the approach of the lower courts to the granting of discovery orders and the scope of deference permitted to foreign laws as the two cases discussed next illustrate. The first case concerned the conflicts between a US courts discovery order and the law of a foreign state. In the case of *In re Grand Jury Proceedings (US v Field)*, a grand jury was investigating possible tax law violations by the defendant.[213] Field, a Canadian citizen and director of a bank located in the Cayman Islands, was served with a subpoena ordering him to testify before the grand jury. Field refused, contending that such testimony would violate the Cayman Islands' bank secrecy laws. In ordering compliance with the discovery order, the court considered the

211 Law No. 80-538 of July 16, 1980, 1980 J.O. 1799.

212 Although the Supreme Court reversed the lower courts, the grounds for reversal did not concern the validity of the discovery order. The court reversed the discovery order primarily on the good-faith efforts of the petitioner to comply with the discovery order, suggesting that a finding that a party courted legal impediments would have a crucial bearing on the justification for the dismissal of an action.

213 532 F.2d 404 (5th Cir. 1976).

vital national interests of the states involved and found that the vital investigatory function of the grand jury was dependent upon its ability to obtain evidence. Furthermore, the court noted that in the US, investigatory bodies are given wide discretion in obtaining information concerning bank activities. Finally, the court noted that the Cayman law permitted disclosure of such information for domestic investigations, but not for international investigations.

In contrast, the court in the case of *US v First National Bank of Chicago* recognized the relevance of the foreign law with respect to US discovery rules.[214] The defendant challenged an Internal Revenue Service summons on the ground that compliance with the summons would subject the bank's employees in Greece, who were to provide the requested documents, to substantial criminal penalties under Greek law. The issue raised in the case was whether criminal law sanctions under Greek law were a bar to the US discovery proceedings. The Court recognized the relevance of the foreign law with respect to US discovery rules and held that the Greek Bank Secrecy Act prevailed over the Internal Revenue Service summons.[215] One possible explanation for the discrepancy between the two US cases may turn on the whether the parties against whom the discovery order is the party facing the sanctions or whether the sanctions will be imposed upon a third party. In *re Grand Jury Proceedings*, the party asserting the privilege was also the party under investigation.

The courts in the UK have refrained from compelling disclosure by companies operating in nations that otherwise reject the open exchange of commercial information, preferring to temper production on the likelihood of success in obtaining the information. In *Lonrho Ltd. v Shell Petroleum Co. Ltd.*, Shell failed to comply with a discovery request.[216] Shell claimed that it lacked control over the respective records, which were held by its subsidiaries in South Africa and that production of the documents would make them liable in local criminal proceedings for divulging confidential information. The court excused Shell's non-compliance, holding that the documents were not under its immediate control. This deference to local jurisdictional concerns espoused by the Lonrho court appears to be a recurring theme. In the case of *R v Grossman*, the Court of Appeal set aside an order for disclosure directed towards a British Bank operating in the Isle of Man.[217] The Court of Appeal deferred to the Isle of Man judiciary, upholding its refusal as a rightful exercise of sovereignty and noted the unfairness of compelling the defendants to open their records in support of a foreign proceeding.

Despite the seeming disparity in the UK and US approaches to the issue of foreign discovery, both approaches share the common objective of trying to facilitate transnational litigation through the equitable access to relevant information. The US approach seeks to foster cooperation by making its discovery

---

214 699 F.2d 341 (7th Cir. 1983).

215 *Ibid.,* at 346.

216 [1980] 1 W.L.R. 627 (H.L.).

217 [1981] 73 Cr.App.R. 302.

practices widely available. The British approach also seeks to foster cooperation by deferring to the sovereign interests of foreign states. Both states use a test that is supposed to take the various interests at stake and make a decision based on a balancing of those interests. The US courts employ a balancing test to determine the appropriateness of foreign discovery over conflicting foreign law. The UK has specifically rejected the balancing analysis employed by US courts as an impossible task that invariably results in prejudice to foreign litigants, preferring instead to focus on principles of comity and fairness to the litigants.

The methodical approach utilized by the US courts in resolving conflicts of US national interest and the interest of a foreign state is contained in the Restatement (Second) of the Foreign Relations Law. The restatement proposed a list of five factors that should be considered by courts.[218] This approach was utilized in the Second Circuit's decision in *US v First National City Bank*, where First National refused to comply with an order to produce documents located in West Germany issued by a grand jury.[219] The District Court found First National in contempt of the discovery order. This decision was affirmed by the Second Circuit in a decision that the Court asserted relied on the factors proposed by the restatement.

Despite the lip service paid to the factors enumerated by the court, the focus of the court was on the national interests' factor, giving little attention to the other restatement factors. Similarly, in the case of *Banca Della Svizzera*, the court's decision focused on the national interest of the US. In addition, the court determined that US interests overrode the confidentiality interests of the foreign state. The factors considered included the US interest set against that of the Swiss government, which had failed to express any opposition to the order. Other factors considered by the court included the flexibility of the Swiss law and the bad faith of BSI in courting legal impediments weighed in favour of granting the order.

The UK courts have specifically rejected the balancing analysis employed by US courts, preferring instead to focus on principles of comity and fairness to the litigants. This approach of using principles of comity and fairness was utilized in the case of *X AG v A Bank*.[220] The anonymous plaintiffs were non–UK oil corporations who had accounts with the London branch of the defendant, a US bank. The companies were under investigation in the US and refused to produce certain documents. A subpoena was issued to the bank's London branch requiring it to disclose records of the plaintiffs held at the bank's New York office. When the

218 The five factors listed by the testatement include: (i) the vital national interests of each of the states, (ii) the extent and nature of the hardship that inconsistent enforcement actions would impose upon the person, (iii) the extent to which the required conduct is to take place in the territory of the other state, (iv) the nationality of the person, and (v) the extent to which enforcement by action of either state can reasonably be expected to achieve compliance with the rule prescribed by that state. See Restatement (Second) of the Foreign Relations Law of the United States § 40 (1965).

219 396 F.2d 897 (2d Cir. 1968).

220 [1983] 2 All E.R. 464.

London branch expressed its intentions to comply with the subpoena, the plaintiffs obtained injunctions against discovery on grounds that disclosure would severely impair their business. The court, upholding the injunctions, employed a balance of convenience to determine which alternative would entail less harm to all parties. The court balanced the hardship disclosure would have on the plaintiffs against the impediment an injunction would impose on the jurisdiction of the New York court. The court reasoned that the balance of convenience weighed heavily in favour of the plaintiffs, and the injunctions were continued. The court furthermore reasoned that discontinuing the injunctions would foster the enforcement of a penal proceeding in the US. Such courtesy would contradict the international law principle that prohibits enforcement by one nation of another state's penal laws.

State courts are often confronted with legal and practical difficulties in their attempts to obtain evidence, whether written or oral, from foreign litigants or non-party witnesses. Discovery orders of states courts relating to testimonial or documentary evidence situated in foreign states have generated legal and political controversy, not only in the area of private suits but also in the field of agency and grand jury investigations. These potential for competition and conflict have important implications for the successful regulation of transnational bribery. Unfortunately, neither the US or UK courts have developed a methodical approach that addresses the potential for competition and conflict in the exercise of discovery orders.

For instance, comparing the discovery practices of the US and UK suggests that the underlying policy goals, to foster cooperation, are similar. The US approach seeks to foster cooperation by making its discovery practices widely available. The UK approach also seeks to foster cooperation by deferring to the sovereign interests of foreign states. Both systems, however, offer distinct sets of rules governing the role of the court in granting access to the information. The US approach, however, does not effectively reconcile the judicial need for information with the sovereign interests of the foreign states implicated and is therefore unlikely to foster an atmosphere of cooperation. Likewise, the UK approach of plain deference to the foreign jurisdiction, on the other hand, neglects the vital role transnational discovery plays in the attempts to curb transnational bribery and is thus likely to hamper international cooperation efforts to regulate transnational bribery.

Conclusion

This chapter, building on the argument in the preceding Chapter 4 that the vociferous exchanges over the use of multilateral initiatives in the regulation of transnational bribery have produced a polarized set of alternatives that fail to capture the essence much less the complexity of the problem, examined some of the challenges posed by the problem of transnational bribery to the multilateral efforts to curb the practice. Using the OFFP as a case study, the chapter examined the payment transactions under the OFFP and found very little consistency with respect to the characterization of the payments among states that had implemented the OECD Convention. The analysis indicated that the payments would be classified as transnational bribery transactions under the OECD Convention.

Nonetheless, under the implementing legislation of the various signatories to the OECD Convention, the characterisation of the payments was less clear. Particularly, several states utilised the word 'corruptly' in their implementation legislation, importing a moral dimension into the element of the offence of transnational bribery. In some states, the implementing legislation imposed a requirement that utilized the phrase 'law' or 'lawful purpose' without clarity on whether the phrase refers to the law of the state or that of the state where the public official was bribed. The analysis in this chapter also indicated similar issues of clarity with respect to whether the affirmative defence if the payments are permitted or required by the written law of the foreign public official's country.

In most countries, the point of reference for determining whether the payments were permitted would be the law of the public official's country. However, the states implementing the OECD Convention differed with respect to whether there was also a requirement that the laws were written, with some countries broadening this requirement to include all laws, regardless of whether they were written or not. One country broadened this to the extent that the defence would be available if the party making the payment was informed by a source with a sufficient degree of authority that the payment was required or permitted. Another country would permit the defence if the party paying could establish that he would have suffered a disadvantage if the payment was not made.

Given the reliance in some countries on foreign law for the establishment of the affirmative defence, this chapter examined judicial interpretation of the validity of foreign law by the US and UK courts. As a general principle, both the US and UK courts would not challenge the validity of a foreign law. Both jurisdictions would adjudicate disputes that concern the acts of a foreign official, but are precluded from questioning the legality of the actions of a foreign official. Although, the general principle survives, the operation of the principle has been weakened by the tendency of courts in both jurisdictions to examine the acts of the foreign official to determine whether it constitutes a sovereign act. In the UK, the courts will go further and examine the motivations of the sovereign state. In both jurisdictions, a determination that the acts are the valid actions of a sovereign does not oblige them to enforce the act.

Although UK courts have been reluctant to encroach on what they deem to be the province of a foreign state when the foreign law contradicts either UK law or public policy, the courts have shown less reluctance when the claim is that the law violates international law. In the US, the role of international law in determining the validity of the act of a sovereign within the territory of the state is similarly ambiguous. Some courts have held that US courts are not obliged to apply the law of a foreign state when the act violates international law. The decisions in both jurisdictions indicate some restraint on the exercise of jurisdiction out of deference for the interests of other states. The parameters of such restraint are not sufficiently well established, and the task of determining the level of deference falls to the individual discretion of each state, leaving room for conflict among states.

Another area particularly prone to conflict and significantly implicated by the issue of transnational bribery relates to the exercise of jurisdiction by states. Most of the state signatories to the OECD Convention assert both territorial and nationality jurisdiction over the bribery of foreign public officials. Some of the signatories, in recognition of the fact that transnational bribery may have very little connection with a state that seeks to prosecute, have led some states to adopt jurisdiction rules that permit them to exercise jurisdiction under the effects principle.

Despite the potentially expansive nature of effects jurisdiction and corresponding scope for conflict between states, the jurisdictional provisions of the three multilateral conventions do not address the issue of effects jurisdiction and therefore do not provide any guidance for state parties or specify which state party's interests should predominate in the event of a conflict. In practice, therefore, each state party's application of effects jurisdiction with respect to transnational bribery could lead to conflict among the states' parties as to whose jurisdictional limits should apply.

Similar to the conflicts associated with the exercise of jurisdiction, the chapter examined the difficulties associated with the gathering of evidence for litigation of transnational bribery, another area of potential conflict between states. In recognition of the potential for conflict, the multilateral initiatives on corruption establish a broad framework to mediate international cooperation between state signatories with respect to the gathering of evidence. Notwithstanding, there are many areas concerning the gathering of evidence in a foreign state that still remain controversial, particularly the differing views on the scope and exercise of discovery orders. The lack of sufficiently well-established rules of customary international law and the differing views held by states on the permissible scope of discovery orders leaves significant potential for conflicts between states.

Chapter 6
Limits of National Regulation: Liability Regime for Corporations

Having examined some of the difficulties associated with multilateral efforts to regulate transnational bribery and several of the challenges that an effective multilateral framework would have to surmount, this chapter focuses on one area that is yet to be a significant focus of the current multilateral efforts: the liability of corporations for transnational bribery. The importance of the liability of corporations in enforcing the transnational bribery prohibitions is recognized by two of the three multilateral instruments discussed in Chapter 4. Article 2 of the OECD Convention requires signatories to establish, in accordance with its legal principles, the responsibility of legal persons for the bribery of foreign officials.[1]

Similarly, Article 26(1) of the UNCAC mandates state parties to adopt measures, as necessary, to establish liability of legal persons for all the offences established in the convention. The two conventions provide for instances where a state does not recognize criminal liability of corporations. Article 3(2) of the OECD Convention, dealing with sanctions, provides that in circumstances where criminal responsibility is not applicable to legal persons, signatories should ensure that legal persons are subject to effective, proportionate, and dissuasive non-criminal sanctions. The UNCAC in Article 26(4) also requires states to ensure that legal persons held liable are subject to effective, proportionate, and dissuasive criminal or non-criminal sanctions.

In general, most states have made laudable efforts to ensure that their national implementing legislation satisfy the requirements of the multilateral agreements regarding the liability of legal persons. The level of compliance with the requirement that states provide liability for legal persons is high. Most of the states that are signatory to the OECD Convention have provided for either criminal or civil liability for legal persons.[2] In spite of the high level of compliance and convergence on the liability of legal persons in states, substantial differences still

---

1 The Commentary to the Convention provides an opt-out clause, which suggests that if criminal responsibility is not applicable, signatories are not required to establish such criminal responsibility.

2 2007 Compilation of the Recommendations Made in the Phase 2 Report by The Committee on International Investment and Multinational Enterprises: Implementation of the Convention on Combating Bribery of Foreign Public Officials in International Business Transactions and the 1997 Recommendation. Available at the OECD website at http://www.oecd.org/dataoecd/51/45/37171905.pdf. Last visited 23 October 2007.

exist in the levels of effectiveness of the liability regime of legal persons, due in part to the varying levels of enforcement.

One of the primary legal issues that limit the efficacy of prohibitions against transnational bribery is the threshold question of the type of liability regime for criminal conduct by corporations. Where the legal system does recognize the imposition of criminal liability on corporations, the debate often focuses on the potential benefits of prosecuting corporations as opposed to individuals.[3] Other questions debated in academic circles include the means and circumstances required to impute the actions of the agent to the corporation.[4] After the determination that the actions of the agent are those of the corporation the focus often turns to whether or not the parent corporation should be held liable for the actions of the subsidiary.

Quite often, the yardstick of the liability of the parent for the actions of the subsidiary is the involvement of the parent in the affairs of the subsidiary. Here, the courts look beyond the formal separateness to disregard the rule of limited liability commonly referred to as 'piercing or lifting the veil' or 'disregarding the entity'. A prime consideration in decision to pierce the veil concerns whether the corporations are sufficiently affiliated with one another that the veil of limited liability would be lost. Determining whether a corporation controls another is easy when a parent owns all of the stock of a subsidiary, but is more complicated where the parent corporation owns a fraction of the stock.

In the forgoing analysis, the focus will be on two particular characteristics of the modern transnational corporation that present significant challenges to the efforts to impose liability on corporations for engaging in transnational bribery. These challenges include the size and complex structures of transnational corporations. Two important artefacts of the legal system exacerbate these challenges. The first artefact is the separate personality of the corporation and the second is limited liability combined with the ability of one corporation to hold the shares of another corporation. These two artefacts of the corporation are very well-settled principles in most jurisdictions. The first section examines the liability framework for corporations by examining two features of the corporation, limited liability and a separate personality, followed by the development of criminal liability and alternatives to criminal liability for corporations. The second and third sections examine group and structural complexity, two features of transnational corporations that particularly challenge efforts to impose liability on transnational corporations. The fourth section locates shortcomings in an effective liability framework on the prevailing legal conception of the corporation.

3 See Khanna [2000].

4 For a discussion on the imputation of criminal liability see Lederman, E [2000]: 'Models for Imposing Corporate Criminal Liability: From Adaptation and Imitation Toward Aggregation and the Search for Self-Identity', in Vol. 4, *Buffalo Criminal Law Review*, 641.

The Liability Regime for Corporations

Corporate Personality and Limited Liability

An important feature of the early corporation, still prominent in corporate law jurisprudence, is the concept of the separate legal personality of the corporation.[5] Prior to the advent of general incorporation statutes, when each corporation was chartered by a special act of the legislature, the corporation was viewed as an artificial person.[6] In the US, the characterisation of the corporation as an artificial person is illustrated by Chief Justice Marshall in the *Dartmouth College* case where he stated that a 'corporation is an artificial being, invisible, intangible, and existing only in contemplation of law'.[7] In the UK, the *Salomon* case entrenched the separate legal personality of the corporation. In this case, Lord Macnaghten stated that:

> The company is at law a different person altogether from the subscribers to the Memorandum ... the company is not in law the agent of the subscribers or trustee for them.[8]

The statement maintains that the corporation has a legal personality distinct from its shareholders. The implications of a distinct legal personality include the right to perpetual succession, ownership of property, capacity to sue or be sued, and the obligation to comply with the formalities of incorporation.

The concept of the separate personality of the corporation has been buttressed by the political concept of limited liability.[9] Limited liability was introduced in the UK in 1855 as an increasing number of English corporations were seeking incorporation in France and the US to achieve limited liability.[10] The House of Lords, in *Salomon* entrenched the limited liability for corporations in England. In the US, different states pursued different strategies with respect to limited liability. For instance, in Delaware, prior to 1967, the law left it to the certificate of incorporation to determine whether liability would be limited.[11] It was not until

5 See Micklethwait, J & Wooldridge, A [2003]: *The Company: A Short History of a Revolutionary Idea* (London: Weidenfeld & Nicolson), at 55–78 for a description of the history of the corporate form.

6 Blumberg [1990: 292].

7 *Trustees of Dartmouth College v. Woodward*, 17 U.S. (4 Wheat.) 518, (1810) at 636.

8 *Salomon v Salomon & Co.* [1897] A.C. 22 at 51.

9 Blumberg states that the jurisprudential doctrine of the separate corporate personality has been strongly buttressed by the political concept of limited liability. See Blumberg, P [2001]: 'Accountability of Multinational Corporations: The Barriers Presented by Concepts of the Corporate Juridical Entity', in Vol. 24, *Hastings International and Comparative Law Review*, 297, at 297.

10 The Limited Liability Act, 1855 (18 & 19 Vict. c. 133).

11 Act of 10 Mar. 1899, ch. 273, 26, 21 Del. Laws 444.

1967 that statute established limited liability as the default rule.[12] For the French legislature by contrast, limited liability was an essential feature of the corporation as limited liability was recognized with the first codification in 1807.[13] Germany followed France in establishing limited liability in 1861.[14]

Although there is a tendency to equate the two concepts, legal personality and limited liability are distinguishable from one another. A corporation may be a separate person but its shareholders may still have unlimited liability for its debts. Limited liability, on the other hand, means that shareholders are under no obligation other than to the extent of the par value of their shares. The twin concepts of the separate legal personality and limited liability of the corporation form the cornerstone of the law's liability regime for corporations. The view of the court regarding limited liability has a significant impact on the court's imposition of liability on the corporation for transnational bribery. The legal personality of the corporation, on the other hand, determines whom within the corporation and under what circumstances the courts will impose liability on the corporation for transnational bribery.[15]

Corporate Criminal Liability

The criminal liability of corporations featured prominently in the early theoretical arguments over the nature of the personality of the corporation.[16] The UK, prior to the nineteenth century, did not recognize criminal liability for corporations.[17] Criminal liability was imposed on the individual acting on behalf of the corporation

---

12 See 56 Del. Laws 50, 102(6), (1967).

13 Code de Commerce, Art. 33.

14 Pistor, K, Keinan, Y, Kleinheisterkamp, J & West, M [2002]: 'The Evolution of Corporate Law: A Cross-Country Comparison', in Vol. 23, *University of Philadelphia Journal of International Economic Law*, 791, at 801.

15 Pollman, E [2011]: 'Reconceiving Corporate Personhood', in Vol. 2011, *Utah Law Review*, 1629, at 1631–9, traces historical and theoretical developments in the corporation and corporate personhood jurisprudence to show that the roots of the doctrine are based in concerns about the property and contract interests of shareholders.

16 Both Laski and Deiser extensively debated this issue. See Laski, H [1916a]: 'The Personality of Associations', in Vol. 29, *Harvard Law Review*, 404; and Deiser, G [1909]: 'The Juristic Person', in Vol. 57, *University of Pennsylvania Law Review*, 300. See Ohlin, J [2005]: 'Is the Concept of a Person Necessary for Human Rights?,' in Vol. 105, *Columbia Law Review*, 209, at 227, who notes the push for domestic and international criminal liability for corporations.

17 For a general discussion on the development of English corporate criminal liability, see Leigh, L [1969]: *The Criminal Liability of Corporations in English Law* (London: Weidenfeld & Nicholson), at 1–12. Also see Nanda, V [2010]: 'Corporate Criminal Liability in the United States: Is a New Approach Warranted?', in Vol. 58, *American Journal of Comparative Law*, 605, at 608–10, where he traces the origin of Corporate Criminal Liability in the United States, and studies its development over the centuries.

and not on the corporation itself. The situation was similar in continental Europe. The French legal system had rejected corporate criminal liability on the basis that criminal liability was personal rather than vicarious.[18] At the turn of the nineteenth century, courts in the UK changed their position and started to hold corporations liable for the actions of its officers and agents.[19] There were significant theoretical obstacles in the legal system that constrained the imposition of criminal liability on corporations.[20] These included the difficulty of attributing acts and moral blameworthiness to juristic persons, the doctrine of *ultra vires*, and the satisfaction of the requirement of physically bringing the accused corporation to court. These obstacles stifled the imposition of criminal liability on corporations.[21]

In view of the theoretical difficulties in attributing acts to corporations, the early examples of courts imposing criminal liability on corporations in UK and the US involved nonfeasance by public corporations.[22] The courts reasoned that corporations could not commit positive acts, but could, however, fail to act.[23] Sometime in the early nineteenth century, criminal liability was then extended from public corporations to commercial corporations for nonfeasance.[24]

The distinction between positive acts and omissions was abandoned in the middle of the nineteenth century as one of form rather than substance.[25] In the UK, this was accomplished through a ruling in 1846 that corporations could be criminally liable for misfeasance.[26] Holding corporations liable for misfeasance was also adopted in the US with the ruling in two mid-nineteenth century cases.[27]

---

18 Coffee, J [1998]: 'Corporate Criminal Liability: An Introduction and Comparative Survey', in Albin Eser et al., eds, [1998]: Criminal Responsibility of Legal and Collective Entities, Entities – International Colloquium Berlin, 4–6 May 1998. Available at http://www.iuscrim.mpg.de/verlag/online/Band_S78/8-SUBJN-3a.pdf, 9 at 23. Last visited 6 February 2006.

19 See Leigh, L [1982]: 'The Criminal Liability of Corporations and Other Groups: A Comparative View', in Vol. 80, *Michigan Law Review*, 1508, at 1510–11.

20 See Khanna, V [1996: 1479–80].

21 See Robson, R [2010]: 'Crime and Punishment: Rehabilitating Retribution as a Justification for Organizational Criminal Liability', in Vol. 47, *American Business Law Journal*, 115, where she discusses the impediments to holding a corporation criminally liable.

22 See Leigh [1969: 16–18].

23 See Silets, H & Brenner, S [1986]: 'The Demise of Rehabilitation: Sentencing Reform and the Sanctioning of Organizational Criminality', in Vol. 13, *American Journal of Criminal Law*, 329, at 339.

24 See Elkins, J [1976]: 'Corporations and the Criminal Law: An Uneasy Alliance', in Vol. 65, *Kentucky Law Journal*, 73, at 93–5.

25 See Bernard, T [1984]: 'The Historical Development of Corporate Criminal Liability', in Vol. 22, *Criminology*, 3, at 8.

26 *Queen v Great North of England Railway Co.* [1846] 115 E.R. 1294 (Q.B.), at 1298.

27 *Commonwealth v Proprietors of New Bedford Bridge*, 68 Mass. (2 Gray) 339 (1854), and *State v Morris & Essex Railroad Co.*, 23 N.J.L. 360 (1852).

Despite the progress in holding corporations liable for criminal actions, the view persisted that corporations could not be liable for offences requiring intent. This barrier was dismantled in the US through the legal fiction of imputing the motives and intent of the agents or officers of the corporation to the corporation.[28] In the 1909 case of *New York Central & Hudson River Railroad v US*, the Court held that an agent's culpable mental state could be imputed or attributed directly to the corporation.[29] Specific intent crimes remain the last vestige to the imposition of criminal liability on corporations.[30] The imputation of specific intent crimes to corporations is still not widely accepted, although some jurisdictions have recognized that specific intent can be imputed from an individual to a corporation.[31]

In continental Europe, there has been some progress in holding corporations liable for criminal actions.[32] This progress has been made despite the widespread reluctance to impose criminal liability on corporations.[33] For instance, the French Nouveau Penal Code, adopted in 1992, significantly departed from the earlier position that offered a limited scope for the imposition of criminal liability on corporations.[34] Under Article 121-2 of the code, corporations may be held liable for criminal offences.[35] These provisions, however, do not entrench criminal liability for corporations in the legal system. The code provides that corporations are liable only when the particular provision that has been breached explicitly declares that

28 See Ramasastry, A [2002]: 'Corporate Complicity: From Nuremberg to Rangoon: An Examination of Forced Labor Cases and Their Impact on the Liability of Multinational Corporations', in Vol. 20, *Berkeley Journal of International Law*, 91, at 152, for an account of how the issue was resolved by imputing the acts of a natural person to a corporation through vicarious liability.

29 212 U.S. 481 (1909), at 493. See also *US v Illinois Cent. R.R.*, 303 U.S. 239 (1938).

30 See Brickey, K [1984]: *Corporate Criminal Liability: A Treatise on the Criminal Liability of Corporations, Their Officers and Agents* (Deerfield: Clark Boardman Callaghan), at 36.

31 Examples include the case of *Granite Constr. Co. v Superior Court,* 149 Cal. App. 3d 465, at 471–3, 197 Cal. Rptr. 3, at 7–9 (1983). This case notes that corporations have been prosecuted for specific intent crimes and held that a corporation could be prosecuted for manslaughter.

32 See Coffee, J [1994]: 'Emerging Issues in Corporate Criminal Policy', Foreword to Gruner, R [1994]: *Corporate Crime and Sentencing* (Charlottesville: Michie Co.), at xix–xxi for an in-depth discussion on Europe's move toward more expansive corporate criminal liability. For a comparative analysis of developments in common law and civil law jurisdictions, see Wells, C [2001]: 'Corporate Law: Corporate Criminal Liability – Developments in Europe and Beyond'. in Vol. 39, *Law Society Journal*, 62.

33 See Beale, B & Safwat, A [2004]: 'What Developments in Western Europe Tell Us About American Critiques of Corporate Criminal Liability', in Vol. 8, *Buffalo Criminal Law Review*, 89, at 107–16 for a discussion of the adoption of corporate criminal liability by European countries.

34 France amended its code to make corporate criminal liability more easily available. See Coffee, J [1994: i].

35 Art. 121–2 C. Pr. Pen. (1992) [French Penal Code].

the law applies to corporations. Another restriction is that Article 121–2 makes it mandatory that the employee or agent of the corporation is explicitly acting on behalf of the corporation. Similar to the French system, German policy towards corporate liability is very restrictive compared with that of other European nations. Under German law, corporations are not criminally liable for acts of their agents.[36]

Recent discussions in the UK around corporate criminal liability have centred on the liability of corporations for manslaughter. In 1996, the UK Law Commission published proposals for reforming the law on involuntary manslaughter and the institution of a new offence of corporate killing.[37] The UK government took no action until a 1999 reference by the Attorney General to the Court of Appeal regarding whether a non-human defendant could be convicted of manslaughter by gross negligence in the absence of evidence establishing the guilt of a known individual.[38] The Court of Appeal held that the 'identification' model in *Tesco v Nattrass* still served as the basis for corporate criminal liability. Shortly after the Court of Appeal ruling, in May 2000, the UK government issued a consultation paper based on the law commission's recommendations.[39]

Following the consultation, the UK government on 23 March 2005 published a draft Corporate Manslaughter Bill.[40] The proposals by the law commission, the consultations, and the draft bill culminated in the enactment of the Corporate Manslaughter Act, which came into force on 6 April 2008.[41] The Corporate Manslaughter Act abolishes the common law offence of manslaughter by gross negligence as it applies to corporations and institutes a statutory regime for corporate criminal liability in relation to manslaughter by gross negligence.[42]

---

36 For a discussion of corporate criminal liability in Germany, see Hefendehl, R [2000]: 'Corporate Criminal Liability: Model Penal Code Section 2.07 and the Development in Western Legal Systems', in Vol. 4, *Buffalo Criminal Law Review*, 283, at 286.

37 England and Wales Law Commission, 'Legislating the Criminal Code: Involuntary Manslaughter (1996)'. Available at http://lawcommission.justice.gov.uk/docs/lc237_Legislating_the_Criminal_Code_Involuntary_Manslaughter.pdf. Last visited 5 March 2013. For a discussion of the law commission's proposed offence of corporate killing, see Clough, J & and Mulhern, C [2002]: *The Prosecution of Corporations* (Melbourne: Oxford University Press), at 181–2.

38 Attorney-General's Reference (No 2 of 1999) [2000] 3 All E.R. 182.

39 Home Office Consultation Paper [2000] 'Reforming the Law on Involuntary Manslaughter'. Available at http://webarchive.nationalarchives.gov.uk/20100418065544/http://www.homeoffice.gov.uk/documents/cons-2000-invol-manslaughter/consultation-paper2835.pdf?view=Binary. Last visited 5 March 2013.

40 Home Office, Corporate Manslaughter: The Government's Draft Bill for Reform, Cm 6497, March 2005. Available at http://www.parliament.uk/documents/upload/draftbillcorporateman.pdf. Last visited 5 March 2013.

41 Corporate Manslaughter and Corporate Homicide Act 2007 (UK).

42 See Todarello, V [2002]: 'Corporations Don't Kill People – People Do: Exploring the Goals of the United Kingdom's Corporate Homicide Bill', in Vol. 46, *New York Law School Law Review*, 851, at 856–9 for a critique of the proposed framework for corporate manslaughter in the UK.

Individual and Civil Liability as Alternatives to Corporate Criminal Liability

The trend over the last 25 years by European countries has been towards the imposition of criminal liability on corporations. In the US, despite the long-standing imposition of criminal liability on the corporation, the focus appears to be shifting towards the imposition of individual responsibility on corporate officers in addition to the corporation.

Some of the arguments for the imposition of criminal liability on the corporation focus on the expressive function of criminal law, and reason that criminal sanctions are necessary to respond to corporate wrongdoing.[43] Similarly, a social meaning analysis emphasizes that criminal law expresses society's condemnation of prohibited activities.[44] In response to arguments that civil law penalties are just as effective, proponents of criminal liability for corporations have argued that replacing corporate criminal liability with civil liability conveys the message that the right to engage in prohibited activities can be purchased. Criminal liability for corporations also has pragmatic advantages. The imposition of criminal liability on corporations makes available the comprehensive network of law enforcement officers and state prosecutors, a network unavailable to private litigants in civil actions.[45] Another pragmatic advantage of the imposition of criminal liability on corporations is the availability of procedural tools, such as the use of investigative grand juries and the power to compel witness testimonies.

The major argument advanced for criminal liability, though, is preventive and concerns the deterrence effect of criminal sanctions on corporations. The premise of this argument is that criminal sanctions aimed at the corporation will deter misconduct by corporate officers and will prompt corporations to undertake internal disciplinary measures aimed at avoiding liability. The use of criminal sanctions would augment the limited ability of the state to investigate and enforce misconduct by forcing corporations to expend resources on deterring misconduct by corporate employees.[46] Also suggested is the probability that the employer will

---

43 See Friedman, L [2000]: 'In Defense of Corporate Criminal Liability', in Vol. 23, *Harvard Journal of Law and Public Policy*, 833, at 858 for a classic exposition of this argument. This argument is countered by Khanna, who suggests that expressive considerations can be furthered by other, less socially costly, forms of liability. See Khanna, V [2003b]: 'Should the Behavior of Top Management Matter?', in Vol. 91, *Georgetown Law Journal*, 1215 at 1218.

44 Kahan, D [1998]: 'Social Meaning and the Economic Analysis of Crime', in Vol. 27, *Journal of Legal Studies*, 609, at 617.

45 Coffee, J [1981]: '"No Soul to Damn: No Body to Kick": An Unscandalized Inquiry into the Problem of Corporate Punishment', in Vol. 79, *Michigan Law Review*, 386, at 447.

46 See Fisse, B [1981]: 'The Social Policy of Corporate Criminal Responsibility', in Vol. 6, *Adelaide Law Review*, 361, at 371, 382, and 384.

have more direct influence over the conduct of the employee.[47] These internal rules are better equipped to train, supervise, and discipline corporate officers; and inculcate law-abiding norms in the individual, ensuring that the state efficiently achieves the more general preventive effects of habitual individual compliance with legal norms.[48]

The imposition of criminal liability on the corporation serves as additional punishment because of the stigma attached to criminal liability.[49] Criminal stigma can result in an adverse public image, which can affect sales volumes, recruiting, the prestige enjoyed by its corporate officers and employees, and its capacity to raise capital in equity markets. Indeed, the threat of negative publicity may carry more deterrent force than the threat of fines as presently applied. Other justifications for criminal liability for corporations relate to the compensatory and restitution functions of criminal liability.[50] Corporations engaging in bribe transactions provide a typical example of this particular justification for the imposition of criminal liability. The payment of a bribe by a corporation enriches the corporation without resulting in losses that are recoverable by private parties. Although it is possible to create a private right of recovery, a potential limitation is determining who can bring these suits and to whom the recovery belongs in a successful action. Imposing criminal liability on corporations sends a consistent message regarding the tolerance of bribery and may serve to bolster the legitimacy of the legal system.

There are at least two alternatives to the imposition of criminal liability on corporations. The first alternative questions whether the corporation is the appropriate unit for the imposition of liability and proposes that the liability regime focuses on the individual.[51] These arguments for individual liability suggest that the traditional forms and functions of criminal law should not be applied to juridical

---

47 See Stone, C [1980]: 'The Place of Enterprise Liability in the Control of Corporate Conduct', in Vol. 90, *Yale Law Journal*. 1, at 29. He argues that the employer and employment environment have stronger and more immediate influence over the conduct of the employee than the State.

48 See Fisse, B [1981: 396].

49 See Hamdani, A & Klement, A [2008]: 'Corporate Crime and Deterrence', in Vol. 61, *Stanford Law Review*, 271, at 278, where they note that a conviction could have fatal consequences for business entities even when the criminal trial ends with a modest penalty because of a variety of laws and regulations that exclude firms convicted of crimes from participating in certain activities.

50 For instance, see Jacobson, K [2005]: 'Doing Business with the Devil: The Challenges of Prosecuting Corporate Officials Whose Business Transactions Facilitate War Crimes and Crimes Against Humanity', in Vol. 56, *Air Force Law Review*, 167, at 214, suggesting that recognition of corporate criminal and civil liability has allowed victims of human rights abuses to better vindicate their rights.

51 See Lederman, E [1985]: 'Criminal Law, Perpetrator and Corporation: Rethinking a Complex Triangle', in Vol. 76, *Journal of Criminal Law and Criminology*, 285, at 295–324.

persons because they cannot meaningfully be deemed guilty of a criminal offence.[52] Imposing criminal liability on a corporate entity requires resorting to the principles of respondeat superior, rather than individual responsibility, which is the hallmark of criminal law. Accordingly, using the criminal justice system to convict or punish a corporation is undesirable because it obscures the moral content of criminal liability.[53] This critique is consistent with a retributive or desert-based view of the function of criminal law, which imposes punishment based on the offender's moral blameworthiness in order to respond to the wrong manifest in criminal conduct.

The imposition of liability on the individual, rather than the corporation, has also been justified on the basis that imposing liability on the corporation is not consistent with the traditional notion of guilt in criminal law notion of guilt.[54] The shareholders, who ultimately bear the brunt of criminal sanctions against the corporation, are not responsible for the actions of the corporate officers who may be the guilty persons under traditional notions of the criminal law. More so, focusing criminal liability on responsible individuals within the corporation provides better deterrence without unfairly stigmatising the firm or its innocent officers and employees.[55] In this view, the prospect of individual liability for the corporate officers is a much more powerful deterrent than the imposition of financial penalties, which they are likely to treat as nothing more than a cost of doing business. Further, corporate officers are likely to be more sensitive to the stigma associated with a criminal conviction.[56] The imposition of personal liability on corporate officers serves other deterrence functions, such as reinforcing the

52 See, for instance, Fischel, D & Sykes, A [1996]: 'Corporate Crime', in Vol. 25, *Journal of Legal Studies*, 319, at 320, where they state that the corporation is a legal fiction, and legal fictions cannot commit criminal acts. Nor can they possess *mens rea*, a guilty state of mind. A similar argument is made by Khanna when he advocates that corporate criminal liability should be based upon negligence or strict liability because of the incoherence of the concept of corporate *mens rea*. See Khanna, V [1999]: 'Is the Notion of Corporate Fault a Faulty Notion? The Case of Corporate Mens Rea', in Vol. 79, *Boston University Law Review*, 355, at 356.

53 Robinson has made a similar argument suggesting that extending criminal liability to corporation's risks obscuring the moral content of criminal liability. See Robinson, P [2003]: 'The Practice of Restorative Justice: The Virtues of Restorative Process, the Vices of Restorative Justice', in Vol. 2003, *Utah Law Review*, 375, at 384–5.

54 See Mueller, G [1957]: 'Mens Rea and the Corporation – A study of the Model Penal Code on Corporate Criminal Liability', in Vol. 19, *University of Pittsburgh Law Review*, 21, at 28. He argued that punishing body corporate with a fine while possibly acquitting truly responsible individual defendant bears no semblance to principles of penal law.

55 Coffee, J [1980]: 'Making the Punishment Fit the Corporation: The Problems of Finding on Optimal Corporation Criminal Sanction', in Vol. 1, *Northern Illinois University Law Review*, 3, at 25. He suggests that punishing responsible individuals focuses stigma of criminal conviction more on culpable individuals within the corporation and less on the corporation itself.

56 Elkins [1976: 77–8] makes this argument.

notion of personal liability in the organisational context by providing a basis for corporate officers to resist pressures from superiors to engage in wrongful conduct. The imposition of criminal liability on the corporate officers also serves as a sanction on the corporation because the conviction and incarceration of the corporate officers causes the corporation to lose a valuable resource.

The second alternative to corporate criminal liability proposes that the imposition of liability on the corporation should be civil rather than criminal.[57] One argument advanced for substituting criminal liability with civil liability is that civil liability is a more efficient response. In this view, the potency of criminal sanctions over-deters corporations, inducing enterprises to spend more resources on monitoring and compliance than is socially useful.[58] Civil sanctions can be more precisely calibrated, and hence more efficient at matching the costs of compliance with the expected social benefit.

The second argument for the use of civil liability suggests that very little difference exists between civil and criminal liability in terms of consequences to the corporation. Since the corporation cannot be imprisoned, the effect of both types of liability is the imposition of monetary penalties, thus raising the question of whether the use of the criminal process can be justified.[59] Nonetheless, there are at least two differences that do exist between criminal and civil sanctions. First, the stigma or reputational penalty imposed by criminal liability; and second, the availability of procedural safeguards afforded by the criminal law to protect the defendant.[60] These differences can be marshalled as arguments either in support or against the use of criminal liability.

Although the scholarship generally treats the existence of this reputational effect as a given, there has been surprisingly little effort to empirically establish its existence.[61] Assuming the existence of these reputational effects, a variety of concerns about their influence and effect on corporations are discernible. A corporation may suffer unjustifiable reputational harm if convicted of a relatively minor criminal offence. On the other hand, in instances of particularly egregious conduct when reputational harm is warranted, the stigma of criminal liability is

---

57 See Coffee [1981: 388–434] for a detailed argument. Also see Fisse, B [1993]: 'Reconstructing Corporate Law: Deterrence, Retribution, Fault, and Sanctions', in Vol. 56, *Southern California Law Review*, 1141, at 1244.

58 See Fischel & Sykes [1996: 320–21].

59 Although Khanna has noted that the use of the criminal process may be justified in instances where sanctions are high and legal standards uncertain because of the greater procedural protections afforded by the criminal process. See Khanna [1996: 1512–20].

60 See Rosen-Zvi, I & Fisher, T [2008]: 'Overcoming Procedural Boundaries', in Vol. 94, *Virginia Law Review*, 79, where they contrast the procedural protections inherent in criminal prosecutions to those in civil cases brought against large corporations.

61 One study found no effect on share prices of news reports of civil charges and settlements of fraud charges compared with reports of criminal charges. See Block, M [1991]: 'Optimal Penalties, Criminal Law and the Control of Corporate Behavior', in Vol. 71, *Boston University Law Review*, 395, at 413–15.

superfluous and adds very little in terms of extra sanctions on the corporation. Furthermore, the stigma attached to the imposition of criminal liability on the corporation is only effective with corporations that have a good reputation and completely irrelevant to those corporations that already have a bad reputation. Another concern is that reputational harm attaches, regardless of guilt, immediately the criminal charges are filed and may create pressure on an otherwise innocent corporation to plead guilty to reduce the impact of the publicity that accompanies criminal proceedings. This effectively serves to impose a penalty on the corporation without due procedural safeguards.

A more recent justification for civil liability for corporations has suggested that imposing criminal sanctions on a corporation is actually the least costly penalty from the corporation's point of view, raising the concern that criminal liability may under-deter corporate misconduct.[62] This is based on the observation that corporate interests have opposed the expansion of corporate criminal liability less vigorously than enhanced civil liability for corporate entities or criminal liability for corporate officers and agents.[63] The view concludes that the muted response of corporations to the imposition of criminal liability suggests that corporations view criminal penalties as less problematic than other sanctions, and corporate criminal liability may be enacted as a substitute for more effective laws.

Whilst disagreeing with the conclusion in this view, the observation is nonetheless relevant to understanding the effectiveness of the criminal liability regime for corporations. The explanation proposed in this book suggests that the muted response of corporate officers to the imposition of criminal liability is reflective of the collective action problem inherent in a system of dispersed share ownership. The group directly affected by the imposition of corporate criminal liability, the dispersed shareholders are not significantly affected individually to mount meaningful opposition to the imposition of criminal liability on the corporation.

---

62 See Khanna, V [2003b]: 'Corporate Crime Legislation: A Political Economy Analysis', in Discussion Paper No. 03-012, University of Michigan John N. Ohlin Center for Law and Economics. Available at http://digitalcommons.law.wustl.edu/cgi/viewcontent.cgi?article=1362&context=lawreview&sei-redir=1&referer=http%3A%2F%2Fwww.google.com.ng%2Furl%3Fsa%3Dt%26rct%3Dj%26q%3Dcorporate%2520crime%2520legislation%253A%2520a%2520political%2520economy%2520analysis%26source%3Dweb%26cd%3D2%26ved%3D0CDUQFjAB%26url%3Dhttp%253A%252F%252Fdigitalcommons.law.wustl.edu%252Fcgi%252Fviewcontent.cgi%253Farticle%253D1362%2526context%253Dlawreview%26ei%3DLMk1UZ7rJYnbPLfugfAI%26usg%3DAFQjCNE3U_yTiHsZ47XwFpbwzew500Tvyw%26bvm%3Dbv.43148975%2Cd.ZWU#search=%22corporate%20crime%20legislation%3A%20political%20economy%20analysis%22, 3 at 46. Last visited 5 March 2013.

63 See Khanna [2003b: 21–3] for a discussion about the reaction of corporations to the Private Securities Litigation Reform Act of 1995, the Foreign Corrupt Practices Act, and the Sarbanes-Oxley Act.

In many respects, the debate on whether or not to impose criminal liability on corporations is not moot for two reasons. First, with the exception of a few states that still do not impose criminal liability on corporations, the imposition of criminal liability on corporations is virtually ubiquitous. The second is that even in the states where criminal liability is not available for corporations, administrative and civil sanctions are imposed on corporations. Differences between legal systems that recognize corporate criminal liability and those that do not are disagreements over form rather than substance. States that do not recognize corporate criminal liability compensate by imposing a system of civil liability for criminal fines or administrative fines on corporations. These penalties differ from criminal fines only in that they are imposed by an administrative agency, not a criminal court.

In essence, administrative and civil liability can capture the desirable features of corporate criminal liability, including criminal liability's powerful enforcement and information gathering dimensions.[64] The only feature of criminal liability for corporations that cannot be mimicked by administrative and civil liability is the stigma associated with criminal sanctions and retribution. Regardless of the liability regime imposed on corporations, two particular attributes of modern transnational corporations and the response of national legal systems to these attributes exacerbate the difficulties in imposing liability on transnational corporations.[65] These attributes are discussed in the following sections.

Group Complexity, Limited Liability and Piercing the Corporate Veil

The first characteristic of the transnational corporation bearing on the imposition of liability relates to the nature of the relationships between corporations that exist in a parent subsidiary relationship (group complexity). In the US, until the end of the nineteenth century, a corporation could not hold shares in another corporation except where expressly authorized by statute.[66] Corporate groups and holding corporations were unknown.[67] This all changed with the revolution of state corporation law led by New Jersey in the 1890s, when the acquisition

64 For an analysis of a possible middle ground between criminal and civil law, see Brown, D [2011]: 'Criminal Law's Unfortunate Triumph over Administrative Law', in Vol. 7, *Journal of Law and Economic Policy*, 657.

65 See Engle, E [2006]: 'Extraterritorial Corporate Criminal Liability: A Remedy for Human Rights Violations?', in Vol. 20, *St. John's Journal of Legal Commentary*, 287, at 300–301, for a discussion of the particular problems posed in the imposition of criminal liability on transnational corporations.

66 See *Louis K. Liggett Co. v Lee*, 288 U.S. 517, 556 (1933), where the court stated that a corporation could not hold shares in another corporation.

67 See Blumberg, P [1996]: 'The Increasing Recognition of Enterprise Principles in Determining Parent and Subsidiary Corporation Liabilities', in Vol. 28, *Connecticut Law Review*, 295, at 297.

and formation of subsidiaries was freely permitted.[68] In the UK, although there had never been any prohibition against one company holding shares in another in England, limited liability in its modern form was not entrenched until the *Salomon* case in 1897.

The combined effect of allowing corporations to hold shares in another corporation and limited liability is that a corporation with multiple subsidiaries is separate from the parent shareholders or other parts of the corporate group, creating two levels of limited liability that, in effect, shelter the parent corporation as well as the shareholders of the parent. The combined effect opened up the possibility that corporations could control other corporations. Even when the effects of these principles on the liability regime for corporations became clear, it took over half a century after the enactment of the New Jersey statute before the law recognized the existence of corporate groups. Even today, English law does not possess a specific body of law applicable to corporate groups. The absence of any overarching legal principle ensures that the system of regulation is fragmented and complex.

The Inadequacy of the Veil Piercing Response

The legal device developed by the law to counter the effect of the layer of insulation provided by limited liability and cross-share holding by corporations has not been effective in stopping corporations from shielding themselves from liability for transnational bribery. The doctrine of 'piercing the veil' in the US and UK is a creation of the common law and provides that under particular circumstances, the courts will disregard the rule of limited liability by piercing the corporate veil.[69] This situation is distinct from other instances in which owners of a corporation are held liable for the actions of that corporation. For instance, when a shareholder incurs an individual obligation as distinct from the corporation, the imposition of liability will not be based upon the corporate rules of piercing the veil. In contrast,

---

68 See Butler, H [1985]: 'Nineteenth-Century Jurisdictional Competition in the Granting of Corporate Privileges', in Vol. 24, *Journal of Legal Studies*, 129, at 161–2.

69 Several countries operate the veil-piercing doctrine including Australia, Canada, Germany, Argentina, France, and New Zealand. See Presser, S [1997]: *Piercing the Corporate Veil* (New York: Clark Boardman Callaghan). He analyses the differences between veil piercing in common law and civil law countries and provides an overview of veil piercing jurisprudence in five jurisdictions. See Cheng, K [2011]: 'The Corporate Veil Doctrine Revisited: A Comparative Study of the English and the U.S. Corporate Veil Doctrines', in Vol. 34, *Boston College International and Comparative Law Review*, 329, at 342–78, for a detailed comparison between the English and US corporate veil doctrines, focusing on differences in their jurisprudential approaches, treatment of specific case types, and related issues. Also see Albert, D [2002]: 'Addressing Abuse of the Corporate Entity in the People's Republic of China: New Thoughts on China's Need for a Defined Veil Piercing Doctrine', in Vol. 23, *University of Pennsylvania Journal of International Economic Law*, 873, for a general description of the veil piercing doctrine in China.

the doctrine of piercing the veil applies to situations in which the actions are clearly those of the corporation and liability is imposed on the shareholder instead. In those circumstances where the court pierces the corporate veil, the court does not question the legal fiction of a corporation's separate existence distinct from the owner's; rather the court merely disregards the fiction for the particular purpose of imposing liability on the owner.

As the doctrine has been developed entirely by the courts (without legislation), there is a significant lack of uniformity in the application of the doctrine even within different states in the US. Wormser coined the term 'piercing the veil' in 1912.[70] Wormser believed that the corporate form should be ignored only when a corporation was obviously used as a means to perpetuate an injustice. He stated:

> When the conception of corporate entity is employed to defraud creditors, to evade an existing obligation, to circumvent a statute, or advertise or perpetuate a monopoly, or to protect knavery or crime, the courts will draw aside the web of entity, will regard the corporate company as an association of live, up-and-doing, men and woman shareholders, and will do justice between real persons.[71]

From Wormser's perspective, the veil should be pierced to achieve justice and to prevent shareholders from evading their legal obligations. Furthermore, Wormser believed that because of the complexity of corporate relationships, the rules for disregarding this privilege should not be confined to statutory regulations.[72] The rationale being that if the rules were made clear in a statute, people intent on committing injustices could merely factor their actions around the law. Wormser's approach is the basis of the approach for piercing the veil in California.[73] The courts in California apply a two-prong test, commonly referred to as the 'alter ego' doctrine.[74] This test requires first that a unity of interest be present between the shareholders and their corporation so that a separation of them no longer exists. Second, that an inequitable result would follow if the acts objected to by the creditors were treated only as those of the corporation.

All US courts do not uniformly follow the alter ego doctrine. Powell rejected Wormser's broad intuitive approach in favour of a three-prong test, generally called the 'instrumentality rule'. The test was originally developed for parent-subsidiary

---

70 See Wormser, M [1912]: 'Piercing the Veil of Corporate Entity', in Vol. 12, *Columbia Law Review*, 496.

71 *Ibid.*, at 517.

72 See Wormser, M [1927]: *Disregard of the Corporate Fiction and Allied Corporation Problems* (Littleton: F.B. Rothman), at 37–8.

73 See Automotriz del Golfo de California S. A. de C. V. v Resnick, 306 P.2d 1, 3 (Cal. 1957).

74 See Blumberg, P [1987]: *The Law of Corporate Groups: Tort, Contract, and Other Common Law Problems in the Substantive Law of Parent and Subsidiary Corporations* (Boston: Little, Brown), at 6.03.

situations, but many courts apply it to other situations involving the domination of an entity.

The instrumentality doctrine, although similar to the alter ego approach advocated by Wormser, exhibits a subtle difference.[75] The first requirement of the instrumentality doctrine is the mere instrumentality precondition. The instrumentality precondition requires that the subsidiary be completely under the control and domination of the parent. This requirement measures the relationship between the shareholder and the corporation. Generally, mere majority stock ownership will be insufficient to satisfy this element.[76] To establish control over the corporation, the plaintiff would have to establish that the parent dominated not only the finances of the subsidiary, but also the policy and business practice in respect to the transaction in question. In effect, the plaintiff would have to establish that in the transaction in question, the subsidiary did not have a separate mind, will, or existence of its own.

The second requirement of the instrumentality doctrine is the fraud, wrong, or injustice requirement. This requires that the defendant parent's conduct in using the subsidiary be somehow unjust, fraudulent, or wrongful toward the plaintiff.[77] The claimant is required to show that the control exercised by the parent corporation or dominant stockholder was used by the defendant to commit fraud or wrong, to perpetrate the violation of a statutory or other positive legal duty, or perform any other dishonest and unjust act in contravention of plaintiffs' legal right. This second requirement focuses on the relationship between the plaintiff and the corporation.[78]

The third requirement is that the plaintiff suffers actual harm because of the conduct of the defendant parent's conduct. The plaintiff must show that the defendant's control, exerted in a fraudulent, illegal, or otherwise unfair manner toward it, caused the harm suffered. Put another way, the plaintiff must prove that, unless the corporate veil is pierced, it will have been treated unjustly by the defendant's exercise of control and improper use of the corporate form and, in so doing suffered damages.

There are clearly many similarities between both the alter ego and instrumentality doctrines for piercing the corporate veil. Both tests are applied by most courts in the US and are often viewed as interchangeable. They both have

---

75 Powell, F [1931]: *Parent and Subsidiary Corporations: Liability of a Parent Corporation for the Obligations of Its Subsidiary* (Chicago: Callaghan), at 4–6.

76 See *Angelo Tomasso, Inc. v Armor Constr. & Paving, Inc.*, 447 A.2d 406, 412 (Conn. 1982) (*Angelo*) where the court stated that that the key factor in any decision to disregard the separate corporate entity was the element of control or influence exercised by the individual sought to be held liable over the corporate affairs of the corporation.

77 See *Collet v American Nat'l Stores, Inc.*, 708 S.W.2d 273, 284 (Mo. Ct. App. 1986).

78 See Olthoff, M [1995]: 'Beyond the Form – Should the Corporate Veil be Pierced?', in Vol. 64, *University of Missouri at Kansas City Law Review*, 311, at 316–17.

common elements of control and fraud (injustice or unfairness perpetrated on the creditor). These elements are prevalent where domination, undercapitalisation, commingling of assets, or disregard of corporate formalities appears in the facts of the case. However, the existence of one of these criteria alone is often insufficient to justify piercing the veil.

The differences between the alter ego and instrumentality doctrines for piercing the corporate veil are subtler. For instance, in contrast to the alter ego doctrine, the instrumentality rule has an additional element of causation regarding the loss suffered by the creditor.[79] Many courts adopted Powell's approach since it offered bright line tests in lieu of the mist of metaphors that existed in the broader approaches.[80] The danger of both approaches is that they rely heavily on the discretion of individual judges. Commenting on the lack of consistency in the circumstances under which the courts will pierce the corporate veil, Clark stated that:

> Despite the fact that different courts' lists of relevant factors bear a family resemblance to one another, a lawyer surveying a broad range of cases involving attempts to pierce the corporate veil might easily conclude that they are unified more by the remedies sought – subjecting to corporate liabilities the personal assets directly held by shareholders – than by repeated and consistent application of the same criteria for granting the remedy.[81]

The reliance on the discretion of the judge creates uncertainty regarding the instances where the veil will be pierced, which in turn ensures that the liability of a particular parent corporation is less clear.

The lack of uniformity in the application of the doctrine is also present in European legal systems. For example, whilst the volume of litigation in the UK and Germany appears to be considerably lower than in the US, the UK and German judicial opinions that do exist on piercing the veil provide even less guidance than their US counterparts regarding the factors that will trigger veil-piercing.[82] In fact, the only common theme that emerges from a consideration of the law in the US, UK, and Germany is the judicial willingness to intervene to curb an abuse or injustice. In sum, making sweeping generalisations about the circumstances in which the courts will pierce the veil is not only difficult but actually reinforces

79 Causation is not required by those courts using the two-prong alter ego test. See *Vuitch v Furr*, 482 A.2d 811, 816, 820 (D.C. 1984).

80 See Cohen, D [1998]: 'Theories of the Corporation and the Limited Liability Company: How Should Courts and Legislatures Articulate Rules for Piercing the Veil, Fiduciary Responsibility and Securities Regulation for the Limited Liability Company?', in Vol. 51, *Oklahoma Law Review*, 427, at 445.

81 See Clark, R [1986]: *Corporate Law* (Boston: Little, Brown), at § 2.4, 73.

82 See Miller, S [1998]: 'Piercing the Corporate Veil Among Affiliated Companies in the European Community and in the U.S.: A Comparative Analysis of U.S., German, and U.K. Veil-Piercing Approaches', in Vol. 36, *American Business Law Journal*, 73, at 77.

the argument that the law has not adequately responded to the task of regulating transnational bribery by corporations.

In the UK, there are limited sets of circumstances where the courts will pierce the corporate veil. The courts have emphasized that English law insists on the recognition of limited liability and that one is entitled to organize and conduct affairs with the expectation that the court will apply the principle in *Salomon.*[83] Commentators in the UK also agree that the jurisprudence in this area is far from principled.[84] In Germany, the courts recognize that a corporation's separate entity may be disregarded in certain circumstances. There is a body of case law (referred to as Durchgriffshaftung), which provides for piercing the corporate veil in exceptional cases for serious reasons of equity and good faith.[85]

The lack of uniformity in instances where the corporate veil would be pierced ensures that commentators can only offer justifications for the disregard of the legal entity rather than state prerequisites as to when the veil can be pierced. The theories posited by the major commentators are similar and the main differences centre on a defendants' subjective intent and whether piercing the veil requires intentional wrongdoing.[86] Similar to the US, courts in Europe do not adhere to any particular theory and are consistent only in maintaining that the corporate entity can be respected only when its use is consistent with the goals of the legal system and will be disregarded only in exceptional cases if required by equity and good faith.[87] The lack of consistency in instances where the corporate veil has been pierced differs not only in respect to the situation and types of corporations making the claims, but also in respect to the types of situations where the courts have refused to accept the claims.

The lack of uniformity in the application of the doctrine of veil piercing is, however, not the only way in which the legal system fails to respond to the ability of corporations to escape liability for transnational bribery. The corporate law principle of limited liability does not distinguish between circumstances where the shareholder is a natural person or a corporation. The nature of the ultimate shareholder corporation or natural person is irrelevant. For instance, company S is a wholly owned subsidiary of company P. In turn, company P is a publicly held corporation with numerous shareholders. An agent of S bribes a foreign public official resulting in losses to D, a competitor who seeks to hold P liable for the actions of S on a veil piercing theory.

---

83 See *Acatos & Hutcheson v Wattson* [1995] 1 BCLC 218, for an articulation of this view.

84 See Ottolenghi, S, [1990]: 'From Peeping Behind the Corporate Veil to Ignoring it Completely', in Vol. 53, *Modern Law Review*, 338, at 338.

85 For a general discussion of veil piercing in German courts, see Alting, C [1995]: 'Piercing the Corporate Veil in American and German Law – Liability of Individuals and Entities: A Comparative View', in Vol. 2, *Tulsa Journal of Comparative & International Law*, 187.

86 *Ibid.*, at 198.

87 *Ibid.*, at 199.

The question raised is whether the considerations militating against piercing the veil in circumstances where the shareholders are numerous individuals should apply to single corporate shareholders. One would think that the policy considerations implicated in the situation where D is trying to hold liable P's numerous shareholders on a veil-piercing theory would be very different from those involved with S and the law would treat them differently. Notwithstanding, the courts in the US, UK, and Germany apply the same standards in situations where the principle of limited liability is challenged even where the parent is a corporation. The mere fact that a corporation is part of a larger enterprise is insufficient to justify veil piercing.

In a comparison of veil-piercing jurisprudence amongst corporate groups in the US, Germany, and UK conducted by Miller, courts did not make a distinction between situations where the parent is a corporation.[88] She concluded that in general, UK courts appear more hesitant to pierce the corporate veil than US courts. German statutory and case law, on the other hand, provides the greatest opportunity for veil-piercing of a subsidiary corporation. As in the US, veil piercing occurs in the UK where there is a high degree of control by the shareholder. German law appears to take a significantly different approach from UK and US case law, and seems to be the most liberal of all three jurisdictions regarding the circumstances in which the court will pierce the subsidiary's corporate veil. German courts will hold that a parent corporation has dominated a subsidiary and that the parent is liable for the subsidiary's obligation where there is an express agreement stipulating the parent's acceptance of this obligation. In the absence of an express agreement, the courts may still hold the parent corporation liable if there is a finding that the parent was involved in a non-arms-length transaction that was detrimental to the subsidiary.

As such, in German law the parent corporation's conduct does not have to involve intentional misconduct or wrongdoing as it does in the US. The transaction does not have to be fraudulent, illegal, or particularly egregious for the corporate veil to be pierced. In addition, the corporate veil of a subsidiary could be pierced to hold the shareholder liable where the parent had exercised pervasive control over the subsidiary. Some of the more recent case law suggests that parental liability would be imposed only where the parent exercised its control in a manner that was not in the interest of the dependent corporation.

Evaluating the Policy Considerations Concerning Limited Liability

In the US, UK, and Germany, the principles applied in piercing the veil when individuals are the shareholders are directly extended to situations where a parent corporation owns or controls a subsidiary. The unfortunate effect of this automatic extension is that a corporation could avoid liability for the obligations of a subsidiary corporation. Allowing limited liability for corporations holding

---

88 See Miller [1998: 79–83].

shares in another corporation allows the parent corporation to escape liability for transnational bribery. Should the doctrine of limited liability be discarded? From a policy perspective, the very compelling policy considerations justifying limited liability for individual shareholders lose their potency when applied to individual corporate shareholders. The doctrine was developed with the legitimate objective of protecting the many individual shareholders of a corporation from personal liability that they would be exposed to through the ownership of a few shares in a corporation. A consequence of allowing one corporation to hold shares in another corporation is that these corporations can exploit the protection of limited liability to shield the corporation from liability for transnational bribery.

The implication of abolishing the protection of limited liability has been the focus of debate amongst scholars. Those arguing in favour of limited liability can be broadly divided into two camps. First, law and economics scholars argue that the concept of limited liability promotes efficiency in the relationship between corporate constituents. Second, historical advocates argue that limited liability allows people of lesser means access to risk taking ventures presented by corporations.

Easterbrook & Fischel have articulated a comprehensive economic justification in support of maintaining limited liability.[89] Easterbrook & Fischel offer five reasons for retaining the doctrine of limited liability based upon principles of economic efficiency.[90] First, limited liability decreases the need for shareholders to monitor the managers of companies in which they invest because the financial consequences of the corporation failing are limited to the shares they own in that corporation. Second, limited liability provides incentives for managers to act efficiently and in the interests of shareholders by promoting the free transfer of shares. Third, limited liability assists the efficient operation of the securities markets because the prices at which shares are traded do not depend on individual shareholder wealth. Fourth, limited liability permits efficient diversification by shareholders, which in turn allows shareholders to reduce their individual risk. Fifth, limited liability facilitates optimal investment decisions by managers.

The justifications set out by Easterbrook & Fischel provide the basic framework of the arguments relied upon by the advocates of limited liability to demonstrate that limited liability is more efficient than unlimited liability. Limited liability provides incentives for shareholders to hold diversified portfolios. Under such circumstances, managers can hedge against the risk associated with the failure of a particular investment and could do so without exposing each shareholder to the loss of his or her personal wealth. However, if a principle of unlimited liability applied, managers might conservatively reject some investments out of a desire to reduce the risk to shareholders. By definition, this would be a social loss because some risky projects turn out to be beneficial uses of capital. The conclusion is that

---

89 See Easterbrook, F & Fischel, D [1985]: '*Limited Liability and the Corporation*', in Vol. 52, *University of Chicago Law Review*, 90, at 90–109.

90 See Easterbrook & Fischel [1991: 41–3].

limited liability stimulates investment, but it also facilitates an effective allocation of risk or loss amongst investors.[91]

The historical advocates, while agreeing with the efficiency argument, nevertheless make a democratic argument for limited liability. Limited liability, the argument suggests, was designed historically as a means of encouraging the small-scale entrepreneur and of keeping entry into business markets competitive and democratic.[92] This democratic argument suggests that the corporation emerged more for political and philosophical reasons than out of any economic need. Before the proliferation of the corporation, only the wealthy had the privilege of investing in corporations. Limited liability serves the added purpose of opening up risk-taking opportunities to wider group of citizens. In sum, the democratic urge to see the widespread participation of citizens in risk-taking ventures necessitated easy access to corporate form before there was an economic need for the corporate form.

The democratic argument for limited liability is not diametrically opposed to the efficiency argument for limited liability. On the contrary, the democratic argument for limited liability serves as a complement to the efficiency argument. If one accepts the premises of the democratic argument, then it is no longer sufficient to argue that limited liability is inefficient. One must also argue that limited liability is not as democratic, in that it fails to open up risk-taking opportunities to a wide group of citizens as other proposed alternatives. Therefore, according to the democratic argument, limited liability need not be the most efficient regime, so long as there it is the most democratic way to spread access to wealth-making opportunities.

Independent of the democratic argument, some commentators disagree with the argument that limited liability is efficient.[93] The efficiency of the current limited liability regime is certainly contestable on the grounds that another framework could provide the same benefits of limited liability while eliminating its less desirable effects. For instance, Hansmann & Kraakman proposed the replacement of limited liability for shareholders with a pro rata liability regime and system of insurance investors for compensating tort creditors.[94] The substance of this proposal rests on the assumption that the current limited liability regime leaves tort creditors uncompensated, while shareholders externalize the costs of doing business and reap great profits at society's expense. Although the proposal is interesting, it falls short by ignoring one of the central concerns: the issue of

91 Easterbrook & Fischel [1991: 44].

92 See Presser [1997: 4–14] for a detailed exposition of the democratic argument for limited liability.

93 A detailed argument against the efficiency of limited liability is provided by Bratton, W & McCahery, J [1997]: 'An Inquiry into the Efficiency of the Limited Liability Company: Of Theory of the Firm and Regulatory Competition', in Vol. 54, *Washington & Lee Law Review*, 629, at 632.

94 See Hansmann, H & Kraakman, R [1991]: 'Toward Unlimited Shareholder Liability for Corporate Torts', in Vol. 100, *Yale Law Journal*, 1871, at 1923–6.

ratings, which limited liability addresses.[95] This issue will essentially lead one back to the regime of unlimited liability and more pertinently undermine widespread participation in business markets.

The importance of limited liability in fostering widespread access to capital markets is incontrovertible and the argument here is not that limited liability should be abolished. However, the blanket availability of limited liability to individuals or corporations in every situation without definite policy justifications is objectionable. The Easterbrook & Fischel justifications for limited liability are generally valid in the context where the parent corporation is a group of dispersed shareholders. In this context, limited liability encourages risk-taking by management. In some circumstances, limited liability may be justifiable for groups of corporations, such as a situation where a corporation seeks to invest in areas unrelated to the existing businesses of the group. However, this justification would not extend to situations where the corporation is simply seeking to extend activities that it is already undertaking, seeking to hide behind limited liability to avoid the costs of risk-taking entirely, or for engaging in illegal conduct.

The justifications for the blanket application of limited liability are less relevant when the affiliation is between corporations.[96] Several of the central justifications for limited liability are irrelevant in the context where corporations are the shareholders. For instance, the justification for limited liability, in that it provides incentives for managers to act efficiently and in the interests of shareholders by promoting the free transfer of shares, has little or no application to holding corporations and wholly owned subsidiaries.

Another justification for limited liability, excessive monitoring costs, is inapplicable to the situation where the corporation is a shareholder and would directly support the efforts to lower transnational bribery because increasing monitoring is likely to reduce bribes paid by the corporation. Another justification that has been advocated for limited liability is that it assists the operation of the securities market. This justification is largely irrelevant in the case of a wholly owned subsidiary.[97] The fact that limited liability permits efficient diversification by shareholders, which in turn allows shareholders to reduce their individual risk, is less applicable to holding companies because they are less risk averse than individual shareholders. This follows from the fact that the individual shareholders of the holding company still receive the protection of limited liability, which means that they can diversify their investments independently of the holding corporation's liability for the subsidiary.

---

95 The insurance firms in deciding whether to grant liability insurance will rate the chances of the success of the business venture, creating a situation where only the wealthy will be able to obtain insurance coverage.

96 For a detailed exposition of this argument, see Blumberg [1987: 681–92].

97 This justification is still relevant in the case of a partially owned subsidiary where there is a market in which the publicly held shares are traded.

Even in the context of the allocation of risk (another primary justification for limited liability), the policy considerations are different when the shareholder is another corporation.[98] The elimination of limited liability for an affiliated group of corporations, especially for the parent corporation, would not have the effect of subjecting individual stockholders to risks greater than their individual investment. Instead, only the entity responsible for the management of the subsidiary, i.e., the parent, would be held liable, and the larger group of shareholders, including those in the parent, would not be held directly responsible for behaviour over which they have merely theoretical control. In fact, the creditors of a constituent corporation are actually exposed to a greater degree of risk than the creditors of a single corporation. For example, the availability of funds from the other affiliates reduces the practical importance of adequate initial capitalisation for any particular member of the group. The danger of commingling assets and properties is greater between the affiliated corporations than between shareholders and independent corporations. In groups of corporations, there is a greater chance that each corporation's economic viability is tied to that of other members of the group. As such, each particular corporation may be unable to develop the independent profit-making activities expected of freestanding corporate entities.[99]

In fairness, there are some credible arguments regarding the importance of limited liability for affiliate groups of corporations. Hackney & Benson argue that even within corporate groups, though utilized by the parent corporation, limited liability still serves to protect the individual shareholders.[100] The essence of this argument is that the original reason for allowing limited liability for shareholders – that it encourages investment and subdivision of risk by allowing parents to incorporate subsidiaries – still encourages investment even in the context of shareholders as corporations. The investment-encouraging rationale is furthered where the parent shareholders profit from reducing the risks of liability to the parent. The more risk is reduced, the greater their potential profit and the more they are encouraged to invest in the parent's stock.[101]

The implication is that the large number of shareholders allows the loss and, therefore, the risk, to be spread evenly among many investors. Unlimited liability in the group context, however, would concentrate these losses on a small

---

98 For a detailed discussion of the risks associated with liability of the constituent members of an affiliated group of corporations in the context of bankruptcy, see Landers, J [1975]: 'A Unified Approach to Parent, Subsidiary, and Affiliate Questions in Bankruptcy', in Vol. 42, *University of Chicago Law Review*, 589, at 589.

99 *Ibid.*, at 596–7.

100 Hackney, W & Benson, T [1982]: 'Shareholder Liability for Inadequate Capital', in Vol. 43, *University of Pittsburgh Law Review*, 837, at 872–3.

101 See Presser, S [1992]: 'Thwarting the Killing of the Corporation: Limited Liability, Democracy and Economics', in Vol. 87, *Northwestern University Law Review*, 148, at 173–5, which provides an interesting exposition of the investment encouragement potential of limited liability for groups of corporations.

number of shareholders. Placing unlimited liability on the closely held corporation shareholder would likely result in underinvestment.[102] Other arguments put forward in support of limited liability for closely held corporations suggest that limited liability is just as efficient in the context of groups of corporations. One such argument suggests that there is little reason for believing that limited liability in the group context actually externalizes costs.[103]

There are clearly a significant number of justifications for limited liability. In partial defence of the Easterbrook & Fischel's position on limited liability, the focus of their analysis was the publicly held corporation with widely dispersed and unrelated shareholders. Within these publicly held corporations, there is a clear distinction between the shareholders and managers. In situations where the shareholder is another corporation, the distinction is not as clear, as it is difficult to distinguish situations where the corporation is acting as a passive owner or actively directing the actions of the subsidiary.

The preceding discussion suggests that at a minimum, there is a need to rethink some of the aspects of limited liability in the context of corporate groups. The legal principle that a corporation is a separate legal entity, and therefore deserving of limited liability even if it is part of a corporate group, is at odds with the fact that many corporate groups operate as a single entity because of the economic benefits that result from the integration of activities. Most of the previous discussions on limited liability were made in the context of the contractual and tortious liability of corporations.

In the context of transnational bribery by corporations, the reasons for constraining limited liability for corporations are even more compelling. Thus, the view taken here would support limited liability for groups at least as a general rule. The courts can temper the harshness in some cases by piercing the corporate veil. This position is very much in line with that taken by Cary & Eisenberg, who state that piercing the corporate veil can act as a safety valve that takes some of the pressure off of the limited liability rule in cases where the rule is most dubious.[104]

Structural Complexity, Criminal Liability and Attribution

The second characteristic of corporations that presents significant challenges to imposing liability for transnational bribery on corporations is their structural complexity. The feature of the legal system directly challenged by the structural complexity of transnational corporations relates to the doctrines upon which

102 See Leebron, D [1991]: 'Limited Liability, Tort Victims, and Creditors', in Vol. 91, *Columbia Law Review*, 1565, at 1630.

103 See Ribstein, L [1991]: 'Limited Liability and Theories of the Corporation', in Vol. 50, *Maryland Law Review*, 80, at 91–107.

104 See Cary, W & Eisenberg, M [1995]: *Corporations: Cases and Materials* (7th ed.) (New York: Foundation Press), at 191.

the legal system imposes liability on corporations for criminal conduct. Most jurisdictions reject vicarious liability for corporations including, for example, the UK, which operates on the principle of identification liability.[105] The US, on the other hand, will hold a corporation vicariously liable for the criminal acts of its employee-agents committed within the scope of employment with at least some intent to benefit the corporate employer.[106] The ability of the law to impose criminal liability for transnational bribery effectively in these complex webs of transnational corporations has been limited by these complicated management structures.

The Inadequacy of the Vicarious/Identification Liability Response

The complex organisational and management structures of transnational corporations pose a significant challenge to the law with regard to the imposition of criminal liability. This challenge is created because the imposition of criminal liability on a corporation by the law requires that clear distinctions be made regarding responsibility for actions before liability is imposed.[107] There are two basic methods for rendering corporations criminally liable: vicarious liability and identification liability.[108] The two models have their origins in the civil sphere realm of torts before they were subsequently transferred to the criminal law. Although the two models are similar, they are quite different in the manner in which they attribute criminal liability to corporations. The two models start by identifying the persons within the corporation who created the mental and physical foundations for the offence. The models diverge in the different means of transferring liability to the corporation.[109] The different means of transfer utilized by both models have significant consequences regarding the persons within the corporation whose actions may be imputed to the corporation.

The imputation of liability could also be complicated in situations where another corporation directs the actions of the corporation. In the instance where the actions of the corporation are directed by another corporation, the degree of control exercised by one corporation over the other will vary in accordance with a significant range of factors, such as the nature of the relationship between both corporations. This ensures that the determination of liability is dependent on specific market and organisational conditions, often requiring difficult economic

105 See Colvin, E [1995]: 'Corporate Personality and Criminal Liability', in Vol. 6, *Criminal Law Forum*, 1, at 8–18, for a discussion of several common law countries that have rejected the vicarious liability model.

106 Brown [1998: 35].

107 See Kelly-Kilgore, S & Smith, E [2011]: Corporate Criminal Liability', in Vol. 48, *American Criminal Law Review*, 421, at 423–32, where they discuss the principles that guide the law of corporate criminal liability and the elements required to incur liability.

108 See Lederman [2000: 650].

109 *Ibid.*, at 651.

and commercial analysis. The complex organisational and management structure of transnational corporations ensures that establishing responsibility is a difficult and complicated task and poses a challenge to the two models utilized for imputing liability for criminal actions.

The measured pace by which the law adopted criminal liability for corporations was due in part to doctrinal conceptions regarding the application of the criminal law to legal persons. The view being that the criminal law was designed to deal with human deviance resulting from thought and behaviour exclusive to natural persons and not to juristic persons. These doctrinal conceptions are also present in the current debate on the appropriate method for imputing criminal liability on the corporation for the actions of its employers. In legal systems where criminal liability is imposed on the corporation for acts of transnational bribery, the particular doctrine for the imputation of liability often determines whether a corporation is liable for transnational bribery.

The vicarious liability model holds the corporation liable for the conduct of all its officers, employees, and agents acting within the scope of their authority regardless of rank.[110] This imputation of liability is carried out through the device of a legal fiction that deems the activities of an agent as those of the principal. This is achieved through a two-step process. First, there is an examination of the conduct of the agent. Second, once the elements are identified in the agent, they are ascribed to the corporation based on their pre-existing legal relationship. The requisite conditions for the imputation of liability are that the agent acts within the course and scope of his authority. Second, the agent must act in furtherance of the interest of the corporation. Some jurisdictions add a third requirement that the acts must be authorized, tolerated, or ratified by the corporation.[111] The principle of vicarious liability has generally been rejected in the criminal law of most jurisdictions.[112]

In the UK, the preferred doctrine since the 1940s has been based on the doctrine of identification, which imposes direct liability on the corporation. The identification doctrine, in contrast to vicarious doctrine, narrows the scope of liability by restricting the range of persons within the corporation whose actions can be imputed to the corporation. The doctrine would only impute liability to the corporation of the key personnel in the corporation. These personnel are deemed to represent the directing mind of the corporation. Lord Denning, in the case of *H.L. Bolton (Engineering) Co v T.J. Graham & Sons, Ltd*, went as far as equating the corporation with the human body, with the directors and managers representing the mind and will of the corporation.[113]

The range of personnel to whom corporate liability can be imputed varies across jurisdictions. In the English case of *Tesco Supermarkets, Ltd. v Nattrass*, the

---

110 See *US v Basic Constr. Co.*, 711 F.2d 570, 573 (4th Cir. 1983).

111 See Lederman [2000: 655].

112 See, for instance, the Canadian case of *Canadian Dredge & Dock Co. v R. [1985] 1 S.C.R. at 691.*

113 [1957] 1 Q.B. 159, 172.

House of Lords identified the range of personnel as those at the centre of corporate power.[114] This principle has been adopted in other commonwealth jurisdictions, notably Australia[115] and New Zealand.[116] However, the Supreme Court of Canada in *Canadian Dredge & Dock Co. v R*, qualified the application of the principle in Tesco Supermarket. The Court, whilst agreeing with the principle as enunciated by the House of Lords, qualified its application by rejecting the notion that a corporation necessarily has only one directing mind, maintaining that the rule may not accord with the realities of life in Canada.[117]

Since the decision in *Tesco*, the UK courts have further clarified the class of persons sufficiently senior to constitute the directing mind of the corporation.[118] In *Meridian Global Funds Management Asia Ltd v Security Commission*, the Privy Council held that language, provisions, content, and policy of statutory offences would be instructive in indicating whose state of mind would be attributed to the corporation.[119] In essence, the court recognized that there might be instances where the court recognized that the intention of the statute would be defeated by the primary rules of attribution, suggesting that the court would be permitted to depart from *Tesco* and thus left open the possibility that the court would 'fashion a special rule of attribution for the particular substantive rule'.[120]

The loosening of the doctrine of attribution received a significant setback with a 1999 ruling of the Court of Appeal. Following the Southall rail crash, a case was brought against the train operator whose procedure had allowed a malfunctioning high-speed train to be driven by a driver without adequate training.[121] In this case, the court applied a strict and formalistic position with respect to the attribution of fault holding that the identification model in *Tesco* still served as the basis for corporate criminal liability and that that an individual company director had to be named in the indictment.[122]

114 [1972] A.C. 153.

115 See the cases *Hamilton v Whitehead*, 166 C.L.R. 121, 127 (1988) and *Kehoe v Dacol Motors (Pty.), Ltd.*,. 1972 Q.R 59, 74–5 (Queensl. Crim. App. 1971).

116 *Nordik Indus.*, [1976] 1 NZLR 199 at 201.

117 *Canadian Dredge*, at 693, per Justice Estey.

118 The principle in Tesco has also been distinguished on a number of occasions in relation to the scope of an employer's duty under the Health and Safety at Work Act 1974. In *R v British Steel* (1995) 1 W.L.R 1356, the Court of Appeal held that a corporation was not absolved of liability by showing that it had taken steps at a senior level if all practicable steps had not been taken at the operational level. Also see *Tesco Stores Ltd v London Borough of London Borough of Brent* (1993) 2 All E.R. 718, DC; *R v Associated Octel Co Ltd* (1996) 1 W.L.R 1543; and *R v Gateway Foodmarkets Ltd* (1997), IRLR 189.

119 [1995] 2 A.C. 500.

120 *Ibid.*, per Lord Hoffman, at 923–4.

121 See Wells, C, Morgan, D & Quick, O [2000]: 'Disasters: A Challenge for the Law', in Vol. 39, *Washburn Law Journal*, 496, at 507.

122 See *Attorney-General's Reference (No. 2 of 1999)* (2000) (Crim. App. Eng.).

The use of the doctrine of vicarious liability for the imputation of criminal liability on the corporation has been justified based on necessity.[123] In this view, the imposition of liability turns on the relationship between an agent and a corporation, with the notional expectation that the corporation has chosen to delegate his authority and is thus responsible in law. Vicarious liability as the method for imputing liability to a corporation is open to several criticisms. First, criminal law should not have the tort rule equivalent of vicarious liability on the basis that it is unfair.[124] Second, subjecting corporations to criminal liability for the acts of lower-level employees is questionable because the acts of lower-level employees bear very little meaningful connection to the acts of the corporation.[125] More so, holding corporations composed of numerous individuals through the doctrine of vicarious liability invariably leads to liability for the entire corporation based on the activities of a sole agent.[126] Third, in situations where corporate policies encourage criminal behaviour, the vicarious liability model is unable to regulate the agents responsible for the criminal actions adequately.[127] Fourth, the doctrine is both too wide because it attributes the wrongdoings of any employee to the company, and too narrow because it leaves no opportunity to explore company policies.[128] These shortcomings of the model of vicarious liability call into question the continued use of this model in the corporate context.

The identification doctrine is in part a response to some of the perceived shortcomings of the vicarious liability model for imputing liability to corporations. The basis for attribution of criminal liability in the identification liability model does not cloud the basis of identification with a legal fiction and as a result formulates a legal definition that is closer to reality.[129] The identification doctrine ameliorates some of the rigours of vicarious liability doctrine by addressing the issues of culpability in a more analytical manner. The more rigorous analytic manner adopted by the identification liability model therefore appears to be a more adequate reflection of reality in that it recognizes that the actions of certain agents, by virtue of their status, are more likely to reflect the culpability of the corporation. However, the identification doctrine raises two issues. First, setting the criteria for which corporate agents will reflect policies of the corporation. Second, the

123 See Laufer, W [1994]: 'Corporate Bodies and Guilty Minds', in Vol. 43, *Emory Law Journal*, 575, at 654.

124 See Colvin [1995: 6] for a detailed account of this criticism.

125 See Mueller, G [1957]: 'Mens Rea and the Corporation – A Study of the Model Penal Code Position on Corporate Criminal Liability', in Vol. 19, *University of Pittsburgh Law Review*, 21, at 41–6.

126 Moore, J [1992]: 'Corporate Culpability Under the Federal Sentencing Guidelines', in Vol. 34, *Arizona Law Review*, 743, provides a general review of this argument.

127 See Fisse, B [1990]: *Howard's Criminal Law* (5th ed.) (Sydney: Law Book Company), at 603–5, for a detailed exposition of this argument.

128 Wells, C, Morgan, D & Quick, O [2000: 514].

129 See Lederman [2000: 308].

numerous ways in which corporations are organized and the diffusion of decision making within corporations ensures that setting precise rules on the issues will remain a challenge.[130] The second issue is in part one of the reasons why corporate criminal liability has thrived, ensuring that the corporation can be prosecuted in the event of difficulty in finding responsible individuals.

An alternative to both the vicarious and identification liability models that has been proposed is the aggregate model.[131] The primary use of this model is in cases when it is hard to point to a natural person acting within a framework of a legal body whose behaviour and thoughts embody the elements of the offence. The inspiration for this model was adopted from the development of concepts such as collective memory in sociology.[132] In this model, the state of mind and culpability of individual representatives of the corporation are aggregated for imputing criminal liability to the corporation.

The aggregation would involve matching the conduct of one individual with the state of mind or culpability of another individual. Alldridge has articulated a similar concept of broad accessorial liability wherein those acts of an agent that were contemplated by the principal are attributed to the principal.[133] This model was accepted by a US court in the case of *US v Bank of New England*, where the charge related to wilfully failing to file reports of currency transactions exceeding a certain statutory amount.[134] The court, endorsing the aggregate theory in the context of complex organisations, concluded that the bank would be liable if some of its personnel knew about the reporting requirement and disregarded it, even if those personnel who knew of the transactions in issue did not know this requirement.[135] This method of aggregating the actions of an individual with the actions of another to impute liability to the corporation has been rejected in most commonwealth jurisdictions and notably in cases arising from the Zeebrugge ferry accident.[136] The basis for rejecting this model rests on the fact that it would invariably turn the innocent activities of agents into corporate acts or omissions of a criminal nature. A further objection to this model of aggregation is that its usefulness is called into question by the model's reliance on derivative liability.

In fact, all three models exalt a fiction that must be abandoned as they all fail to consider culpability of corporations in relation to advances in organisational theory.

---

130 See Wells, C, Morgan, D & Quick, O [2000: 514] for a similar argument.

131 Described in Colvin [1995: 18–23].

132 See Lederman [2000: 665].

133 Alldridge, P [1990]: 'The Doctrine of Innocent Agency', in Vol. 2 *Criminal Law Forum*, 45, at 54.

134 *821 F.2d 844* (1st Cir.1987).

135 *Ibid.*, at 856.

136 See Wells, C [2001]: *Corporations and Criminal Responsibility* (2nd ed.) (Oxford: Oxford University Press), at Chapter 6; and Colvin [1995: 16–18] for a discussion of this incident. The criminal cases included *R. v H.M. Coroner for East Kent*, [1987] 88 CA. 10 (Q.B); and *R. v P&O Eur. Ferries (Dover), Ltd.*, [1990] 93 CA 72.

Wells has pointed out that the basis of corporate liability in the UK, which assumes that only a few individual officers exert control or have managerial autonomy over the corporation, is at odds with current theories of organisations.[137] Abandoning this fiction for a model based on organisational responsibility would ensure that the determination of corporate culpability is based on whether liability inheres in the organisation itself.[138]

At least four models have emerged in scholarly debates that reject the existing models and instead focus on culpability in relation to features of the corporate form. The first model, proactive corporate fault, focuses on a corporation's practice and procedures in the determination of liability.[139] With its origins in the traditional defence of due diligence, this model imposes liability when a corporation fails to make reasonable efforts to implement policies and procedures that prevent crime. The second model, reactive corporate fault model, shifts the focus of liability from fault prior to the acts to fault in reaction to the act in question.[140]

The third model focuses on the character of the corporation with an enquiry into whether the personality of the corporation encourages its agent or employees to commit criminal acts.[141] This theory modifies the test under vicarious liability to (1) the presence of an illegal policy and an agent who carries out the policy; (2) an illegal act that is committed, authorized, ordered, or endorsed by a high managerial agent; and (3) the implicit ratification or endorsement of the violation by the corporation.[142] The fourth model focuses on the internal decision-making structure of the corporation in order to distil corporate policy. This model imputes liability to the corporation when the act is consistent with the implementation of established corporate policy. The underlying basis for this model is that corporate actions rarely reflect individual choice and are in reality aggregates of individual decisions based on the structure of the corporation and influenced by the organisational culture.[143]

Notwithstanding the fact that the basis for the attribution of liability in the UK remains the identification doctrine, the recently passed Corporate Manslaughter

---

137 Wells [2001: 157].

138 See Colvin [1995: 22–3] for a similar argument.

139 Proponents of this model include Fisse. See Fisse, B [1983]: 'Restructuring Corporate Criminal Law: Deterrence, Retribution, Fault, and Sanctions', in Vol. 56, *Southern California Law Review*, 1141.

140 See Fisse, B [1983: 1195–7].

141 This model's chief proponent includes commentators such as Bucy, P [1991]: 'Corporate Ethos: A Standard for Imposing Corporate Criminal Liability', in Vol. 75, *Minnesota Law Review*, 1095; Foerschler, A [1990]: 'Corporate Criminal Intent: Toward a Better Understanding of Corporate Misconduct', in Vol. 78, *California Law Review*, 1287; and Moore [1992].

142 See Moore [1992: 768–9].

143 See French, P [1984]: *Collective and Corporate Responsibility* (New York: Columbia University Press), at 44.

Act provides for a form of organisational liability.[144] Section 3 provides that an organisation is guilty of an offence under the Act if the way in which its activities are managed or organized by its senior management is a substantial element in causing a person's death. The wording of the section suggests that courts will look to the liability of the whole corporation and how the corporation was run as an organisation. Although the liability provisions contained in the Act only apply to the offence of manslaughter, the principles relating to the derivation of liability for corporations may well be adopted in relation to the liability framework for corporations in relation to other offences such as transnational bribery.

Evaluating the Policy Considerations Concerning Vicarious and Identification Liability

The jurisprudential controversy over the exact nature of the corporation as a legal institution, prior to the recent exposition, has gone through three distinct views of the nature of the corporation. The first, the fiction theory of the corporation, viewed the corporation as an artificial entity with an existence distinct from its incorporators.[145] Conflated with the fiction theory of the corporation was the view that the corporation is a state concession and owed its existence to the state rather than to the private initiative of the incorporators. Inherent in the grant of the concession was the fact that corporations lacked any power beyond those conferred by the state.[146] Even the replacement of the express grant of the right to incorporate by a mechanical procedure was not considered a diminution in the role of the state in the regulation of corporations.[147]

On the contrary, the pervasive adoption of general incorporation statutes reinforced the idea that the corporation was an artificial creation of the state. Some of these incorporation statutes were distinct in the protection they afforded people who were harmed by corporations. A New York incorporation statute, for instance, imposed liability on the shareholder for debts owed to the corporation's employees.[148] Many of these incorporation statutes included specific limitations on the activities that could be carried out by the corporation, and the courts construed these powers very narrowly through the *ultra vires* doctrine.[149] The idea of the

144 Corporate Manslaughter and Corporate Homicide Act 2007 (UK).

145 Blumberg, P [1990]: 'The Corporate Entity in an Era of Multinational Corporations', in Vol. 15, *Delaware Journal of Corporate Law*, 283, at 292.

146 *Ibid.*, at 293.

147 Foster, N [2000]: 'Company Law Theory in Comparative Perspective: England and France', in Vol. 48, *American Journal of Comparative Law*, 573, at 583.

148 N.Y. Stock Corp. Law § 57 (consol. 1909).

149 Hurst, J [1970]: *The Legitimacy of the Business Corporation in the Law of the United States, 1780–1970* (Charlottesville: University of Virginia Press), at 37–44, identified these restrictions to include limitations on the duration and the capitalisation of corporations. Other limitations included the requirement for and enforcement of specific single corporate-purpose descriptions with a narrow interpretation of the *ultra vires* doctrine.

corporation as an artificial creature of the state provided a theoretical basis for the imposition of liability on the corporation rather than individuals.[150]

The second view, the aggregate theory, is the notion of the corporation as a product of private initiative. Eventually, this theory supplanted the view of the corporation as a creation of the state.[151] This basis in private initiative, despite its rejection of the role of the state, did not involve the suggestion that the corporation was not a separate legal entity of its own, separate and different from its shareholders with the rights traditionally recognized by the common law.[152] Rather, the aggregate notion of the corporation emphasized that corporate property rights were similar to individual property rights and therefore entitled to the same protections. Despite the fact that the aggregate theory decreased the validity of the fiction/concession theory's doctrinal foundation for the imposition of regulation on the corporation, it did not present a complete defence against the arguments for the imposition of regulation on corporations.

The growth in the size of corporations and the dispersal of share ownership reduced shareholders' active participation in the management of the corporation, thus leaving the operations of the corporation to professional managers. This shift in the internal relationship between management and shareholders rendered the partnership analogy, which the aggregate theory was based on, untenable. The justification for regulation was that the weak position of the corporation's shareholders required the imposition of liability on the corporation's management.[153] It is important to note that the focus of liability is not on the corporation but rather on the corporation's management to hold them accountable to the shareholders who could not impose these duties themselves.

The aggregate theory was rejected in exchange for the third notion of the corporation, the entity theory.[154] This theory views the corporation as a juridical unit with rights much like those of a natural person. The entity theory is similar to the fiction/concession theory with its focus on a corporation's separate existence from its incorporators. However, the entity theory differs from the fiction/concession theory with respect to one particular component crucial to the liability of corporations. The entity theory emphasizes the private initiative of the owners rather than the state concession emphasized by the fiction/concession. These rights extend both beyond the circumstances of the corporation's legal creation by the state and the claims or interests of the corporation's incorporators.

---

150 See Thoennes, K [2005]: 'Frankenstein Incorporated: The Rise of Corporate Power and Personhood in the United States', in Vol. 28, *Hamline Law Review*, 203, at 204–5, where she discusses the impact of artificially created corporations.

151 See Millon, D [1990, April]: 'Frontiers of Legal Thought I: Theories of the Corporation', in Vol. April 1990, *Duke Law Journal*, 201, at 202.

152 See the *Railroad Tax Cases,* 13 F. 722 C.C.D. Cal. (1882), at 758.

153 See Mark, G [1987]: 'The Personification of the Business Corporation in American Law', in Vol. 54, *University of Chicago Law Review*, 1441, at 1453.

154 Millon [1990: 211–16].

In sum, although the fiction theory does not actively promote the liability of individuals within the corporation, it is marked in contrast with the entity theory, which denies liability for the individuals within the corporation. The essence of the entity theory that constrains the individual liability is based on the contention that corporations are unique individuals separate from their human creators. This argument states that the distinction between the corporation and its owner, and the nature of the corporation as a separate entity, implies that the corporation, as a citizen, owes duties to the state analogous to those owed by natural persons, not as individuals but as a collective.

The understanding in the early twentieth century was that the fiction theory was pro-liability while the entity theory was anti-liability. The pro-liability assumptions of the fiction theory were based on the supposition that the origins of the corporation from the state entitled the state to regulate the corporation freely.[155] Conversely, the corporation as private initiative (aggregate) of individuals should not be subject to state regulation because regulation would restrict the freedom of contract of the individuals. This initial understanding of the liability bias of the two theories dominated comparisons, even though it was clear to many that the predominance of the fiction theory had not engendered an effective regulatory regime for corporations.[156]

Notwithstanding the pro-liability potential of the fiction/concession theory, Laski noted that the theory had 'fail[ed] to regulate [corporations] with the ease that might be desired'.[157] The criticisms of the fiction/concession theory revolved around the theory's premise of the corporation as a concession of the state.[158] The dominance of the fiction theory did not succeed in fostering a regime that would curb the power of corporations. On the contrary, corporate power had grown to staggering proportions under the fiction paradigm. The fiction theory could not foster a liability regime to curb the growth of corporate power, in part because the theory could not provide an adequate account of criminal responsibility of corporations. The fiction theory, Deiser concluded, was a 'venerable and decrepit survival' of a by-gone age, inadequate to cope with the realities of modern corporate life.[159]

Despite the seemingly pro-regulatory stance of the fiction/concession theory, the conceptual limitations of the theory ensured that the theory was unable to provide an adequate basis for the regulation of corporations.[160] The theoretical foundations

155 Hager, M [1989]: 'Bodies Politic: The Progressive History of Organizational "Real Entity" Theory', in Vol. 50, *University of Pittsburgh Law Review*, 575, at 579–80.

156 *Ibid.*, at 625–6.

157 Laski [1916a: 407].

158 Corporations, if created by state authorisation, could not possess their own 'personality' or 'will'. Secondly, there was a theoretical difficulty with the criminal acts and the doctrine of *ultra vires*.

159 Deiser [1909: 313].

160 Laski [1916a: 407].

of corporate criminal liability that were based on notions of negligence and moral fault with an individualistic perception of the corporation were incompatible with the emerging large-scale corporate enterprises. The entity theory, Laski argued, would provide an escape from the individualistic interpretation used as a premise for corporate liability inherent in the fiction/concession theory.[161] More pertinently, the agency and master servant doctrines being utilized by the common law to attribute criminal liability on corporations were only a covert move towards an entity theory of the corporation.[162]

In retrospect, the entity theory of the corporation offered a better theoretical basis for the imposition of criminal liability on corporations than the fiction/concession theory. The view of the common law that a corporation could not be criminally liable because it did not have a mind as an artificial being and could not be legally responsible for *ultra vires* acts, were relics of the fiction/concession theory and therefore shortcomings of the fiction/concession theory.[163]

The entity theory responded to these shortcomings because the entity could have a guilty conscience or at least the criminal liability of its incorporators could be imputed to the corporation. Furthermore, a corporation as an entity meant that its powers were a natural attribute of its own and not the product of state recognition and therefore liable for criminal acts.[164] Furthermore, it is clear that the logic of the real entity theory was used to liberate rather than restrain corporate conduct. For instance, the demise of the *ultra vires* doctrine and the constitutional restrictions on corporations were a result of the triumph of the entity theory of the corporation.[165] The entity theory facilitated the spread of corporations beyond the states of their incorporation. This was in contrast to the restrictions of the fiction/concession theory. Under the fiction/concession theory, the corporation as a state creation was not required to be recognized by another state.[166] On the other hand, a corporation as an autonomous entity whose powers do not derive from any one state was free to move across states.[167] The spread of corporations across state lines in the US was a precursor to the spread of the modern transnational corporation. The entity theory

161 Laski [1916b]: 'The Basis of Vicarious Liability', in Vol. 26, *Yale Law Review*, 105, at 121–2.

162 Laski [1916a: 416].

163 Hager [1989: 587, 593].

164 *Ibid.*, at 592–611.

165 See Horwitz, M [1985]: 'Santa Clara Revisited: The Development of Corporate Theory', in Vol. 88, *West Virginia Law Review*, 173, at 189 for a detailed account of this argument.

166 Corporations were denied the power to act beyond the borders of the states that chartered them. See *Bank of Augusta v Earle*, 38 U.S. (13 Pet.) 519 (1839), at 588.

167 The US Supreme Court rejected that idea that a corporation could not move across states in several cases decided in 1910. See *Southern Ry. v Greene*, 216 U.S. 400, 416–17 (1910); *Ludwig v Western Union Tel. Co.*, 216 U.S. 146, 164 (1910); *Western Union Tel. Co. v Kansas*, 216 U.S. 1, 18 (1910); *Pullman Co. v Kansas*, 216 U.S. 56 (1910).

significantly enhanced the private law, anti-regulatory conception of corporate law, and justified the early twentieth century relaxation of the regulation of corporations.

Theoretical Constraints on the Liability Framework for Corporations

Historically, the prevailing theory of the corporation has consistently had an impact on the appropriate liability regime for regulating corporations. A tapering of the essential elements of the debate on the nature of corporate personality in corporate law theory discussed in the previous section suggests that the debate is characterized by ideological distinctions of the corporation on two particular dimensions.

The first difference relates to the personality of the corporation and is characterized by the ideological distinction between the corporation as an artificial creation of the state and the corporation as a natural product of private initiative. The personality of the corporation is inherent in the conflict between the fiction/concession theory of the corporation, which views the corporation as an artificial creation of the state and the aggregate theory, which views the corporation as a product of private initiative. The issue raised is whether the state or private initiative should govern the regulatory regime for corporations.

The second difference relates to the liability of the corporation and is characterized by the ideological distinction between the corporation as an entity with a real existence separate from its shareholders and other participants, or as a mere aggregation of natural individuals without a separate existence. The liability of the corporation is inherent in the conflict between the aggregate theory of the corporation, which views the corporation as an aggregation of its natural members, and the entity theory, which views the corporation as an entity with a separate existence distinct from the natural persons that constitute the corporation. The issue raised is whether the individual or group is the appropriate unit for the imposition of liability on the corporation.

The personality and criminal liability of the corporation are critical to the regulation of transnational bribery by corporations and define the effectiveness of the regulatory framework to curb transnational bribery by corporations. In the following sections, two related arguments about the impact of corporate theories on the liability framework are presented. First, conceiving of the corporation as an entity appears to bolster the capacity of the corporation to evade liability. Second, the fiction/concession conception of the corporation constrains the imposition of criminal liability on the individuals within the corporation for transnational bribery.

Entity Conceptions of the Corporation Promote Evasion of Liability

The entity theory played a significant role in the development of the doctrine of limited liability.[168] Fiction/concession theory, the dominant paradigm of the

168 See Horwitz [1985: 205, 207–14].

corporation prior to the entity theory, eschewed the corporation as an entity distinct from its incorporators, a view that presented a theoretical challenge to the doctrine of limited liability. The concept of the corporation as a separate entity, on the other hand, rationalized the notion that the liability of the corporation could be separate from that of the shareholders.

The liability of a corporation for transnational bribery committed by the subsidiary and the circumstances under which the courts should pierce the corporate veil depends on the position of the court on limited liability. If the court believes that limited liability is unjustified, there would be enhanced inclination for piercing the corporate veil and thus holding the parent liable for transnational bribery by the subsidiary. On the other hand, if the view of the court is that limited liability is desirable, there would be reluctance to pierce the veil and hold the parent liable.

Whether or not limited liability is a desirable policy outcome is in turn influenced by the dominant description of the corporation. Under the entity concept, for instance, the doctrine of limited liability and the notion of the corporation as a separate entity are revered, even if the parent of the subsidiary is also a corporation. The fiction/concession theory, with its failure to recognize a distinct entity, would eliminate limited liability because a non-existent entity would be liable for the transnational bribery, while the liability of the very real shareholders would be limited to their paid-up capital. Entity conceptions of the corporation constrain the capacity of the law to regulate corporations in two significant ways. First, the emergence of the entity theory with its emphasis on private initiative advocated a diminutive role for the state in the regulation of corporations. Second, the entity theory played a significant role in justifying the emergence of the doctrine of limited liability.[169] The combined effect of decreased regulation and the increased prospect of the evasion of liability have severely weakened the capacity of the regulatory regime to curb transnational bribery by corporations.

The capacity of corporations to evade liability for transnational bribery as a result of the entity concept of the corporation has been exacerbated by the evolution of transnational corporations as complex networks of subsidiary corporations.[170] As discussed in the preceding section, the corporate law principle of limited liability does not distinguish between circumstances where the shareholder is a natural person or a corporation. The failure to distinguish between a corporation as a separate legal entity and therefore deserving of limited liability even if it is part of a corporate group is based on the entity concept. Commentators have noted how the failure to make the distinction between a person and a corporation as a shareholder has ensured that the law, in its piercing the veil jurisprudence, has

169 *Ibid.*, at 221.

170 Commentators have argued for a rethink of the way that we view corporations. See Ripken, S [2009]: 'Corporations Are People Too: A Multi-Dimensional Approach to the Corporate Personhood Puzzle', in Vol. 15, *Fordham Journal of Corporate and Financial Law*, 97, where she proposes an interdisciplinary view of corporations.

failed to adequately deal with the dynamic and commercial reality of corporate groups.[171] The failure to distinguish between instances where the shareholder is a person or a corporation permits a corporation to shield itself from liability for its own wrongdoing, even when the general principle justifying limited liability, concern for the protection of inactive shareholders, does not apply.

In sum, the entity concept of the corporation views corporations as legal institutions, emphasising that they are legal 'persons' and that this legal form defines the nature of the entity. This entity concept bolsters the capacity of corporations to evade liability for transnational bribery by articulating a view of the corporation that is at odds with the reality of the modern transnational corporation. The shortcoming of the regulatory regime for transnational bribery is based on the incongruity of applying traditional standards developed by the legal system regarding limited liability for individuals and applying them wholesale to situations involving the relations between various groups of corporations. The automatic extension to corporate groups of limited liability has undermined the liability regime for corporations engaging in transnational bribery.[172] The entity theory of the corporation bolsters the capacity of corporations to evade liability for transnational bribery by shielding themselves with the doctrine of limited liability.

Fiction/concession and Entity Conceptions of the Corporation Constrain the Imposition of Liability

The basis for the establishment of criminal liability on corporations discussed previously demonstrates that the prevailing liability framework for corporate criminal liability has oscillated between two distinct doctrinal views of the corporation: the view of the corporation as a collective of individuals or the corporation as being an entity independent of its constituents. These two doctrinal distinctions represent fundamentally different views on the imposition of criminal liability on the corporation. There are two distinct components to attaching criminal liability to a corporation. The first is identifying fault: who is responsible, the individual, or the corporation? The second component is the imposition of criminal liability: upon which one of them, the individual or corporation, should criminal liability be imposed?

With regard to the derivation of fault for criminal liability, the law has been influenced by the fiction/concession theory with the corporation viewed as a fiction and the individuals within the corporation as the only subjects of the

171 See Blumberg, P [1995]: *Multinational Challenge to Corporation Law: The Search for a New Corporate Personality* (Oxford: Oxford University Press), at 121–50.

172 These issues are not limited to corporate criminal liability for transnational bribery and arise across the entire range of the law, covering areas as diverse as classical tort liability, contract liability, environmental liability, product liability, labour liability, tax liability, competition liability, penal liability, and bankruptcy liability.

criminal law.[173] On the other hand, in the imposition of criminal liability, the law has adopted the entity concept of the corporation and separates the corporation's liability from those of the individuals within the corporation. The assumptions that the corporation's liability must be derivative and that the corporation must retain criminal liability are challenged in this argument. The regulatory regime should be switched, using the fiction/concession paradigm for imposing liability and the entity conception for identifying fault.

Treating the corporation as a fiction/concession for the purpose of deriving liability underestimates the complexity of the modern corporation and presents challenges in identifying fault within a complex corporate structure. The method for determining the liability of the corporation based on the fiction/concession theory would view the corporation as a collective. In this view, corporate responsibility is derivative, first located in an individual actor and then imputed to the corporation. On the one hand, if the corporation is viewed as an independent entity, the responsibility of the corporation is primary and not dependent on the responsibility of any individual within the corporation. The law relying on the fiction/concession conception of the corporation uses vicarious and identification models for the imputation of liability; both models treat corporate criminal liability as a derivative form of liability. Liability is derivative because it requires that an individual of the corporation from whom liability may be imputed to the corporation commit the initial offence. The substantive difference between the models is the positions of the people within the corporation that criminal liability may be imputed.

Despite the seemingly broad ambit of these two models, identifying the person responsible for transnational bribery within large transnational corporations is a complex endeavour.[174] Even in instances where there is overwhelming evidence that the bribe has been paid by the corporation, determining the agent to attribute the intent to pay the bribe is difficult. The identification liability model, in particular, distorts the allocation of criminal liability in complex transnational corporations.[175] Often, the decision to bribe a foreign public official is made at the level of a subsidiary or by middle management. In the identification liability model, the corporation would only be liable for transnational bribery authorized by senior officials within the corporation. The most salient criticism of both models is the fact that corporation's liability is hinged on the conduct of corporate personnel rather than on the presence of corporate fault.

173 See Alschuler, A [2009]: 'Two Ways to Think About the Punishment of Corporations', in Vol. 46, *American Criminal Law Review*, 1359, at 1367–9, where he makes the mainstream argument that a corporation is a mere fiction that cannot be punished, and that it is innocent shareholders who are forced to bear the direct burden of criminal sanctions.

174 See Coffee, C [1981: 417], where he indicates the difficulties identifying the truly blameworthy individual in many instances of corporate misbehaviour.

175 Fisse, B & Braithwaite, J [1993]: *Corporations, Crime, and Accountability* (Cambridge: Cambridge University Press), at 47, make a similar argument.

In the area where the law should treat the corporation as an aggregate, the imposition of liability, the focus is on the corporation rather than the individual within the corporation as the primary unit of liability. Treating the corporation as an entity for the purposes of imposing liability exaggerates the unity of the corporation and ensures that no particular constituent of the corporation bears the sanctions for transnational bribery. One of the significant changes in the nature of the modern corporation has been the rise of managerial power resulting from the separation of ownership and control in the corporation. The separation of ownership and control creates a moral hazard in that the managers who control the corporation may use their power for their self-interest rather than the interest of the owners. The issue of transnational bribery illustrates the moral hazard because the payment of the bribe by the manager is against the interest of the corporation.

The entity theory of the corporation has constrained the corporate liability for transnational bribery by focusing criminal liability on the group rather than on the individual. The lack of individual responsibility has been a source of criticism for the current regime for corporate criminal liability. The vicarious liability approach is both over-inclusive, as it permits unreasonable imputations against low-level employees; and yet under-inclusive, where corporate practices or policies actually encourage criminal acts, and no single employee's actions may be identified as culpable.[176] Treating the corporation as an entity reduces the responsibility for criminal liability for transnational bribery, as no particular individual within the corporation is responsible when the corporation engages in transnational bribery. This lack of individual liability requires a revised conception of the corporation to ensure responsibility within corporations for transnational bribery.

Conclusion

Modern transnational corporations have evolved into complex entities, and two facets of their complexity are particularly relevant to the liability regime for transnational bribery. The first facet of the complexity of these corporations relates to the legal nature of the relationship between two or more groups of corporations. The legal doctrine directly implicated by the complexity of the relationships of these transnational corporations is the doctrine of piercing the veil. The doctrine of piercing the veil is devised from the very well-settled principle of the limited liability of the corporation. The principle of limited liability holds that the corporation is a separate legal entity and therefore deserving of limited liability even if it is part of a corporate group.

The principles applied in piercing the veil where individuals are the shareholders are directly extended to situations where a parent corporation owns or controls a subsidiary. Allowing limited liability for corporations holding shares in another corporation allows the parent corporation to escape liability for

176 Laufer [1994: 659].

transnational bribery. The wholesale extension of the principle of limited liability to corporate groups is at odds with the fact that many corporate groups operate as a single entity simply because of the economic benefits that result from the integration of their activities. This extension allows a corporation to avoid liability for the obligations of a subsidiary corporation.

The second facet of complexity of these transnational corporations is internal to the corporation and relates to the organisational and managerial structure of these corporations. The complex organisational and management structures utilized by transnational corporations pose a significant challenge to the law with regard to the imposition of criminal liability. The ability of the law to impose criminal liability effectively for transnational bribery on the appropriate corporation in these complex webs of transnational corporations has been limited because of the complicated management structures.

The feature of the legal system directly challenged by the structural complexity of transnational corporations relates to the doctrines upon which the legal system imposes liability on corporations for criminal conduct. The two major doctrines utilized for the imposition of liability on the corporation are the doctrines of vicarious or identification liability. The challenge to the law pertains to the fact that the imposition of criminal liability on a corporation requires that clear standards be met regarding responsibility for actions before criminal liability is imposed. The complex organisational and management structures of transnational corporations ensure that establishing responsibility is often a difficult and complicated task, which poses a challenge to the two models used for imputing liability for criminal actions.

Chapter 7

Liability for Bribery within the Agency Framework of the Contracts Theory

The problem of transnational bribery is frequently analyzed in the context of criminal liability of the perpetrators for their action. The incidents of transnational bribery by corporations nonetheless raise serious questions about the quality and effectiveness of the governance of corporations. There is a theoretical justification for dealing with transnational bribery in the context of corporate governance rather than solely as an issue of individual wrongdoing. As Baer notes, once one assumes that the root cause of corporate misconduct is that managers and officers cannot achieve performance goals without resorting to some variety of fraud or intentional wrongdoing, then the problem of corporate misconduct is inevitably also an issue of corporate governance.[1] Efforts to stem transnational bribery can only follow two general directions. First, changes could acknowledge that directors and managers should control corporations and that efforts should be directed towards ensuring that these directors and managers do not engage in transnational bribery. This is the traditional method for analyzing corporate wrongdoing. The second direction, which entails analyzing corporate misconduct from a corporate governance perspective, would ensure that changes to the current system focus on empowering shareholders by providing them with better ways to monitor and influence corporate managers. The inherent logic to the corporate governance perspective is that lasting solutions require a reassessment of the allocation of powers between the various constituents of the corporation. Far-reaching changes to the problem of transnational bribery can only be achieved after we look beyond the narrow confines of corporate criminal liability to the very structure of corporate law.

The objective of this chapter is to develop and evaluate a supplementary explanation for the failure of the current multilateral regime to curb transnational bribery by corporations. In the argument developed in this chapter, it is maintained that the inefficacies of the current multilateral efforts stem from the failure of these initiatives to provide adequate direction to national legal systems for the implementation of an effective regime to hold transnational corporations liable for bribery. This point has not been given sufficient attention in the ongoing debate about the current multilateral efforts against transnational bribery. This argument is predicated on the assumption that aspects of domestic structures will invariably

1 Baer, M [2010]: 'Organizational Liability and the Tension Between Corporate and Criminal Law', in Vol. 19, *Journal of Law & Policy*, 1, at 14.

influence the level of effectiveness of these multilateral initiatives independently from the level of compliance of any state.

The significance of the liability of corporations to the effectiveness of the OECD Convention was explicitly recognized by the *Travaux Préparatoires* to the Convention. According to the Chair of the OECD Working Group on Bribery, beyond individual wrongdoing, corporate liability was exactly the issue that needed to be tackled if the OECD Convention was to be successful in changing attitudes towards transnational bribery.[2] He further notes that additional reasons were given for corporate liability. Citing the example of Bulgaria, he noted that the examiners in the Phase 2 evaluation observed that '"corporate entities" were "frequent vehicles for the payment of bribes"', and went on to say that 'the use of elaborate financial structures and accounting techniques to conceal the nature of transactions is commonplace'.[3]

Buttressing the observations of the Chair of the Working Group, commentators have suggested that '… in relation to corruption cases in particular, it is, however, very often the legal person (typically the company or corporation) which drives, and benefits from, corrupt activity"'.[4] Notwithstanding the significance of the framework for corporate liability, the Chair of the Working Group acknowledged that differences in the application of corporate liability across different legal systems resulted in the OECD negotiations opting for a broad common denominator.[5] Despite the significance of the liability of corporations in preventing transnational bribery, the articles of the OECD Convention did not articulately define minimum standards to be implemented by the State Parties with respect to the imposition of corporate liability.[6]

In analysing the liability framework for corporations, the argument in the last chapter suggested that legislation regulating transnational bribery by corporations has ossified the conception of a corporation as an 'entity'. Developments in corporate law theory, however, have challenged what is known as the 'entity' conception of the corporation. The entity conception utilized in the liability regime for transnational bribery by corporations is at variance with the complex and internally conflicted transnational corporations that are widespread in transnational commercial transactions. Granted, contemporary corporate law theory has not provided a unified or all-encompassing account of the nature of corporations. Contemporary law theory has nonetheless discarded the formalistic 'entity theory' of the corporation upon which regulations prohibiting transnational

2 See Pieth, M [2007]: 'Article 2 – The Responsibility of Legal Persons'. In Pieth, M, Low, L & Cullen, P (eds.) [2007]: *The OECD Convention on Bribery: A Commentary*. Cambridge: Cambridge University Press. Available on the OECD website at http://www.oecd.org/dataoecd/27/34/39200754.pdf at 5. Last visited 4 March 2013.

3 *Ibid.*, at 6.

4 Nicholls, C, Daniel, T, Polaine, M & Hatchard, J [2006: 415].

5 Pieth, M [2007: 6].

6 See Nicholls, C, Daniel, T, Polaine, M & Hatchard, J [2006: 416] where they state that the liability of legal persons is central to the enforcement of the OECD Convention.

bribery are modelled. The entity theory has been replaced by a 'contracts theory' of the corporation.

The contracts theory, relying on agency principles, deconstructs the corporation into component parts of the corporation's human participants. The contracts theory of the corporation suggests that the corporation should not be treated as an entity, but as a network of contracts between various constituencies. The analytical basis for devising regulation under the contracts theory examines legislative options to determine their effect on relationships that exist between the constituent parts of the corporation. Pertinent to the regulation of transnational bribery, this concept of the corporation recognizes that the different constituents of a corporation have different and sometimes conflicting incentives. The liability framework of corporations engaging in transnational bribery should thus be designed to take account of the conflicting incentives of the various constituents of the corporation. Holding shareholders liable for transnational bribery may seem a radical expansion of the current liability regime. Nonetheless, the foundations of an expanded shareholder duty have been laid in existing case law and new regulations.

The first section sketches the contracts theory of the corporation. The second section applies the insights of the agency framework to transnational bribe transactions by corporations. The third section proposes an alternate liability framework for transnational corporations. The argument proffered, that an effective liability framework to curb transnational bribery by corporations should be based on the contracts theory of the corporation, relies on three assumptions. First, if some or all of the rights of the various corporate constituents arise from or are subject to contract, the current emphasis on the prohibition of transnational bribery through the imposition of criminal liability as a preference-shaping device has a limited role in shaping the specification of these rights. Second, acceptance that the corporation is a network of contracts suggests that the theory describing the legal rules applicable to these corporate contracts would be equally useful in the analysis of how corporate criminal liability could be used to shape the preferences of the corporation's various constituents. Third, the approach implicit in contractual expositions of the corporation highlights many erroneous assumptions implicit in the current regime of criminal liability for the regulation of transnational bribery by corporations.

Analytical Foundations of the Contracts Theory and Agency Framework

In the early 1930s, Berle & Means set out to describe what they saw as the major trend of modern publicly held corporations, namely the separation of ownership and control.[7] This concept of the corporation influenced corporate legal theory

7 Berle, A, & Means, G, [1932]: *The Modern Corporation and Private Property* (New York: Macmillan), at 124.

in two significant ways.[8] First, it recast the central conundrum of corporate law as the separation of ownership and control. The shift in power to management gave managers control over property that was, in actuality, owned by someone else. Second, this concept hypothesized that the concentration of economic power coupled with the separation of ownership and control had the effect of eroding legal control over managers of the corporation.

This formulation of the central conundrum of corporate law as a separation between ownership and control has become attenuated by the size and complexity of the modern corporation. This is because attaching responsibility and locating the source of control over corporate operations is more pronounced in large complex corporations. Modern corporate law vests managers with wide discretionary control over the activities of the corporation. The limited rights of shareholders to challenge the decisions of management are protected by the business judgement rule and shielded by exculpatory statutes that limit the liability of managers for bad business decisions.[9] The only real power possessed by shareholders is the right to vote, but given the diffuse ownership of corporations, there is little incentive for shareholders to act in concert (collective action problem). These shareholders would benefit from monitoring the conduct of managers, but individually, none of them has the incentive to do so.

Much of the recent work on corporate law theory has built on the initial insights of Berle & Means, but extended their thinking in two ways particularly relevant to the regulation of transnational bribery by corporations. First, contemporary corporate law posits that the manager has far less autonomy than was described by Berle & Means because the manager's own self-interest would lead him to install various monitoring and bonding devices in order to maximize the value of his own investment in the corporation.[10] Second, recent scholarship has rejected the view of the corporation as being owned by shareholders in favour of a view of the corporation as an equilibrium position achieved through bargaining among the various participants, including managers, shareholders, and creditors.[11]

---

8 See Tsuk, D [2005]: 'From Pluralism to Individualism: Berle and Means and 20th-Century American Legal Thought', in Vol. 30, *Law & Social Inquiry*, 179, for a general discussion of modern legal scholarship's interpretation of the foundational analysis of corporations by Berle and Means.

9 For a discussion of the ramifications of the business judgement rule, see Bainbridge, S [2004]: 'The Business Judgment Rule as Abstention Doctrine', in Vol. 57, *Vanderbilt Law Review*, 83.

10 See Alchian, A & Demsetz, H [1972]: 'Production, Information Costs and Economic Organization', in Vol. 62, *American Economic Review*, 777; Cheung, S [1983]: 'The Contractual Nature of the Firm', in Vol. 26, *Journal of Law and Economics*, 1; and Fama, E [1980]: 'Agency Problems and the Theory of the Firm', in Vol. 88, *Journal of Political Economy*, 288.

11 See Fama, E & Jensen, M [1983]: 'The Separation of Ownership and Control', in Vol. 26, *Journal of Law and Economics*, 301; Jensen & Meckling, [1976]: 'Theory of the

The disaggregation of the corporation into constituent parts is the crucial intellectual contribution provided by the contracts theory of the corporation.

The intellectual foundation provided by the concept of the central conundrum of the corporation by Berle & Means were developed much around the same time as Coase developed his insights into the nature of the corporation.[12] Coase suggested that corporations exist to reduce transaction costs and that corporations would integrate to the extent required to take advantage of savings in transaction costs.[13] Coase had already started to conceive of the corporation as a series of relationships. From the basic notion that there were different constituents within a corporation, it was not long before commentators started to describe the role and functions of the various constituents of the corporation. The insights provided by Coase regarding the relationship between the corporation and the rest of the world were extended by Alchian & Demsetz to explain the internal dynamics of the corporation.[14] They suggested that corporations were designed to solve the problems associated with rewards in a system where individual inputs are unobservable because each team member's performance is impossible or prohibitively expensive to monitor. The solution to this problem was outside monitoring by principals whose incentives would be the residual earnings of the team. Jensen & Meckling built on the monitoring analysis framework suggested by Alchian & Demsetz by implying that the corporation was more than a device for the elimination of market transactions.[15] Their view of the corporation described the corporation as a vehicle that served as the basis for contracting relationships characterized by the existence of divisible residual claims on the assets and cash flow of the organisation.

Taken together, the contributions of Alchian & Demsetz on the one hand and Jensen & Meckling on the other erased the boundary between the corporation and the outside world. The erasure of the boundary essentially permitted Coase's analysis to be applied to the entire landscape of the corporation such that even the relationships between all the constituents of the corporation were a negotiated agreement. From Jensen & Meckling's standpoint, the boundaries of the corporations as developed by Coase were meaningless.[16] They suggested that the corporation in reality was only a multitude of complex relationships (a nexus of contracts) between various participants. These sets of implicit or explicit contracts and the legal interpretation of these contracts governed the actions of the various

---

Firm: Managerial Behavior, Agency Costs, and Ownership Structure', in Vol. 3, *Journal of Financial Economics*, 305.

12 See Bainbridge, S [2002]: 'The Board of Directors as Nexus of Contracts', in Vol. 88, *Iowa Law Review*, 1, at 9–10, for a discussion of the early Berle/Means concepts of separation of ownership and control, the Coase theory, and the nexus of contracts model. He states that the origins of the nexus of contracts model can be traced to Coase's famous article.

13 Coase, R [1937]: 'The Nature of the Firm', *Economica*, repr. in Stigler, G & Boulding, K (eds.) [1952]: *Readings in Price Theory* (Homewood: Richard D. Irwin), 386.

14 Alchian & Demsetz [1972].

15 Jensen & Meckling [1976].

16 *Ibid.*, 310.

constituents making up the corporation. Thus, reference to the corporation as an entity masked the importance of these contracts.

The analysis of the corporation as a nexus of contracts spawned the analysis of relationships between the constituents of corporations within an agency framework.[17] Jensen & Meckling recognized the potential conflicts that arise between managers and shareholders because of share ownership dispersal.[18] The managers do not necessarily have incentives to act in the best interests of the shareholder. Accordingly, shareholders would incur costs to monitor the manager's performance. The likelihood that self-interested managers would deviate from the best interests of the shareholders would prompt both parties to provide incentives for managers to be loyal by bonding themselves to the corporation. They argued further that it was in the interest of management to convince potential shareholders, by bonding, that the corporation would minimize agency costs.[19] However, despite monitoring by the shareholders, alignment between the interests of both parties was impossible, and these divergences were referred to as residual losses. The sum total of the monitoring, bonding costs, and residual losses are the agency costs of the relationship.[20] Furthermore, these agency costs can be reduced through monitoring, bonding, and incentive compensation.[21] This agency view of the contracts theory advocated by Jensen & Meckling buttresses the voluntary nature of the corporation and cautions that the liability regime for transnational bribery by corporations is cognisant of the terms upon which the various constituents have contracted to participate in the corporation.

Applying the Contracts Theory and Agency Analysis to Transnational Corporate Bribery

The premise of the current regime for transnational bribery is that for deterrence purposes, a corporation should be held liable for the bribe transactions carried out by its agent. The regulatory regime prohibiting transnational bribery imposes liability on the corporation for the actions of its employees through the mechanism of vicarious liability.[22] This is based on the assumption that it is efficient to hold the corporation liable for transnational bribes based on the entity conception of

---

17 For a detailed account of the evolution of the contract theory of the corporation, see Bolodeoku, I [2005]: 'Contractarianism and Corporate Law: Alternative Explanations to the Law's Mandatory and Enabling/Default Contents', in Vol. 13, *Cardozo Journal of International and Comparative Law*, 433, at 445–51.

18 Jensen & Meckling [1976: 312–19].

19 The cost associated with reducing misappropriation.

20 Jensen & Meckling [1976: 308].

21 *Ibid.*, 325.

22 Yockey, J [2011]: 'Solicitation, Extortion, and the FCPA', in Vol. 87, *Notre Dame Law Review*, 781, at 808–12, argues that the FCPA enforcement policies raise unique corporate governance and compliance challenges and ultimately pose a risk of over deterrence.

the corporation. This view holds that transnational bribery is deterred efficiently if the corporation is held liable because holding the corporation liable forces the internalisation of social costs of engaging in a bribe transaction. The imposition of liability on the corporation operates as a direct sanction on the actual wrongdoer, the corporation. The direct application of the sanction to the corporation deters the management from engaging in bribe transactions. The entity concept of the corporation for liability for transnational bribery supports this view that imposing vicarious/identification criminal liability on the corporation invariably reduces the incidence of bribery. This deterrence model is based on the assumption that even where risk-averse managers are relatively free from shareholder monitoring, and where the corporation is not threatened with insolvency, risk-averse corporate managers would refrain from pursuing the wealth interests of shareholders by unlawful means. Since these are the prevailing conditions at most large corporations, bribery should not be a significant social problem. Nonetheless, corporations engage in transnational bribery; this is because this standard deterrence model does not apply to a bribe transaction.[23]

The preceding deterrence model breaks down when applying the contracts theory of the corporation to analyse the transnational bribery corporations. In a typical bribe transaction, the manager alone makes the choice of whether or not to pay a bribe to secure a lucrative contract. This decision is influenced by the risk that the refusal to pay the bribe will result in the loss of the contract to a competitor who is willing to pay the bribe. The decision to pay the bribe is much riskier to the manager than it is to the shareholder, but the payment of the bribe is the only way in which the manager can obtain the lucrative contract. The payoff to the manager is much higher than the potential gains to the shareholder in the event that the contract is secured because the relative benefit of the bribe is divided among the other shareholders. In this scenario, the manager's preference for the high-risk/high-payoff strategy conflicts with that of the shareholders, who have no desire to risk the consequences of bribery for very little payoff.

The conclusion that management may sometimes behave in a risk-preferring fashion may appear to contradict the basic premise that managers tend to be more risk averse than shareholders with regard to the corporation. Yet, there is no contradiction. The manager's utility function remains constant, but whether he will disdain a desirable risk or accept an excessive one depends on the expected benefits from the risk incurred in each case. In a transnational bribery transaction, the expected benefit is high and thus the rational utility-maximising manager is more likely to pay the bribe to secure the contract.

---

23 See Meeks, W [2006]: 'Corporate and White-Collar Crime Enforcement: Should Regulation and Rehabilitation Spell an End to Corporate Criminal Liability?', in Vol. 40, *Columbia Journal of Law and Social Problems*, 77, at 87, where he states that recent corporate scandals have shown that policing corporate crime through traditional enforcement techniques such as post hoc punitive fines and sanctions has been ineffective to achieve the goals of deterrence and punishment.

The insights from the agency theory caution against treating the corporation in the context of a bribe transaction as an entity with a single interest. On the contrary, the corporation is composed of various constituents with different and sometimes conflicting interests. The current model for the regulation of transnational bribery makes two erroneous assumptions relating to transnational bribery by corporations. First, transnational corporations often have groups of widely dispersed shareholders or are subsidiaries of another corporation. Where the shareholders are dispersed, they face collective action problems. In cases where the shareholders are dispersed as well as where another corporation is the shareholder, an additional level of agency costs is introduced.

Second, the model oversimplifies the principal-agent problem of transnational corporations, viewing the principal as a single owner-manager of a corporation who hires agents to perform various tasks on his behalf. The principal also decides what measures the corporation will take to deter wrongful acts by the agents. On the contrary, the modern corporation is a structurally complex organisation with elaborate layers of managerial structures developed to oversee their activities. Although managers decide how the corporation will deter bribery, another layer of agency costs is introduced when middle-level managers commit the bribery as opposed to senior managers.

With regard to the first erroneous assumption relating to transnational bribery implicit in the current liability regime, the shareholders in a corporation do not represent a monolithic group with undifferentiated interests and incentives.[24] For instance, within the corporation, there is a distinction between the undiversified shareholders and diversified shareholders. Undiversified shareholders hold an investment portfolio dominated by the shares of one or a small number of corporations. These portfolios are highly risky as the fortunes of the shareholders are closely linked to that of the single corporation. The typical undiversified shareholder is an investor with controlling interests in the corporation. In this scenario, the undiversified investor maximizes personal utility by maximising the market value of that single corporation. Undiversified shareholders would also include holding corporations and, more importantly for this analysis, the corporation's management. The diversified shareholder, on the other hand, is typically risk-averse and seeks a diversified portfolio of investments in order to reduce risk.[25] Nevertheless, investors in any particular corporation will each have different preferences in terms of risk and income. The interests of these

---

24 For a detailed account of the argument that shareholders do not have a single and uniform interest, see Stout, L & Blair, M [2006]: 'Specific Investment: Explaining Anomalies in Corporate Law', in Vol. 31, *Journal of Corporate Law*, 719. See also Hayden, G & Bodie M [2010]: 'Shareholder Democracy and the Curious Turn Toward Board Primacy', in Vol. 51, *William and Mary Law Review*, 2071, at 2095–6, where they discuss the possible divergence in shareholders' interests.

25 For present purposes, it is sufficient to state that the greater the number of different securities held by an individual, the lower the risk.

diversified shareholders are maximized when management maximizes the corporation's value.

With regard to the second erroneous assumption relating to transnational bribery implicit in the current liability regime, shareholders are not the only constituents of a corporation that may have conflicting interests. Managers are also not a monolithic group, and the interests of middle managers may differ from those of senior management. The investment of management in the corporation differs distinctively from that of the shareholder in that it is inherently non-diversifiable. This stems from investment in firm-specific specialisation and the disproportionate level of investment, as the manager's job is typically his most important investment. The interests of senior managers are often more closely aligned with those of the undiversified shareholder than with those of the diversified shareholder for the following reasons. First, there is a greater investment of firm-specific capital in the corporation by senior managers. Second, senior managers' compensation tends to be based more on firm quarterly or annual financial results than that of middle managers, who are compensated more on their individual or departmental performance. Conversely, middle managers interests may more closely be aligned with those of the diversified shareholder. The sum effect of these varying interests is that both senior and middle managers will make decisions to maximize their personal utility. While the senior managers may receive personal satisfaction from maximising shareholder value, the personal utility of middle managers is not tied to the market value of the corporation.

Not only does the current model regulating transnational bribery by corporations fail to distinguish between the interests of the different shareholders and managers, the model fails to distinguish between the preferences and incentives of groups of managers and shareholders within the corporation. In this construct, unlike a shareholder, whose utility is enhanced by maximising share prices, a manager's utility is more dependent upon such factors as job security and his corporation's latest quarterly results, factors that encourage risky behaviour such as engaging in a bribe transaction.[26]

Shareholders and managers thus have divergent interests with respect to bribe transactions. The divergence of interests among different categories of shareholders may itself give rise to a whole host of agency costs. These differing interests further complicate the agency cost analysis. When an undiversified shareholder, including a parent, is present, a corporation will be more likely to choose excessively risky, socially costly activity in the form of engaging in a bribe transaction. When corporate ownership is dispersed, that tendency will be reduced. The reasons for this include, first, when corporate ownership is dispersed, senior managerial risk aversion is likely to temper shareholder tendency to take

---

26 Eisenberg, M [1989]: 'Contractual Freedom in Corporate Law: Articles and Comments: The Structure of Corporation Law', in Vol. 89, *Columbia Law Review*, 1461, at 1472, refers to the interaction between shareholder wealth maximization and managerial job security as positional conflicts.

excessive risks. By comparison, an undiversified shareholder by virtue of his control over the corporation may more easily compel managers to indulge his risk-taking preferences to maximize profit.

Second, an undiversified shareholder will be better able to strategically time dividend payments or equity sales to assure that the benefits from risky corporate activity are vested in the shareholders before lawsuits are filed against the corporation. Finally, because a controlling shareholder obtains special benefits from corporate activities, such a shareholder will be more likely to encourage a corporation to take excessive risks. Thus, when faced by a bribe transaction, the undiversified shareholder would prefer the riskier corporate activity by the payment of the bribe while the diversified shareholder would not favour such activity because the marginal benefit from the corporate activity to the undiversified shareholder will be higher. The problem is even more acute where the undiversified shareholder is a corporation. A corporation's parent, for example, could compel the corporation to pay dividends promptly when the corporation is engaged in very risky activities. The parent also might simply sell the subsidiary. This would mean that the parent (as well as other shareholders) could potentially lock in benefits from the bribe transaction before the transaction is prosecuted.

The excessive desire for risk-taking by the undiversified shareholder can be tempered by senior managerial risk aversion, which theoretically should dampen the tendency of the undiversified shareholder to select excessively risky activity. Unless constrained to do so by shareholders, however, senior managers are unlikely to engage in a bribe transaction because that would mean putting their (undiversified) jobs at risk whilst the benefit goes to the corporation's shareholders. Consequently, senior managers might not maximize profits in the strictest sense, which in this case would involve not engaging in a bribe transaction whose downside costs could be subsidized by limited liability. Senior managers might prefer to forego the bribe transaction and simply maintain profit levels and their jobs, even if such an approach does not obtain every possible profit dollar for stockholders. This, in turn, is tempered by middle managerial risk-taking preferences, as they have not invested as much capital in the firm, as discussed previously.

This discussion suggests that, as with diversified shareholders, senior managers will be more risk-averse and less likely to engage in a bribe transaction than would middle management and the undiversified shareholder. The difference in interests among managers, however, is probably not as acute as that among shareholders. Because senior management has a greater influence on corporate policy, there is likelihood that their interest would have a greater effect on corporate behaviour than those of middle managers. The traditional supplement to the agency problem, discussed previously, has been the discipline provided by the possibility of takeover.[27] This disciplining effect operates by a process of adverse selection whereby third parties learn that a corporation has bad managers, take

27 The notion that the market for corporate control provides a disciplining effect on potentially inefficient managers is attributed to Henry Manne. See Manne, H [1965]:

over the corporation, and install better managers who will increase the value of the corporation. However, this disciplining effect by third-party bidders is ineffective in mitigating the moral hazard situation presented by bribe transactions. The basis for the ineffectiveness is that if the prevailing incentive scheme fails to eliminate the possibility of moral hazard, it is inferred that any other rational manager in a similar position would act in the same manner. Replacing the manager would be irrelevant, as the new manager facing the same incentive scheme would behave in the same manner. Thus, even if ongoing moral hazard inefficiency is known by the market and reflected in the corporation's stock price, it may not be profitable for informed third parties to mount a takeover effort.

This reluctance to discipline managerial moral hazard becomes even more pronounced if potential third-party bidders cannot easily observe whether managers are succumbing to moral hazard incentives. Therefore, the agency cost in a bribe transaction-setting needs to be structured to contend not only with adverse selection problems but with moral hazard problems as well. The only way to mitigate moral hazard problems is to improve the incentive scheme facing the manager and there is nothing inherent in takeover or replacement system to achieve this result. Furthermore, it is conceivable that efforts to solve adverse selection problems by replacing senior managers could exacerbate the managerial moral hazard. Senior managers are often privy to information useful in controlling the moral hazard of middle managers. Replacing incumbent senior managers on adverse selection grounds could heighten the moral hazard problems presented by middle managers.

Viewing the corporation as a nexus of contracts alters the traditional deterrence model for inducing corporations to comply with the prohibitions against transnational bribery. This perspective suggests that each of the contracts is subject to efficient breach.[28] Altering the liability regime to increase the cost of one particular type of breach will increase the level of compliance. The cost is increased by altering the liability regime to raise the level of monitoring of parties to the contract. The rationale is to overcome the perverse incentive of the corporate officers to decrease monitoring in order to reduce the number of violations detected, even though the sanctions on detection are more severe.

In summary, the assertion that corporate agents have weaker incentives to commit bribery than individuals while bearing the full risk of punishment is flawed because the agents must share the gains from the bribe with the other corporate constituents. This is because this scenario does not take into account the private benefits derived from aspiration levels set by the senior management. Recognising the influence of differing incentives, risk preferences, and monitoring functions fundamentally changes the analysis of the prohibitions of transnational bribery by corporations. The regulatory regime for curbing transnational bribery

---

'Mergers and the Market for Corporate Control', in Vol. 73, *Journal of Political Economy*, 110, at 117.

28 There will be some circumstances in which the contracting party can derive more benefit from breaching the contract than from performing it.

assumes that the imposition of liability on the corporation should lead to a reduction in bribe transactions. Analysing the corporation as a nexus of contracts reveals that prohibiting transnational bribery by corporations will not necessarily reduce its occurrence and may indeed exacerbate the problem. The current regime presents constituents who should be playing a monitoring role with the potentially perverse incentive that increasing their monitoring role would ensure that they risk bearing liability and the cost of the imposition of liability. This perverse incentive calls into question the underlying regime regulating transnational bribery by corporations.[29]

To illustrate the significance of the corporate criminal liability framework to the effectiveness of legislation and to buttress the argument that the OECD Convention would be more effective if a different basis for corporate liability were adopted, this section examines the impact of the Sarbanes-Oxley Act (a liability framework premised on the contracts theory of the corporation) and its effect on FCPA enforcement actions.[30] The Securities Act of 1933 ('Securities Act') and the Securities Exchange Act of 1934 ('Exchange Act') impose obligations on companies listed on the US stock exchange to provide a variety of reports relating to their financial position.[31] The Exchange and Securities Acts provided the framework upon which the reporting obligations of corporations were determined. This regime was substantially altered in July 2002 with the passage of the Sarbanes-Oxley Act of 2002. The objective of the Sarbanes-Oxley Act is to protect investors in listed companies by improving the accuracy and reliability of corporate disclosures under the securities laws. The main provision of the Sarbanes-Oxley Act is incentive driven and requires the disclosure of knowledge of wrongdoing and certification of financial reports by the chief executive officers (CEOs) and chief financial officers (CFOs).[32] The certification requirement mandates the CEOs and CFOs to certify the following in each annual or quarterly report. First, that the signing officer has reviewed the report. Second, based on the officer's knowledge, the report does not contain any untrue statement of a material fact or omit to state a material fact necessary in order to make the statements made misleading. The act imposes direct criminal penalties on CEOs and CFOs who certify reports knowing that they do not comply with the act. The penalties for knowing inaccuracies in the reports filed by the CEO and CFO include a fine of up to five million dollars, 20 years' imprisonment, and forfeiture of incentive-based compensation and profits from sale of securities to the corporation.[33]

---

29 A similar argument has been made by Arlen, who argues that a strict regime of vicarious corporate liability can have the perverse effect of discouraging socially desirable corporate monitoring. See Arlen, J [1994]: 'The Potentially Perverse Effects of Corporate Criminal Liability', in Vol. 23, *Journal of Legal Studies*, 833, at 848–9.

30 Sarbanes-Oxley Act of 2002, Pub. L. No. 107-204, 116 Stat. 745 (2002) (codified at 15 U.S.C. §§ 7201–66 (2002).

31 See Securities Exchange Act of 1934 Section 12(b)(1)(D)–(G), 15 U.S.C Section 78l(b)(1)(D)–(G).

32 See Section 302 of the act, titled 'Corporate responsibility for financial reports.'

33 See 18 U.S.C.A. § 1350 (2004).

In contrast to the regulations prohibiting transnational bribery by corporations, the Sarbanes-Oxley Act is premised on a model of the corporation that draws on the corporation as a nexus of contracts. The view of the corporation as a nexus of contracts suggests that each of the contracts among the constituents of a corporation is subject to efficient breach.[34] The strategy for regulatory compliance adopted by the Sarbanes-Oxley Act is to increase the cost of breaching the monitoring function by one of the contracting parties within the corporation. The Sarbanes-Oxley Act therefore attempts to regulate the actions of the corporation by altering the incentives of the key constituents in the corporation.

Sarbanes-Oxley has already had a noticeable impact on FCPA compliance practices with respect to the investigation of potential FCPA violations and disclosure issues.[35] The certification requirements of the Sarbanes-Oxley Act extend to cover violations of the FCPA provisions. Although Sarbanes-Oxley does not refer to the FCPA, the certification requirements for CEOs and CFOs under Section 302 requires the periodic certifications to state any fraud, whether or not material, involving persons with a significant role in corporate internal controls were disclosed auditors and the Board of Directors. Section 406 requires a code of corporate ethics for senior financial officers, defined to include compliance with legal obligations. Section 906 contains new criminal penalties for false certifications. The periodic certifications must identify any corrective actions with respect to significant deficiencies and material weaknesses in internal controls or other factors that could significantly affect internal controls. The certification requirement removes responsibility for oversight from management and imposes a monitoring obligation on the Board of Directors and auditors. Prior to the certification requirements imposed by the Sarbanes-Oxley Act, corporations discovering violations of the FCPA provisions could opt to remediate these issues without disclosure to enforcement officials.

The increase in the level of compliance with the reporting requirements that occurred after the passage of the Sarbanes-Oxley Act suggests that the law can contribute to reducing the incidence of transnational bribery if the punishment imposed is sufficient to deter the conduct of responsible parties within the corporation. With the certification requirements imposed by the Sarbanes-Oxley Act, compliance was increased because the CEO and CFO could be held criminally

---

34 An efficient breach of contract occurs whenever the breaching party profits from the breach after compensating the other party for his or her expectation interest. Applied to regulatory law, the doctrine suggests that a corporation would evade economic regulations whenever it is profitable to do so. See Posner [1998: 118–20].

35 See Low, L, Bonheimer, O & Lorello, D [2007]: 'The Uncertain Calculus of FCPA Voluntary Disclosures'. Paper presented to the American Conference Institute 17th National Conference, 27 & 28 March 2007, at 2–6. Available at http://apps.americanbar.org/intlaw/spring07/World%20Bank%20Anticorruption%20Programs/Low%20-%20The%20Uncertain%20Calculus%20of%20FCPA%20Voluntary%20Disclosures.pdf. Last visited 4 March 2013.

responsible for non-compliance. The claim here is not that the Sarbanes-Oxley Act has reduced the incidence of fraud within corporations. Rather, the claim is that the Sarbanes-Oxley Act has increased the level of monitoring within the corporation by recognising that parties within the corporation are best placed to foster oversight over the reporting activities of the corporation.[36] Granted, the Sarbanes-Oxley Act merely insisted on reporting; however, the crucial underlying assumption for the regulation of transnational bribery by corporation is that the reporting process itself decreases unethical behaviour.

The Proposed Liability Regime for Transnational Corporations for Bribery

This book has argued that the legal responses to transnational bribery by corporations have been ineffective. Even worse, the analysis indicates that the incongruity of the legal responses may serve to exacerbate the occurrence of transnational bribery by corporations. The occurrence of transnational bribery is exacerbated because the current legislative framework does not make any allowance for the differing preferences of the various constituents of the corporations and therefore allows the corporation to shield itself from liability. The argument presented suggests that the failure to make allowance for the constituent parties comprising the corporation is based on the tendency to view the modern corporation as a single monolithic entity rather than an entity with constituent parts, which often have different and sometimes conflicting interests.

The varying and sometimes conflicting interests on the liability regime for transnational bribery by corporations have had a significant impact on its effectiveness. A radical revision of the usual norms of legal accountability as applied to corporations is required if any meaningful progress in curbing transnational bribery is to be achieved. For instance, in the discussion on limited and criminal liability of the corporations in the preceding chapters, several commentators defended the current regime of limited shareholder liability in general and, by necessary implication, the criminal liability regime for corporations. Other commentators proposed pro rata unlimited shareholder liability for corporate actions. Even these proposals for pro rata unlimited shareholder liability do not go far enough because regimes of liability coupled with the prohibitions against transnational bribery by corporations do not adequately account for the differences in incentives and transaction costs that influence either different shareholders or managers in a corporation.

36 See Westbrook, A [2011]: 'Enthusiastic Enforcement, Informal Legislation: The Unruly Expansion of the Foreign Corrupt Practices Act', in Vol. 45, *Georgia Law Review*, 489, at 510–15, where she argues that Sarbanes-Oxley has led to more vigorous enforcement of the FCPA as the greater disclosure requirements have led corporations to err on the side of caution by reporting borderline transactions rather than risk the consequences of non-disclosure in the event of an investigation.

There is some consensus in the literature that the arguments espoused in favour of limited liability for publicly traded corporations do not apply for closely held corporations and parent-subsidiary groups. Bainbridge, for instance, notes that holding a parent liable for a subsidiary's conduct will not discourage investor diversification or cause the parent's shareholders to invest excessively in firm monitoring.[37] Similarly, commentators have argued that shareholders in closely held firms should be liable for corporate torts and that vicarious liability should extend to directors of publicly traded corporations.[38] This proposal has gained very few adherents. The main criticisms revolve around the chilling effect that potential tort liability would have in deterring qualified persons from becoming directors.[39] Although Kraakman alluded to the possible benefits of managerial liability, suggesting its potential usefulness in some contexts – where enterprise liability fails as a legal control, for instance.[40] In a later article, he rejects managerial liability and dismisses managerial liability as inefficient.[41] The argument to extend vicarious liability to (nonshareholder) directors or other managers of publicly traded corporations has gained very little traction or adherents.

One proposal does depart from conventional wisdom on the subject by proposing the abolishment of limited liability for corporate torts. In a 2002 law review article, Mendelson set forth a comprehensive critique of the cost and benefits of limited liability. Extending the literature on the arguments about the efficacy of limited liability, she argued that the efficiency-based arguments in favour of limited shareholder liability fail to take into account qualitative differences among shareholders.[42] The analytical foundation for Mendelson's proposal is Berle's and Means's model of the management-controlled corporation.[43] In these corporations, the diffuse shareholders cannot influence the decision-making process of

37 Bainbridge [2001: 569].

38 Halpern, P, Trebilcock, M & Turnbull, S [1980]: 'An Economic Analysis of Limited Liability in Corporation Law', in Vol. 30, *University of Toronto Law Journal*, 117, at 148–9.

39 Hansmann & Kraakman [1991: 1929] argue that managerial liability will lead to mass resignations from boards. See also Thompson, R [1994]: 'Unpacking Limited Liability: Direct and Vicarious Liability of Corporate Participants for Torts of the Enterprise', in Vol. 47, *Vanderbilt Law Review*, 1, at 31–2, where he argues that liability should not be extended to shareholders because it will have a significant negative effect on the ability of shareholders to diversify and therefore will remove the advantage of standardized share-pricing necessary for liquid financial markets for shares.

40 Kraakman [1984]: 'Corporate Liability Strategies and the Costs of Legal Controls', in Vol. 93, *Yale Law Journal*, 857.

41 Hansmann, H & Kraakman, R [1991]: 'Toward Unlimited Shareholder Liability for Corporate Torts', in Vol. 100, *Yale Law Journal*, 1879, at 1928–9.

42 Mendelson, N [2002]: 'A Control-Based Approach to Shareholder Liability for Corporate Torts', in Vol. 102, *Columbia Law Review*, 1203, at 1214–17.

43 Berle & Means [1991]: *The Modern Corporation and Private Property* (8th ed.) 65–6, at 47–65.

the corporation. Mendelson argued rightly that this model of management-controlled corporations is not reflective of the ownership structure of most public corporations. She maintains that the efficiency-based justifications for limited liability apply only to small, passive investors and does not justify limited liability for controlling shareholders for corporate torts harms social utility.[44] She proposes that all shareholders with the capacity to control corporate activity be held liable for corporate torts and tort-like statutory violations, as this would be the most efficient way to reduce excessively risky corporate behaviour.[45] This model distinguishes between shareholders with the capacity to direct or influence corporate tort behaviour and shareholders who lack this capacity. Shareholders will be defined as having the capacity to control if they have a significant portion of corporate shares or if they exercise actual control over the corporate operations. The dispersed shareholders who by virtue of the collective action problem do not have control over the corporation will be shielded from any liability exceeding their initial investment in the corporation.

Anabtawi and Stout have also called for greater shareholder responsibility. They note that changes in financial markets, in business practice, and in corporate law have given minority shareholders in public companies greater power than they have ever enjoyed before. They argue that greater shareholder power should be coupled with greater shareholder responsibility. Specifically, they suggest that the rules of fiduciary duty traditionally applied to officers and directors and, more rarely, to controlling shareholders should be applied to activist minority investors as well.[46] This suggestion is based on rapidly gaining acceptance that promoting shareholder democracy may serve as a useful counterweight to managerial misconduct.[47] Bebchuck has argued that the current state of corporate law has significantly curtailed the ability of shareholders to participate in directing corporate activity. As a normative prescription, he advocates that the system is reformed to ensure greater participation by shareholders in the management of the corporation.[48]The proposal is not far removed from the trend towards the adoption of corporate law practices designed to increase shareholders' participation that includes the hiring of independent directors and the removal of staggered boards.

In the current liability regime for corporations, the corporation is arguably being held liable for the transnational bribery transactions by its agents that it sought to prevent. From this perspective, the critical policy issue turns on how heavily the liability regime should tax the corporation to induce it to monitor transnational

44 Mendelson [2003: 1219–32].

45 *Ibid.*, at 1271–9.

46 Anabtawi, I & Stout, L [2008]: 'Fiduciary Duties for Activist Shareholders', in Vol. 60, *Stanford Law Review*, 1255, at 1260.

47 See Bebchuck, L [2005]: 'The Case for Increasing Shareholder Power', in Vol. 118, *Harvard Law Review*, 833, a major proponent of shareholder democracy.

48 Bebchuk, L [2006]: 'Letting Shareholders Set the Rules', in Vol. 119, *Harvard Law Review*, 1784, at 1784–5.

bribery transactions by its agent. From this perspective, it is arguable that severe penalties to encourage monitoring may not necessarily be justified. From an efficiency perspective, it would be a waste of resources to spend an extraordinarily large amount to prevent a small monetary loss. In the context of corruption in general and transnational bribery in particular, these economic efficiency arguments must be viewed with scepticism. As discussed in Chapter 2, the effects of corruption are particularly difficult to quantify. More importantly, many of the effects of corruption, such as a loss of confidence in the system by citizens, are intangible and therefore would not show up on the standard efficiency calculation.

The analysis of the liability framework for corporations engaging in transnational bribery from the perspective of the contracts theory of the corporation and within the agency framework changes the basis for the imposition of liability on the corporation for transnational bribery. The perspective of the corporation through the lens of the contracts theory suggests that when a corporation has engaged in transnational bribery, a particular constituent without the knowledge or consent of the other contracting parties has engaged in the bribe transaction. In the decision on imposing liability, the analysis should change from the pertinent question under the current framework – when to impute the actions of the agent to the corporation, to the question – what liability a non-participating constituent in a contract should face for the acts of bribery of another constituent of the corporation.

From the analysis of the corporation from the agency perspective, it is clear that the efficacy of the prohibitions on transnational bribery is dependent on the monitoring functions of the constituents of the corporation. Transnational bribery by a corporation is not analogous to an individual committing bribery. Transnational bribery is not committed by a corporation, but by agents of the corporation. These agents are rational self-interested utility-maximizers whose incentives may not align with those of other constituents of the corporation. In truth, the bribe transaction will benefit the corporation, but this is merely incidental and not the purpose for engaging in the bribe.

This characterisation recognizes that certain constituents are sometimes in the position to monitor and influence others, thus requiring a more complicated role for the prohibition of transnational bribery than has been acknowledged. To stem the occurrence of transnational bribery by corporations, the regulatory framework must both prohibit transnational bribery and induce the constituents of the corporation to implement monitoring, preventive (making bribery less attractive), and policing (increasing the likelihood of detection) mechanisms. The regime for regulating transnational bribery can only be effective to the extent that it incorporates these mechanisms. The question for regulators remains how much liability is required to induce the corporation to undertake the optimal amount of monitoring. The key to designing an effective regulatory regime for curbing transnational bribery by corporations is to ensure that the current prohibitions against transnational bribery engender the appropriate level of monitoring by the right constituent of the corporation.

The grafting of a disclosure and certification requirement (similar to the Sarbanes-Oxley Act) onto the existing criminal or civil prohibitions would eliminate many of the difficulties associated with regulating transnational bribery by corporations. As discussed previously, the two major difficulties with the liability regime for transnational corporations engaging in bribe transactions concern the difficulties in determining unto whom within the organization the liability should be imposed, and the requisite relationship between groups of affiliated corporations.

The imposition of a disclosure and certification requirement regarding knowledge of the payment of bribes directly addresses these problems by imposing a duty on officers within the corporation to ensure that subordinates are not engaging in transnational bribery. The imposition of a certification requirement also addresses the issue of the perverse incentive that prompt senior officials to look the other way because knowledge of bribe payments subjects them to liability. The imposition of the disclosure and certification requirement reverses the cost calculus of corporate officers from a focus on the performance of the corporation. Instead, the corporate officers will have to consider whether they wish to violate the anti-bribery provisions by either not reporting the bribe transactions or attesting to his knowledge and consent of the bribery transaction.

Designing the appropriate level of monitoring and the proper participant requires the disaggregation of the risk preference and incentives of the various constituents of the corporation and determining the least cost monitor amongst the various constituents of the corporation. The book argues that holding minority shareholders (criminally) liable for bribery may prove useful in reducing the prevalence of transnational bribery by corporations. This is because the imposition of criminal liability on the minority shareholders in effect imposes an obligation on these shareholders to monitor the activities of the members of the corporation likely to engage in bribe transactions. The imposition of criminal liability on the minority shareholder would ensure that the preferences of the minority shareholder are aligned with those of the regulators in ensuring that the corporation does not engage in bribe transactions.

The viability of the revisions to the liability regime that governs corporations draws support from Easterbrook & Fischel's salient empirical claim about the purpose and effect of the law on corporations. They optimistically observe that the common law has a tendency to produce efficient solutions to agency costs in corporations.[49] The challenge for developing an effective liability regime to curb the incidence of transnational bribery by corporations is to design a liability regime that capitalizes on this tendency of the law to produce efficient outcomes.

The resolution of the question of the liability of a non-participating constituent is dependent on the monitoring obligations sought to be imposed, by either contract or the law on the non-participating constituent. There is a fundamental difference between the liability of an agent of the corporation engaging in a bribe transaction and other constituents of the corporation who failed to deter the agent.

49 Easterbrook & Fischel [1991: 22].

The law may decide to deter the agent unconditionally, but the question raised is whether unconditional deterrence should also be applied to the other constituents of the corporation. In other words, to what extent should other constituents in the corporations be encouraged by the law to invest resources in monitoring the activities of managers to prevent them from committing transnational bribery? The costs that arise from monitoring due to the inability of a corporation to control the behaviour of its employees who engage in bribery could be regarded as agency costs.

Characterising these bribe transactions as agency costs alters the traditional analysis of the effects of criminal sanctions on a corporation. The current system ignores the distinction between the liability of the agent who engages in the bribe transaction and the other constituents who are liable for failing to invest sufficient resources in monitoring.

Fischel & Sykes suggest that a corporation should be penalized to the point equal to the social cost of the crime adjusted for the probability of non-detection.[50] Beyond this point, the return from monitoring and compliance will exceed the social return through over-compliance. Despite the cost imposed by bribery, the goal of the legal system is not to impose an arbitrarily large penalty on the corporation. Except in situations where the corporation can effectively transfer the penalty to the agent, an arbitrarily large penalty in excess of the social harm will induce excessive investment in monitoring and prevention. These costs will be ultimately transferred to the society through higher prices and the resulting welfare losses are exactly the effects the regulation of bribery seeks to prevent.

Unconditional deterrence may be appropriate for the agent engaging in a bribe transaction, but will rarely be appropriate for a constituent who fails to monitor.[51] Analysing bribery as an agency cost suggests that the imposition of liability on the corporation should not be designed to deter only, but also to provide incentives for the corporation to monitor, detect, and prevent the agents of the corporation from engaging in bribery. It cannot be the goal of the prohibitions on transnational bribery to ensure that all the constituents of the corporation invest infinite resources on the prevention of transnational bribery by agents. Rather, the level of monitoring required is the amount required to ensure that marginal cost of monitoring does not exceed the marginal social gain from the reduced social harm of bribery. In terms of the level, a penalty equal to the social harm caused by the agent adjusted for the probability of detection will suffice.

Once the level of monitoring is determined, the challenge that remains is to create the incentives for the least cost monitor to engage in the appropriate level of

50 Fischel, D & Sykes, A [1996]: 'Corporate Crime', in Vol. 25, *Journal of Legal Studies*, 319, at 320–21.

51 Conditional deterrence refers to the deterrence of breaches in which the costs to the victim of the breach are greater than the benefits to the breaching party. Unconditional deterrence is deterrence regardless of the costs caused by the harm. See Posner [1998: 357—8].

monitoring. Who then is the least cost monitor? The analysis of who is the least cost monitor is related to an important justification for the imposition of liability on the corporation – that is, the imposition of liability is a means of indirectly sanctioning agents. The assumption is that a corporation found liable for bribery would then sanction the agent. In this context, there might be an effect of deterrence on the action of the agent. However, this deterrent effect is tempered by the effect it has on monitoring mechanisms. There are costs associated with detecting bribery, and constituents of the corporation are often in the best position to detect transnational bribery. As a result, the imposition of liability on the corporation will affect the monitoring function of the constituents of the corporation. Thus devising an efficient regime to regulate transnational bribery is substantially more complicated than the traditional analysis indicates. One of the areas where the design of a liability regime for corporations may be able to benefit is current research into patterns of ownership of corporations.[52]

The shares of most corporations are typically held by large institutional investors who are better positioned to obtain and analyse corporate information and prevent the corporate constituents from engaging in transnational bribery. Recent empirical research into patterns of share ownership suggests that the small-diversified shareholder is no longer the typical shareholder in modern corporations.[53] In fact, the small diversified shareholder accounts for less than 40 percent of corporate equity holdings and do not hold most corporate equity in corporations today. The more typical shareholder is either a large institutional investor or another corporation; these parties hold the majority of the shares of corporations.[54] Institutional investors at best have the capacity to control, and at worst are in the position to monitor and exert influence over the operations of managers who might engage in transnational bribery.[55]

More importantly for the prevalence of transnational bribery, the interests of these institutional investors are currently aligned with those of the managers likely to engage in a bribe transaction. The institutional shareholder will be more inclined to favour a risky bribe transaction because of a general ability to reap a share of corporate benefits in excess of a pro rata share. Meanwhile, under the current

---

52 LaPorta, R, Lopez-De-Silanes, F & Schleifer, A [1999]: 'Corporate Ownership Around the World', in Vol. 54, *Journal of Finance*, 471, at 491–511, present empirical evidence illustrating the different corporate ownership patterns in various countries.

53 *Ibid.*, at 471–2.

54 Institutional investors hold 49.8 percent of all outstanding corporate equities. See NYSE Facts, available on the website http://www.nyxdata.com/nysedata/asp/factbook/viewer_edition.asp?mode=table&key=2673&category=12. Last visited 5 March 2013.

55 See Booth, R [2001]: 'Theory Informs Business Practice: Who Owns a Corporation and Who Cares?', in Vol. 77, *Chicago-Kent Law Review*, 147, at 150–52, where he distinguishes between shareholders as either passive investors or active managers. He notes that the interests of the two types of shareholders may diverge and therefore questions whether the stockholder ownership theory applies to both types of shareholders.

liability regime for corporations, not only is limited liability fully available to the institutional investors but any consequence of engaging in the bribe transaction is also diffused amongst all the shareholders. Consequently, the presence of an institutional shareholder creates an incentive for the corporation to externalize more costs than if the corporation's equity is diffusely held by small diversified shareholders.

The revision to the liability regime proposed is the imposition of liability on the controlling shareholder for transnational bribery by the corporation. The moral hazard created by the current system, which imposes corporate criminal sanctions on managers who engage in bribe transactions, is clearly affected by the pattern of share ownership of the corporation. A liability regime targeting those who exercise control would explicitly address the differences in shareholder risk preference. Furthermore, targeting those who have the capacity to influence the direction of the corporation is more likely to address limited liability's moral hazard in the context of transnational bribery by the corporation. The fact that dispersed shareholders are rarely involved in management election and business decisions leaves the controlling shareholders as the single and direct influence on corporate business decisions. These controlling shareholders have access to information and the capacity to monitor and influence the actions of management and are therefore not affected by the collective action problems experienced by dispersed shareholders. The effectiveness of the control-based liability regime is based on two separate but requisite components. First, the control-based liability regime should improve the incentive of shareholders to monitor the managers. Second, and of equal importance, the control-based liability regime could only function if the managers are responsive to the directives of the controlling shareholder.

With regard to incentives, the targeting the controlling shareholder is likely to improve the incentives of the shareholders to monitor managers by aligning the interest of the controlling shareholder against that of the managers to engage in a bribe transaction through the imposition of liability for transnational bribery. This is because in comparison with the existing limited liability and corporate criminal liability regimes system, proposed revised regime is more likely to compel the controlling shareholder to internalize the costs of middle management's engagement in transnational bribery transactions. Control-based liability in the specific context of liability for transnational bribery would ensure that the differences in preferences and incentives amongst the different groups of shareholders and managers are aligned with those of both the risk-averse senior management and small shareholders to disfavour transnational bribery. The imposition of liability on the controlling shareholder would ensure that the controlling shareholder exercises a monitoring function on the moral hazards associated with middle managers faced with the prospect of a bribe transaction.

The second requirement for the effectiveness of the control-based liability regime, in addition to increased monitoring, is the responsiveness of managers to the direction of the controlling shareholder. This question is particularly apt because these shareholders, unlike the parents of subsidiaries, seldom exercise direct control over the day-to-day activities of the corporation. This raises the question why a control-based regime can assume this. Once again, current corporate law scholars attest to the influence of the controlling shareholder on the activities of the corporation. Recent corporate law research indicates that a variety of corporate mechanisms, share price for instance, encourage both middle and senior managers to be responsive to shareholders. If shareholders faced liability for bribe transactions, share prices would incorporate available information about the full extent of the corporation's policies. Senior managers, in turn, would then have as much incentive to consider the full-expected social costs of engaging in bribery. In addition, shareholders facing contingent liability would presumably demand more information about the practices of the corporation as the information would have greater importance in valuing shares and provide incentive for senior managers to consider the bribery risks associated with their policies. Indeed, if shielding shareholders from liability is justified because they have insufficient control over managers, it would seem to follow that there should be no liability for corporations whose agents engage in bribery, a position that has very little support.

The discussion has thus far focused on the arguments associated with imposing liability on controlling shareholders for transnational bribery. More difficult to assess are the social costs that may arise from the shareholder's incentives to avoid liability for transnational bribery. One such possible concern of the imposition of control base liability on shareholders is that it would thrust onto them the risk of criminal liability for conduct that they will find hard to assess, or to prevent by monitoring management. Notwithstanding, the controlling shareholder in the corporation is the most appropriate constituent of the corporation because they have lower information costs than the individual shareholder, a greater influence over managerial decision-making, and the ability to benefit more from corporate transnational bribery than the individual shareholder.

A significant issue in the revisions relates to the level of control required to trigger liability for transnational bribery by the corporation. The US courts have given some direction on the definition of a controlling shareholder holding that a controlling shareholder includes a stockholder owning a majority of the voting power of the corporation, a stockholder owning less than a majority but a sufficiently large block to exercise de facto control (for example, where the other shares are widely held), and a stockholder with effective control of the board of directors by contract.[56] A determination of whether a particular shareholder possesses the capacity to control the corporation would be made if the shareholder possessed significant ownership or if it exercised actual control over the activities of the corporation. The exercise of actual control by virtue of ownership suggests the ability to control the corporation in other respects. These include involvement in the selection of the corporation's board of directors, the exercise of authority over significant asset sales, or participation in other major corporate decisions.

56 Kahn v. Lynch Communication Sys., Inc., 638 A.2d 1110, at 1114–15 (Del. 1994).

The possession of significant ownership, on the other hand, would ensure that the shareholder maintained a monitoring function over the activities of the corporation's managers. The American Law Institute takes the position that a controlling influence should be assumed where there is ownership and/or possession of the power to vote more than 25 percent of the corporation's shares.[57] The SEC has publicly noted the widely held belief that the ownership of 20 percent voting power in a widely held company in most instances constitutes control.[58]

Whether a particular minority shareholder has the capacity to control the corporation might depend on the total value of the corporation, and consequently the value of the shareholder's holdings. Other factors include whether there is a majority shareholder, the relationship with the minority shareholder or between other minority shareholders, or the relationship between that shareholder's board representatives and those of the other shareholders. Regarding the time when shareholder liability would be assessed, an occurrence rule imposing liability on a shareholder with the capacity to control the corporation at the time of the bribe transaction would appropriately encourage those in positions of control to monitor and influence corporate decision-making.

The regime proposed would abolish limited liability for transnational bribery by corporations only when a shareholder actually controls the corporation or owns a large enough stake to exercise control over the corporation. Some of the liability should be borne by the agents or senior management, but there is no reason to believe that this will always be the case, as the prevailing liability regime necessarily presumes. It will remain the responsibility of the courts to determine which costs are borne equitably and efficiently by a corporation and its shareholders and which are not. Shareholders who benefit from a bribe transaction should not be able to spread the cost amongst other constituents of the corporation by hiding behind existing corporate governance mechanisms.

This proposal is not as radical as it might first appear. Courts already pierce the veil in corporations when there is a shareholder who dominates the corporation to the extent that the person and the corporation are one in the same. More pertinently, there is already a small but growing set of practices that hold controlling persons liable for actions that they did not affect but could have avoided.[59] These controlling person obligations have found root in regulatory statutes that extend liability to controlling persons who would not otherwise be liable under traditional corporate, tort, or agency law principles. An essential hallmark of these regulatory statues

---

57 American Law Institute Project [1994]: *Principles of Corporate Governance: Analysis and Recommendations* (St. Paul: American Law Institute), para 1.10 and 1.10(b).

58 Brudney, V [1983]: 'Equal Treatment of Shareholders in Corporate Distributions and Reorganizations', in Vol. 71, *California Law Review*, 1072, at 1074, suggesting that the owner of 5 percent or 10 percent of the outstanding voting power may possess control.

59 See Thompson, R [1994: 27–8], where he highlights the trend towards holding corporate managers accountable for the failure to monitor or supervise employees who commit torts or statutory violations.

is that they often impose criminal or civil liability without a demonstration of intent or negligence. For instance, the Securities Act of 1933, in Section 11, holds anyone who signs the registration statement, anyone serving as a director at the time the registration statement is filed, and every person named in the registration statement as about to become a director liable for any materially misleading registration statements.[60] Similarly, any person who controls a liable corporation is also responsible for its securities violation, unless the controlling person acted in good faith.[61] Finally, Section 16(b) of the 1934 Act holds controlling persons strictly liable for short-swing trading in equity securities.[62] The SEC views 'control' the possession, direct or indirect, of the power to direct or cause the direction of the management and policies of a person, whether through the ownership of voting securities, by contract, or otherwise.[63] According to Carson, the legislative history of the statute evinces that control can exist through ownership of shares, by virtue of a contract, and an agency relationship.[64] The American Law Institute (ALI) has taken the view that a shareholder could be considered a controlling person if he exercises a controlling influence over the management or policies of the corporation.[65] The threshold at which this control would be presumed is where the shareholder either alone or pursuant to an arrangement with others, has the power to vote more than 25 percent of the shares of a corporation.[66]

To the extent that a corporation already has an effective monitoring mechanism, low penalties would be appropriate, even if the monitoring mechanism occasionally fails to detect transnational bribery. This is because there would seem to be little value in exacting a large penalty on a corporation that has made extensive efforts to prevent and deter transnational bribery by its agents, as the deterrence of the corporation depends entirely upon the deterrence of the individual agents. One potential shortcoming in the analysis, however, is that it assumes that the corporation is truly interested in monitoring transnational bribery by its agents.

In fact, if penalties were reduced to reflect the adoption of a monitoring mechanism to expose and deter transnational bribery, this would provide an incentive for corporations to develop cosmetic monitoring mechanisms to detect transnational bribery, so that they can benefit from the bribe transactions and at the same time incur only modest penalties if the bribe transactions are detected. This

60 See 15 U.S.C. 77k (2000).

61 Section 15 of the 1933 Act and Section 20 of the Securities Exchange Act of 1934. See 15 U.S.C. 77o; 15 U.S.C. 78t.

62 See 15 U.S.C. 78p(b).

63 17 C.F.R. ßß 240.12b-2(f), 230.405 (2002).

64 L C Carson II [1996]:, 'The Liability of Controlling Persons Under the Federal Securities Acts', Vol. 72 *Notre Dame Law Review* 263, 274 (1996) citing H.R. No. 73-1383, at 26 (1934), cited in *In re Enron Corp. Sec., Derivative & ERISA Litig.*, No. H-01-3624, 2003 U.S. LEXIS 1668, at *32 (S.D. Tex. Jan. 28, 2003)).

65 *Principles of Corporate Governance Analysis and Recommendations* ß 1.10(a)(2) (ALI) (1994).

66 *Ibid.*, ß 1.10(b).

argument is similar to the traditional analysis of strict liability versus a negligence-based system of tort law. Holding corporate officers liable for transnational bribery under the disclosure and certification requirement essentially amounts to a strict liability regime, whilst the existing corporate liability regime is similar to a negligence-based system. Generally, economists recognise that under either regime, rational actors will take precautions only up to the point where the expected liability equals the precaution and avoidance costs. The arguments for a negligence system over strict liability is that it achieves the same level of monitoring without making the corporation an insurer for acts that it cannot prevent.

Conclusion

A transformation is required of the domestic rules of corporate liability that currently enable corporations to shield themselves from criminal liability for transnational bribery. The design of these domestic regulations did not contemplate that the activities of these corporations would have a transnational dimension. The thesis offers two suggestions that will improve the efficacy of the current regulatory framework to curb transnational bribery by corporations. The first suggestion is obvious – design better laws. The goal, however, is to ensure that a simple check is placed on the tendency of regulatory policies to be influenced by political expediency rather than by available evidence. The second suggestion is subtler – ensure that any new law that passes the design test is compatible with the already existing legal prescriptions. To be sure, these two requirements for new efforts to regulate transnational bribery by corporations, one a design test and the other a compatibility test, should inform further efforts to regulate transnational bribery by corporations.

Chapter 8
Conclusion

The current framework of the multilateral efforts to curb transnational bribery by corporations is unable to effectively tackle the problem of transnational bribery by corporations. It is important that the liability regime for the regulation of transnational bribery by corporations is influenced by science rather than political expediency. Unfortunately, the development of the liability regime for corporations engaging in transnational bribery has generally been accepted to be the result of political expediency rather than that of empirical information. Corruption, transnational bribery being one example, is a multifaceted and complex phenomenon often deeply rooted in the social, political, and economic systems of a country. The regulation of transnational bribery by corporations provides a framework for analyzing the critical dimensions of the interaction between the norms in various domestic communities and the transnational context of these interactions.

The analysis of this interaction indicates that policy initiatives that make a straightforward intuitive attempt to control actors within a complex social system, without giving due deference to the social forces shaping individual preferences within those systems, are prone to fail. This is not to suggest that the current system is completely inadequate; rather the point is that there is further research required on corporate compliance and deterrence before an optimal liability regime can be determined. More pertinently, the review of the literature conducted clearly indicated that the current liability regime governing the liability of corporations for transnational bribery has not received the same rigorous analysis that has been applied to the regulation of corporations in other contexts. One of the recommendations proposed is that the design of the liability regime for corporations draws ideas from mainstream research on corporations.

The focus of the current regulatory regime to curb transnational bribery has almost exclusively been on the imposition of criminal prohibitions backed with deterrent sanctions on corporations engaging in transnational bribery. This regulatory regime has been widely acknowledged as being ineffective in curbing the prevalence of transnational bribery. There have been two main criticisms of the regulatory framework, both of which relate to the disparities in the ability of states to respond to the problem of transnational bribery. First, the domestic regimes where transnational bribery occurs are often too weak to pursue adequate regulation. Second, the home states of the transnational corporations engaging in transnational bribery, which are often in a better position to enforce the transnational regulatory regime, are hampered by the prevailing notions of sovereignty and jurisdiction, undermining the cross-jurisdictional cooperation requisite to effective regulation.

In response to these criticisms, through multilateral institutions and organizations, states have made considerable efforts to galvanize the international cooperation required to regulate transnational bribery by corporations. These efforts resulted in the adoption of three major multilateral agreements in which state signatories agreed to enact legislative provisions to tackle corruption in general. A simple comparison of the levels of compliance with the various multilateral agreements indicates that where the targets set by the agreements were low, the level of compliance was high. This is unfortunate because although levels of compliance with the conventions have been high, they have not adequately dealt with the issue of transnational bribery.

Different explanations have been presented to explain the failure of the multilateral efforts to regulate transnational bribery. Some critics of the current multilateral initiatives argue that they are ill conceived and that fundamental flaws in the multilateral initiatives are the reason why they will fail to curb transnational bribery. The proponents of the current multilateral initiatives, in contrast, laud the current multilateral initiatives. They argue that transnational bribery damages the quality of transnational relationships thus endangering global security. These proponents locate the inefficacy of the current multilateral initiatives in the level of enforcement of these initiatives. In many respects, the debate is inconclusive. The critics of the multilateral initiatives overstate the problem: the multilateral initiatives alone cannot be the cause of the inefficacy. They also overplay their preferred solution of strengthening domestic capacity: Strengthening domestic capacity alone will not increase the efficacy of the regulatory regime. The proponents understate the problem: they advocate a transnational regulatory regime without fully exploring its relational and process characteristics. The proponents also tend to avoid sustained consideration of solutions as they fail to spell out the essential characteristics of how the proposed transnational regulatory regime would work in practice.

Utilising the OFFP as a case study, the book examined the transactions in the Programme to illustrate some of the major problems associated with making the multilateral initiatives to curb transnational bribery effective. For instance, despite the multilateral initiatives, there were still inconsistencies with respect to the application of different national regulations to the same set of facts, even in countries that had implemented one of the major multilateral initiatives. Other problems explored to illustrate the challenges that the multilateral initiatives would need to surmount included the recognition of foreign law by domestic courts; assertion of jurisdiction, particularly on the basis of the effects doctrine; and the gathering of evidence located in foreign jurisdictions for use in domestic litigation. These problems highlighted the potential scope for conflict between states in the regulation of transnational bribery.

In essence, although the international community has succeeded in fostering consensus on the substantive aspects of transnational bribery, there are nonetheless significant procedural impediments to the efficient operation of these multilateral initiatives. Immediately apparent was the fact that the multilateral initiatives do not address both the policy and procedural concerns that would effectively mediate the conflicts between states in the regulation of transnational bribery. The principal effect of the failure is to nullify the deterrent aspect of the prohibitions against transnational bribery through under-enforcement by individual states.

To advance the central argument, a different focus for future efforts to curb transnational bribery, the book examined one area that has received very little attention in the current multilateral initiatives, the liability regime for transnational corporations. The focus advocated involves an augmented analysis of the primary participants in transnational bribery transactions, corporations, and an alteration of the existing regulatory regime to alter the behaviour of these corporations.

The analysis of the current liability regime for transnational bribery by corporations indicates that the current regime allows the decision-makers within these transnational corporations to shield themselves from criminal liability for transnational bribery. These transnational corporations have developed complex relationships amongst groups of corporations that pose challenges to the ability of the law to impose liability. Transnational corporations have also developed complex non-hierarchical structures where establishing control poses challenges to the law in terms of who within the corporation is liable for transnational bribery.

Modern transnational corporations have evolved into complex entities, and two facets of their complexity are particularly relevant to the liability regime for transnational bribery. The first facet of the complexity of these corporations relates to the legal nature of the relationship between two or more groups of corporations. The legal doctrine directly implicated by the complexity of the relationships of these transnational corporations is the doctrine of piercing the veil. The doctrine of piercing the veil is devised from the very well settled principle of the limited liability of the corporation. The principle of limited liability holds that the corporation is a separate legal entity and therefore deserving of limited liability, even if it is part of a corporate group. The principles applied in piercing the veil where individuals are the shareholders are directly extended to situations where a parent corporation owns or controls a subsidiary. Allowing limited liability for corporations holding shares in another corporation allows the parent corporation to escape liability for transnational bribery. The wholesale extension of the principle of limited liability to corporate group is at odds with the fact that many corporate groups operate as a single entity simply because of the economic benefits that result from the integration of their activities. This extension allows a corporation to avoid liability for the obligations of a subsidiary corporation.

The second facet of complexity of these transnational corporations is internal to the corporation and relates to the organisational and managerial structure of these corporations. The complex organisational and management structures utilized by transnational corporations pose a significant challenge to the law with regard to the imposition of criminal liability. The ability of the law to impose criminal liability effectively for transnational bribery on the appropriate corporation in these complex webs of transnational corporations has been limited because of the complicated management structures in these transnational corporations.

The feature of the legal system directly challenged by the structural complexity of transnational corporations relates to the doctrines upon which the legal system imposes liability on corporations for criminal conduct. The two major doctrines utilized for the imposition of liability on the corporation are the doctrines of vicarious or identification liability. The challenge to the law pertains to the fact that the imposition of criminal liability on a corporation requires that clear standards be met regarding responsibility for actions before criminal liability is imposed. The complex organisational and management structure of transnational corporations ensure that establishing responsibility is often a difficult and complicated task and poses a challenge to the two models utilized for imputing liability for criminal actions.

Corporate law theory has played an important role in the development of the liability regime for transnational corporations engaging in bribery. The twin concepts of the separate legal personality and limited liability of the corporation form the cornerstone of the law's liability regime for corporations. These two concepts have played a significant role in the development of the regulatory regime for corporations. On the one hand, the view of the court regarding limited liability has a significant impact on the courts' imposition of liability on the corporation for transnational bribery. The legal personality of the corporation, on the other hand, determines whom within the corporation and under what circumstances the courts will impose liability on the corporation for transnational bribery. The normative implications of the concepts of limited liability and legal personality are encapsulated within the corporate law theory discourse in the debate about the nature of the corporation.

Tapering the essential elements of the debate on nature of the corporation in corporate law theory suggests that the debate is characterized by the ideological distinction of the corporation on two particular dimensions. The first dimension relates to the personality of the corporation and is characterized by the ideological distinction between the corporation as an artificial creation of the state and the corporation as a natural product of private initiative. The issue raised is whether the state or private initiative should govern the regulatory regime for corporations.

The second dimension relates to the liability of the corporation and is characterized by the ideological distinction between the corporation as an entity with a real existence separate from its shareholders and other participants, or as a mere aggregation of natural individuals without a separate existence. The issue raised is whether the individual or group is the appropriate unit for the imposition of on the corporation. The personality and criminal liability of the corporation have significant normative implications, are critical to the regulation of transnational bribery by corporations, and ultimately define the effectiveness of the regulatory framework to curb transnational bribery by corporations.

Unfortunately, on the dimension relating to the personality of the corporation and concerned with identifying fault, the liability regime for corporations has been influenced by the fiction/concession theory with the corporation viewed as a fiction and the individuals within the corporation as the culpable parties in identifying criminal liability. On the dimension relating to liability and concerned with the imposition of liability, the law has adopted the entity conception of the corporation separating the corporation's liability from those of the individuals within the corporation. The assumptions that the corporation's liability must be derivative and that criminal liability must be retained by the corporation have been called into question by contemporary theories of the corporation that view the corporation as a nexus of contracts. The current liability regime's treatment of the corporation as a fiction/concession for the purpose of deriving liability underestimates the complexity of the modern corporation and presents challenges in identifying fault within a complex corporate structure. Similarly, treating the corporation as an entity for the purposes of imposing liability exaggerates the unity of the corporation and ensures that no particular constituent of the corporation bears the sanctions for criminal actions.

The current liability regime regulating transnational bribery by corporations has ossified these outdated perceptions of the corporation in devising the liability regime for transnational bribery. These perceptions of the corporation are at a variance with the complex and internally conflicted transnational corporations that are widespread in transnational commercial transactions. These formalistic conceptions of the corporation bolster the capacity of the corporation to evade liability and constrain the imposition of criminal liability on the individuals within the corporation for transnational bribery. Granted, contemporary corporate law theory is still yet to provide a unified all-encompassing account of the nature of corporations. Contemporary law theory has nonetheless discarded the formalistic theories of the corporation on which the regulations prohibiting transnational bribery are modelled. The conception of the corporation as a nexus of contracts suggests that the corporation should be treated as a network of contracts between various constituencies. More pertinently for the regulation of transnational bribery, this conception of the corporation recognizes that the different constituents of a corporation have different and sometimes conflicting incentives. The contracts theory, relying on agency principles, deconstructs the corporation into component parts composed of the corporation's human participants.

Bibliography

Abbott, F [1997]: 'Foundation-Building for Western Hemispheric Integration'. In Vol. 17, *North Western Journal of International Law and Business*, at 900.

Ajayi, K [1997]: 'On the Trail of a Spectre – Destabilisation of Developing and Transitional Economies: A Case Study of Corruption in Nigeria'. In Vol. 15, *Dickinson Journal of International Law*, at 545.

Akehurst, M [1972]: 'Jurisdiction in International Law'. In Vol. 46, *British Yearbook of International Law*, at 145.

Ala'i, P [2000]: 'The Legacy of Geographical Morality and Colonialism: A Historical Assessment of the Current Crusade Against Corruption'. In Vol. 33, *Vanderbilt Journal of Transnational Law*, at 877.

Alam, M [1991]: 'Some Economic Costs of Corruption in LDCs'. In Vol. 27, *Journal of Development Studies*, at 89.

Alam, M [1989]: 'Anatomy of Corruption: An Approach to the Political Economy of Underdevelopment'. In Vol. 48, *American Journal of Economics and Sociology*, at 441.

Alam, M [1995]: 'A Theory of Limits on Corruption and Some Applications'. In Vol. 48, *Kyklos: International Review for Social Science*, at 419.

Alatas, S [1990]: *Corruption: Its Nature, Causes and Functions*. Aldershot: Ashgate.

Albert, D [2002]: 'Addressing Abuse of the Corporate Entity in the People's Republic of China: New Thoughts on China's Need for a Defined Veil Piercing Doctrine'. In Vol. 23, *University of Pennsylvania Journal of International Economic Law*, at 873.

Alchian, A & Demsetz, H [1972]: 'Production, Information Costs and Economic Organization'. In Vol. 62, *American Economic Review*, at 777.

Alchian, A & Demsetz, H [1973]: 'The Property Rights Paradigm'. In Vol. 33, *Journal of Economic History*, at 174.

Alfert, R [1992]: 'Hostes Humani Generis: An Expanded Notion of U.S. Counterterrorist Legislation'. In Vol. 6, *Emory International Law Review*, at 171.

Alldridge, P [1990]: 'The Doctrine of Innocent Agency'. In Vol. 2, *Criminal Law Forum*, at 45.

Alldridge, P [2000]: 'Reforming the Criminal Law of Corruption'. In Vol. 11, *Criminal Law Forum*, at 287.

Alschuler, A [2009]: 'Two Ways to Think About the Punishment of Corporations'. In Vol. 46, *American Criminal Law Review*, at 1359.

Alting, C [1995]: 'Piercing the Corporate Veil in American and German Law – Liability of Individuals and Entities: A Comparative View'. In Vol. 2, *Tulsa Journal of Comparative & International Law*, at 187.

American Law Institute Project [1994]: *Principles of Corporate Governance: Analysis and Recommendations*. St. Paul: American Law Institute.

Andreski, S [1978]: '*Kleptocracy as a System of Government in Africa,* in Political Corruption'. In Heidenheimer, A (ed.) [1978]: *Political Corruption: Readings in Comparative Analysis*. New Brunswick: Transaction Books, at 346–57.

Andvig, J & Karl, O [1990]: 'How Corruption May Corrupt'. In Vol. 13, *Journal of Economic Behavior and Organization*, at 63.

Anton, A [1956]: 'The Introduction into English Practice of Continental Theories on the Conflict of Laws'. In Vol. 5, *International & Comparative Law Quarterly*, at 534.

Areeda, P & Turner, D [2000]: *Antitrust Law: An Analysis of Principles and their Application*. New York: Aspen Law and Business, at 167.

Arlen, J [1994]: 'The Potentially Perverse Effects of Corporate Criminal Liability'. In Vol. 23, *Journal of Legal Studies*, at 833.

Babcock, H [1997]: 'Democracy's Discontent in a Complex World: Can Avalanches, Sandpiles, and Finches Optimize Michael Sandel's Civic Republican Community?' In Vol. 85 *Georgia Law Journal*, at 2085.

Bader, M & Shaw, B [1983]: 'Amendment of the Foreign Corrupt Practices Act'. In Vol. 15, *New York University Journal of International Law and Politics*, at 627.

Baer, M [2010]: 'Organizational Liability and the Tension Between Corporate and Criminal Law'. In Vol. 19, *Journal of Law & Policy*, at 1.

Bainbridge, S [1996]: 'Participatory Management Within a Theory of the Firm'. In Vol. 21, *Journal of Corporate Law*, at 657.

Bainbridge, S [2002]: 'The Board of Directors as Nexus of Contracts'. In Vol. 88, *Iowa Law Review*, at 1.

Bainbridge, S [2004]: 'The Business Judgment Rule as Abstention Doctrine'. In Vol. 57 *Vanderbilt Law Review*, at 83.

Baker, D [1974]: 'Antitrust and World Trade: Tempest in an International Teapot?' In Vol. 8, *Cornell International Law Journal*, at 16.

Balen, M [2003]: *The Secret History of the South Sea Bubble: The World's First Great Financial Scandal*. New York: Fourth Estate, HarperCollins.

Barack, B [1981]: *The Application of the Competition Rules of the European Economic Community to Enterprises and Arrangements External to the Common Market*. London: Kluwer Law International.

Bardhan, P [1997]: 'Corruption and Development: A Review of Issues'. In Vol. 35, *Journal of Economic Literature*, at 1320.

Barnett, R [1986]: 'A Consent Theory of Contract'. In Vol. 86, *Columbia Law Review*, at 269.

Barrett, E [1947]: 'The Doctrine of Forum Non Conveniens'. In Vol. 35, *California Law Review*, at 386.

Bayley, D [1966]: 'The Effects of Corruption in a Developing Nation'. In Vol. 19, *Western Political Quarterly*, at 719.

Beale, B & Safwat, A [2004]: 'What Developments in Western Europe Tell Us About American Critiques of Corporate Criminal Liability'. In Vol. 8, *Buffalo Criminal Law Review*, at 89.

Bebchuk, L [2005]: 'The Case for Increasing Shareholder Power'. In Vol. 118, *Harvard Law Review* at 833.

Bebchuk, L [2006]: 'Letting Shareholders Set the Rules'. In Vol. 119, *Harvard Law Review*, at 1784.

Becker, G [1968]: 'Crime and Punishment: An Economic Approach'. In Vol. 76, *Journal of Political Economy*, at 169.

Berle, A & Means, G [1932]: *The Modern Corporation and Private Property*. New York: Macmillan.

Bernard, T [1984]: 'The Historical Development of Corporate Criminal Liability'. In Vol. 22, *Criminology*, at 3.

Bhagwati, J [1982]: 'Directly Unproductive, Profit-Seeking (DUP) Activities'. In Vol. 90, *Journal of Political Economy*, at 988.

Bialos, J & Husisian, G [1997]: *The Foreign Corrupt Practices Act: Coping with Corruption in Transitional Economies*. New York: Oceana Publications.

Bixby, M [2010]: 'The Lion Awakes: The Foreign Corrupt Practices Act – 1977 to 2010'. In Vol. 12, *San Diego International Law Journal*, at 89.

Black, B [1990]: 'Shareholder Passivity Reexamined'. In Vol. 89, *Michigan Law Review*, at 520.

Black, B [1992]: 'Agents Watching Agents: The Promise of Institutional Investor Voice'. In Vol. 39, *University of California Los Angeles Law Review*, at 811.

Blair, P [1929]: 'The Doctrine of Forum Non Conveniens in Anglo-American Law'. In Vol. 29, *Columbia Law Review*, at 1.

Blakey, R [1983]: 'The RICO Civil Fraud Action in Context: Reflection on Bennett v. Berg'. In Vol. 58, *Notre Dame Law Review*, at 237.

Bliss, C & Rafael, D [1997]. 'Does Competition Kill Corruption?' In Vol. 105, *Journal of Political Economy*, at 1001.

Bliss, J & Spak, G [1989]: 'The Foreign Corrupt Practices Act of 1988: Clarification or Evisceration?' In Vol. 20, *Law and Policy in International Business*, at 441.

Block, M [1991]: 'Optimal Penalties, Criminal Law and the Control of Corporate Behavior'. In Vol. 71, *Boston University Law Review*, 395.

Blumberg, P [1986]: 'Limited Liability and Corporate Groups'. In Vol. 11, *Journal of Corporate Law*, at 573.

Blumberg, P [1987]: *The Law of Corporate Groups: Tort, Contract, and Other Common Law Problems in the Substantive Law of Parent and Subsidiary Corporations*. Boston: Little Brown.

Blumberg, P [1990]: 'The Corporate Entity in an Era of Multinational Corporations'. In Vol. 15, *Delaware Journal of Corporate Law*, at 283.

Blumberg, P [1995]: *Multinational Challenge to Corporation Law: The Search for a New Corporate Personality*. Oxford: Oxford University Press.

Blumberg, P [1996]: 'The Increasing Recognition of Enterprise Principles in Determining Parent and Subsidiary Corporation Liabilities'. In Vol. 28, *Connecticut Law Review*, at 295.

Blumberg, P [2001]: 'Accountability of Multinational Corporations: The Barriers Presented by Concepts of the Corporate Juridical Entity'. In Vol. 24, *Hastings International and Comparative Law Review*, at 297.

Bolodeoku, I [2005]: 'Contractarianism and Corporate Law: Alternative Explanations to the Law's Mandatory and Enabling/Default Contents'. In Vol. 13, *Cardozo Journal of International and Comparative Law*, at 433.

Bonneau, J [2011]: 'Combating Foreign Bribery: Legislative Reform in the United Kingdom and Prospects for Increased Global Enforcement'. In Vol. 49, *Columbia Journal of Transnational Law*, at 365.

Booth, R [2001]: 'Theory Informs Business Practice: Who Owns a Corporation and Who Cares?' In Vol. 77, *Chicago-Kent Law Review*, at 147.

Borchers, P [1990]: 'The Death of the Constitutional Law of Personal Jurisdiction: From Pennoyer to Burnham and Back Again'. In Vol. 24, *University of California Davis Law Review*, at 19.

Born, G [1992]: 'A Reappraisal of the Extraterritorial Reach of U.S. Law'. In Vol. 24, *Law and Policy in International Business*, at 1.

Born, G & Hoing, S [1990]: 'Comity and the Lower Courts: Post-Aerospatiale Applications of the Hague Evidence Convention'. In Vol. 24, *International Law*, at 393.

Born, G & Westin, D [1992]: *International Civil Litigation in United States Courts: Cases and Materials.* Cambridge, MA: Kluwer Law and Taxation Publishers.

Boswell, N [1996]: 'Combating Corruption: Focus on Latin America'. In Vol. 3, *South-Western Journal of Law and Trade in the Americas*, at 179.

Bratton, W [1989a]: 'The "Nexus of Contracts" Corporation: A Critical Appraisal'. In Vol. 74, *Cornell Law Quarterly*, at 407.

Bratton, W [1989b]: 'The New Economic Theory of the Firm: Critical Perspectives from History'. In Vol. 41, *Stanford Law Review*, at 1471.

Bratton, W & McCahery, J [1997]: 'An Inquiry into the Efficiency of the Limited Liability Company: Of Theory of the Firm and Regulatory Competition'. In Vol. 54, *Washington & Lee Law Review*, at 629.

Braucher, R [1947]: 'The Inconvenient Federal Forum'. In Vol. 60, Harvard Law Review, at 908.

Brickey, K [1984]: *Corporate Criminal Liability a Treatise on the Criminal Liability of Corporations, their Officers and Agents*. Deerfield: Clark Boardman Callaghan.

Brilmayer, L [1986]: 'Carolene, Conflicts, and the Fate of the "Insider-Outsider"' In Vol. 134, *University of Philadelphia Law Review*, at 1291.

Brilmayer, L [1987]: 'The Extraterritorial Application of American Law: A Methodological and Constitutional Appraisal'. In Vol. 50, *Law and Contemporary Problems*, at 311.

Brilmayer, L [1988]: 'Related Contacts and Personal Jurisdiction'. In Vol. 101, *Harvard Law Review*, at 1444.

Brilmayer, L [1989]: 'Consent, Contract, and Territory'. In Vol. 74, *Minnesota Law Review*, at 1.

Brilmayer, L, Haverkamp, J, Logan, B, Lynch, L, Neuwirth, S & O'Brien, J [1988]: 'A General Look at General Jurisdiction'. In Vol. 66, *Texas Law Review*, at 721.

Brilmayer, L & Paisley, K [1986]: 'Personal Jurisdiction and Substantive Legal Relations: Corporations, Conspiracies, and Agency'. In Vol. 74, *California Law Review*, at 1.

Brown, D [2011]: 'Criminal Law's Unfortunate Triumph over Administrative Law'. In Vol. 7, *Journal of Law and Economic Policy*, at 657.

Brooks, M & Heijdra, B, [1991]: 'Dividing the Spoils'. In Policy Paper No. 20. Australian Institute for Public Policy.

Brown, H [1994]: 'The Foreign Corrupt Practices Act Redux: The Anti-Bribery Provisions of the Foreign Corrupt Practices Act'. In Vol. 12, *International Tax & Business Law*, at 279.

Brown, H [1995]: 'Vicarious Criminal Liability of Corporations for the Acts of Their Employees and Agents'. In Vol. 41, *Loyola Law Review*, at 260.

Brown, H [1998]: 'Parent-subsidiary Liability under the Foreign Corrupt Practices Act'. In Vol. 50, *Baylor Law Review*, at 1.

Brown, H [1999]: 'The Extraterritorial Reach of the U.S. Government's Campaign Against International Bribery'. In Vol. 22, *Hastings International and Comparative Law Review*, at 407.

Brown, H [2001]: 'Extraterritorial Jurisdiction Under the 1998 Amendments to the Foreign Corrupt Practices Act: Does the Government's Reach Now Exceed Its Grasp?'. In Vol. 26, *North Carolina Journal of International Law & Commercial Regulation*, at 239.

Brown, W [1905]: 'The Personality of the Corporation and the State'. In Vol. 21, *Law Quarterly Review*, at 365.

Brownlie, I [1990]: *Principles of Public International Law* (4th ed.). Oxford: Clarendon Press.

Brudney, V [1983]: 'Equal Treatment of Shareholders in Corporate Distributions and Reorganizations'. In Vol. 71, *California Law Review*, at 1072.

Brudney, V [1985]: 'Corporate Governance, Agency Costs and the Rhetoric of Contract'. In Vol. 85, *Columbia Law Review*, at 1403.

Brunetti, A, Kisunko, G & Weder, B [1997]: 'Institutional Obstacles for Doing Business Data Description and Methodology of a Worldwide Private Sector Survey'. World Bank Policy Research Working Paper, at 1759.

Buckley, P & Casson, M [1985]: *The Economic Theory of the Multinational Enterprise*. London: Macmillan.

Bucy, P [1991]: 'Corporate Ethos: A Standard for Imposing Corporate Criminal Liability'. In Vol. 75, *Minnesota Law Review*, at 1095.

Burger, E & Holland, M [2006]: 'Why the Private Sector is Likely to Lead the Next Stage in the Global Fight Against Corruption'. In Vol. 30, *Fordham International Law Journal*, at 45.

Burley, A [1992]: 'Law Among Liberal States: Liberal Internationalism and the Act of State Doctrine'. In Vol. 92, *Columbia Law Review*, at 1907.

Buscaglia, E [2001]: 'An Analysis of Judicial Corruption and Its Causes: An Objective Governing-Based Approach'. In Vol. 21, *International Review of Law and Economics*, at 233.

Buscaglia, E & Dakolias M [1999]: 'An Analysis of the Causes of Corruption in the Judiciary'. In Vol. 30, *Law and Policy in International Business Law and Policy in International Business*, at 95.

Butler, H [1985]: 'Nineteenth-Century Jurisdictional Competition in the Granting of Corporate Privileges'. In Vol. 24, *Journal of Legal Studies*, at 129.

Butler, H & Ribstein, L [1990]: 'Opting Out of Fiduciary Duties: A Response to the Anti-Contractarians'. In Vol. 65, *Washington Law Review*, at 1.

Canfield, G [1917]: 'The Scope and Limits of the Corporate Entity Theory'. In Vol. 17, *Columbia Law Review*, at 128.

Carney, W [1988]: 'Controlling Management Opportunism in the Market for Corporate Control: An Agency Cost Model'. In Vol. 63, *Wisconsin Law Review*, at 385.

Carr, I [2007]: 'Corruption in Africa: Is the African Union Convention on Combating Corruption the Answer?' In Vol. 7, *Journal of Business Law*, at 111.

Carrington, P [2010]: 'Enforcing International Corrupt Practices Law'. In Vol. 32, *Michigan Journal of International Law*, 129.

Cary, W & Eisenberg, M [1995]: *Corporations: Cases and Materials* (7th ed.). New York: Foundation Press.

Casey, S [2005]: 'Balancing Deterrence, Comity Considerations, and Judicial Efficiency: The Use of the D.C. Circuit's Proximate Cause Standard for Determining Subject Matter Jurisdiction over Extraterritorial Antitrust Cases'. In Vol. 55, *American University Law Review*, at 585.

Chanda, P [2004]: 'The Effectiveness of the World Bank's Anti-Corruption Efforts: Current Legal and Structural Obstacles and Uncertainties'. In Vol. 32, *Denver Journal of International Law and Policy*, at 315.

Cheffins, B [1999]: 'Using Theory to Study Law: A Company Law Perspective'. In *Cambridge Law Journal*, at 197.

Cheng, K [2011]: 'The Corporate Veil Doctrine Revisited: A Comparative Study of the English and the U.S. Corporate Veil Doctrines'. In Vol. 34, *Boston College International and Comparative Law Review*, at 329.

Cheshire, G & North, P [1987]: *Private International Law* (11th ed.). London: Butterworth.

Cheung, S [1983]: 'The Contractual Nature of the Firm. In Vol. 26, *Journal of Law and Economics*, at 1.

Chow, D [1987]: 'Rethinking the Act of State Doctrine: An Analysis in Terms of Jurisdiction to Prescribe'. In Vol. 62, *Washington Law Review*, at 397.

Clark, R [1986]: *Corporate Law.* Boston: Little Brown.

Clough, J & Mulhern, C [2002]: *The Prosecution of Corporations.* Melbourne: Oxford University Press.

Coase, R [1937]: 'The Nature of the Firm'. *Economica.* In Stigler, G & Boulding, K (eds.) [1952]: *Readings in Price Theory.* Homewood: Richard D. Irwin, at 386.

Coffee, J [1980]: 'Making the Punishment Fit the Corporation: The Problems of Finding on Optimal Corporation Criminal Sanction'. In Vol. 1, *Northern Illinois University Law Review*, at 3.

Coffee, J [1981]: 'No Soul to Damn: No Body to Kick: An Unscandalized Inquiry into the Problem of Corporate Punishment'. In Vol. 79, *Michigan Law Review*, at 386.

Coffee, J [1994]: 'Emerging Issues in Corporate Criminal Policy'. Foreword to Gruner, R [1994]: *Corporate Crime and Sentencing.* Charlottesville: Michie Co.

Coffee, J [1998]: 'Corporate Criminal Liability: An Introduction and Comparative Survey'. In Eser, A, et al. (eds.) [1998]: *Criminal Responsibility of Legal and Collective Entities*. International Colloquium Berlin, May 4–6, 1998.

Coffee, J [2007]: 'Law and the Market: The Impact of Enforcement'. In Vol. 156, *University of Pennsylvania Law Review*, 229.

Cohen, D [1998]: 'Theories of the Corporation and the Limited Liability Company: How Should Courts and Legislatures Articulate rules for Piercing the Veil, Fiduciary Responsibility and Securities Regulation for the Limited Liability Company?' In Vol. 51, *Oklahoma Law Review*, at 427.

Colangelo, A [2007]: 'Constitutional Limits on Extraterritorial Jurisdiction: Terrorism and the Intersection of National and International Law'. In Vol. 48, *Harvard International Law Journal*, at 121.

Colare, J [2006]: 'The Evolving Domestic and International Law against Foreign Corruption: Some New and Old Dilemmas Facing the International Lawyer'. In Vol. 5, *Washington University Global Studies Law Review*, at 1.

Collins, J [1979]: 'Opportunities for and Obstacles to Obtaining Evidence in England for Use in Litigation in the United States'. In Vol. 13, *International Law*, at 27.

Colvin, E [1995]: 'Corporate Personality and Criminal Liability'. In Vol. 6, *Criminal Law Forum*, at 1.

Conison, J [1994]: 'What Does Due Process Have to Do with Jurisdiction'? In Vol. 46, *Rutgers Law Review*, at 1071.

Cooke, C [1950]: *Corporation Trust and Company*. Manchester: Manchester University Press.

Coppel, J [1993]: 'A Hard Look at the Effects Doctrine of Jurisdiction in Public International Law'. In Vol. 6, *Leiden Journal of International Law*, at 73.

Cox, S [1991]: 'Would that Burn Had Not Come to Be Done Insane! A Critique of Recent Supreme Court Personal Jurisdiction Reasoning, An Explanation of Why Transient Presence Jurisdiction Is Unconstitutional, and Some Thoughts About Divorce Jurisdiction in a Minimum Contacts World'. In Vol. 58, *Tennessee Law Review*, at 497.

Cragg, A [1998]: 'Business, Globalization, and the Logic and Ethics of Corruption'. In Vol. 53, *International Journal*, at 643.

Cressey, D [1988]: 'The Poverty of Theory in Corporate Crime Research'. In Vol. 1, *Advances in Criminological Theory*, at 31.

Crutchfield, B & Dundas, M [1980]: 'Responsibilities of Domestic Corporate Management Under the Foreign Corrupt Practices Act'. In Vol. 31, *Syracuse Law Review*, at 865.

Crutchfield, B & Lacey, K [2006]: 'The Changing Face of White-Collar Crime: Investigation of Halliburton Co./Tskj's Nigerian Business Practices: Model for Analysis of the Current Anti-Corruption Environment on Foreign Corrupt Practices Act Enforcement'. In Vol. 96, *Journal of Criminal Law & Criminology*, at 503.

Cullen, P [2007]: 'Article 5 – Enforcement'. In Pieth, M, Low, L & Cullen, P (eds.) [2007]: *The OECD Convention on Bribery: A Commentary*. Cambridge: Cambridge University Press, at 289.

Culp, M [1933]: 'Process in Actions Against Non-Residents Doing Business Within a State'. In Vol. 32, *Michigan Law Review*, at 909.

Cummings, S [1986]: 'International Mass Tort Litigation: Forum Non Conveniens and the Adequate Alternative Forum in Light of the Bhopal Disaster'. In Vol. 16, *Georgia Journal of International & Comparative Law*, at 109.

Dainow, J [1935]: 'The Inappropriate Forum'. In Vol. 29, *Illinois Law Review*, at 867.

Dalton, M [2006]: 'Efficiency V. Morality: The Codification of Cultural Norms in the Foreign Corrupt Practices Act'. In Vol. 2, *New York University Journal of Law & Business*, at 583.

David, L, Strudler, A & Wasserman, D [1992]: 'Moral Responsibility in the Age of Bureaucracy'. In Vol. 90, *Michigan Law Review*, at 2348.

Davis, K [1999]: 'Self-Interest and Altruism in the Deterrence of Transnational Bribery'. In Olin Working Paper No. 99-22.

Davis, K [2012]: 'Why Does the United States Regulate Foreign Bribery: Moralism, Self-Interest, or Altruism?' In Vol. 67, *New York University Annual Survey of American Law*, at 497.

De Michele, R [2004]: 'The Follow-Up Mechanism of the Inter-American Convention Against Corruption, A Preliminary Assessment: Is the Glass Half Empty?' In Vol. 10, *Southwestern Journal of Law and Trade in the Americas*, at 295.

Deberardine, V [1984]: 'Foreign Corrupt Practices: Creating an Exception to the Act of State Doctrine'. In Vol. 34, *American University Law Review*, at 203.

Defleur, M [1995]: 'Corruption, Law and Justice'. In Vol. 23, *Journal of Criminal Law and Justice*, at 243.

Deiser, G [1909]: 'The Juristic Person'. In Vol. 57, *University of Pennsylvania Law Review*, at 300.

Delaney, P [2006]: 'Transnational Corruption: Regulation Across Borders'. In Vol. 47, *Virginia Journal of International Law*, at 413.

Demsetz, H [1988] *Ownership Control and the Firm: The Organization of Economic Activity*. Oxford: Basil Blackwell.

Dewey, J [1926]: 'The Historical Background of Corporate Legal Personality'. In Vol. 35, *Yale Law Journal*, at 655.

Dicey, A & Morris, J [1987]: *Dicey and Morris on the Conflict of Laws*. London: Sweet & Maxwell.

Dickerson, C [1999]: 'Political Corruption: Free-Flowing Opportunism'. In Vol. 14, *Connecticut Journal of International Law*, at 393.

Ditton, J [1977]: 'Alibis and Aliases: Some Notes on the "Motives" of Fiddling Bread Salesmen'. In Vol. 11, No. 2, *Sociology*, at 233.

Donaldson, T & Dunfee, T [1994]: 'Toward a Unified Conception of Business Ethics: Integrative Social Contracts Theory'. In Vol. 19, *Academy of Management Review*, at 252.

Donaldson, T & Dunfee, T [1999]: *Ties That Bind: A Social Contracts Approach to Business Ethics.* Boston: Harvard University Press.

Dowd, M & Eichelberger, T [1984]: 'Recent Decision: International Law – Act of State Doctrine: An Emerging Corruption Exception in Antitrust Cases?' In Vol. 59, *Notre Dame Law Review*, at 455.

Doyle, M [1997]: *Ways of War and Peace.* New York: W.W Norton & Company.

Dubois, A [1938]: *The English Business Company After the Bubble Act 1720–1800.* New York and London: Oxford University Press.

Duncan, C [2000]: 'The Foreign Corrupt Practices Act Amendments: Moral Empiricism or Moral Imperialism'. In Vol. 1, *Asian Pacific Law & Policy Journal*, at 14.

Dundas, M & Crutchfield B [1980]: 'Historical Analysis of the Accounting Standards of the Foreign Corrupt Practices Act'. In Vol. 10, *Memphis State Law Review*, at 499.

Dunfee, T [1999]: 'Social Contracts and Marketing Ethics'. In Vol. 63, *Journal of Marketing*, at 14.

Dunning, J [1981]: *International Production and the Multinational Enterprise.* London: George Allen & Unwin.

Dunning, J [1992]: *Multinational Enterprises and the Global Economy.* London: Addison Wesley.

Earle, B & Cava, A [2009]: 'Are Anti-Corruption Efforts Paying Off? International and National Measures in the Asia-Pacific Region and Their Impact on India and Multinational Corporations'. In Vol. 31, *University of Hawaii Law Review*, at 59.

Easterbrook, F & Fischel, D [1985]: 'Limited Liability and the Corporation'. In Vol. 52, *University of Chicago Law Review*, at 90.

Easterbrook, F & Fischel, D [1986]: 'Close Corporations and Agency Costs'. In Vol. 38, *Stanford Law Review*, at 271.

Easterbrook, F & Fischel, D [1991]: *The Economic Structure of Corporate Law.* Boston: Harvard University Press.

Edgardo Campos, J et al. [1999]: 'The Impact of Corruption on Investment: Predictability Matters'. In Vol. 27, *World Development*, at 1059.

Eisenberg, M [1984]: 'New Modes of Discourse in the Corporate Law Literature'. In Vol. 52, *George Washington Law Review*, at 819.

Eisenberg, M [1989]: 'Contractual Freedom in Corporate Law: Articles and Comments: The Structure of Corporation Law'. In Vol. 89, *Columbia Law Review*, at 1461.

Eisenberg, M [1999]: 'Symposium: Team Production in Business Organizations: The Conception That the Corporation Is a Nexus of Contracts, and the Dual Nature of the Firm'. In Vol. *24 University of Iowa Journal of Corporation Law*, at 819.

Elkins, J [1976]: 'Corporations and the Criminal Law: An Uneasy Alliance'. In Vol. 65, *Kentucky Law Journal*, at 73.
Elliot, K [1998]: 'The Problem of Corruption: A Tale of Two Countries'. In Vol. 18, *Journal of International Law & Business*, at 524.
Engle, E [2006]: 'Extraterritorial Corporate Criminal Liability: A Remedy for Human Rights Violations?' In Vol. 20, *St. John's Journal of Legal Commentary*, at 287.
Estreicher, A [1993]: 'Beyond Agency Costs: Managing the Corporation for the Long Term'. In Vol. 45, *Rutgers Law Review*, at 513.
Faigman, D [1989]: 'To Have and Have Not: Assessing the Value of Social Science to the Law as Science and Policy'. In Vol. 38, *Emory Law Journal*, at 1005.
Fama, E [1980]: 'Agency Problems and the Theory of the Firm'. In Vol. 88, *The Journal of Political Economy*, at 288.
Fama, E & Jensen, M [1983]: 'The Separation of Ownership and Control'. In Vol. 26, *Journal of Law and Economics*, at 301.
Fantaye, D [2004]: 'Fighting Corruption and Embezzlement in Third World Countries'. In Vol. 68, *Journal of Criminal Law*, at 170.
Field, S & Jorg, N [1991]: 'Corporate Liability and Manslaughter: Should We Be Going Dutch?' In *Criminal Law Review*, at 156.
Fischel, D [1982]: 'The Corporate Governance Movement'. In Vol. 35, *Vanderbilt Law Review*, at 1259.
Fischel, D & Sykes, A [1996]: 'Corporate Crime'. In Vol. 25, *Journal of Legal Studies*, at 319.
Fisher, H (ed.) [1911]: *The Collected Papers of Frederic William Maitland.* London: Cambridge University Press.
Fisse, B [1981]: 'The Social Policy of Corporate Criminal Responsibility'. In Vol. 6, *Adelaide Law Review*, at 361.
Fisse, B [1983]: 'Restructuring Corporate Criminal Law: Deterrence, Retribution, Fault, and Sanctions'. In Vol. 56, *Southern California Law Review*, at 1141.
Fisse, B [1990]: *Howard's Criminal Law* (5th ed.). Sydney: Law Book Company.
Fisse, B [1993]: 'Reconstructing Corporate Law: Deterrence, Retribution, Fault, and Sanctions'. In Vol. 56, *Southern California Law Review*, at 1244.
Fisse, B& Braithwaite, J [1988]: 'The Allocation of Responsibility for Corporate Crime: Individualism, Collectivism and Accountability'. In Vol. 11, *Sydney Law Review*, at 469.
Fisse, B & Braithwaite, J [1993]: *Corporations, Crime, and Accountability.* Cambridge: Cambridge University Press.
Fitzmaurice, G [1957]: 'The General Principles of International Law Considered from the Standpoint of the Rule of Law'. Reprinted in Harris, D [1998]: *Cases and Materials on International Law*. London: Sweet and Maxwell.
Fletcher, G [1985]: 'Paradoxes in Legal Thought.' In Vol. 85, *Columbia Law Review*, at 1263.
Foerschler, A [1990]: 'Corporate Criminal Intent: Toward a Better Understanding of Corporate Misconduct'. In Vol. 78, *California Law Review*, at 1287.
Ford, H [1958]: *The Rise and Growth of American Politics*. New York: Macmillan.

Formoy, R [1923]: *The Historical Foundations of Modern Company Law*. London: Sweet and Maxwell.

Fort, T & Noone, J [2000]: 'Gifts, Bribes, and Exchange: Relationships in Non-Market Economies and Lessons for Pax E-Commercia'. In Vol. 33, *Cornell Journal of International Law*, at 515.

Foster, N [2000]: 'Company Law Theory in Comparative Perspective: England and France'. In Vol. 48, *American Journal of Comparative Law*, at 573.

Fox, G [1992]: 'Reexamining the Act of State Doctrine: An Integrated Conflicts Analysis'. In Vol. 33, *Harvard International Law Journal*, at 521.

Franko, L [1976]: *The European Multinationals*. London: Harper & Row.

Fraser, B [1983]: 'Adjudicating Acts of State in Suits Against Foreign Sovereigns: A Political Question Analysis'. In Vol. 51, *Fordham Law Review*, at 722.

Freeman, J [2006]: 'The Razor's Edge in Cafta's Bribery Provision: Is the U.S. Really Concerned About Eliminating Corruption?' In Vol. 13, *Southwestern Journal of Law and Trade in the Americas*, at 189.

French, P [1984]: *Collective and Corporate Responsibility*. New York: Columbia University Press.

Friedman, L [1973]: *A History of American Law*. New York: Touchstone.

Friedman, L [2000]: 'In Defense of Corporate Criminal Liability'. In Vol. 23, *Harvard Journal of Law and Public Policy*, at 833.

Freidrich, C [1966]: 'Political Pathology'. In Vol. 37, *Political Quarterly*, at 70.

Gantz, D [1998]: 'Globalizing Sanctions Against Foreign Bribery: The Emergence of a New International Legal Consensus'. In Vol. 18, *North-Western Journal of International Law & Business*, at 457.

Garber, P [1990]: 'Famous First Bubbles'. In Vol. 4, *Journal of Economic Perspectives*, at 2.

Gayed, J [2003]: '"Corruptly": Why Corrupt State of Mind Is an Essential Element for Hobbs Act Extortion Under Color of Official Right'. In Vol. 78, *Notre Dame Law Review*, at 1731.

George, G [1990]: 'In Search of General Jurisdiction'. In Vol. 64, *Tulane Law Review*, at 1097.

Gerber, D [1984]: 'Beyond Balancing: International Law Restraints on the Reach of National Laws'. In Vol. 10, *Yale Journal of International Law*, at 185.

Geu, T [1998]: 'Chaos, Complexity, and Coevolution: The Web of Law, Management Theory, and Law Related Services at the Millennium'. In Vol. 65, *Tennessee Law Review*, at 137.

Gevurtz, F [1987]: 'Commercial Bribery and the Sherman Act: The Case for Per Se Illegality'. In Vol. 42, *University of Miami Law Review*, at 365.

Gibb, A [1926]: *The International Law of Jurisdiction in England and Scotland*. Edinburgh: W. Hodge & Co.

Giddens, A [1990]: *The Consequences of Modernity*. Palo Alto, CA: Stanford University Press.

Glynn, P, Stephen, K & Moisés, N [1997]: 'The Globalization of Corruption'. In K Elliott (ed.) [1997]: *Corruption and the Global Economy*. Washington D.C.: Institute for International Economics, at 7.

Goldbarg, A [2000]: 'The Foreign Corrupt Practices Act and Structural Corruption'. In Vol. 18, *Boston University International Law Journal*, at 273.

Goldsmith, J [1999]: 'Part III: Separation of Powers in Foreign Affairs: The New Formalism in United States Foreign Relations Law'. In Vol. 70, *Colorado Law Review*, at 1395.

Gower, L [1997]: *Gowers Principles of Modern Company Law* (6th ed.). London: Sweet & Maxwell.

Greanias, G & Windsor, D [1982]: *The Foreign Corrupt Practices Act: Anatomy of a Statute.* Lexington: Lexington Books.

Green, S [2006]: *Lying, Cheating and Stealing – A Moral Theory of White Collar Crime*. Oxford: Oxford University Press.

Guggenheim, K [1996]: 'Corruption, Not Revolutions or Coups, Topples Governments These Days'. In *Los Angeles Times*, Oct. 6, 1996, at A4.

Hackney, W & Benson, T [1982]: 'Shareholder Liability for Inadequate Capital'. In Vol. 43, *University of Pittsburgh Law Review*, at 837.

Hager, M [1989]: 'Bodies Politic: The Progressive History of Organizational "Real Entity" Theory'. In Vol. 50, *University of Pittsburgh Law Review*, at 575.

Halberstam, M [1985]: 'Sabbatino Resurrected: The Act of State Doctrine in the Revised Restatement of U.S. Foreign Relations'. In Vol. 79, *American Journal of International Law*, at 68.

Halpern, P, Trebilcock, M & Turnbull, S [1980]: 'An Economic Analysis of Limited Liability in Corporation Law'. In Vol. 30, *University of Toronto Law Journal*, at 117.

Hamdani, A & Klement, A [2008]: 'Corporate Crime and Deterrence'. In Vol. 61, *Stanford Law Review*, at 271.

Hansen, C [1993]: 'The Duty of Care, the Business Judgment Rule, and the American Law Institute Corporate Governance Project'. In Vol. 48, *Business Law*, at 1355.

Hansmann, H & Kraakman, R [1991]: 'Toward Unlimited Shareholder Liability for Corporate Torts'. In Vol. 100, *Yale Law Journal*, at 1871.

Hart, H [1954]: 'Definition and Theory in Jurisprudence'. In Vol. 70, *Law Quarterly Review*, at 37.

Hart, O [1989]: 'An Economist's Perspective on the Theory of the Firm'. In Vol. 89, *Columbia Law Review*, at 1757.

Hatchard, J [2007]: 'Countering Corruption and Enhancing Human Rights: Responsibilities of the Corporate Sector in the African Context'. Paper presented at the Business, Accountability and Human Rights Conference, 16–17 January 2007, Johannesburg, South Africa.

Hayden, G & Bodie, M [2010]: 'Shareholder Democracy and the Curious Turn Toward Board Primacy'. In Vol. 51, *William and Mary Law Review*, at 2071.

Hazeltine, H (ed.) [1936]: *F.W Maitland, Selected Essays.* Cambridge: Cambridge University Press.

Hefendehl, R [2000]: 'Corporate Criminal Liability: Model Penal Code Section 2.07 and the Development in Western Legal Systems'. In Vol. 4, *Buffalo Criminal Law Review*, at 283.

Heidenheimer, A. [1970]: *Political Corruption: Readings in Comparative Analysis*. New York: Holt, Rinehart, and Winston.

Heifetz, D [2002]: 'Japan's Implementation of the OECD Anti-Bribery Convention: Weaker and Less Effective Than the U.S. Foreign Corrupt Practices Act'. In Vol. 11, *Pacific Rim Law and Policy Journal*, at 209.

Heimann, F [1997]. 'Combatting International Corruption: The Role of the Business Community'. In K Elliott (ed.) [1997]: *Corruption and the Global Economy*. Washington D.C.: Institute for International Economics, at 147.

Hellman, J, Jones, G & Kaufmann, D [2000]: 'Beyond the "Grabbing Hand" of Government in Transition: Facing up to "State Capture by the Corporate Sector". In Vol. 11 (2), *Transition: The Newsletter about Reforming Economies*, at 8.

Hendrix, S [2005]: 'New Approaches to Addressing Corruption in the Context of U.S. Foreign Assistance with Examples from Latin America and the Caribbean'. In Vol. 12, *Southwestern Journal of Law and Trade in the Americas*, at 1.

Henkin, L [1964]: 'The Foreign Affairs Power of the Federal Courts: Sabbatino'. In Vol. 64, *Columbia Law Review*, at 805.

Henn, H & Alexander, J [1983]: *Laws of Corporations and Other Business Enterprises*. St Paul: West Publishing Co.

Henning, P [1995]: 'Maybe It Should Just Be Called Federal Fraud: The Changing Nature of the Mail Fraud Statute'. In Vol. 36, *British Columbia Law Review*, at 435.

Henning, P [2001]: 'Public Corruption: A Comparative Analysis of International Corruption Conventions and United States Law'. In Vol. 18, *Arizona Journal of International and Comparative Law*, at 793.

Hess, D & Dunfee, T [2000]: 'Symposium Fighting International Corruption & Bribery in the 21st Century; Fighting Corruption: A Principled Approach; The C2 Principles (Combating Corruption)'. In Vol. 33, *Cornell International Law Journal*, at 593.

Hessen, R [1979]: 'A New Concept of Corporations: A Contractual and Private Property Model'. In Vol. 30, *Hastings Law Journal*, at 1327.

Hogarth, J [1995]: 'Developments in Criminal Law and Criminal Justice: Bribery of Officials in Pursuit of Corporate Aims'. In Vol. 6, *Criminal Law Forum*, at 557.

Hohfeld, W [1909]: 'Nature of Stockholders' Individual Liability for Corporate Debts'. In Vol. 9, *Columbia Law Review*, at 285.

Holt, J [2007]: 'The International Law Exception to the Act of State Doctrine: Redressing Human Rights Abuses in Papua New Guinea'. In Vol. 16, *Pacific Rim Law & Policy Journal,* at 459.

Hongju Koh, H [1999]: 'How Is International Human Rights Law Enforced?' In Vol. 74, *Indiana Law Journal*, at 1397.

Hood, N, and Young, S [1979]: *The Economics of the Multinational Enterprise.* London: Longman.

Hornbeck, S [1996]: 'Transnational Litigation and Personal Jurisdiction over Foreign Defendants'. In Vol. 59, *Albany Law Review*, at 1389.

Horwitz, M [1985]: 'Santa Clara Revisited: The Development of Corporate Theory'. In Vol. 88, *West Virginia Law Review*, at 173.
Hovenkamp, H [1989]: 'Antitrust's Protected Classes'. In Vol. 88, *Michigan Law Review*, at 1.
Hovenkamp, H [1998]: 'The Classical Corporation in American Legal Thought'. In Vol. 76, *Georgia Law Journal*, at 1593.
Huntington, S [1968]: *Political Order in Changing Societies.* New Haven: Yale University Press.
Huntington, S [1979]: 'Modernization and Corruption'. In Epko, M (ed.) [1979]. *Bureaucratic Corruption in Sub-Saharan Africa: Toward a Search for Causes and Consequences*. Washington D.C.: University Press of America, at 313.
Hurst, J [1970]: *The Legitimacy of the Business Corporation in the Law of the United States, 1780–1970*. Charlottesville: University of Virginia Press.
Husted, B [1994]: 'Honor Among Thieves: A Transaction-Cost Interpretation of Corruption in Third World Countries'. In Vol. 4, *Business Ethics Quarterly*, at 17.
Jackson, J [2003]: 'Sovereignty-Modern: A New Approach to an Outdated Concept'. In Vol. 97, *American Journal of International Law*, at 782.
Jacobson, K [2005]: 'Doing Business with the Devil: The Challenges of Prosecuting Corporate Officials Whose Business Transactions Facilitate War Crimes and Crimes Against Humanity'. In Vol. 56, *Air Force Law Review*, at 167.
Jatto, L [2010]: 'Africa's Approach to the International War on Corruption: A Critical Appraisal of the African Union Convention on Preventing and Combating Corruption'. In Vol. 10, *Asper Review of International Business and Trade Law*, at 79.
Jensen, M & Meckling, W [1976]: 'Theory of the Firm: Managerial Behavior, Agency Costs, and Ownership Structure'. In Vol. 3, *Journal of Financial Economics*, at 305.
Johnson, O [1975]: 'An Economic Analysis of Corrupt Government, With Special Application to Less Developed Countries'. In Vol. 28, *Kyklos: International Review for Social Science*, at 47.
Johnston, J [1993]: 'The Influence of the Nature of the Firm on the Theory of Corporate Law'. In Vol. 18, *Journal of Corporate Law*, at 213.
Johnston, M [1982]: *Political Corruption and Public Policy in America.* Monterey: Brooks/Cole Publishing Company.
Johnston, M [1986]: 'The Political Consequences of Corruption: A Reassessment'. In Vol. 18, *Comparative Politics*, at 459.
Johnston, M [1996]: 'The Search for Definitions: The Vitality of Politics and the Issue of Corruption'. In Vol. 149, *International Social Science Journal*, at 321.
Johnston, M [1997]: 'Public Officials, Private Interests, and Sustainable Democracy: When Politics and Corruption Meet'. In K Elliott (ed.) [1997]: *Corruption and the Global Economy.* Washington D.C.: Institute for International Economics, at 61.

Johnston, M (ed.) [2005]: *Civil Society and Corruption: Mobilizing for Reform*. Lanham: University Press of America.

Johnston, M [2012]: 'Why Do So Many Anti-Corruption Efforts Fail?' In Vol. 67, *New York University Annual Survey of American Law*, at 467.

Jones, H [1953]: 'International Judicial Assistance: Procedural Chaos and a Program for Reform'. In Vol. 62, *Yale Law Journal*, at 515.

Jordan, J [2000]: 'Universal Jurisdiction in a Dangerous World: A Weapon for All Nations Against International Crime'. In Vol. 9, *Michigan State University-DCL Journal of International Law*, at 1.

Jordan, J [2011a]: 'Recent Developments in the Foreign Corrupt Practices Act and the New UK Bribery Act: A Global Trend Towards Greater Accountability in The Prevention of Foreign Bribery'. In Vol. 7, *NYU Journal of Law & Business*, at 845.

Jordan, J [2011b]: 'The Adequate Procedures Defense Under the UK Bribery Act: A British Idea for the Foreign Corrupt Practices Act'. In Vol. 17, *Stanford Journal of Law, Business & Finance* at 25.

Kahan, D [1998]: 'Social Meaning and the Economic Analysis of Crime'. In Vol. 27, *Journal of Legal Studies*, at 609.

Karelis, K [1989]: 'The Act of State Doctrine: Reconciling Justice and Diplomacy on a Case-by-Case Basis'. In Vol. 43, *University of Miami Law Review*, at 1169.

Kauffman, S [1995]: *At Home in the Universe: The Search for Laws of Self-Organization and Complexity*. Oxford: Oxford University Press.

Kaufmann, D & Paul, S [1995]: 'Privatization and Corruption in Transition Economies'. In Vol. 50, *Journal of International Affairs*, at 419.

Kelly-Kilgore, S & Smith, E [2011]: 'Corporate Criminal Liability'. In Vol. 48, *American Criminal Law Review* 421.

Kennedy, D. [1999]: 'The International Anti-Corruption Campaign'. In Vol. 14, *Connecticut Journal of International Law*, at 455.

Khanna, V [1996]: 'Corporate Criminal Liability: What Purpose Does It Serve?' In Vol. 109, *Harvard Law Review*, at 1477.

Khanna, V [1999]: 'Is the Notion of Corporate Fault a Faulty Notion?: The Case of Corporate Mens Rea'. In Vol. 79, *Boston University Law Review*, at 335.

Khanna, V [2000]: 'Corporate Liability Standards: When Should Corporations be Held Criminally Liable?'. In Vol. 37, *American Criminal Law Review*, at 1239.

Khanna, V [2003a]: 'Corporate Crime Legislation: A Political Economy Analysis'. In Discussion Paper No. 03-012, University of Michigan John N. Ohlin Center for Law and Economics.

Khanna, V [2003b]: 'Should the Behavior of Top Management Matter?' In Vol. 91, *Georgetown Law Journal*, at 1215.

Kim, H [1999]: 'The Errand Boy's Revenge: Helms-Burton and the Supreme Courts Response to Congress's Abrogation of the Act of State Doctrine'. In Vol. 48, *Emory Law Journal*, at 305.

Kim, J [1999]: 'Korean Implementation of the OECD Bribery Convention: Implications for Global Efforts to Fight Corruption'. In Vol. 17, *University of California Pacific Basin Law Journal*, at 245.

Kim, J & Kim, J [1997]: 'Cultural Differences in the Crusade Against International Bribery: Rice-Cake Expenses in Korea and the Foreign Corrupt Practices Act'. In Vol. 6, *Pacific Rim Law and Policy Journal*, at 549.

Kirgis, F [1988]: 'Understanding the Act of State Doctrine's Effect'. In Vol. 82, *American Journal of International Law*, at 58.

Klich, A [1996]: 'Bribery in Economies in Transition: The Foreign Corrupt Practices Act'. In Vol. 32, *Stanford Journal of International Law*, at 121.

Klitgaard, R [1988]: *Controlling Corruption.* Los Angeles: University of California Press.

Knudsen, M [1988]: 'Jurisdiction Over a Corporation Based on the Contacts of a Related Corporation: Time for a Rule of Attribution'. In Vol. 92, *Dickson Law Review*, at 917.

Koch, R [2005]: 'The Foreign Corrupt Practices Act: It's Time to Cut Back the Grease and Add Some Guidance'. In Vol. 28, *Boston College International and Comparative Law Review*, at 379.

Koehler, M [2010]: 'The Facade of FCPA Enforcement'. In Vol. 41, *Georgetown Journal of International Law*, at 907.

Kofele-Kale, N [2006]: 'Change or the Illusion of Change: The War Against Official Corruption in Africa'. In Vol. 38, *George Washington International Law Review*, at 697.

Korn, H [1999]: 'The Development of Judicial Jurisdiction in the United States: Part 1'. In Vol. 65, *Brooklyn Law Review*, at 935.

Kraakman, R [1984]: 'Corporate Liability Strategies Liability Strategies and the Costs of Legal Controls'. In Vol. 93, *Yale Law Journal*, at 857.

Krueger, A [1974]: 'The Political Economy of the Rent-Seeking Society'. In Vol. 64, *America Economic Review*, at 291.

Krueger, A [1993a]: *Political Economy of Policy Reform in Developing Countries*. Cambridge, MA: MIT Press.

Krueger, A [1993b]: 'Virtuous and Vicious Circles in Economic Development'. In Vol. 83, *American Economic Review*, at 351.

Lacey, K & Crutchfield, B [2003]: 'Crackdown on Money Laundering: A Comparative Analysis of Feasibility and Effectiveness of Domestic and Multilateral Policy Reforms'. In Vol. 23, *Northwestern Journal of International Law and Business*, at 263.

Ladd, J [1970]: 'Morality and the Ideal of Rationality in Formal Organizations'. In Vol. 54, *Monist*, at 488.

Lambsdorff, J [2007]: *The Institutional Economics of Corruption and Reform: Theory, Evidence and Policy*. Cambridge: Cambridge University Press.

Landers, J [1975]: 'A Unified Approach to Parent, Subsidiary, and Affiliate Questions in Bankruptcy'. In Vol. 42, *University of Chicago Law Review*, at 589.

Landes, D [1999]: *The Wealth and Poverty of Nations: Why are Some So Rich and Others So Poor?* New York: W.W. Norton & Company.

Landes, W & Posner, R [1987]: *The Economic Structure of Tort Law.* Boston: Harvard University Press.

Lanham, D [1987]: 'Bribery and Corruption'. In *Essays in Honour of J C Smith*, Consultation Paper No 145.

Laski, H [1916a]: 'The Personality of Associations'. In Vol. 29, *Harvard Law Review*, at 404.

Laski, H [1916b]: 'The Basis of Vicarious Liability'. In Vol. 26, *Yale Law Review*, at 105.

Laufer, W [1994]: 'Corporate Bodies and Guilty Minds'. In Vol. 43, *Emory Law Journal*, at 575.

Laufer, W & Strudler, A [2000]: 'Corporate Intentionality, Desert, and Variants of Vicarious Liability'. In Vol. 37, *American Criminal Law Review*, at 1285.

Lederman, E [1985]: 'Criminal Law, Perpetrator and Corporation: Rethinking a Complex Triangle'. In Vol. 76, *Journal of Criminal Law and Criminology*, at 285.

Lederman, E [2000]: 'Models for Imposing Corporate Criminal Liability: From Adaptation and Imitation Toward Aggregation and the Search for Self-Identity'. In Vol. 4, *Buffalo Criminal Law Review*, at 641.

Leebron, D [1991]: 'Limited Liability, Tort Victims, and Creditors'. In Vol. 91, *Columbia Law Review*, at 1565.

Leff, N [1979]: 'Economic Development through Bureaucratic Corruption'. In Epko, M (ed.) [1979]. *Bureaucratic Corruption in Sub-Saharan Africa: Toward a Search for Causes and Consequences.* Washington D.C.: University Press of America, at 8.

Leigh, L [1969]: *The Criminal Liability of Corporations in English Law*. London: Weidenfeld & Nicholson.

Leigh, L [1982]: 'The Criminal Liability of Corporations and Other Groups: A Comparative View'. In Vol. 80, *Michigan Law Review*, at 1508.

Leiken, R [1996]: 'Controlling the Global Corruption Epidemic'. In Vol. 105, *Foreign Policy*, at 55.

Lev, E [1993]: 'European Community Competition Law: Is the Corporate Veil Lifted Too Often?' In Vol. 2, *Journal of Transnational Law & Policy*, at 199.

Levin, M [1994]: 'Judicial Jurisdiction in International Civil Litigation'. In Vol. 6, *International Quarterly*, at 66.

Levmore, S [1982]: 'Monitors and Freeriders in Commercial and Corporate Settings'. In Vol. 92, *Yale Law Journal*, at 49.

Lewin, J [1998]: 'The Genesis and Evolution of Legal Uncertainty About "Reasonable Medical Certainty"'. In Vol. 57, *Maryland Law Review*, at 380.

Leys, C [1965]: 'What Is the Problem About Corruption?' In Vol. 3, *The Journal of Modern African Studies*, at 215.

Lindgren, J [1988]: 'The Elusive Distinction Between Bribery and Extortion: From the Common Law to the Hobbs Act'. In Vol. 35, *University of California Los Angeles Law Review*, at 815.

Lindgren, J [1993]: 'The Theory, History, and Practice of the Bribery-Extortion Distinction'. In Vol. 141, *University of Pennsylvania Law Review*, at 1695.

Little, J [1987]: 'Up with Torts'. In Vol. 24, *San Diego Law Review*, at 861.

Loken, K [2001]: 'The OECD Anti-bribery Convention: Coverage of Foreign Subsidiaries'. In Vol. 33, *George Washington International Law Review*, at 325.

Low, L [1998]: 'The Foreign Corrupt Practices Act: How to Comply Under the New Amendments and the OECD Convention'. American Bar Association Center for Continuing Legal Education.

Low, L [2003]: 'The Anti-Corruption Laws of the United States and Mexico'. In Vol. 11, *United States-Mexico Law Journal*, at 149.

Low, L, Bonheimer, O & Lorello, D [2007]: 'The Uncertain Calculus of FCPA Voluntary Disclosures'. Paper presented to the American Conference Institute 17th National Conference, March 27–28, 2007.

Lowell Brown, H [1998]: 'Parent -Subsidiary Liability Under the Foreign Corrupt Practices Act'. In Vol. 50, *Baylor University Baylor Law Review*, at 1.

Lowenfeld, A [1979]: 'Public Law in the International Arena: Conflict of Laws, International Law, and Some Suggestions for Their Interaction'. In Vol. 163, *Recueil Des Cours*, at 311.

Lowenfeld, A [1989]: 'U.S. Law Enforcement Abroad: The Constitutional and International Law'. In Vol. 83, *American Journal of International Law*, at 880.

Macey, J [1991]: 'Agency Theory and the Criminal Liability of Organizations'. In Vol. 71, *Boston University Law Review*, at 315.

Machen, A [1911]: 'Corporate Personality'. In Vol. 24, *Harvard Law Review*, at 253.

Mann, F [1973]: *Studies in International Law.* Oxford: Oxford University Press.

Manne, H [1965]: 'Mergers and the Market for Corporate Control'. In Vol. 73, *Journal of Political Economy*, at 110.

Manzi, M [1990]: 'Dow Chemical Co. v. Castro Alfaro: The Demise of Forum Non Conveniens in Texas and One Less Barrier to International Tort Litigation'. In Vol. 14, *Fordham International Law Journal*, at 819.

Marceau, J [2007]: 'A Little Less Conversation, a Little More Action: Evaluating and Forecasting the Trend of More Frequent and Severe Prosecutions Under The Foreign Corrupt Practices Act'. In Vol. 12, *Fordham Journal of Corporate & Financial Law*, at 285.

Mark, G [1987]: 'The Personification of the Business Corporation in American Law'. In Vol. 54, *University of Chicago Law Review*, at 1441.

Marong, A [2002]: 'Toward a Normative Consensus Against Corruption: Legal Effects of the Principles to Combat Corruption in Africa'. In Vol. 30, *Denver Journal of International Law and Policy*, at 99.

Marris, R & Mueller, D [1980]: 'The Corporation, Competition, and the Invisible Hand'. In Vol. 18, *Journal of Economic Literature*, at 32.

Martin, K & Walsh, S [1996]: 'Beware the Foreign Corrupt Practices Act'. In Vol. 13, *International Commercial Litigation*, at 25.

Matthews, J [1997]: 'Power Shift'. In Vol. 76, *Foreign Affairs*, at 50.

Mauro, P [1995]: 'Corruption and Growth'. In Vol. 106, *Quarterly Journal of Economics*, at 681.

Mauro, P [1996]: 'The Effects of Corruption on Growth, Investment, and Government Expenditure: A Cross Country Analysis, in Corruption and the Global Economy'. In K Elliott (ed.) [1996]: *Corruption and the Global Economy.* Washington D.C.: Institute for International Economics, at 83.

Mauro, P [1997]: 'The Effects of Corruption on Growth, Investment, and Government Expenditure: A Cross-Country Analysis'. In K Elliott (ed.) [1997]: *Corruption and the Global Economy.* Washington D.C.: Institute for International Economics, at 83.

Mayer, C [1990]: 'Personalizing the Impersonal: Corporations and the Bill of Rights'. In Vol. 41, *Hastings Law Journal*, at 577.

Mbaku, J [1994]: 'Bureaucratic Corruption and Policy Reform in Africa'. In Vol. 19, *Journal of Social Political and Economic Studies*, at 149.

McClean, D [1992]: *International Judicial Assistance.* Oxford: Oxford University Press.

McClenahen, J [1998]: 'Bribery Remains Widespread'. In *Industry Week*, Oct. 19, 1998, at 16.

McDermott, C [1999]: *Criminal Law.* Dublin: Butterworths.

McMullan, M. [1961]: 'A Theory of Corruption'. In Vol. 9, *Sociological Review*, at 181.

Meeks, W [2006]: 'Corporate and White-Collar Crime Enforcement: Should Regulation and Rehabilitation Spell an End to Corporate Criminal Liability?' In Vol. 40, *Columbia Journal of Law and Social Problems*, at 77.

Mehren, A [1983]: 'Adjudicatory Jurisdiction: General Theories Compared and Evaluated'. In Vol. 63, *Boston University Law Review*, at 279.

Mendelson, N [2002]: 'A Control-Based Approach to Shareholder Liability for Corporate Torts'. In Vol. 102, *Columbia Law Review*, at 1203.

Merryman, J [1985]: *The Civil Law Tradition.* Palo Alto, CA: Stanford University Press.

Mertus, J [1999]: 'From Legal Transplants to Transformative Justice: Human Rights and the Promise of Transnational Civil Society'. In Vol. 14, *American University International Law Review*, at 1335.

Micklethwait, J & Wooldridge, A [2003]: *The Company: A Short History of a Revolutionary Idea.* London: Weidenfeld & Nicolson.

Miller, S [1998]: 'Piercing the Corporate Veil Among Affiliated Companies in the European Community and in the U.S.: A Comparative Analysis of U.S., German, and U.K. Veil-Piercing Approaches'. In Vol. 36, *American Business Law Journal*, at 73.

Millon, D [1990]: 'Frontiers of Legal Thought I: Theories of the Corporation'. In April 1990, *Duke Law Journal*, at 201.

Minda, G [1989]: 'The Jurisprudential Movements of the 1980's'. In Vol. 50, *Ohio State Law Journal*, at 599.

Moohr, G [1994]: 'Mail Fraud and the Intangible Rights Doctrine: Someone to Watch Over Us'. In Vol. 31, *Harvard Journal on Legislation*, at 153.

Moore, J [1992]: 'Corporate Culpability Under the Federal Sentencing Guidelines. In Vol. 34, *Arizona Law Review*, at 743.

Moravcsik, A. [1997]: 'Taking Preferences Seriously: A Liberal Theory of International Politics'. In Vol. 51, *International Organization*, at 513.

Morrissey, D [2007]: 'The Fight Against Corruption by International Organizations'. In Vol. 39, *George Washington International Law Review*, at 165.

Muchlinski, P [1995]: *Multinational Enterprises and the Law.* London: Blackwell Publishers.

Mueller, G [1957]: 'Mens Rea and the Corporation – A Study of the Model Penal Code'. In Vol. 19, *University of Pittsburgh Law Review*, at 21.

Murphy, K, Schleifer, A & Vishny, R [1993]: 'Why Is Rent-Seeking So Costly to Growth'? In Vol. 83, *The American Economic Review*, at 409.

Murphy, M [1995]: 'International Bribery: An Example of an Unfair Trade Practice?' In Vol. 21, *Brook Journal of International Law*, at 385.

Nanda, V [2010]: 'Corporate Criminal Liability in the United States: Is a New Approach Warranted?' In Vol. 58, *American Journal of Comparative Law*, at 605.

Nekam, A [1938]: *The Personality Conception of the Legal Entity.* Boston: Harvard University Press.

Nesbit, J [1998]: 'Transnational Bribery of Foreign Officials: A New Threat to the Future of Democracy'. In Vol. 31, *Vanderbilt Journal of Transnational Law*, at 1273.

Nicholls, C, Daniel, T, Polaine, M & Hatchard, J [2006]: *Corruption and Misuse of Public Office.* New York: Oxford University Press.

Nichols, P [1997]: 'Outlawing Transnational Bribery Through the World Trade Organization'. In Vol. 28, *Law & Policy in International Business*, at 305.

Nichols, P [1999a]: 'Are Extraterritorial Restrictions on Bribery a Viable and Desirable International Policy Goal Under the Global Conditions of the Late Twentieth Century?' In Vol. 20, *Michigan Journal of International Law*, at 451.

Nichols, P [1999b]: 'Regulating Transnational Bribery in Times of Globalization and Fragmentation'. In Vol. 24, *Yale Journal of International Law*, at 257.

Nichols, P [2000]: 'The Myth of Anti-Bribery Laws as Transnational Intrusion'. In Vol. 33, *Cornell International Law Journal*, at 627.

Nichols, P [2001]: 'The Fit Between Changes to the International Corruption Regime and Indigenous Perceptions of Corruption in Kazakhstan'. In Vol. 22, *University of Pennsylvania Journal of International Economic Law*, at 863.

Nichols, P [2004]: 'Corruption as an Assurance Problem'. In Vol. 19, *American University International Law Review*, at 1307.

Nichols, P [2011]: 'The Perverse Effect of Campaign Contribution Limits: Reducing the Allowable Amount Increases the Likelihood of Corruption in the Federal Legislature'. In Vol. 48, *American Business Law Journal*, at 77.

Nichols, P [2012a]: 'The Psychic Costs of Violating Corruption Laws'. In Vol. 45, *Vanderbilt Journal of Transnational Law*, at 145

Nichols, P [2012b]: 'The Business Case for Complying with Bribery Laws'. In Vol. 49, *American Business Law Journal*, at 325.

Noonan, J [1984]: *Bribes.* Los Angeles: University of California Press, Berkeley.

Nye, J [1979]: 'Corruption and Political Development: A Cost-Benefit Analysis'. In Ekpo, M (ed.) [1979]: *Bureaucratic Corruption in Sub-Saharan Africa: Toward a Search for Causes and Consequences.*_Washington D.C.: University Press of America, at 411.

O'Connor, S [2004]: 'Be Careful What You Wish For: How Accountants and Congress Created the Problems of Auditor Independence'. In Vol. 45, *Boston College Law Review*, at 741.

Ohlin, J [2005]: 'Is the Concept of a Person Necessary for Human Rights?' In Vol. 105, *Columbia Law Review*, at 209.

Ohnesorge, J [1999]: 'Ratcheting Up the Anti-Corruption Drive: Could a Look at Recent History Cure a Case of Theory-Determinism?' In Vol. 14, *Connecticut Journal of International Law*, at 467.

Oldenburg, P [1987]: 'Middlemen in Third-World Corruption: Implications of an Indian Case'. In Vol. 39, *World Politics*, at 508.

Olson, M [1996]: 'Big Bills Left on the Sidewalk: Why Some Nations are Rich, and Others Poor'. In Vol. 10, *Journal of Economic Perspectives*, at 3

Olson, M [2000]: *Power and Prosperity: Outgrowing Communist and Capitalist Dictatorships*. New York: Basic Books.

Olthoff, M [1995]: 'Beyond the Form – Should the Corporate Veil be Pierced?' In Vol. 64, *University of Missouri at Kansas City Law Review*, at 311.

Omestad, T [1997]: 'Bye-Bye to Bribes: The Industrial World Takes Aim at Official Corruption'. In *US News & World Report*, Dec. 22, 1997, at 42.

Opara, I [2007]: 'Nigerian Anti-Corruption Initiatives'. In Vol. 6 *Journal of International Business and Law*, at 65.

Ottolenghi, S [1990]: 'From Peeping Behind the Corporate Veil to Ignoring it Completely'. In Vol. 53, *Modern Law Review*, at 338.

Ouzounov, N [2004]: 'Facing the Challenge Corruption, State Capture, and the Role of Multinational Businesses'. In Vol. 37, *John Marshall Law Review*, at 1181.

Parseghian, L [1991]: 'Defining the 'Public Act' Requirement in the Act of State Doctrine'. In Vol. 58, *University of Chicago Law Review*, at 1151.

Perdue, W [1987]: 'Sin, Scandal, and Substantive Due Process: Personal Jurisdiction and Pennoyer Reconsidered'. In Vol. 62 *Washington Law Review*, at 479.

Peters, J & Welch, S [1978]: 'Political Corruption in America: A Search for Definitions and Theory'. In Vol. 72, No 3, *American Political Science Review*, at 974.

Phillips, M [1994]: 'Reappraising the Real Entity Theory of the Corporation'. In Vol. 21, *Florida State University Law Review*, at 1061.

Picciotto, S [1997]: 'Networks in International Economic Integration: Fragmented States and the Dilemmas of Neo-Liberalism'. In Vol. 17, *Northwestern Journal of International Law and Business*, at 1014.

Pieth, M, Low, L & Cullen, P (eds.). [2007]: *The OECD Convention on Bribery: A Commentary*. Cambridge: Cambridge University Press.

Pines, D [1994]: 'Comment, Amending the Foreign Corrupt Practices Act to Include a Private Right of Action'. In Vol. 82, *California Law Review*, at 185.

Pistor, K, Keinan, Y, Kleinheisterkamp, J & West, M [2002] 'The Evolution of Corporate Law: A Cross-Country Comparison'. In Vol. 23, *University of Philadelphia Journal of International Economic Law*, at 791.

Pollman, E [2011]: 'Reconceiving Corporate Personhood'. In Vol. 2011, *Utah Law Review*, at 1629.

Pollock, F [1911]: 'Has the Common Law Received the Fiction Theory of Corporations?' In Vol. 27, *Law Quarterly Review*, at 219.

Posadas, A [2000]: 'Combating Corruption Under International Law'. In Vol. 10, *Duke Journal of Comparative & International Law*, at 345.

Posner, R [1980]: 'The Ethical and Political Basis of the Efficiency Norm in Common Law Adjudication'. In Vol. 8, *Hofstra Law Review*, at 487.

Posner, R [1981]: 'The Present Situation in Legal Scholarship'. In Vol. 90, *Yale Law Journal*, at 1113.

Posner, R [1998]: *Economic Analysis of Law* (5th ed.). New York: Aspen Law and Business.

Powell, F [1931]: *Parent and Subsidiary Corporations: Liability of a Parent Corporation for the Obligations of Its Subsidiary*. Chicago: Callaghan.

Prentice, D [1996]: 'Veil Piercing and Successor Liability in the United Kingdom'. In Vol. 10, *Florida Journal of International Law*, at 469.

Presser, S [1992]: 'Thwarting the Killing of the Corporation: Limited Liability, Democracy and Economics'. In Vol. 87, *Northwestern University Law Review*, at 148.

Presser, S [1997]: *Piercing the Corporate Veil*. New York: Clark Boardman Callaghan.

Quah, J [1997]: 'Singapore's Experience in Curbing Corruption'. In Heidenheimer, A, Johnston, M & Vine, V (eds.) [1997]: *Political Corruption: A Handbook*. New Brunswick, NJ: Transaction Publishers, at 841.

Radin, M [1932]: 'The Endless Problem of Corporate Personality'. In Vol. 32, *Columbia Law Review*, at 643.

Radin, M [1982]: 'Property and Personhood'. In Vol. 34, *Stanford Law Review*, at 957.

Rajagopal, B [1999]: 'Corruption, Legitimacy and Human Rights: The Dialectic of the Relationship'. In Vol. 14, *Connecticut Journal of International Law*, at 495.

Ramasastry, A [2002]: 'Corporate Complicity: From Nuremberg to Rangoon: An Examination of Forced Labor Cases and Their Impact on the Liability of Multinational Corporations'. In Vol. 20, *Berkeley Journal of International Law*, at 91.

Ramsey, M [1998]: 'Acts of State and Foreign Sovereign Obligations'. In Vol. 39, *Harvard International Law Journal*, at 1.

Randall, L [1997]: 'Multilateralization of the Foreign Corrupt Practices Act'. In Vol. 6, *Minnesota Journal of Global Trade*, at 657.

Rashid, S [1981]: 'Public Utilities in Egalitarian LDC's: The Role of Bribery in Achieving Pareto Efficiency'. In Vol. 34, *Kyklos: International Review for the Social Sciences*, at 448.

Ribstein, L [1991]: 'Limited Liability and Theories of the Corporation'. In Vol. 50, *Maryland Law Review*, at 80.

Richards, S & Topp, R [1999]: 'Federal Criminal Conflict of Interest'. In Vol. 36, *American Criminal Law Review*, at 631.

Riechenberg, K [1988]: 'The Recognition of Foreign Privileges in United States Discovery Proceedings'. In Vol. 9, *Northwestern Journal of International Law & Business*, at 81.

Ripken, S [2009]: 'Corporations Are People Too: A Multi-Dimensional Approach to the Corporate Personhood Puzzle'. In Vol. 15, *Fordham Journal of Corporate and Financial Law*, at 97.

Robertson, R [1992]: *Globalization: Social Theory and Global Culture*. London: Sage.

Robinson, M [2012]: 'Global Approach to Anti-Bribery and Corruption, An Overview: Much Done, But a Lot More to Do'. In Vol. 37, *Thurgood Marshall Law Review*, at 303.

Robinson, N & Sattar, N [2012]: 'When Corruption is an Emergency: "Good Governance" Coups and Bangladesh'. In Vol. 35, *Fordham International Law Journal*, at 737.

Robinson, P [2003]: 'The Practice of Restorative Justice: The Virtues of Restorative Process, the Vices of Restorative Justice'. In Vol. 2003, *Utah Law Review*, at 375.

Robson, R [2010]: 'Crime and Punishment: Rehabilitating Retribution as a Justification for Organizational Criminal Liability'. In Vol. 47, *American Business Law Journal*, at 115.

Rockwell, L [1997]: 'The Right To Pay Bribes'. In *Journal of Commerce*, 23 May 1997, at 6A.

Roe, M [1996]: 'Chaos and Evolution in Law and Economics'. In Vol. 109, *Harvard Law Review*, at 641.

Rose, C [1988]: 'Crystals and Mud in Property Law'. In Vol. 40, *Stanford Law Review*, at 577.

Rose, C [2012]: 'The Corner House Case and the Incomplete Incorporation of the OECD Anti-Bribery Convention in the United Kingdom'. In Vol. 20, *Tulane Journal of International and Comparative Law*, at 351.

Rose-Ackerman, S [1978]: *Corruption: A Study in Political Economy.* New York: Academic Press.

Rose-Ackerman, S [1996]: 'Democracy and "Grand" Corruption'. In Vol. 48. No. 149, *International Social Science Journal*, at 365.

Rose-Ackerman, S [1997a]: 'The Political Economy of Corruption'. In K Elliott (ed.) [1997]: *Corruption and the Global Economy.* Washington D.C.: Institute for International Economics, at 31.

Rose-Ackerman, S [1997b]: 'The Role of the World Bank in Controlling Corruption'. In Vol. 29, *Law and Policy in International Business*, at 93.

Rose-Ackerman, S [1999] *Corruption and Government: Causes, Consequences and Reform.* Cambridge: Cambridge University Press.

Rose-Ackerman, S & Billa, B [2007]: "Treaties and National Security". In John M. Olin Center for Studies in Law, Economics, and Public Policy, Research Paper No. 351.

Rosenthal, D & Yale-Loehr, S [1984]: 'Two Cheers for the ALI Restatement's Provisions on Foreign Discovery'. In Vol. 16, *New York University Journal of International Law & Politics*, at 1075.

Rosen-Zvi, I & Fisher, T [2008]: 'Overcoming Procedural Boundaries'. In Vol. 94, *Virginia Law Review*, at 79.

Rosgow, A & Laswell, H [1978]: 'The Definition of Corruption.' In Heidenheimer, A (ed.) [1978]: *Political Corruption: Readings in Comparative Analysis.* New Brunswick: Transaction Books, at 54.

Ross, G [1933]: 'The Shifting Basis of Jurisdiction'. In Vol. 17, *Minnesota Law Review*, at 146.

Rossbacher, H & Young, T [1997]: 'The Foreign Corrupt Practices Act Within the American Response to Domestic Corruption'. In Vol. 15, *Dickenson Journal of International Law*, at 509.

Rubin, E [1988]: 'The Practice and Discourse of Legal Scholarship'. In Vol. 86, *Michigan Law Review*, at 1835.

Rubin, N [1998]: 'A Convergence of 1996 and 1997 Global Efforts to Curb Corruption and Bribery in International Business Transactions: The Legal Implications of the OECD Recommendations and Convention for the United States, Germany, and Switzerland'. In Vol. 14, *American University International Law Review*, at 257.

Ruzindana, A [1997]: 'The Importance of Leadership in Fighting Corruption in Uganda'. In K Elliott (ed.) [1997]: *Corruption and the Global Economy.* Washington D.C.: Institute for International Economics, at 133.

Ryznar, M & Korkor, S [2011]: 'Anti-Bribery Legislation in the United States and United Kingdom: A Comparative Analysis of Scope and Sentencing'. In Vol. 76, *Missouri Law Review*, at 415.

Salbu, S [1997]: 'Bribery in the Global Market: A Critical Analysis of the Foreign Corrupt Practices Act'. In Vol. 54, *Washington & Lee Law Review*, at 229.

Salbu, S [1999a]: 'Battling Global Corruption in the New Millennium'. In Vol. 31, *Law & Policy in International Business*, at 47.

Salbu, S [1999b]: 'The Foreign Corrupt Practices Act as a Threat to Global Harmony'. In Vol. 20, *Michigan Journal of International Law*, at 419.

Salbu, S. [1999c]: 'Extraterritorial Restriction of Bribery: A Premature Evocation of the Normative Global Village'. In Vol. 24, *Yale Journal of International Law*, at 223.

Salbu, S [2000]: 'A Delicate Balance: Legislation, Institutional Change, and Transnational Bribery'. In Vol. 33, *Cornell Journal of International Law*, at 657.

Salbu, S [2001a]: 'Information Technology in the War Against International Bribery and Corruption: The Next Frontier of Institutional Reform'. In Vol. 38, *Harvard Journal on Legislation*, at 67.

Salbu, S [2001b]: 'Transnational Bribery: The Big Questions'. In Vol. 21, *Journal of International Law & Business*, at 435.

Schachter, S [1997]: 'The Decline of the Nation-State and Its Implications for International Law'. In Vol. 36, *Columbia Journal of Transnational Law*, at 7.

Schane, S [1986]: 'The Corporation Is a Person: The Language of a Legal Fiction'. In Vol. 61, *Tulane Law Review*, at 563.

Scheppele, K [1999]: 'The Inevitable Corruption of Transition'. In Vol. 14, *Connecticut Journal of International Law*, at 509.

Schleifer, A & Vishny, R [1993]: 'Corruption'. In Vol. 108, *Quarterly Journal of Economics*, at 599.

Schroth, P [2002]: 'The United States and the International Bribery Conventions'. In Vol. 50, *American Journal of Comparative Law*, at 593.

Schroth, P [2005]: 'The United Nations Convention Against Doing Anything Serious about Corruption'. In Vol. 12, *Journal of Legal Studies in Business*, at 1.

Schwartz, R [1994]: 'And Tomorrow? The Torture Victim Act'. In Vol. 11, *Arizona Journal of International and Comparative Law*, at 271.

Scott, J [1972]: *Comparative Political Corruption.* Englewood Cliffs, NJ: Prentice Hall.

Scott, J [1979]: 'Corruption, Machine Politics, and Political Change'. In Ekpo, M (ed.) [1979]: *Bureaucratic Corruption in Sub-Saharan Africa: Toward a Search for Causes and Consequences.* Washington D.C.: University Press of America, at 101.

Scott, K [1983]: 'Corporation Law and the American Law Institute Corporate Governance Project'. In Vol. 35, *Stanford Law Review*, at 927.

Segal, P [2006]: 'Coming Clean on Dirty Dealing: Time for a Fact-Based Evaluation of the Foreign Corrupt Practices Act'. In Vol. 18, *Florida Journal of International Law*, at 169.

Shahid Alam, M [1989]: 'Anatomy of Corruption: An Approach to the Political Economy of Underdevelopment'. In Vol. 48, *American Journal of Economics and Social Science*, at 441.

Shaw, B [2000]: 'The Foreign Corrupt Practices Act and Progeny: Morally Unassailable'. In Vol. 33, *Cornell International Law Journal*, at 689.

Shaw, M [1991]: *International Law* (3rd ed.). Cambridge: Cambridge University Press.

Shihata, I [1997]: 'Corruption – A General Review with an Emphasis on the Role of the World Bank'. In Vol. 15, *Dickinson Journal of International Law*, at 451.

Silets, H & Brenner, S [1986]: 'The Demise of Rehabilitation: Sentencing Reform and the Sanctioning of Organizational Criminality'. In Vol. 13, *American Journal of Criminal Law*, at 329.

Singer, M [1981]: 'The Act of State Doctrine of the United Kingdom: An Analysis, with Comparisons to United States Practice'. In Vol. 75, *American Journal of International* Law, at 283.

Slaughter Burley, A [1993]: 'International Law and International Relations Theory: A Dual Agenda'. In Vol. 87, *American Journal of International Law*, at 205.

Smith, S [1987]: 'The Critics and the "Crisis": A Reassessment of Current Conceptions of Tort Law'. In Vol. 72, *Cornell Law Review*, at 765.

Smith, V [1974]: 'Economic Theory and Its Discontents'. In Vol. 64, *American Economic Review*, at 320.

Snider, S & Kidane, W [2007]: 'Combating Corruption Through International Law in Africa: A Comparative Analysis'. In Vol. 40, *Cornell International Law Journal*, at 691.

Sorauf, F [1994]: 'Politics, Experience and the First Amendment: The Case of American Campaign Finance'. In Vol. 94, *Columbia Law Review*, at 1348.

Spahn, E [2009]: 'International Bribery: The Moral Imperialism Critiques'. In Vol. 18, *Minnesota Journal of International Law*, at 155.

Spalding, A [2010]: 'Unwitting Sanctions: Understanding Anti-Bribery Legislations as Economic Sanctions Against Emerging Markets'. In Vol. 62, *Florida Law Review*, at 351.

Speck, P [1987]: 'Forum Non Conveniens and Choice of Law in Admiralty: Time for an Overhaul'. In Vol. 18, *Journal of Maritime Law & Commerce*, at 185.

Spiegelberger, W [2006]: 'Russian Roulette: Doing Business in Russia in Compliance With Anti-Bribery Laws and Treaties'. In Vol. 2, *New York University Journal of Law & Business*, at 819.

Starek, J [1989]: *Introduction to International Law.* London: Butterworths.

Stephan, P [1999]: 'Rationality and Corruption in the Post-Socialist World'. In Vol. 14, *Connecticut Journal of International Law*, at 533.

Stevenson, D & Wagoner, N [2011]: 'FCPA Sanctions: Too Big to Debar?' In Vol. 80, *Fordham Law Review*, at 775.

Stigler, G [1970]: 'The Optimum Enforcement of Laws'. In Vol. 78, *Journal of Political Economics*, at 526.

Stiglitz, J & Edlin, A [1992]: 'Discouraging Rivals: Managerial Rent Seeking and Economic Insufficiencies'. In National Bureau of Economic Research Working Paper No. 4145.

Stoljar, S [1973]: *Groups and Entities: An Inquiry into Corporate Theory.* Canberra: Australian National University Press.

Stone, C [1980]: 'The Place of Enterprise Liability in the Control of Corporate Conduct'. In Vol. 90, *Yale Law Journal*, at 1.

Story, J [1834]: *Commentaries on the Conflict of Laws.* Boston: Hilliard, Gray & Co.

Stout, L & Blair, M [2006]: 'Specific Investment: Explaining Anomalies in Corporate Law'. In Vol. 31, *Journal of Corporate Law*, at 719.

Strauss, A [1995]: 'Beyond National Law: The Neglected Role of International Law of Personal Jurisdiction in Domestic Courts'. In Vol. 36, *Harvard International Law Journal*, at 373.

Sundack, T [1988]: 'Republic of Philippines v. Marcos: The Ninth Circuit Allows a Former Ruler to Invoke the Act of State Doctrine Against a Resisting Sovereign. In Vol. 38, *American University Law Review*, at 225.

Surjadinata, K [1998]: 'Revisiting Corrupt Practices from a Market Perspective'. In Vol. 12, *Emory International Law Review*, at 1021.

Sutton, R [1997]: 'Controlling Corruption Through Collective Means: Advocating the Inter-American Convention Against Corruption'. In Vol. 20, *Fordham International Law Journal*, at 1427.

Swadron, R [1987]: 'The Bhopal Incident: How Courts Have Faced Complex International Tort Litigation'. In Vol. 5, *Boston University International Law Journal*, at 445.

Swanson, T [2007]: 'Greasing the Wheels: British Deficiencies in Relation to American Clarity in International Anti-Corruption Law'. In Vol. 35, *Georgia Journal of International and Comparative Law*, at 397.

Sykes, A [1981]: 'An Efficiency Analysis of Vicarious Liability Under the Law of Agency'. In Vol. 91, *Yale Law Journal*, at 168.

Tanzi, V [1994]: 'Corruption, Governmental Activities and Markets'. International Monetary Fund Working Paper No 94/99.

Tarullo, D [2004]: 'The Limits of Institutional Design: Implementing the OECD Anti-Bribery Convention'. In Vol. 44, *Virginia Journal of International Law*, at 665.

Teubner, G [1988]: 'Enterprise Corporatism: New Industrial Policy and the "Essence" of the Legal Person'. In Vol. 36, *American Journal of Comparative Law*, at 130.

Thoennes, K [2005]: 'Frankenstein Incorporated: The Rise of Corporate Power and Personhood in the United States'. In Vol. 28, *Hamline Law Review*, at 203.

Thomas, C [1999]: 'Does the "Good Governance Policy" of the International Financial Institutions Privilege Markets at the Expense of Democracy?' In Vol. 14, *Connecticut Journal of International Law*, at 551.

Thompson, D [1993]: 'Mediated Corruption: The Case of the Keating Five'. In Vol. 87, No. 2, *American Political Science Review*, at 369.

Thompson, R [1994]: 'Unpacking Limited Liability: Direct and Vicarious Liability of Corporate Participants for Torts of the Enterprise'. In Vol. 47, *Vanderbilt Law Review*, at 1.

Thoumi, F [1987]: 'Some Implications of the Growth of the Underground Economy in Columbia'. In Vol. 29, *Journal of International Studies and World Affairs*, at 35.

Tilman, R [1979]: 'Emergence of Black-Market Bureaucracy: Administration, Development, and Corruption in the New States'. In Ekpo, M (ed.) [1979]: *Bureaucratic Corruption in Sub-Saharan Africa: Toward a Search for Causes and Consequences.* Washington D.C.: University Press of America, at 341.

Timmeny, W [1982]: 'An Overview of the FCPA'. In Vol. 9, *Syracuse Journal of International Law and Commerce*, at 235.

Todarello, V [2002]: 'Corporations Don't Kill People – People Do: Exploring the Goals of the United Kingdom's Corporate Homicide Bill'. In Vol. 46, *New York Law School Law Review*, at 851.

Trachtman, J [1994]: 'Conflict of Laws and Accuracy in the Allocation of Government Responsibility'. In Vol. 26, *Vanderbilt Journal of Transnational Law*, at 975.

Trimble, P [1990]: 'International Law, World Order, and Critical Legal Studies'. In Vol. 42, *Stanford Law Review*, at 811.

Tronnes, R [2000]: 'Ensuring Uniformity in the Implementation of the 1997 OECD Convention on Combating Bribery of Foreign Public Officials in International Business Transactions'. In Vol. 33, *George Washington International Law Review*, at 97.

Tsuk, D [2005]: 'From Pluralism to Individualism: Berle and Means and 20th-Century American Legal Thought'. In Vol. 30, *Law & Social Inquiry*, at 179.

Tullock, G [1967]: 'The Welfare Costs of Tariffs, Monopolies and Theft'. In Vol. 5, *Western Economic Journal*, at 224.

Turner, C [1964]: *Russell on Crime* (12th ed.). London: Stevens & Son, at 381.

Turner M [2006]: 'Most Iraq Oil-for-Food Scandal Perpetrators Go Unpunished'. *Financial Times*, 9 December 2006.

Tushnet, M [1988]: *Red, White, and Blue: A Critical Analysis of Constitutional Law*. Boston: Harvard University Press.

Twitchell, M [1988]: 'The Myth of General Jurisdiction'. In Vol. 101, *Harvard Law Review*, at 610.

Tyler, A [2011]: 'Enforcing Enforcement: Is the OECD Anti-Bribery Convention's Peer Review Effective?' In Vol. 43, *George Washington International Law Review*, at 137.

Utset, M [1995]: 'Towards a Bargaining Theory of the Firm'. In Vol. 80, *Cornell Law Review*, at 540.

Vernon, R [2001]: *Sovereignty at Bay: The Multinational Spread of Us Enterprises* (Rise of International Business). London: Routledge.

Villalta, P [2007]: 'Unethical Conduct in the Performance of International Government Contracts: AWB Ltd. and the United Nations Oil-for-Food Programme'. In Vol. 37, *Public Contract Law Journal*, at 59.

Vogl, F [1998]: 'The Supply Side of Global Bribery'. In Vol. 35, *World Bank Finance & Development*, at 30.

Voxman, W [1992]: 'Jurisdiction Over a Parent Corporation in its Subsidiary's State of Incorporation'. In Vol. 141, *University of Pennsylvania Law Review*, at 327.

Wade, R [1982a]: 'Irrigation Reform in Conditions of Populist Anarchy: An Indian Case'. In Vol. 14. *Journal of Development Economics*, at 285.

Wade, R [1982b]: 'The System of Administrative and Political Corruption: Canal Irrigation in South India'. In Vol. 18, *Journal of Development Studies*, at 287.

Wade, R [1985]: 'The Market for Public Office: Why the Indian State Is Not Better at Development'. In Vol. 13, *World Development*, at 467.

Walsh, J [1998]: 'A World War on Bribery'. In *Time International* , 22 June 1998, at 16.

Waterbury, J [1979]: 'Endemic and Planned Corruption in a Monarchical Regime'. In Ekpo, M (ed.) [1979]: *Bureaucratic Corruption in Sub-Saharan Africa: Toward a Search for Causes and Consequences.* Washington D.C.: University Press of America, at 355.

Watson, G [1998]: 'The OECD Convention on Bribery'. In *Insight*, Mar. 1998, at 1.

Watts, C [1991]: 'Corporate Legal Theory Under the First Amendment: Bellotti and Austin'. In Vol. 46, *University of Miami Law Review*, at 317.
Webb, P [2005]: 'The United Nations Convention Against Corruption: Global Achievement or Missed Opportunity?' In Vol. 8, *Journal of International Economic Law*, at 191.
Wei, S [1997a] 'How Taxing Is Corruption on International Investors?' National Bureau of Economic Research, Working Paper No. 6030.
Wei, S [1997b]: 'Why Is Corruption So Much More Taxing than Tax? Arbitrariness Kills'. In National Bureau of Economic Research, Working Paper No. W6255.
Weinstein, J [1990]: 'The Dutch Influence on the Conception of Judicial Jurisdiction in 19th Century America'. In Vol. 38, *American Journal of Comparative Law*, at 73.
Wells, C [2001a]: 'Corporate Law: Corporate Criminal Liability – Developments in Europe and Beyond'. In Vol. 39, *Law Society Journal*, at 62.
Wells, C [2001b]: *Corporations and Criminal Responsibility* (2nd ed.). Oxford: Oxford University Press.
Wells, C, Morgan, D & Quick, O [2000]: 'Disasters: A Challenge for the Law'. In Vol. 39, *Washburn Law Journal*, at 496.
Werhane, P [1985]: *Persons, Rights, and Corporations.* Englewood Cliffs, NJ: Prentice Hall.
Werlin, H [1973]: 'The Consequences of Corruption: The Ghanaian Experience'. In Vol. 88, *Political Science Quarterly*, at 71.
Westbrook, A [2011]: 'Enthusiastic Enforcement, Informal Legislation: The Unruly Expansion of the Foreign Corrupt Practices Act'. In Vol. 45, *Georgia Law Review*, at 489.
Whincop, M [2000]: 'Three Positive Theories of International Jurisdiction'. In Vol. 24, *Melbourne University Law Review*, at 379
Wight, J [1994]: 'An Evaluation of the Commercial Activities Exception to the Act of State Doctrine'. In Vol. 19, *Dayton Law Review*, at 1265.
Wilkins, M [1970]: *The Emergence of Multinational Enterprise: American Business Abroad from the Colonial Era to 1914.* Boston: Harvard University Press.
Willard, H [1970]: *The Legitimacy of the Business Corporation in the Law of the United States 1780–1970.* Charlottesville: University Press of Virginia.
Williams, C [2002]: 'Corporate Social Responsibility in an Era of Economic Globalisation'. In Vol. 35, *UC Davis Law Review*, at 705.
Williams, R [1987]: *Political Corruption in Africa.* Aldershot: Gower Publication
Williams, R [1999a]: 'New Concepts for Old'. In Vol. 20, *Third World Quarterly*, at 503.
Williams, R [1999b]: 'The New Politics of Corruption'. In Vol. 20, *Third World Quarterly*, at 487.
Williamson, O [1979]: 'Transaction-Cost Economics: The Governance of Contractual Relations'. In Vol. 22, *Journal of Law and Economics*, at 233.
Windsor, D & Getz, K [1999]: 'Regional Market Integration and the Development of Global Norms for Enterprise Conduct'. In Vol. 38, *Business and Society*, at 415.

Windsor, D & Getz, K [2000]: 'Multilateral Cooperation to Combat Corruption: Normative Regimes Despite Mixed Motives and Diverse Values'. In Vol. 33, *Cornell International Law Journal*, at 731.

Wiseman, C [1993]: 'Reconstructing the Citadel: The Advent of Jurisdictional Privity'. In Vol. 54, *Ohio State Law Journal*, at 403.

Wolf, P [1995]: 'International Securities Fraud: Extraterritorial Subject Matter Jurisdiction'. In Vol. 8, *New York Journal of International Law*, at 1.

Wood, G [1995]: 'Ethics at the Purchasing/Sales Interface: An International Perspective'. In Vol. 4, *International Marketing Review*, at 7.

Wormser, M [1912]: 'Piercing the Veil of Corporate Entity'. In Vol. 12, *Columbia Law Review*, at 496.

Wormser, M [1927]: *Disregard of the Corporate Fiction and Allied Corporation Problems*. Littleton: F.B. Rothman.

Wurmnest, W [2005]: 'Foreign Private Plaintiffs, Global Conspiracies, and the Extraterritorial Application of U.S. Antitrust Law'. In Vol. 28, *Hastings International and Comparative Law Review*, at 205.

Yockey, J [2011]: 'Solicitation, Extortion, and the FCPA'. In Vol. 87, *Notre Dame Law Review*, at 781.

Zervos, A [2006]: 'Amending the Foreign Corrupt Practices Act: Repealing the Exemption for "Routine Government Action" Payments'. In Vol. 25, *Penn State International Law Review*, at 251.

Index

For Product Safety Concerns and Information please contact our EU representative GPSR@taylorandfrancis.com Taylor & Francis Verlag GmbH, Kaufingerstraße 24, 80331 München, Germany

Batch number: 10725973

Printed by Printforce, the Netherlands